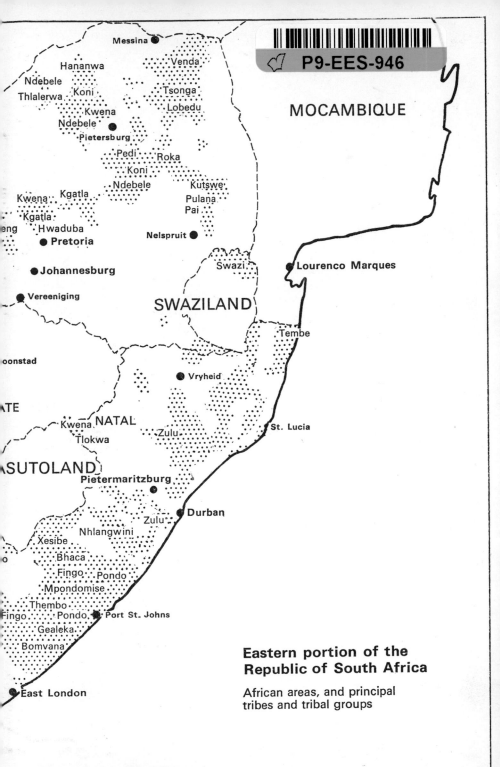

Messina

Hananwa

Ndebele
Thlalerwa Koni

Kwena
Ndebele

Pietersburg

Venda

Tsonga
Lobedu

MOCAMBIQUE

Pedi Roka
Koni
Ndebele Kutswe
Kwena Kgatla Pulana
Kgatla Pai
eng Hwaduba
● Pretoria Nelspruit ●

● Johannesburg

● Vereeniging

SWAZILAND

oonstad

ТЕ

Kwena NATAL
Tlokwa

SUTOLAND
Pietermaritzburg

Xesibe
Bhaca
Fingo Pondo
Mpondomise
Thembo
Fingo Pondo Port St. Johns
Gealeka
Bomvana

● East London

Swazi

Tembe

Vryheid

Zulu St. Lucia

Zulu
Nhlangwini

● Durban

Lourenco Marques

Eastern portion of the Republic of South Africa

African areas, and principal
tribes and tribal groups

100   200   Miles

FROM UNION TO APARTHEID

Margaret Ballinger

FROM UNION
TO APARTHEID

A Trek to Isolation

PRAEGER PUBLISHERS

New York · Washington

323.119
B192f

BOOKS THAT MATTER
Published in the United States of America in 1969
by Praeger Publishers, Inc.
111 Fourth Avenue, New York, N.Y. 10003
© 1969 in Cape Town, South Africa by Margaret Ballinger
All rights reserved
Library of Congress Catalog Card Number: 76–79558

Printed in Great Britain

DR MARGARET BALLINGER

To my husband

Contents

Part III

Epilogue

List of Illustrations

Author's Note

Certain forms generally used in the text would seem to call for some explanation—e.g. Natives Representative Council, Natives Land Act and Native Representatives.

The two former derive from the relevant statutes. The latter is standardised on established practice, Hansard, platform and press.

References to the various population groups are also as far as possible standardised on current practice. In earlier days, the term 'native' was generally used in respect of the Black population. It then tended to become Native, with the older form also occurring. Later the term African came into use, by the choice of the people themselves. The Nationalist Party found this unacceptable and began to use the word Bantu. But Bantu is a plural form, meaning people, which makes its use ungrammatical when applied to one person.

The use of capitals in respect of groups may seem capricious. The growing practice now is to use capitals in both noun and adjectival associations, e.g. 'Whites' and 'non-White persons'. In the case of quotations, I have generally transcribed precisely as originally printed.

Capitals for Native Representatives has been standardised on the model of Members of Parliament.

PUBLISHER'S NOTE

Standardised Forms

Native Representatives
Natives Representative Council (i.e. without apostrophe).
See Rogers & Linington, Strydom.
This is the form Hansard used—NOT Strydon.

In the early days, the term NATIVE was generally used. Later we began to use the term AFRICAN. The Nationalist Party found this unacceptable and began to use BANTU, but Bantu is a plural form which makes its use ungrammatical when applied to one person.

Preface

When Dr. Verwoerd, in 1959, announced his intention to abolish all African representation in the South African Parliament as from June 30th, 1960, Nuffield College, Oxford, invited me to spend a year thereafter as an associate fellow of the College writing something of my experiences as a member of Parliament representing Africans. This book is the outcome of the effort this invitation initiated.

It is essentially a personal record, reflecting my own view of events and developments over the twenty-three years during which the special representation provided for in General Hertzog's settlement of what was commonly referred to as the Native problem functioned. While the final disappearance of an African franchise which had existed since the beginning of Parliamentary institutions in South Africa must have made the occasion an appropriate stopping point for review and stock-taking, there were special circumstances of the year 1960 which made it particularly appropriate for the purpose. It was the jubilee year of the Union of South Africa, that political reintegration of a country lamentably divided on emotional issues in the nineteenth century and but recently emerged from the distresses of the Anglo-Boer war. This was an occasion which a wholly Afrikaner Government proposed to mark by country-wide celebrations designed to illustrate what half a century of Union had achieved in drawing together the two white groups in the community. It was also the year of Dr. Verwoerd's announcement as Prime Minister of his intention to hold a referendum on the still highly contentious issue of the conversion of the Union into a republic. And most immediately important as it transpired, it was the year of that demonstration of the Africans' interpretation of the record of fifty years of Union which was to result in the tragic incidents of Sharpeville and Langa and to convert a jubilee year into a year of crisis, challenging the most serious evaluation of that record by every conscientious citizen.

This book reflects my own effort in that regard. Its starting point, and its conclusions, are those of a liberal bred in the tradition of the old Cape Colony. That was a tradition founded on the assumption of the common humanity, the common rights and therefore the common loyalties of all members of a complex society. I believe that our departure from it after Union, and particularly after 1948, in favour of a policy of separation—apartheid—based on the contention that differences of race and cultural inheritance are fundamental and antipathetic in association, has been the major tragedy of our history in this twentieth century.

The crisis of 1960 seemed to suggest something of this to many others besides professing liberals. The result, however, was not a change of course but more strenuous efforts by those in power to apply the policy more effectively and thus to prove anxieties as to its virtue unfounded and unjustified. Nothing that this has achieved over the succeeding years has led me to revise my attitude to the policy itself or to change my view of the cost which it has exacted and continues to exact in increasing measure from the people of South Africa both individually and collectively.

Here I wish again to express my appreciative thanks to Nuffield College for their invitation to me to embark upon this study. I also wish to thank the Oppenheimer Trust for a grant towards its completion, and Mr. Leo Marquard, Mr. David Welsh and Mr. Walter Mears for their kindness in reading through the script and offering helpful suggestions for its improvement. I am also extremely grateful to Miss Maggie Rodger for the care and efficiency with which she contended with all the difficulties of my manuscript.

Introduction

The world has learnt a good deal over the last few years about the complex make-up of South Africa. Experience, however, suggests that a descriptive exercise is still a useful preface to any consideration at least of the politics of this highly controversial country.

It is a country of 472,859 square miles with a population of some 16,000,000 people; that is, it is a large country with a comparatively small population. The racial composition of this population is its most significant feature, with its distribution, both geographical and economic, almost if not equally significant.

According to the last complete census, taken in 1960, the European (white) population numbered 3,088,492, Africans, 10,927,922, Asians 477,125 and Coloured persons, that is, people of mixed origin, 1,509,258. These figures give a ratio of just over three Africans to one European, or if we include all non-White groups in the calculation, four non-Whites to one white. On the other hand, if the Asian and Coloured groups were combined with the Whites as belonging to more developed stocks than the Africans—as they were encouraged to count themselves in the formative days of a segregation policy directed immediately at the Africans—the ratio would be in the region of two Africans to one of the other group.

However, accepting colour as the line of division, as indeed it is in South Africa today, this country has the highest proportion of Whites to non-Whites of any country south of the Sahara, the geographical line of division commonly used in discussing the problems of Africa as Africa, although perhaps less appropriate in these days of the Organisation for African Unity than it used to be. Its neighbour, Southern Rhodesia, comes next with something in the region of seventeen Africans to one white person. The only other countries within this geographic range with established white populations of any size are Northern Rhodesia, now become Zambia, and Kenya. The proportion there of Africans to Whites is of course very considerably higher, indeed so much so as virtually to place these states in a different category which recent shifts of power within them would seem to justify. They see themselves as essentially parts of and belonging to Africa both culturally and emotionally.

By contrast, the Republic of South Africa looks out from Africa to the Western world for its cultural and emotional associations. This it does, even though the majority, now something over 60 per cent of the dominant white population which exercises a monopoly control of power in this country, claims also to be essentially African. This is a claim reflected in the name which it has assumed for itself, that of Afrikaner, and for the language which it speaks, Afrikaans. However, even as Afrikanerdom claims to be a product of Africa, and has resented the use of the word African to denote the black population group in the country, it claims also to be the torch-bearer of Western Christian civilisation on the continent of Africa. Diverse in origin, Hollanders, refugee French Huguenots, and Germans seeking a livelihood and adventure in the service of the great Dutch East India Company which founded the first settlement at the Cape in the mid-seventeenth century, in the isolation of the days of slow travel and communication and over the wide spaces of this sparsely populated land, these early settlers did in fact develop a character and a culture of their own, and a language to express them. This, under various influences and at various times, has encouraged a sense of separateness from all the other groups that has been of profound political significance.

The rest of South Africa's white population, the English speaking section, while largely derived from immigrant British stocks which followed the assumption of sovereignty over the country by Britain in 1806, includes also numerous other elements, attracted later to the country by the discovery of diamonds and gold towards the end of the nineteenth century. With origins also diverse, in the context of a developing industrial society and with a language of widely international range, this group has tended both in character and in culture to remain composite and comprehensive rather than to develop any consciously specific character of its own.

While the small European population thus presents—and seems likely to continue to present—two clear strains, the assumption has been generally made that in fact they form one group within which the line of division must and will disappear. Among the large African population, there are also lines of division. These are tribal and linguistic. In terms of present Government policies, however, the assumption is that these dividing lines will not and must not disappear. Dr. Verwoerd's government, in its planning for the future, identified eight main groups within the African population[1] between which, it maintained, the differences are sufficiently great to call for permanent separation between them.

It also postulated separation between the white and the non-white groups in the population and between one non-white group and another. The declared purpose and intention of this policy of separation is to guarantee the survival of the small white group against the menace of black numbers in at least part of the area now covered by the Republic of South Africa. In the meantime, all these groups are comprehended within the Republic. Their distribution within the country presents certain features of some considerable interest and importance.

The Republic of South Africa—until 1961 the Union of South Africa—consists of four provinces: the Cape Province, which was the original colony occupied by the Dutch East India Company, and taken over by the British in 1806; the two ex-Boer Republics of Transvaal and Orange Free State established by members of the older white population who could not accommodate themselves to the new rule; and Natal, which was established as a British colony after the danger of Voortrekker occupation of its port, Durban, became apparent to the British authorities at the Cape and in Britain. Thus the history of the Cape goes back over 300 years; the other Provinces are something over 100 years old.

Today, the white population of all the Provinces is mixed in some degree, with the Orange Free State predominantly Afrikaner and Natal predominantly English in speech and sentiment. Of the Coloured population the vast majority, some 88 per cent according to the 1960 census, are in the Cape. They are in fact a Cape people as their name implies—they are usually known as the Cape Coloureds. They were originally a by-product of slavery, the Dutch East India Company having early sought to solve its labour problems in its Southern African outpost by the introduction of slaves from its Far Eastern possessions and from other parts of Africa, partly because the indigenous populations, Hottentots and Bushmen, were

---

[1] Reduced in terms of the Promotion of Bantu Self Government Act (46 of 1959) to seven for administrative purposes.

B

small in numbers and difficult to harness and partly because the
Company did not wish to saddle itself with the responsibilities of
territorial sovereignty.

The Asian population belongs predominantly to Natal and is
likely to continue to do so. There is a small Asian community in
the Transvaal which owes its origin to British control of the old
Transvaal republic in the eighties of last century. The Free State
has always determinedly closed its doors against Asian immigration
and denies rights of domicile to Asians. Within the country as a
whole, there is generally a complete embargo on the movement of
Asians across the Provincial boundaries except on a temporary
basis and they by permit only. There is now a complete ban on
Asian immigration from without.

The African population, like the European population, is distributed over all the Provinces. The 1960 census returns show nearly
3,000,000 in the Cape Province, including the Transkei, 2,155,000
in Natal, 4,600,000 in the Transvaal and just over a million in the
Free State. But it is not the numerical distribution between the
Provinces that goes to make up the significance of the distribution
of the African population; it is its distribution between Native
reserves, now generally referred to by the Government as their
homelands or heartlands, and the rest of the country now commonly
called the European area.

The Native reserves comprise those areas of which Africans are
in recognised occupation in terms of a policy of territorial separation
that goes back formally to 1913. In that year, the first government
of the Union of South Africa passed a Natives Land Act,[1] the purpose
of which was to limit the acquisition of land by the growing African
population, or even the occupation of land by them on other than
a service tenancy basis. It was to take over twenty years for the
political forces supporting this policy of territorial separation as
between Africans and Europeans to decide what the Africans'
share in this deal should be. In 1936, it was eventually agreed that
areas amounting to some 7,250,000 morgen should be released for
purchase by Africans or for the settlement of Africans—this to be
added to the already occupied areas which had been scheduled in
the 1913 Act, amounting to some 10,000,000 morgen. When the
quota should be completed, it would give to the Africans some 13
per cent of the area of the country. However, when the second Native

[1] Act 27 of 1913.

Land Act[1] was passed embodying this proposition, the then United Party Government under the premiership of General Hertzog found it impossible to specify a considerable part of the proposed allocation[2] and after another thirty-odd years, the gap still remains to be filled. In the intervening years some 3,009,806 morgen of land have been purchased by the Government for the extension of the scheduled reserves.[3] In the meantime, however, the reserves themselves have acquired a new importance by the emphasis which has been laid on their function within the apartheid policy. In terms of that policy, these are indeed to be the homelands of the Africans, within which they must seek their economic and social advance and satisfy their political ambitions. Soon after its accession to power in 1948, Dr. Malan's Nationalist Government set up a Commission the function of which was to explore the position and to make recommendations as to how this objective could be advanced. Reporting in 1955, it found that the reserves consisted of some 260 separate and generally fragmented areas which 'save for a few blocks like the Transkei and Vendaland are so scattered that they form no foundations for community growth'.[4]

Particularly significant is the proportion of the African population which can presently claim domicile in these areas. Again the Government's own authorities establish the facts of the case. These put the proportion at some 40 per cent, the remaining 60 per cent being not domiciled in the so-called white areas—for the law does not permit the acquisition of domicile by Africans in these areas, even of Africans born in them—but living and working there and entirely dependent upon them for their homes and the occupations which sustain them.

Nor is this the whole story. The reserves are generally undeveloped rural areas with a high population density. In 1964, the Transkei showed 84 Africans to the square mile, the Ciskei, 91 as against 33 persons for the country as a whole and 19·1 for the Cape Province

[1] Native Trust and Land Act 18 of 1936.
[2] According to a Socio-Economic Commission (U.G. 61/1955) appointed in 1949, the area still to be released was 1,903,831 morgen (vide Summary of the Report, p. 46, para. 41). In 1967, Mr. A. H. Vosloo, the Deputy Minister of Bantu Development, opening the South African Bureau of Racial Affairs (SABRA) conference of that year on the subject of the consolidation of the Bantu homelands, said there were still 1,545,632 morgen to be found to fill the promised quota. 1 morgen = 2·11654 acres.
[3] And 1,842,924 morgen Crown land vested in the Native Trust. Vide Report of Controller and Auditor for year 1964 (Part III, RR 57/64, p. 553).
[4] Socio-Economic Commission (U.G. 61/1955)—Summary, p. 180, para. 13.

of which these reserves form part.[1] Still largely practising traditional
methods of agriculture and pastoral farming on uneconomic
holdings, they cannot sustain even the very modest standard of
living they have achieved so far save by the regular export of
labour. Thus there flows from the reserves a continuous stream of
migrant workers seeking employment where it may be found. To
quote the Government's own Commission again, it was found that
this flow accounted for absence from the reserves *at any one time* (my
italics) of 12 per cent of their total population, which in significant
economic terms represented more than 40 per cent of the male
population between the ages of 15 and 64 years.[2] There has been
nothing to change the pattern appreciably since this report was made
in 1955. A growing African population in the reserves still seeks and
must seek avenues of employment outside its homelands to survive,
and an expanding national economy relies more and more on its
ability to draw on this source of labour.

Here it seems important to underline what people without
personal experience of the country generally fail to appreciate—that
South Africa is a highly developed industrial state. It is the only
one of its kind in Africa, with Rhodesia a distant second in the
process of development. The extent of its industrialisation is
reflected in the degree of urbanisation of all its populations. Most
recent figures show that over 83 per cent of both the European and
the Asian groups are now urban. For the Coloured people, the percentage figure is just over 68. For the Africans, it is approximately
32.[3] This comparatively low figure represents a significant change in
the economic character of the African population which would
undoubtedly have been considerably more marked but for political
influences which have operated to restrain the process of African
urbanisation, of which in recent years the application of the policy
of apartheid has been the most determined.

The spectacular rise of the country in little more than half a
century from a group of comparatively poor rural communities
to a rich, largely urbanised society with a highly diversified
economy has been the combined achievement of all its racial
groups. In the process of change set in motion by the discovery of
diamonds and gold, leading to an impressive development of second-

[1] *South African Statistical Year Book 1964,* Tables 77 and 98.
[2] Ch. 13, para. 7, p. 53, Summary of Socio-Economic Commission's Report
(U.G. 61/1955).
[3] *South African Statistical Year Book 1964,* Table 108.

ary industry which now produces some 25 per cent of the national income, the whites have contributed capital, enterprise, initiative and skill while the other groups have mainly contributed the labour on which the whole development has been based. The Asian community indeed has, here as elsewhere, done something more than that. It was first introduced, much against the will of the then Indian Government, as indentured labour to meet the labour needs of a developing sugar industry in Natal which the local African population, the Zulus, could not then be induced to supply. The descendants of these workers today still provide a small proportion of the unskilled labour of the Province, but generally they are to be found in the ranks of the semi-skilled and to an increasing degree in the ranks of the skilled in industry and trade.[1] They are also the market gardeners of the Province.

In the wake of the indentured labourers came free immigrants, mainly Muslim traders. These latter have developed into a considerable economic force, occupying a conspicuous place in the commercial life of the chief city, Durban, where the Asian population now exceeds the white. They also constitute the main trading element in all the smaller towns of the Province.

In the Transvaal the Asians have long been an important factor in the commercial life of all the urban areas, this being the class which entered the province in the eighties.[2]

The Cape Coloured people supplied most of the agricultural labour and generally did the unskilled and much of the semi-skilled work of the old Cape Colony. They still meet the needs of agriculture but in declining measure, tending to shift in the fashion typical of societies in process of industrialisation into better paid urban occupations. Here, like the Asians in Natal, in response to the labour needs of an expanding economy, they are breaching skilled levels hitherto jealously reserved by custom for white workers.[3]

Moving in where any opportunity offers to fill the place of the other advancing groups, and under the pressure of their own need to find employment, the Africans supply the bulk of the unskilled labour throughout the country, and provide the broad

[1] Vide *Official Year Book of Union of South Africa, No. 30*, p. 213.
[2] This situation is changing in terms of the Group Areas legislation under which Indians are being called upon to move both for purposes of residence and the conduct of business to areas specially designated for them.
[3] They have always performed much of the skilled work in building—a position which has now become precarious under the system of job preservation designed to protect white workers.

foundation on which the whole South African economic and social system rests. The mining industry has always been based on African labour. In 1956, its labour force averaged 500,000 Africans as against 73,000 whites. Today Africans constitute something over 60 per cent of the labour force in manufacturing as well. Nor is it only in industry that they have come to play this enormous, indeed this vital part. According to a recent Government Commission of enquiry[1] into European occupancy of the rural areas, four-fifths of the rural population outside the Native reserves is African, and in its hands is concentrated most of the production of the nation's food.

It is this highly economically integrated society to which Afrikaner Nationalism, which has been in political control of the country since 1948, is committed to apply the policy of apartheid, separation. So far, it has achieved an almost complete political separation in the purely negative sense that Africans and Asians have no representation in the Parliament which makes laws for the whole country. The Cape Coloured community have four elected representatives in the House of Assembly and two in the Cape Provincial Council, all by law white.[2] According to declared government policy, not only the Africans but all the racial groups in the country must seek their political and social advance in their own areas. Where, to say nothing of when, the Africans are to achieve a framework for this development still remains a secret which the Government has not so far been induced to share with the rest of the country or with the Africans themselves. The Government to which the Socio-Economic Commission made its report, that of Mr. J. G. Strydom, with the voice of Dr. H. F. Verwoerd, repudiated the Commission's proposals for the consolidation of the fragmented reserves in order to produce units of potential community growth. Since then, repeated requests for a clear statement as to the boundaries of the future independent African states to which the Government, first under Dr. Verwoerd himself and now under Mr. Vorster, is committed, have been completely unavailing.

So far as the Coloured and Asian groups are concerned, the where and the when are even more problematical, since as communities they have no territorial foundations, however inadequate,

[1] European Occupancy of Rural Areas (Annexure No. 865/1960). (Printed but not numbered.)
[2] These are now due to disappear at the end of the present Parliament, see Epilogue.

on which to begin to build any semblance of an independent existence.

In the meantime, in the relentless pursuit of an objective which fails to achieve any practical or precise definition, revolutionary changes are being made in the character of the South African state which threaten to cut it off from Africa and Europe alike, and indeed to leave it friendless in a race-conscious world profoundly hostile to both its philosophy and its practice. An attempt to trace the course and to assess the nature of these changes as they came within the range of my personal experience constitutes the essential purpose of this book. Its starting point is that of a liberal; its conclusions are still those of a liberal. In the course of the years, I found nothing to modify my belief that a broad-based democratic system progressively embracing politically all the elements in our complex society is not only the way to peace; it is the only way in which we can fulfil our essential destiny which is, at whatever price of pride or privilege, to help to carry the torch of Western Christian civilisation, with its emphasis on the value of the individual irrespective of race or colour, to the uttermost ends of the earth.

PART I

I

The Representation of Natives Act, 1936 [1]

I was elected to the South African House of Assembly in 1937 in terms of a Representation of Natives Act passed by the South African Parliament in 1936, and I took my seat together with my colleagues at the beginning of 1938. I continued to be a member of Parliament in the same capacity and for the same constituency until June 1960, when not only this representation but all representation of Africans in the South African Parliament came to an end under the provisions of an Act of Dr. Verwoerd's Nationalist Government called the Promotion of Bantu Self-Government Act.[2] Thus the period of my Parliamentary experiences covers an episode in South African political history. But it is an episode in the purely temporal sense—that is, as having a precise beginning and a definite end. In the historical sense, its significance is deeply rooted in the past, and it is still exercising a considerable influence on the course of events in this country.

The Representation of Natives Act for the first time provided for the representation of the African population of the whole of South Africa in the South African Parliament. This it did by the institution of four new seats in the upper chamber, the Senate, to be filled by elected representatives of Africans. The constituencies for these seats were to be the Cape Province excluding the Transkei, the Transkei, the Province of Natal including Zululand, and the Orange Free State and Transvaal Provinces functioning as one constituency. The Act also created three new seats in the House of Assembly, but these were to be filled by representatives of Africans in the Cape Province only. It further established two new seats in the Provincial Council of the Cape Province to be filled by representatives of Africans of that Province.

Only British subjects of European descent were to be eligible for election to these seats.

Finally the Act created an entirely new institution, the Natives

---

[1] General reference on this chapter—*Native Administration in the Union of South Africa*, by Howard Rogers of the Department of Native Affairs; second edition revised by P. A. Linington, G.P.–S 4438, 1948–9.
[2] Act 46 of 1959.

Representative Council. This was to consist of twenty-three members. Seven of these were to be the senior administrative officers of the Department of Native Affairs; the other sixteen were to be Africans. Of these sixteen, twelve were to be elective, three from each of the constituencies created for the election of Senators. The machinery for their election was to be substantially the same as in the case of the Senate representation. The remaining four were to be nominated by the Government, one from each of the constituencies.

The representatives of the Africans in the House of Assembly and the Provincial Council were to be elected by individual vote cast in secret ballot. The voters were to be persons with the qualifications which had pre-existed for all non-Europeans in the Cape Province and, before 1930, for all voters in that Province: that was, males of twenty-one years and over who could read and write and either occupied a house of the value of £75 or had earned £50 in wages in the year.

For the Senate, the process of election was much more complicated. Here the net was spread much more widely to take in all taxpayers, which meant all males of eighteen years and over. In each constituency, there was to be an electoral college which, except in the Transkei, was to operate through a series of units. These units were mainly already recognised and largely elected local government entities. In the Native Reserves, Local Councils where they existed, Native Reserve Boards of Management, Chiefs and Headmen functioned in this capacity; in the urban areas, the Native Advisory Boards which were supposed to be constituted in all Native townships were given the responsibility of casting the local vote. Only in respect of farm labourers in so-called European area, that is Africans in rural areas outside Native Reserves, was it deemed necessary to create new machinery. Here, for each election, the local administrative officer, the Magistrate or Native Commissioner, was called upon to summon the taxpayers in his district to a meeting at which they should elect an electoral committee which was to constitute the area unit.

In the election itself, each of these units was empowered to cast a vote the numerical value of which was determined by the number of taxpayers which it represented, this vote ostensibly reflecting the will of the majority of these taxpayers. The units themselves might consist of from one to eight or nine persons. The number of votes they might cast could vary from between as few as seven to some tens of thousands. For example, in 1953, in the last election held under the system, in the Transvaal–Orange Free State constituency, one unit alone, consisting of nine persons, cast a vote of 52,000.

In the Transkei, the elected members of the Transkeian General Council, some eighty-one persons, functioned as the Electoral College for both the Senate and the Natives Representative Council.

In order presumably to discourage irresponsible entrants for the Senatorial election, the Act provided that candidates had to secure a percentage of the votes of the electoral college as a condition of valid nomination. In practice this produced a system of double election. Nomination itself became a contest which revealed the strength of the competitors and the election campaign proper thereafter inevitably resolved itself into a further contest among the accepted candidates to hold their own votes and to win over those of their opponents. A contested election took a minimum of four months to complete and could extend over seven months, and, unlike the traditional electoral practice, there was no defined limit of the amount of money that might be spent and no return of expenses was demanded of the contestants.

For election of the African members of the Natives Representative Council, the units constituting the electoral colleges were grouped in three sections, urban, rural, and reserve, each of which elected one of the three elective members for the constituency.

The Africans' representatives in Parliament and the Cape Provincial Council were elected for five years irrespective of the duration of their respective bodies and, with one exception, they enjoyed all the rights of other members, including in respect of the Parliamentary representatives, the right to vote on questions of confidence in the Government; that is, they could help to vote a government out of office without themselves having to submit to re-election in the event of a consequent general election. The exception to their powers was the right to vote for the other elected members of the Senate. Under the Act of Union, the Senate consisted of forty members, thirty-two of whom were elected on the basis of eight for each Province. The electors in this case were the members of Parliament and of the Provincial Council for the respective Province, each of whom exercised his vote under the system of a single transferable vote—a system designed to make the upper chamber as far as possible a reflection of the balance of political forces within the general electorate.

In addition to the thirty-two elected members, the Senate included eight nominated members, four of whom were to be selected, according to the Act of Union, by reason of their thorough acquaintance, by reason of their official experience or otherwise, with the reasonable wants and wishes of the Coloured races of South Africa.

Natives Representative Council

Like the members of Parliament and the Cape Provincial Council, the members of the Natives Representative Council held their seats for a fixed term of five years. Their functions were purely advisory, but all proposed legislation affecting Africans was to be submitted to the Council for consideration and report. Any other matter might be referred to it by the Minister of Native Affairs and the Council could itself recommend to Parliament, or to any Provincial Council as the case might be, legislation which it considered to be in the interests of the African people. To it were to be submitted on the eve of every ordinary session of Parliament, or as soon thereafter as possible, a statement of the estimates of expenditure for the ensuing year in respect of all aspects of Native affairs, together with an estimate of all revenues to be derived from sources other than Parliamentary allocation and a statement of the Minister's proposals as to how all such revenues should be allocated. This latter was a provision designed to cover the use of various sectional and local trusts that had come into existence from time to time and which now, with the progressive unification of administrative practice in Native affairs, were being placed under centralised control. Every report of the Council was to be submitted to the Minister who should lay it before Parliament. If the report related to matters concerning a Provincial Council, a copy of such report was to be sent to the Administrator of the Province for submission to his Council.

The Council was to sit under the chairmanship of the Secretary for Native Affairs. The official members of the Council were entitled to participate in all debates but exercised no vote. The Chairman similarly had no ordinary vote but could exercise a casting vote in the event of an equal division between the African members.

The members of the Native Affairs Commission could also attend the meetings of the Council and could speak but could not vote.

Here it may be appropriate to explain the character and the functions of the Native Affairs Commission, since it occupied a special position in the general organisation of political business as it affected Africans and was to play an important part in the history of this whole phase of South African Native policy to which this experiment in group representation belongs.

Constituted in terms of a Native Affairs Act passed in 1920[1] by the first Smuts Government, the Commission, which was to be a permanent part of the machinery of government in the field of Native affairs, may be regarded, as might the four nominated Senators, as an effort to fill the gap left by the absence of Parliamentary representation of the mass of the African population. Its functions and duties set it apart from, and in important respects above, the general departmental organisation. In the language of the Act, these were to 'include the consideration of any matters relating to the general conduct of the administration of Native affairs and of legislation in so far as it may affect the Native population, and the submission to the Minister of Native Affairs of its recommendations on any such matter'. While departmental administration was explicitly excluded from its purview, it was empowered to consider and make recommendations in respect of 'any matter of administrative routine' which the Minister himself might submit to it.

The potentially significant range of these functions was underlined by the provision that 'if in regard to any matter, the Minister does not accept the recommendation of the Commission, or takes any action contrary thereto, the Commission may require that such matter, together with a memorandum of its views thereon, be submitted to the Governor-General, and thereupon if the Governor-General does not accept the Commission's recommendation, the Commission may require that all papers relative to the matter be laid before both Houses of Parliament and the Minister, if such request is made, shall lay such papers before both Houses'.

The Act went further and provided that where a question had been decided at any meeting of the Commission by the casting vote of the chairman or the deputy chairman, any member who dissented from the decision of the Commission might request that his views as stated by him in writing should be recorded and laid before both Houses of Parliament, and the Minister was under

[1] Act 23 of 1920.

obligation to accede to his request. Since the Act laid down that
the Minister or his nominee should be chairman of the Commission,
these provisions were clearly intended to give to the Commissioners
a degree of independence in the field of Native Affairs that could
over-ride the Minister himself.

That the Commission was to be a working body of very considerable power and importance, 'in permanent attendance subject to
the discretion of the Chairman', the Act went on to specify a number
of matters on which its recommendation was to be an essential
condition of Ministerial action. These included for example the
establishment of local and general Native Councils in Native
reserves, that is, the whole development of local government machinery. Later, in 1925, when the right of taxing Africans was taken
away from the Provinces and concentrated in the hands of the
central government by the Native Taxation and Development
Act of that year, the Minister of Native Affairs was required to
consult the Commission in regard to the administration of the
Native Development Account constituted under the Act. Later still,
in 1936, when the Native Trust and Land Act was passed, it was
laid down that in administering the South African Native Trust
which the Act created and into which the Native Development
Account was now merged, the Minister must act in consultation
with the Commission. As all reserve land was vested in this Trust,
this meant in effect that the Commission had practically a controlling interest in the methods of use of what, in terms of the segregation
policy, might be called the African estate, including the Native
Trust Account established under the Act for the 'settlement, support,
benefit and material and moral welfare of the Natives of the Union'.

For these responsible tasks, the members of the Commission
were to be remunerated at the rate of £1000 (R2000) per annum, a
higher allowance than was then paid to members of Parliament.
In addition they were to receive travelling allowances and subsis-
tence allowances when on the Commission's business, on the scale
applicable to the Civil Service.

Most significantly, it was provided under the Act that a member
of either House of Parliament might be appointed to the Commission
and 'though he receive remuneration as such, he shall not be deemed
to hold an office of profit under the Crown within the Union'.
When the Commission was first instituted its members, who by
Statute were to be not less than three and not more than five, were

not recruited from the political field. They were in fact chosen mainly from the upper ranks of the administration, and chosen for their special experience of and among Africans. Latterly, however, the practice had grown up of making Parliamentary appointments to this office and when the new machinery constituted under the Representation of Natives Act came into operation, of its four members, three were members of the governing party in the House of Assembly. When, within a year, it was decided to appoint a fifth member to help to meet the increasing volume of work which was being referred to the Commission as the segregation policy got under way, he also was drawn from the Parliamentary ranks. Prominent among the Parliamentary members was Mr. Heaton Nicholls, United Party member for Zululand, under whose forceful guidance the Commission came to occupy a position of great importance in the lives of the African community.

With members of the Commission appointed for five years, the outbreak of war in 1939, bringing about a change in government which put General Smuts in office in place of General Hertzog, gave rise to a situation in which two of its members became part of the official opposition.[1] There was, of course, provision in the constituting act for resignation and for removal of members; but in the case of removal, a full statement of the reasons therefore had to be laid before both Houses of Parliament. The two members who followed General Hertzog out of the United Party did not choose to resign, and General Smuts did not choose to dismiss them. Indeed three years later he re-appointed one of these members, General Conroy, at the conclusion of his first term of office—an action which was not very favourably viewed by a good many of his own followers.

If it had been difficult for anyone outside the ranks of the governing party to see why General Conroy had been appointed to the Commission in the first instance, it was more difficult still to see why General Smuts should challenge the emotions—and aspirations— of his own followers by renewing this appointment. No doubt the explanation was to be found in his anxiety to gather in as much support as he could from the ranks of a still very divided opposition. At that time General Conroy was leader in the House of a small Afrikaner Party, followers of Mr. Havenga who, with General Hertzog, had resigned his own seat in Parliament in 1940; and General Smuts was preparing for his first appeal to the electorate

[1] Mr. J. F. T. Naudé and General E. H. Conroy.

C

after the fateful vote in September 1939, which had brought him into office and South Africa into the war. It was an appointment that made little difference to the Commission so far as one could judge, and with the disappearance from Parliament of the Afrikaner Party at the election in 1943, we as Native Representatives ceased to be actively conscious of it except as an additional justification of our claim, early publicised by us in the House of Assembly, that the establishment of the Parliamentary representation of Africans and of the Natives Representative Council had made the existence of the Native Affairs Commission itself redundant. It was a view which the Prime Minister did not accept, for reasons that one might argue had little to do with Native affairs.

2

The Emergence of 'Purified' Nationalism

The establishment of the system of representation embodied in the Representation of Natives Act was the culmination of a struggle which goes back in South African history for a century. It was indeed intended to bring that struggle to an end—the struggle over the appropriate place of Africans—Natives as they were still called—in our mixed society.

It was on this question that South Africa had split up in the first half of the nineteenth century, when, after the advent of the British, the attempt to establish effective administrative control over the Colony, the abolition of slavery, and the progressive extension of the frontier made the legal position and the rights of persons of colour a very live issue. The direction which this new preoccupation with what would now be called human rights gave to the process of adjustment between the established white population and its new rulers touched deep sentiments and prejudices in a community that had grown up with slavery and had largely been a law unto itself in its relations with other non-White groups. There were indeed many of the older population who could not accomodate themselves to it. They therefore decided to go out and establish new states for themselves where their own conception of the appropriate relationship between black and white should prevail, where the principle of no equality in church or state should be the recognised and accepted foundation on which the frame of the constitution should be raised.

With their departure, the Cape Colony, already set in the contrary direction, progressively evolved a multi-racial society which, by the time of the unification of the four states which had come to divide the wide spaces of South Africa between them, was already operating successfully on the basis of a non-colour-bar Parliamentary system inspired and illuminated by British experience. It is true, there had been periodic agitations about the 'blanket' vote as the boundary of the Colony moved eastwards to take in large black populations who had had no experience of European life and ways, and the franchise qualifications, significantly low

35

when a Legislative Assembly was first established in 1854, had been raised on more than one occasion with the intention of making access to the voters' roll more difficult for persons of colour; but the limitations imposed tests of civilisation and not of colour.

The forces behind the divergence of practice between the Cape and the states which the intransigents had created to the north, the Boer republics of Transvaal and the Orange Free State, were still operative after the Anglo-Boer War, when Union became a matter of practical politics. Indeed they might be said to have acquired a new strength through use. For a time, it seemed that those differences would form an insuperable obstacle to the realisation of unification. In the end, the danger was only scotched by the acceptance of a compromise under which it was agreed that each contracting party should maintain its own system—with one significant surrender demanded of, and reluctantly agreed to by, the Cape, that of the right of people of colour to stand for Parliament as well as to vote for it. The Parliament of the new Dominion of South Africa which the Act of Union was to establish was to be an all-white Parliament even if non-whites might still cast votes for the candidates in what was now to be the Cape Province.

In 1910, the new state, in spite of all the anxieties attendant upon its birth, was hopefully launched in its way. Time, it was argued in interested quarters, and the progress of the human spirit would resolve its implicit conflict, particularly in the matter of political rights, and that in a way appropriate to an advancing civilisation. In fact, the compromises to meet the demands of the North were not to prove the beginning of that broadening out of freedom which seemed the predestined course of twentieth century development. On the contrary, it was only the first move in a determined struggle to establish a uniform pattern in black-white relations in South Africa which should give to the believers in inequality the victory they had failed to win a century earlier. The next move was to be an indirect attack on the Cape position in the enfranchisement of European women in 1930, on the qualification of age only, followed by the establishment of adult suffrage for white men also. These tactics greatly reduced the value of the votes of the non-Whites in the Cape and created a new and highly significant discrimination in the Cape system.

By this time the abolition of the African's franchise in the Cape had become a plank in the platform of the Nationalist Party formed by General Hertzog in 1914 and with a Nationalist Government now in office,[1] this was a matter of immediate political importance. Indeed the situation had only been held to that point by the entrenchment of its non-white franchise which had been conceded to the Cape at Union. This laid down the necessity of a two-thirds majority of both Houses of Parliament sitting together for the disfranchisement of any person on the grounds of race or colour only. As the two major parties then stood, General Smuts's South African Party and General Hertzog's Nationalists, the Government was not within measurable distance of the requisite majority. But circumstances were to change that position almost abruptly. On the back of the great depression and the gold price crisis was to come coalition between, and then fusion of, the two parties; and in 1936, the old Cape African franchise disappeared, part, and a most significant part, of the price to General Smuts of the new alliance. And with its going, South Africa accepted officially the policy of segregation which, applying to Africans only, was soon to be elevated to the status of the South African way of life as between White and non-White generally. I wrote of this at the time as the Voortrekkers' return. All that it could and would involve in the context of a twentieth century which itself was to take such unexpected turns, we had yet to discover. To others more intimately familiar than I was with the various facets of our political life and the personalities who were then shaping it, some at least of what has eventuated has perhaps been less unexpected. In my education and experience, there had been nothing to prepare me for the course which events have taken at least in these latter years since the close of the war and the opening of the second phase of Nationalist government in South Africa.

For years before my entry into Parliament I had indeed had a strong and active interest in one aspect of our political life, the course of Native policy. Derived from Scottish radical stock, and brought up in the Eastern Province of the Cape with its liberal traditions, I was convinced that the real interest and responsibility of South African politics lay in implementing the liberal principle, and in building on a democratic foundation a common society out of all the diverse elements which compose our very complex population. Of the inner conflicts within the white community that

[1] The Pact Government—Nationalist Party in alliance with the (white) Labour Party. Came to office in 1924.

kept the stream of South African life in a constant state of turbulence, I was of course conscious, but they did not achieve the same significance in my mind. Essentially urban in my personal associations[1] and without party political affiliations to bring me into immediate contact with the progressively competitive political forces which the country's past history had thrown up, I was more aware of and preoccupied with the need to see our problems as a whole, of which the use and the needs of our large black population were basic, than of the emotional forces that were to make that almost a secondary objective. Looking back therefore over the record of the years, particularly the earlier years in which I was in Parliament, and reviewing the conditions under which the Native Representatives entered Parliament, I have been startled to discover how violent and how deep these conflicts were, how well-defined the course of Afrikaner nationalism as we have since learnt to know it already was, and the extent to which the road to what I regard as our unhappy present had already been charted. From the moment I entered Parliament and came into contact with the personalities who were shaping our destinies, I could no longer remain ignorant of or indifferent to the part that Afrikaner-Afrikaner relationships were already playing in our national life. Whatever the subject of discussion and argument, behind it, underneath it, around it eddied the currents of inter-Afrikaner reactions. Everything else seemed indeed of secondary (or at best contingent) importance. And already the essence of the conflict had become, not whether Afrikaner nationalism should dominate South Africa but whether dominating Afrikaner nationalism should absorb or exclude the other elements in the population.

The history of this conflict can be traced back beyond the Anglo-Boer War, at least to the formation of the Bond in the old Cape Colony in 1879. This, the first organisation of those who were to call themselves Afrikaners but who at that time were generally referred to as Dutch South Africans, was initially a movement for cultural ends. Almost immediately, however, with what seems to be an implicit logic of the Afrikaner spirit, which has repeated itself again and again since, it took on a political complexion. Anti-British in sentiment and republican in objective, it sought to estab-

---

[1] I was educated in the then very English towns of Port Elizabeth and Grahamstown and spent the years of my academic professional life at what was then Rhodes University College and later at the University of the Witwatersrand.

lish common ground with its fellows beyond the Cape frontier in the Boer Republics, ground which might provide the foundation for a united independent Dutch South Africa.

Almost immediately, there emerged that dualism that has charac-terised Afrikanerdom ever since. J. H. Hofmeyr, Onze Jan, the leading Dutch political figure in the Cape Colony, early established a controlling interest in the organisation and drew it back to a policy of a broad inclusive South Africanism taking in the English section of the population and accepting the British connection. Appreciating the way in which the British empire was shaping towards an association of progressively free and equal partners, he no doubt felt that this was the soundest, and the most hopeful direction for Dutch ambitions to take. Since any greater and freer South Africa must inevitably be a predominantly Dutch South Africa by the very force of numbers, the older population had nothing to lose and much to gain by such a course. But while the Bond itself accepted this lead, the idea of an exclusive, anti-British Dutch (Afrikaner) nationalism did not die, for President Kruger would have none of Hofmeyr's inclusive South Africanism, and the circumstances of the Jameson Raid and the Anglo-Boer War were to strengthen the Kruger influence.

From this time onwards, the possibilities fluctuated between an inclusive intra-commonwealth nationalism operating within the main stream of Western culture and an exclusive extra-common-wealth republican nationalism in which form and content alike should be Afrikaner. It is a conflict which has been implicit in practically the whole of the life of South Africa since Union, rising to the explicit level after 1933 where it tended to remain there-after, achieving its essential victory in 1961 when, after thirteen years of a wholly Afrikaner nationalist Government, the Union of South Africa became the Republic of South Africa, outside the British Commonwealth.

In the early years, the tide ran clearly and strongly in favour of an inclusive, co-operative 'Western' South Africanism. Botha and Smuts were deeply committed to this line of development. For them, after their earlier experiences and with the British post-war con-cession of self-government to encourage them, the primary need and essential objective was to weld the two white stocks into a nation strong enough to take advantage of the opportunities which this situation offered. Out of misfortune had come a South Africa re-united, and under Boer leadership, with freedom to develop its own shape and character, and with the military and economic advantages of membership of a large and rich family of nations to help to sustain and develop it.

As early as 1912, however, the exclusive objective began to raise its head again. The Orange Free Stater, General Hertzog, could not accept the co-operation policy of the Transvaal generals, Botha and Smuts. For him, the life of South Africa, even of white South Africa, could not run in one stream—at least not until the two converging streams which were to constitute it were of equal strength. The Afrikaner stream was, by comparison with the English stream, economically poor and emotionally depressed by recent defeat. It must be revived and strengthened before co-operation could even be considered. So the new National party formed under his leadership in 1914 was a party of and for Afrikaans-speaking South Africans dedicated to the objective not of a united nation but of a united Afrikanerdom. Its binding force would be not only a language and a culture rooted in South African soil but a way of life essentially South African, freed from the extraneous forces which, it was claimed, had for a century sought to shape it in a foreign mould, and imbued with a determination to stamp its impress indelibly on this re-united South Africa. It is true that, latterly, General Hertzog himself could be found giving a new accent to the need for a wider nationalism that would take in both white groups. Indeed, it was a working alliance between his wholly Afrikaans Party and an English-speaking Labour Party which brought office within his reach in 1924, and first coalition and then fusion with General Smuts's South African Party, in the early thirties, which kept him in office as leader of the new United South African National Party until September 1939. Indeed, except as a bid to get and to keep the two white groups together, this latter political adventure has no reasonable explanation. For General Smuts, there can be little doubt that this was the determining motive for what to all appearances was an unprecedented sacrifice at that time, since the tide was running strongly against the Hertzog Government and the reins of office were practically dropping into his hands. For General Hertzog, the increasing evidence of his need to draw some support from the English-speaking section of the population if he was to achieve his final ambitions no doubt dictated his readiness to accept an alliance with his old political enemy, an alliance with the attraction not only of keeping him in office but in the leadership as well.

It is important however to note that, as his biographer Professor C. M. van den Heever records, as early as 1930 he had said that after the Imperial Conferences of 1926 and 1930, there was no reason why Dutch and English speaking South Africans should not be consolidated in the spirit of a South African people. That was the remaining task of the National Party. If it failed in that, he said, then its days were over.[1]

But not all his colleagues were prepared for alliance with their old opponents. While Transvaal, Free State and Natal Nationalists in their provincial conferences, where the decision for each lay in terms of the federal constitution of the Party, endorsed their leader's decision to convert coalition into fusion of the two major parties, the Cape would have none of it. Led by Dr. Malan, they preferred to go into the wilderness rather than accept a permanent alliance with their old opponent, General Smuts. Afrikaner South Africa lives by slogans. The one for this occasion was 'Let those who belong together be together', and Dr. Malan's answer to the messages that came to the Nationalists of the Cape from the other Provinces urging them to unite was that General Smuts and his people of the South African Party did not belong with the Nationalist Party; that they still did not accept the basic objectives of that Party—the right of secession, the right of neutrality in the event of war and the right to make republican propaganda. In vain General Hertzog argued that since the Commonwealth Prime Ministers' Conference in 1926, the two first of these had been achieved and acknowledged, that the third, which Smuts had rejected in 1920 on the occasion of an earlier effort to reach agreement between his Party and Nationalism, had been accepted as part of the bargain out of which the United Party was to grow—that in fact the policy of the new United South African National Party was to be essentially that of the old Nationalist Party. In vain also did General Hertzog's Transvaal supporters argue that if indeed the right to secede was still in doubt, it could be achieved and could only be achieved by an alliance with the English-speaking section of the population which would, they claimed, put an end to 'racialism'—in this context, relations between English- and Afrikaans-speaking South Africans.

[1] C. M. van den Heever, *General J. B. M. Hertzog*, p. 248.

In vain also did they argue that only with the assistance of General Smuts and his party members could the Nationalists gain their immediate major objective of establishing a legislative framework for segregation in the field of race relations—that is, as between white and black. This meant initially the abolition of the Cape Province non-White franchise; but this could only be achieved in terms of the entrenchment in the Constitution, which so far no one had proposed to sidestep, on which indeed the leaders had recently pledged South Africa's honour, if support could be obtained outside the Nationalist Party ranks. That support, it was argued, would not be forthcoming so long as the Smuts Party remained independent, since that Party had too much to gain from a vote which had consistently gone its way.

While the majority of his Parliamentary supporters followed General Hertzog into the new United South African National Party, a 'purified' National Party under Dr. Malan gave new life to the oldest Afrikaner ideal of an independent republic clear of all external political ties and influences. More immediately important was the fact that there continued to be a completely Afrikaans party in South Africa, and one deeply committed to the policy of segregation in race relations. This it professed to believe would as inevitably be compromised in the new association as would other basic objectives of their Nationalism, since many members of the Smuts Party, it contended, were infected with 'liberal' ideas of foreign origin and inspiration.

Thus things stood when the first representatives of Africans went to Parliament when, with the assistance of the Smuts section of the new United Party, General Hertzog did succeed in getting rid of the Cape African vote and in establishing what he claimed was the effective framework of a permanent segregation policy. The Malanites, even while they supported him in this legislation, were to claim that the policy had in fact been compromised in more ways than one, of which the most important was on the political front. Here General Hertzog's first move had been to provide representation for Africans in the Senate only, a proposition with which the Malanites were in agreement; but he early substituted for it another proposition which conceded both House of Assembly and Provincial Council representation to the Cape African population, a concession which the Malanites accusingly and bitterly laid at the door of General Smuts.

These were not very propitious omens for a 'liberal' cause. However, two things which I, and those who shared my views, hoped for in South Africa still seemed possible, to encourage us to take on a seemingly impossible task. The first of these was that the two white groups might indeed come together to create one community able to face its developing racial problems in a truly national rather than a sectional spirit; and secondly and contingently, that a sane policy of black-white relations that would commend itself on both sides of the colour line might yet be reached.

So far as the first of these hopes was concerned, the wide and deeply emotional acceptance of the fusion of the two major parties seemed to give it fair justification. The country was already weary of political contention concerned with emotional issues rather than with practical needs, particularly where the practical needs were so great. Poor whiteism had haunted the country for a generation and more, with all its tragedies, and dangers, underlined in the circumstances of the great depression of the late twenties and early thirties. As for the second of our hopes, and the essential one, where European poverty had earlier accentuated colour prejudice and encouraged a segregation policy with all its discriminations, the economic prosperity which rapidly followed our departure from the gold standard was already alleviating the worst acerbities of black-white relations. Already, with expanding industry offering more and better jobs, Government pressure on private employers to implement a white labour policy—the Nationalist cure for white distress—was being relaxed, and the argument in favour of the need to develop all our natural resources, of which the most important was our human resources, was getting a chance at least to be heard.

It was against the background of these trends, slight perhaps but seemingly real, and convinced that sooner or later all our racial groups must be welded into one democratic community if South Africa was to fulfil its destiny, that African leaders and white liberals alike decided to try to use the new machinery, designed to support segregation, to propagate our view of the alternative and the right road for South Africa.

3

First Election of Native Representatives

The first election for the seats created under the 1936 Representation of Natives Act took place in November 1937, with a general election pending in May 1938. When the Act was passed, Parliament in its wisdom had decided that elections to be held under it should not take place simultaneously with 'white' elections. The reason for this arrangement was ostensibly to avoid the danger of these elections being influenced by or infected with the fever of the general election. It was also a gesture towards the much publicised ideal of 'taking Native Affairs out of politics'. This has always in effect meant trying to isolate the African from the party political life of the country, a proposal which appealed particularly to the Nationalists in view of their failure ever to attract any substantial part of the Cape African vote.

Perhaps the most significant feature of this first election, and one which was to give its colour to the whole of this representation, was the type of candidate chosen by the Africans. Although most of the seven persons elected had had some party affiliation at some time only one had been to any extent previously active in party politics. That was the Senator elected for the Cape Province, Senator Karl Malcomess. I myself had never been associated with any party. By tradition and instinct, I should have been drawn to the Labour Party; but the South African Labour Party was at that time no home for anyone with my views on colour. I had had therefore to refuse the offer of a Parliamentary seat years earlier made by Mr. Madeley, leader of the Labour Party, at a time when Labour had seats to give. A similar offer was made to my husband at the same time, with the same result.

Four of us elected in 1937 were what I suppose might have been called academic liberals.[1] We had all been closely associated through Joint Councils of Africans and Europeans, with the fight against the Hertzog policy, the principles of which we repudiated, and had decided to contest these seats in the hope of using the

[1] Dr. Edgar Brookes and Mr. J. D. Rheinallt Jones to the Senate, Mr. D. B. Molteno and myself to the House of Assembly.

44

Parliamentary platform to expose what we regarded as its dangers. This we did individually and independently of one another, each making our case as we saw it and no doubt placing emphasis where our special interests dictated. My own election address committed me to the 'ideal of eventual equal citizenship for Europeans and non-Europeans in South Africa, based on the abolition of all colour bar legislation'. As specific objectives, it proposed among other things the extension of the then existing political rights in the Cape Province to the other Provinces of the Union as a stepping stone to uniform rights for all people, free access to land for all sections of the population on equal terms, equal educational facilities for all, the inclusion of the African worker in the industrial machinery of the country, the establishment of a minimum wage for African workers in urban areas based on the cost of keeping a family without the need of the mother to go out to work leaving her children unattended, no taxation of Africans under twenty-one years of age and no taxation of any wage regarded as less than enough for a family to live on.

The election itself was a gruelling experience I should not like to repeat. Under the Act, the Cape Province had been divided into three electoral circles. I had chosen the eastern circle, since it included the area in which I had spent my childhood and had received most of my education, and in which I had had my earliest professional experience: that was as lecturer in charge of the Department of History at Rhodes University College, which was then a constituent College of the University of South Africa. Geographically the smallest of the three circles, it yet covered an area approximately equal to that of England and Scotland together. In addition to two out of the three large urban areas of the Cape Province, Port Elizabeth and East London, and a large range of the smaller towns, it included all but two of the Native reserves in the Province outside the Transkei. The border area where black and white had originally met and where the process of Bantu colonisation of South Africa, spreading south-westward, had been held by the white colonial stream moving east, it was—and is still—an area of dense African population pressing heavily on unexpanding and undeveloped land, a situation which made problems of poverty immediate and extensive.

It included also extensive white farming areas with a considerable African farm labour population, areas which had been purposely developed nearly a century earlier with the express intention of breaking up the border tribes and building a composite society in the hope of bringing to an end the costly frontier clashes which had for so long afflicted the old Cape Colony.

It thus represented every aspect of African life and every point of contact between black and white in our highly complex and rapidly changing society. Later it was to be enormously extended, westward, to take in part of the Cape Midlands and the only reserves in the original Cape Western Circle, those of the far north-west which bordered on the Bechuanaland Protectorate.[1] As counter balance, East London City went over to the Transkei. It was a change I did my best to induce the Smuts Government not to make, since it seemed to me that these seats, which by law were limited to three, should each as far as possible be representative in some degree of all sections of the African population. But the Act had provided for a five-yearly delimitation,[2] and that not on the basis of population but of registered voters. The qualifications for voters, however, had been determined originally for a white society and failed to take account of the special features of African society, even when they came to be applied to Africans specifically; for instance, earnings and the value of immovable property, whether owned or occupied, but not movable property such as cattle, the 'property' of the re-serves, and indeed the only wealth of the African population.[3] By 1948 when the new delimitation came into effect, there were few houses in any urban Native township worth less than £75 (R150), while it proved difficult for many rural dwellers to establish such a value for the huts which constituted their dwelling; and few could establish earnings of £50 (R100) per annum. Thus while the urban vote increased as wages, and particularly the value of property increased, the rural vote showed a tendency to remain static or even to decline, until in 1948 East London alone had more voters than the whole of the Transkei. Indeed Wynberg, a suburb of Cape Town, had more voters than the Transkei.

The enormous extension of the Eastern Circle which the conse-

[1] Now Botswana.
[2] In 1942, the Native Appeal Court which constituted the delimitation Com-mission in terms of the Representation of Natives Act advised no change in the boundaries of the constituencies on the ground that the African population was in a state of transition involving movement of people from country to town and within the country generally the nature and extent of which had not yet been established. In 1947, it accepted the situation and recommended the changes noted above.
[3] For qualifications for registration as a voter, see p. 28.

quent delimitation involved was, of course, of major importance to me. In fact it made it impossible for me to maintain, over my later years in Parliament, the intimate personal contacts that I had established over the first ten years. Indeed, if I had had any serious opposition to meet either in 1948 or in 1956, I should have found it difficult if not impossible to face a contest over so vast an area. An election even in a constituency the size and character of the original Cape Eastern Circle was in the best of circumstances bound to make great demands on a candidate. In the circumstances which actually prevailed, these demands seemed endless. They included the need to create some sort of an organisation in a field over which no organisation existed, covering an electorate that was not constituted to assist in such an undertaking.

On the initiative of the Rev. James Calata, who was destined to play a considerable—and to him costly[1]—role in later African political activities, I was invited to stand for election by the Cape division of the now banned African National Congress. This sponsorship was a strong factor in my favour, but it did not solve my problem of organisation. That remained my own affair. What it did for me, however, was to provide me with an election agent, who was to prove a tower of strength to me throughout this election and a staunch and valued friend throughout the rest of his life. Indeed I have always felt that only A. Z. Tshiwula's confidence, encouragement, and unstinted, undemanding and ever cheerful service kept me going through the months of campaigning over the enormous field which this first election involved; and that among people who were as new to me as I was to them. He had an unrivalled knowledge of his own people. He knew, and was known and respected by, all the leading personalities among them and could evaluate their character and their influence. Having decided to back the surprising, indeed revolutionary decision of the African National Congress to support a woman candidate, he brought all this knowledge and experience into my service. On the basis of his experience as a voter on the old common roll, he organised committees at all the focal points in the constituency. Into these he gathered both those who could be depended upon and those whom, less reliable, it would be useful to have under observation. And where and when it was discovered that my committees and those

---

[1] He was among those arrested on a charge of Treason in 1956. He is now in the ranks of banned persons, i.e. ordered to desist from all political action.

of other candidates showed a tendency to overlap, his patience and tact smoothed over the rough places created by my intolerance and my failure to understand all the temptations to which voters were subjected, of which the desire to be on the winning side was possibly not the least. He suffered with me all the difficulties and discouragements consequent upon what is generally known as 'African time', in which we were to be met alternatively with the claim that meetings arranged with great care and much labour had been fixed too early in the day or—on the following occasion, in the same area, and on the strength of this experience—too late!—or had in general been organised too far ahead or not far enough ahead. When these things tried my spirit badly, he could always take them philosophically, encouraging me with the assurance that no matter how small the audience, the important people were there, and they would carry the word back to all the others. He religiously attended all my meetings, a remarkable feat of endurance which I myself could only sustain by doing my best to forget his presence, since over so vast an area and so long a period of campaigning, there was a limit to the amount of variation that I or any one could introduce into a programme, no matter how vast.

There was only one service he could not perform satisfactorily for me—that was to interpret. It was an important service since all speeches had to be interpreted into Xhosa, the Bantu language of the area—the practice even where the speaker was qualified to speak in the local language, as I was not. Tshiwula, although well-educated as Africans go, and a good speaker of English, had not mastered the art—and it is indeed an art—of current interpretation. His inadequacy in this regard was accentuated by a slight tendency to stammer as he sought for the appropriate word until the audience began to grow restive, and it seemed better to curtail the whole performance than to try their patience too much. As he himself was only too conscious of his deficiency in this field, only the failure of the most determined efforts to get a competent interpreter from the audience induced him to undertake this office, and he welcomed the termination of the effort with even more satisfaction and relief than those who had to listen to him.

This matter of interpretation of speeches is one of the more exacting experiences that speakers in mixed African-European meetings have to get to grips with. Africans find it less exacting than Europeans, at least than English-speaking Europeans, to whom my

experience is mainly confined in this regard. Africans, like all pre-
literate people I imagine, are facile speakers. Indeed, in any meeting,
given enough time, practically every African would make a speech,
a circumstance that itself involved a considerable strain on the
candidate in an election where, in my experience, the best moment
in any meeting was the final one, particularly if the vote of confidence was sure and solid, but even if it was not. But for those who
are not practised speakers, or not experienced in this field, the technique of speaking with an interpreter is one that has to be learnt,
since the interpretation goes on sentence by sentence, which creates
obvious difficulties of construction and continuity in which the
interpreter is as important as the speaker. Looking back on my
wide experience in this regard, what impresses me is the high level
of effective interpretation that was produced among all the varied
audiences that an adventure of this kind threw up. Practically all
were competent, some were very good, a few were brilliant. Among
the latter I remember particularly Mr. Theo B. Lugisa, a headman
in the East London location who had been a prominent member
of the I.C.U.,[1] the African trade union my husband had come to
South Africa to advise. It was a pleasure to listen to oneself being
put over in a critical election by Lugisa. Such colourful force and
volubility could not fail to carry conviction. And East London was
one of my danger spots in that first election, since there, those who
had hived off from the I.C.U. after my husband's arrival were
strongly supporting my most dangerous opponent—an additional
reason for my pleasure in Lugisa's performance.

Possibly the most impressive and artistic interpreter I ever had
in the constituency was Professor Jabavu, father of Miss Noni
Jabavu. I remember opening an agricultural show in which he was
interested; indeed I believe he had issued the invitation. He performed the function of interpreter for me on that occasion. It was a
performance that delighted the audience. It had only one slight
drawback from my point of view, and that was that, being a
teacher, as well as an expert in the vocal arts in which Africans
excel—he organised and led all the community singing at Fort
Hare, the Native University College where he was Professor of
Classics—he not only added colour to my businesslike address,
but also a good deal of what he thought might be said both by
way of comment and elaboration, the whole interspersed with

[1] Industrial and Commercial Workers' Union.

D

appropriate jokes of which he was not the least appreciative. It was all done with fine oratorical flourishes which left me feeling that the show had been well and truly opened, but I was not sure that it had been opened by me.

The election was hotly contested. While in the neighbouring constituencies the fight was a straight one between two contestants, in the Eastern Circle there were four competitors besides myself. No doubt the attraction here was the smaller size and the apparently more compact character of the constituency. Two of the contestants had already had some experience of Parliament, one as a Labour member of the Pact Government[1] and one under General Smuts in the parliament which preceded the advent of General Hertzog to power.[2] A third was a retired magistrate from the Transkei,[3] and the fourth, Mr. Duncan, was the proprietor of a country hotel.

My own candidature occasioned a great deal of comment in interested 'white' circles in which the dominating note was complete scepticism about my chances of success. Africans, it was asserted, certainly African men, would never vote for a woman—and African men only were the voters in this election.

In a situation of this kind, it is difficult to put a finger on any deciding factor. All the candidates were equally personally unknown to the majority of the voters. In the long run, I fancy the contest swung in my favour for a combination of reasons, of which possibly the most important were my own participation over a number of years in the fight to retain the old Cape franchise, and the circumstances of my husband's arrival in South Africa and his continuing efforts as Secretary of the Friends of Africa to help the emergent African worker in his struggle to improve his very burdensome lot. All these activities, and particularly my share in my husband's work in the industrial field, which more and more absorbed me when my marriage terminated my appointment on the staff of the University of the Witwatersrand, gave me a knowledge of the day to day problems of the lives of the African people which, in the political and social circumstances of South Africa, is not readily available to the ordinary white citizen. Indeed, I have always felt that one of the greatest arguments against a segregation policy is the ignorance which it fosters among those who pursue it. In terms

[1] Mr. J. Stewart.
[2] Mr. W. Stuart—later to represent the Transkei in the House of Assembly.
[3] Mr. Frank Brownlee, the author of a delightful book, altogether too little known. —*The Cattle Thief*.

of this policy it is true to say that, generally speaking, those who govern do not know how those whom they govern live.

If I had another advantage in the field it was that I had no political past to live down. First, I could say that I had never been a member of any political party because all the parties hitherto represented in Parliament up to that time had supported some colour bar or another. This certainly stood me in good stead. And, as I have already said, I was particularly fortunate in my election agent.

Finally, in an election for male voters only, the African woman's voice was not without influence. Wherever I went, I was interested to try to see life from the African woman's point of view and to try to show the women their own situation from my point of view. It was an effort I found highly rewarding both personally and politically; for the African woman in South Africa was a person to be reckoned with. She is often educated better than her brothers, certainly in the rural areas where cattle herding in open lands made and still makes great demands on the male youth of the kraal, and although without much in the way of legal rights she was—and, where she still gets the same opportunities—she is, very generally a person of some independence of character with the will to assert it. So while much play was made by my opponents of the disaster into which the Xhosas had been led in their struggle against the invading Whites, in the days of the frontier wars, by the false prophetess Nongqausa,[1] their influence was strongly exercised on my behalf.

[1] In 1856, when an uneasy peace had been established on the eastern frontier of the Cape Colony between the Colony and the Xhosas, a girl named Nongqausa claimed to have met at the river where she went to draw water, a number of men who differed greatly in appearance from the people she was accustomed to see. Her uncle, to whom she told of her experience, himself went to the place and there saw the strangers and conversed with them. The meeting was repeated on successive days. On the fourth day he recognised among the party a brother long dead. According to the story, the strangers then informed him that they were the eternal enemies of the white man come from battlefields beyond the seas to help the Xhosas to drive out their white neighbours. The condition of their assistance was that the people should kill and eat their fattest cattle. Later according to Nongqausa and her uncle, who now professed to be the channel of communication between the spirit world and the Xhosa nation, the command was that all cattle should be killed and all grain destroyed for on a given day, new and lovelier cattle and finer grain would come out of the earth and the heroes of the past would come to help them to rid the land of the white invaders.

The story spread and was received throughout the land, and over the succeeding months, the destruction of the nation's resources was hopefully pursued. On the appointed day, the sun rose and set on a starving people to whom not conquest of but supplication to their competitors for the land, for food, for work, for any means of keeping body and soul together, was all that was left to a broken nation.

At every meeting they formed an important part of the audience, and their views on all that was said were widely canvassed throughout the constituency.

Thus, in the end, we defied the prophecies of those who 'knew the Native' and were certain a woman could not win. The margin was not a great one in actual figures. The whole vote was only 2870. Of this I got 1118, putting me 157 votes ahead of the runner-up. I had entered the contest reluctantly when the provisions of the Act stipulated a residential qualification in the Cape Province for candidates, a qualification which I had but my husband had not. I had never entertained any desire to enter Parliament. Now it had happened, and in exceptional circumstances which made the question 'what next' more pertinent and immediate than is usual for a new member. Both I and my colleagues were soon to discover how complicated the answer to it was to be.

4

First Experiences on the Parliamentary Front

Among the successful candidates in this first election under the Representation of Natives Act, there was none with any Parliamentary experience. We had thus to find our own way through Parliamentary procedure and practice as well as to establish our relationship with one another. Here I may say that, from the beginning, we strove to work together and succeeded sufficiently effectively, certainly for the first ten years during which the representation changed little, to make a considerable impression at least of team work. We did our best to resolve any differences of opinion behind the scenes, and on no occasion could we be found voting on opposite sides. This was, I believe, quite an achievement since, in the circumstances, we tended to be strongly individualistic.

In that regard, I was exceptionally fortunate in the colleagues with whom this first election brought me into association in the House of Assembly, Mr. Gordon Hemming from the Transkei and Mr. D. B. Molteno, a young barrister from the Western Cape. When Mr. Molteno entered Parliament, he was its youngest member. But, inheriting a strong political tradition—his grandfather had been the first Prime Minister of the old Cape Parliament—he had been as actively associated at the Cape with the struggle against the abolition of the Cape Native franchise and the formalising of the segregation policy as I had been in the Transvaal. We had therefore a good deal of common ground and common experience on which to build a working partnership.

To that experience, Mr. Hemming, an extremely able and highly respected attorney from Umtata, added his invaluable knowledge of the Transkei and its people gained over many years' residence and work in that territory. I use the word 'added' advisedly for from the beginning Mr. Hemming implicitly endorsed the idea of a partnership and, throughout the years, helped to cement such a partnership with good nature, tolerance and a bonhomie which endeared him to all who knew him. His death in 1946, after an illness largely due to his effort, in the first year of the war, to

53

prepare himself for a military service beyond his physical capacity, was a very great blow to us.

So far as Parliament itself was concerned, it is interesting—and important—to remember its composition. Indeed it is essential to do so in order to appreciate the problems of adjustment which we had to meet. The United Party, with General Hertzog as Prime Minister, supported by his two lieutenants, Mr. Havenga at Finance and Mr. Oswald Pirow, then at Railways, and with General Smuts as Deputy Prime Minister with the portfolio of Justice, held 117 seats in a House which numbered 150 apart from us. The official Opposition led by Dr. Malan had twenty seats, the Dominion Party under Colonel C. Stallard's leadership held five seats and the Labour Party, under the leadership of Mr. Walter Madeley, four seats.

The Dominion Party, like Dr. Malan's Nationalist Party, owed its origin to the coalition between General Hertzog and General Smuts and to a large extent to the same issues, although for different reasons. Like Dr. Malan, Colonel Stallard was not satisfied that the rights of secession and neutrality were implicit in the 1926 Commonwealth Prime Minister's declaration. But in his opinion they should not be. So while Dr. Malan desired to make that situation explicit and secure, which he contended could best be achieved through the establishment of a republic, Colonel Stallard was entirely opposed to any loosening of the bonds between the Dominions and Britain. Indeed his own wish was to see these bonds drawn as tightly as possible so that the component parts should become increasingly integrated, to a point at which imperial federation might become the natural development. In the circumstances, he would have nothing to do with the right to propagate republicanism which the South African Party had felt compelled to accept as part of the bargain of fusion.

Of immediate importance to us was the fact that whatever else might differentiate them, all these parties were essentially 'white' parties, that is, not only were their members all white and, except in the Cape where the Coloured people were still enfranchised on the common roll,[1] elected by white voters; they were all committed to a greater or lesser degree, or in one way and another, to colour bar policies. The Botha-Smuts Government had laid the founda-

[1] But with the old qualifications—those which also governed the African electorate. See p. 28.

tions of the segregation policy in the 1913 Native Land Act, which restricted the African's right to land to limited and as yet undefined areas, and the 1923 Natives (Urban Areas) Act, which first embodied the idea of the developing urban areas as 'white' preserves to which the Native population could and should come as servants and in which they should only remain so long as they continued to serve. When the Smuts Government eventually gave place to General Hertzog's first Government in 1924, it had on the stocks a Class Areas Bill designed to apply the principle of compulsory residential separation to all racial groups. The new Nationalist-Labour Pact Government celebrated its advent to power by a Mines and Works Act Amendment[1] under which still today Africans may not achieve those certificates of competency which are the essential prerequisites of the right to do skilled jobs on the mines. That was followed in 1932 by a Native Service Contract Act[2] which strengthened the hold of the white farmer on his black labour by making the labourer's contract of service, where it involved the right to put up huts to accommodate his family, cover the service not only of the labourer himself but of all his minor children. All these measures together were the foundation on which General Hertzog had built his comprehensive programme of segregation, which only needed the abolition of the Cape common roll Native franchise to enable him to apply it uniformly over the whole country—which meant in effect to the Cape Province. In his efforts to achieve this objective he had the whole-hearted support of Colonel Stallard, who had in fact been largely responsible for the form of the Urban Areas legislation, while Mr. Madeley, leading what had always been essentially a 'white' labour party, claimed that he and his Party were committed to a policy of complete separation of Black and White. It is true, Colonel Stallard could not always take all his Party with him on colour issues; and not many members of the Labour Party would have been prepared to die in the last ditch for total segregation—or indeed even to spend much time on what was regarded even in their ranks as an academic programme designed to rationalise their white labour politics. But the days when Colonel Stallard's support of Dr. Malan's proposition that African representation in the House of Assembly should be abolished finally tore the Dominion Party in shreds lay nearly ten

[1] Act 25 of 1926.
[2] Act 24 of 1932.

years ahead, by which time the Labour Party was well on the way to changing its whole attitude, character and atmosphere and had lost its leader in the process. In the meantime, both parties had found little or no difficulty in accepting General Hertzog's programme, and their benches could still produce speeches on colour that differed little in content from those of their most reactionary Nationalist neighbours.

In a set-up of this kind, with Government and Opposition alike committed to policies which, with their implications of discrimination and racial exclusiveness, Africans could not accept, the immediate problem for this first group of representatives of Africans was how a statutory fractional representation should conduct itself if it was to achieve anything for those who had elected it. What tactics should it pursue that would justify any hope of useful service? Our earliest Parliamentary experiences were to raise this issue in very practical form.

We entered Parliament in a short pre-election session with parties lining up for their first contest since coalition. Usually in South Africa, Parliament meets in the first half of the year, sits for approximately six months and then goes into recess for the rest of the year. In election years, however, it has become customary to vary this practice, that is where a Parliament has run its full course of five years and the date of the election is thus more or less fixed. On such occasions, Parliament has met for a short pre-election session primarily concerned to put through a part appropriation, and has met again in the latter part of the year to consider the budget and to pass any legislation which the Government feels it requires forthwith. The foundations of this practice were being laid when we joined the ranks of the legislators.

But if our first session was brief, and the range of its business officially limited, it produced enough to show us thus early just what our hopes of influencing policy in a more liberal direction would have to contend with. The Government, with the significantly autocratic temper of all large majorities, which instinctively claim to be national in their range and appeal, began by taking all the time of the session for its own business—that is by voting out all the time normally provided for private members' motions. The proposition did not go unchallenged. The argument put forward in support of it was that this was in effect an extraordinary session, to be followed after the election by a full session of the normal pattern, in which at that time two out of the five sitting days in each week were, for a considerable part of the session, given over to private members. In any case, the Government contended, the financial measures would give the Oppositions all the opportunity they needed to expound and publicise their election programmes, as indeed they did. When these measures were through, there was no doubt of the character of the impending contest or of the challenge which we ourselves were going to have to meet.

South Africa has not one budget but two. It has a general budget and what was then a railways and harbours budget which has now become a transport budget. For transport is a function of Government in South Africa. This makes the Government itself the largest single employer of labour after the mining industry. In the circumstances, particularly in the circumstances of this country, it provides a fruitful field of party competition and contention in which sectional interests easily rise to the surface as we were thus early to discover. The great depression of the late twenties and early thirties had hit South Africa with exceptional force. In so doing, it had aggravated seriously the already too serious problem of poor Whiteism, reducing the inadequate opportunities then available to the rural Whites drifting townwards under the combined pressure of the collapse in commodity prices and the competitive cheapness of Native labour itself forced more and more into the labour market through increasing numbers and too little land.

In its efforts to combat White poverty, the first Nationalist Government[1] had already extensively applied a White labour policy in the public services, of which transport was the largest and most important. Its immediate response to this crisis was to extend this policy wherever possible. With falling revenues, this meant giving preference to White workers in respect of any work available. While wage rates had perforce to be reduced for all grades in the service, every effort was made to maintain and, wherever possible, to increase the actual numbers of White labourers employed. Where its own resources came to an end, the Department took in workers subsidised by the Department of Labour as a special unemployment relief scheme.

But if South Africa went into the trough of depression more rapidly and more deeply than some other countries, it also emerged

[1] See p. 37.

with exceptional speed and vigour, thanks to its gold. The Minister of
Railways, Mr. Oswald Pirow, could therefore present his partial
budget in 1938 in terms of mounting surpluses and with happy
references to 'the extraordinary prosperity this country now enjoys'.[1]
This, he claimed with supporting figures, was being effectively
shared by all the employees in the service of the Department.

All of which might have been expected to lend a mellow air to the
discussions, and to complicate the business of opposition. But even
if there had been no pending election to stimulate competition, it
soon became apparent that 'purified' Nationalism had enough
stock-in-trade to provide it with a fighting platform of high emotional content that could function as effectively in prosperity as in
adversity. This was the distresses, the needs, the claims and the
rights of Afrikanerdom. These had been the binding force of the old
Nationalist Party. Since that Party had split, claims to be the in-
heritors of its mantle had been a progressively competitive issue,
exacerbating the already bitter relationship between old friends. In
the pre-election atmosphere, it was given full rein. At once the
Opposition launched an attack on the Minister of Railways on
three fronts, notably none of them concerned with the mechanics of
running a large public service which in terms of the Constitution is
supposed to be conducted on business principles.

The first accusation was that the Minister, in his new-found
alliance with mining magnates and big business generally—the
Nationalist conception of the Smuts section of the United Party—
was throwing the White workers to the wolves and piling up profits
out of cheap Black labour. They quoted figures to prove that the
railway service was becoming progressively blacker and that those
Whites who had succeeded in retaining a place in the lower levels
of the service—Afrikaners—had had a shamefully inadequate share
in the prosperity of the service. Those in the upper levels, by implication unilingual English-speaking personnel, had fared signally
better, they claimed. Here the second line of attack emerged—
that the Government had departed from the policy of enforced
bilingualism which, with the White labour policy, had been a
corner stone of the old Nationalist policy.

The final accusation was that the Minister was trying to destroy
Spoorbond, the organisation which the Afrikaans workers on the
railways had created to look after their own interests. This, they said,

[1] Hansard, Vol. 31, Col. 457 *et seq.*

he had set out to do because that organisation was an Afrikaans organisation founded on Christian national lines and reflected the Afrikaner spirit, whereas he wished to force the Afrikaans worker into an organisational pattern dictated by English-speaking artisans.

For days, argument surged and eddied repetitively around these three topics in a debate in which the Minister's responses to the challenges made to him were as significant to us as the challenges themselves. Giving his own figures to disprove the accusation that he was changing the ratio of non-White to White workers in the railway service, he took his stand determinedly on the maintenance of the White labour policy. Indeed he claimed that, with mounting revenues, it had been possible to develop that policy in a way that the old Nationalist Party had never been able even to dream of. Not only had all depression cuts in the wages of White workers been restored; new levels of wages and other rewards had been given to all levels. In addition, plans had now been elaborated and were being implemented to make the railway service a career for White youths as it had never been before. So far as bilingualism was concerned, again there had been, not a departure from the old Nationalist policy, but a more effective application of the policy with the support of the English-speaking element of the United Party—'one of the real fruits of co-operation' between Hertzogites and Smutsites. As for Spoorbond, the Minister declared that far from wishing to destroy this expression of the Afrikaans spirit, his main concern was to keep the Opposition from dragging it into politics, and that to their chagrin he had succeeded in establishing a friendly and co-operative relationship with the organisation which had effectively countered their disruptive influence.

In fact the Minister's case on all points of argument was that the new party, the United Party, was carrying on the programme of the old Nationalist Party with a new effectiveness due to the support of the English-speaking electorate, a contention strongly supported by other Government speakers from both sections of the Party.

It was into this argument that my colleague, Mr. Molteno, and I decided to adventure with our maiden speeches. It seemed an appropriate occasion not only to air a case with which I at least had been much preoccupied in the preceding years, that of the non-White, particularly the African workers on the railways, but also to state our attitude to the white labour policy in general. Everywhere the depression had fallen on the African worker with a particular force the extent of which was gradually being at least partially revealed by official statistics. The Department of Census and Statistics had reported that in the private sector of the economy, efforts to keep the level of white employment fairly stable had succeeded in holding the fall at 4 per cent; for non-Europeans, on the other hand, there had been a fall of 12 per cent. The situation in public employment was amply revealed by the Minister's own statements as to what had occurred in the railway service. In reply to the accusations which had been levelled at him, he instanced that between 1933, when the United Party took over from the Nationalists, to 1937, the number of European labourers in permanent or temporary service in his department had risen from 12,636 to 14,390, while the number of Native labourers had fallen from 36,254 to 23,534. 'Thus in a period of four years,' he proudly declared, 'we have increased the number of Europeans who have got a career on the railways by about 2000 while we have reduced the number of natives (sic) by about 12,000.'[1] He did not need to inform his audience that the Natives who remained in the service did not belong to categories with careers before them in the service, nor did he say what had happened to those who could no longer look for employment in this service. But he could add to his laurels the replacement of 743 natives who had performed a specialised job, that of hammer men, by 701 Europeans at an extra cost of £54,000 (R108,000) per annum, a cost which white South Africa could now afford and was apparently happy to pay without query as to the fate of those who had been displaced.

Nor was this drive to keep up White employment at the expense of non-White workers the whole story. When the rates of pay of White workers in the Department's service had been cut by from 2 per cent to 10 per cent in the depression, those of non-Whites suffered cuts of from 14 per cent to 20 per cent, with the surprising further discrimination that while the cuts in European wage rates were essentially temporary, the Minister declared the cuts in non-European rates to be a permanent reduction, and all pressure from outside Parliament to secure their restoration on the flowing tide of prosperity had been unavailing. The justification for this discrimination had never been made clear. The Minister's reply to representations made to him in this regard had been that the cuts in the

[1] Hansard, Vol. 31, Col. 735.

rates paid by his department to its non-European workers were an adjustment in line with the cost of living and with the rates prevailing in private employment. To anyone familiar with the pressures of life on the African worker this could never have seemed more than a frivolous response, since nowhere did the customary rates paid to Africans approximate a living standard. That it could be said by a Cabinet Minister and meet little or no criticism in political circles demonstrated the weakness, political and economic, of the African worker and of the African population as a whole.

The whole situation also demonstrated the characteristic thinking of White South Africa, which was to be one of the main obstacles we as Native Representatives were to have to meet: that is, that poverty in one section of the community can be cured by shifting it to another, what Professor Herbert Frankel has pertinently called the economic frontier mentality.[1]

Incidentally, until the advent of the present series of Nationalist Governments, it was only in Government service that wage rates could be and were determined in terms of race. In fact, the industrial legislation operative at that time in the private sector of the economy specifically excluded race as a determining factor in wage agreements gazetted under statute and administered under the aegis of the Department of Labour.

It was in the light of all these facts that Mr. Molteno and I proceeded to make for the first time in Parliament what was to become our standard case over all the years of our political life. It was a case which, alas, is still pertinent and is still being made, with less effect even now than it should achieve where so many proofs of its soundness have been provided over the years. It began with a plea for justice for the non-European worker on the railways—on the principle that a community has a responsibility for all its members; surely non-White workers with the need and the will to work had a right to consideration of that need and assistance to satisfy it that was as great as that of any other section of the population. It ended with insistence upon the interdependence of all sections of the community. How could South Africa hope, we asked, to find jobs for a growing White population except on the increasing effectiveness of the non-Whites both as producers and consumers—particularly for Whites with the standards of South African Whites? Was

[1] S. Herbert Frankel, 'The Tyranny of Economic Paternalism in Africa'. Supplement to *Optima*, December 1960.

not the greatest danger to Whites and White standards in South Africa the very cheapness of Black labour?

We could not complain of the hearing we received. It was courteous and attentive. The response was less encouraging. The leader of the Labour Party indeed spent a minute of two endorsing our general thesis that starvation wages are the enemy of progress, but he linked it with a call for a national minimum wage of 10s. per day—in a country where, and at a time when African workers were fortunate to earn 27s. per week—and for complete segregation, territorial, economic and political, of the African population. The members of the official Opposition left the argument where it was and continued with their own line of attack as if we had not spoken. One member of their team alone made any reference to our case, Mr. Bruckner de Villiers of Stellenbosch, and that was to say he hoped the Minister would not do what we asked since to improve the position of the non-European workers on the railways would only encourage the drift from country to town and make it more difficult for the farmers to get labour. The Minister himself, with polite commendation of the general line of our argument and what he and his colleagues seemed to regard as the unexpected moderation of its presentation, assured us that the Government was no worse, if no better, than private employers in its treatment of its non-European employees and that as conditions improved in the private sector of the economy, they would keep pace in the public sector; in other words, that the Government would follow but would not lead any effort to improve the economic status of the unenfranchised majority of the population.

Several of the older members who had followed General Smuts into fusion, notably Mr. Morris Alexander who represented a Cape Town seat with a considerable Coloured community, and Mr. Morris Kentridge, a Johannesburg member and an erstwhile Labourite, did put forward a plea in support of our case from the Government benches, but their speeches suffered the same fate as ours—they were drowned in the welter of argument between the Hertzogites and the Malanites as to who were the real defenders and promoters of Afrikanerdom, the faithful upholders of Nationalist principle and policy. Everything else was of secondary importance. We were being taught our first lesson in the practical politics of our country.

5

First Session Continued

The impressions our first major debate left on my mind as to the forces we as Native Representatives would have to meet in any effort to establish our case were markedly heightened by the course of the second financial debate, the only other major debate of this session. Here again the central theme was an inter-Afrikaner one, indeed the same one, that is, which section of the old Nationalist Party, those in the United Party or those on the 'purified' benches, was carrying on the true Nationalist policy.

It began with a typically lengthy amendment by Dr. Malan which in the light of subsequent developments has a special significance. Its first paragraph was a demand that the Government embark forthwith on an effective large-scale scheme to place the landless farming population back on the land and 'an effective mortgage redemption scheme' designed to 'place the farming industry in general upon a sound economic basis'—a back-to-the-land policy which was still the typical answer of South Africa to the unfamiliar problems of industrialisation. This of course related to Whites only. It then called for the application of the policy of segregation 'consistently, by providing inter alia for separate residential areas for Europeans and non-Europeans in urban areas, coupled with a proper and adequate national housing scheme, separate spheres of employment for all sections of the population as far as possible, the limitation of employment in definite directions to European labour and/or in accordance with an equitable quota for Europeans and non-Europeans, legislation against mixed marriages and the employment of Europeans by non-Europeans, and finally separate representation of coloured voters in the legislative bodies'.[1]

The smaller Opposition groups naturally used the occasion to put up their own special programmes. With the Dominionites, it was a demand that the Government should take 'no further administrative or legislative steps . . . calculated to weaken the position of the Union as a part of the British Empire or wound the feelings of

[1] Hansard, Vol. 31, Col. 754.

those who appreciate the vital importance of that connection as
the sole means of providing for the safety and security of the Union'.
The leader of the Labour Party, with an amendment even longer than
Dr. Malan's, began with a demand for legislation to prevent anti-
democracy and racial propaganda.[1] (Here again 'racial' refers not
to Black-White relations but to relations between the two sections
of the White population.) It went on to an elaborate programme of
increased wages, shorter hours, lower prices of food and rent,
higher old age pensions, all to be pinned together by a state bank,
and ended with the proposal of complete separation 'of natives
and Europeans territorially, socially and economically by providing
sufficient suitable land whereon the native population can develop
along its own lines with assistance—financial and otherwise—as
far as may be required'.[2]

These programmes did indeed provoke some discussion among
the old South African Party members of the United Party, the
Dominionites' with some acrimony, the Labour Party's with
little seriousness. At best, however, these were but side-shows. The
essential interest of the occasion for most of the members lay in the
Malanite challenge to the Government.

The gist of the case made by Dr. Malan himself was that Afrikaners were being forced into the towns by the pressures of rural
poverty, there to compete with non-Europeans of lower living standards but with urban skills and experience. This situation was
fraught with great dangers for the Whites, he contended, and must
be tackled from two directions. As many of the urban immigrants
as possible must be put back on the land, and for the rest, for those
for whom this was not possible, there must be housing and employment provision based on a separation that would prevent all social
contact between the races since such contact must constitute a
threat to the purity of the White race. And where administrative
action might still not be entirely effective in this regard, the law
must come in to reinforce it by making all marriages between
White and non-White illegal.

He wound up a lengthy speech on this wide field with a few
words on the subject of separate representation of the enfranchised
Coloured population. Contending that the policy of segregation
must be applied consistently or not at all, he declared 'If you do not

[1] Hansard, Vol. 31, Col. 821.
[2] Hansard, Vol. 31, Col. 770.

want to apply that segregation to legislative bodies, then you are not entitled to apply it consistently to industrial and economic matters'[1]—on the principle presumably of taking from him who hath not even that which he hath. This was a logic with which we were to become more and more familiar as time went on.

This initiated an increasingly acrimonious debate in which the Malanite Nationalists threw at their erstwhile friends two further accusations of departure from the straight and narrow path of Afrikaner nationalism. The first was in regard to their attitude to the proposition that the Cape Coloureds should be removed from the voters' roll as the Africans had been removed in 1936. This, they contended, had been adopted as Nationalist party policy by the Provincial Congresses of the Party some years before fusion, that was while General Hertzog was still their leader, but General Hertzog was clearly now retreating from that position under the pressure of his new friends. The second point at which there was failure to maintain the appointed course was in the purchase of land for Natives. This they argued with increasing virulence had never been the policy of the Nationalist Party. Segregation, yes; limitation of land open to Native occupation and acquisition, yes; but purchase of land by the Government for the Natives, an emphatic no. The land released from the restrictions of the 1913 Land Act was for purchase by the Natives themselves if and where they could afford to acquire it. From this point, it was a short step to the sort of argument that tends to develop on all such occasions in South Africa, that the White man's money was being spent on Black people while nothing was being done for necessitous Whites.

Since part of the segregation policy was the intention to keep the Africans out of the towns and to remove them from proximity to Europeans, the obvious counter argument was, how do you achieve this purpose in respect of a people so lacking in resources except under a system of assisted land settlement? This argument was indeed put up by the Hertzogites, but with less conviction than it might have been, since farmers on both sides of the House had a simpler and cheaper solution of that problem, namely to send the urban and the reserve surplus alike to augment their labour supply which the conditions offered failed of themselves to attract.

Particularly vocal on the subject of the purchase of land for Natives and on the whole policy of the development of the reserves,

[1] Hansard, Vol. 31, Col. 759.

E

with which it had been linked as part of the compensation for the restrictive aspects of both the Land laws and the Urban Areas Act, was the Transvaal Nationalist, Mr. J. G. Strydom, destined later to become Prime Minister in succession to Dr. Malan.

Mr. Strydom had already shown his colours in the Railway debate. On that occasion he had castigated the Minister concerned for allowing railway carriages normally reserved for White passengers to transport Blacks. Nor was he placated by the Minister's explanation that this had resulted from a temporary shortage of rolling stock and the urgent need to transport labourers for the mines, and that the coaches had been duly fumigated before being put into circulation again for their original purpose. He then produced a new grievance, which was that the same crockery had been used on the Natal service for Asiatics and Whites.

On this occasion,[1] Mr. Strydom was not only emphatic in his contention that the old Nationalist Government under which General Hertzog's legislative programme had taken shape had never contemplated purchasing land for Natives. He had been studying the report of the Native Affairs Department as well as the debates in the first session of the new Natives Representative Council, and he was volubly and violently critical of the way in which the plans for the rehabilitation of the reserves were going. He was shocked to discover that these plans had led not only to the purchase of some pedigree livestock—poultry and cattle—for an experimental farm and an agricultural school (what came to be referred to later as the cock and bull story); they had even involved the purchase of a 2-ton lorry, a 12-h.p. engine and dynamo and a motor tractor. The idea of an engine and a dynamo called forth the exclamation 'Just imagine, electricity for natives.'[2] As for the tractor, which was apparently not to be used to combat soil erosion as someone had tried to tell him, but for communal cultivation, 'I should have thought,' cried Mr. Strydom, 'that the natives could be taught to use their hands if it were necessary to prepare the land, but now they have to be taught to use tractors for that purpose.' He had no objection to the Natives learning to cultivate their land a little better in their areas, he declared, but 'when we find that money is spent for motor tractors etc. for communal cultivation of land, then we call a halt.' This was not only an unwarrant-

[1] Hansard, Vol. 31, Col. 1052 *et seq.*
[2] Hansard, Vol. 31, Col. 1710 *et seq.*

able extravagance, a squandering of the White man's money; it was also a danger to the established pattern of South African life. In his own words, 'While our object is not to allow the natives to become Europeans, we find that the Government is buying motor tractors, ploughs and harrows for the natives and spending £550 (R1100) for the purpose . . .' If the Government went on in this way, he argued, the natives would soon cease to be labourers and become farmers, with disastrous effects on White farming, where the problem of markets was already a serious one.

If anything was needed to complete the discouraging impression of this our first session, it was provided by the Opposition's move to delete from the estimates a contribution of £2000 (R4000) to a fund sponsored by the Society of Friends for the relief of distress among children who were the victims of the civil war in Spain. By the time the session came to an end, it was clear that we were facing a particularly unpleasant election in which appeals to colour prejudice were again going to play a major part as they had done in the 1929 election, when the old Nationalist Party produced a Black Manifesto as its principal election weapon.

Nor was the attitude shown by the Government itself a ground for consolation. In face of the determined attacks of the Opposition, its general tone was defensive and apologetic. Would a sweeping victory at the polls, of which there was every prospect, make a difference? Would it give the now not so new alliance the inner security and the confidence needed to withstand the onslaughts of old friends and enable its combined elements to find a road forward that would take cognisance of the new forces coming into operation both at home and abroad which were making the old patterns of South African life as lived in the Northern Provinces and already pressing down on the South, increasingly obviously obsolete? We could but wait and see with what optimism we could muster.

6

A New Parliament But Old Attitudes

The election which took place in May 1938 saw the return of the United Party with a majority which, if not quite as massive as before the election, was yet large enough to justify the claim that the country wanted, and was well set on the road to achieve, true national unity as between the two White groups in the population. It now held 111 out of the 150 'White' seats. But if the smaller parties had gained little, in two cases at least their gains were significant. The Nationalists had increased their number from twenty to twenty-seven, the Dominion Party from five to eight. The Nationalist gains were mainly in the Cape Province. In the Free State the Party gathered in two new seats. In the Transvaal it lost one seat and Mr. Strydom came back as its sole member in that Province. Thus the official Opposition was predominantly a party of the Cape Province. The Dominionites, on the other hand, with one exception, were all from Natal, indeed all from Durban and its environs. The one exception was from East London in the Cape Province.

With the official Opposition calling the tune, the election itself had been fought on two highly explosive issues both of which had been foreshadowed in the previous session. One was, as we anticipated, the question of colour where the emphasis was now being laid on the danger to White civilisation of the Cape Coloured franchise. The other, which was to assume major importance in the near future, was the implications of South Africa's so-called sovereign status out of which the new party alignment had grown and to which the threatening international situation lent special point. The Dominionites had little interest in the colour issue, but they were deeply concerned about the implications of sovereign independence; it was indeed their very *raison d'être*.

By the time Parliament met, in July, for its short post-election session, the first flush of satisfaction over their great victory had passed from the ranks of the United Party and there were already signs that the unity of the Party was not as deep or secure as its joint leadership was anxious to claim. Indeed, for weeks before the

68

opening of the session, there had been widespread agitation among the old South African Party members who had voted hopefully and enthusiastically for the two generals marching into the future shoulder to shoulder, and there was considerable anxiety about where their chosen path was going to take them.

The trouble revolved round flags and anthems. The immediate occasion was later to be explained as a series of unfortunate mistakes and misunderstandings about the hoisting of the Union Jack and the playing of God Save the King at Defence Headquarters on Union Day, May 31st. Flags and anthems were still highly explosive issues, closely bound up with the rival interpretations of South Africa's status and the conflicting views as to South Africa's ultimate destiny. It was not a long time as these things go since the country had reached the verge of civil war over the question of flags. The advent of the Nationalist Party to power in 1924 had been followed immediately by pressure for a national flag to replace the Union Jack which was regarded by the Party and its followers as the symbol of Afrikaner defeat and subjection. English sentiment was still sufficiently strong, however, to make the reaction to this proposition, particularly in Natal, a serious matter. In the end, the worst was avoided by a compromise negotiated by Dr. Malan as Minister of the Interior under which it was agreed that the Union should have a flag of its own but that this flag and the Union Jack should both be flown on appropriate occasions under regulations designed to respect the feelings of both sections of the white population.

Since then, the idea of a South African national anthem had begun to take shape in Nationalist circles, threatening a revival of the emotions which the flag issue had provoked. The formation of the United Party encouraged the hope that future developments on this front would be achieved without bitterness and even with consent. Had not the Transvaal message to the Cape to accept fusion argued that 'without racialism', that is, without English-Afrikaner divisions, the English could be brought even to agree to secession which, divided, they would never accept? But fusion had still to be proved the deathblow to racialism as understood in this context, and that would take time. In the meantime, under and behind the formation of the United Party, there were scarcely conscious anxieties initiated and stimulated by the emergence of the Dominion Party on the one side and the 'purified' Nationalists on the other. The old Smutsites were uneasy about the republican leanings of their new bed-fellows, while the Hertzogites were restless under the accusation of making concessions to imperialists and thus surrendering the Nationalist objective of full republican independence.

How near the surface these anxieties were had already been revealed in our first session as the result of an unheralded innovation in the proceedings attending the official opening of the session. This was the playing of Die Stem van Suid-Afrika,[1] a song which was steadily acquiring the status of a national anthem among the Afrikaans-speaking section of the population, as well as God Save the King. Who was responsible for suggesting the innovation is still a matter of conjecture. The decision, however, had been the Prime Minister's and that in a very real sense; he had discussed his proposal with some of his friends but he had not, it seemed, consulted his Cabinet on the subject. If some of them knew of the plan, to others, when the episode occurred, it was as great a surprise as it was to the Oppositions.

These circumstances, which at once came to light, inevitably tended to bring to the surface feelings of alarm and uncertainty among the non-Nationalist members of the Party. As it was, two impending events casting advance shadows seemed to give the innovation a special emotional content and significance. The first of these derived from the fact that this year, 1938, was the centenary year of the Great Trek, that episode in South African history around which so much Afrikaner sentiment and emotion has been woven. The occasion was to be celebrated by a whole series of events designed to commemorate the struggles, the sacrifices and the achievements of those who, rather than accommodate themselves to ways which offended their sense of the fitness of things, had gone out into the wilderness to build new homes and new states that should enshrine their own ideals. The central event was to be a series of pious pilgrimages in the steps of these pioneers, and that in the traditional fashion, by ox-wagon. These new treks were to converge on a site outside Pretoria where the whole celebration would culminate in the laying of the foundation stone of a great monument which should stand as a lasting tribute to all who had taken part in this historic movement. There was a good deal of

[1] Die Stem van Suid-Afrika (The Voice of South Africa) is now the official anthem of the Republic of South Africa.

talk of the 'national' character which the celebrations should take. The question was, would they indeed be national in the broadest sense, which in this context meant embracing the whole white population? Would this be an occasion for rejoicing in a common heritage or would it be an occasion for emphasising differences in tradition? Would it bring white South Africans together or would it drive them apart?

The other menacing element in the situation was the gathering clouds of war. If war did indeed come, how united, how divided would it find us?

All this had been the background in the pre-election session to two significant and related moves on the Parliamentary front. The first of these was a series of questions addressed by the Leader of the Dominion Party to the Prime Minister, of which the essential one was whether the playing of Die Stem at the opening of the session was intended as a recognition of that song as the national anthem of South Africa. The second was a debate initiated by the leader of the official Opposition, Dr. Malan, on the international situation and its implications for South Africa, through which the right and the need of a sovereign independent nation to have an anthem of its own came and went as a repetitive refrain.

These two occasions had been mainly notable for the efforts of the leaders of the United Party to satisfy both sections of the electorate and thus to cut the ground from under the feet of the Opposition groups in the forthcoming election. Replying to Colonel Stallard on the anthem, General Hertzog proclaimed that South Africa had in law no national anthem. For the English-speaking people, he said, God Save the King was a national anthem; for the Afrikaans-speaking people it could never fulfil that function. For them, including himself, Die Stem was rapidly coming to be accepted as their national anthem. He hoped that one day it would be so for all South Africans. In the meantime, to meet the practical situation he sought a compromise similar to that reached on the flag. This was that both God Save the King and Die Stem should be played on appropriate public occasions. But in recognition of the feelings and emotions of the Afrikaans-speaking group in the population, he defined God Save the King not as an anthem but as a prayer for the King and Die Stem as the song that spoke to the heart of the people.

On the subject of the international situation, General Smuts, who in this field was the Government's spokesman, disagreed with the contention which Dr. Malan had put forward that the League of Nations was dead and that we needed to take stock of our position in the light of this circumstance. The League might appear to be dead but he did not believe that it was dead. That being the case, we were bound, he said, by one great instrument and that was the Covenant of the League of Nations. If any liability should arise for South Africa in regard to war, we were bound as signatories to the Treaty to discharge our liabilities. Theoretically legally, we had no other liability, and it would depend upon circumstances whether we would take an active part in any war that might eventuate. He quoted Locarno as showing that our obligations in regard 'even to British wars' was undefined and that it would depend on the circumstances of each particular case whether South Africa or any of the other dominions would take part. The question therefore, he contended, remained an open question for the people of this country, a statement with which he obviously hoped to damp down argument on this highly explosive topic.

The result of the election suggested that for the great majority of the electorate, these declarations had proved as effective as their authors had hoped. In the circumstances, the episodes of May 31st were particularly unfortunate—the more so in that Mr. Oswald Pirow as Minister of Defence was the Minister concerned, whose German background encouraged anxieties as to his real intentions, and raised doubts in various quarters as to the genuineness of the 'mistakes' which the Government was later at pains to explain away. The story which burst upon the public on the evening of the 31st May was that, in the presence of several thousands of people gathered at Defence Headquarters at Roberts Heights, near Pretoria, to celebrate the Union's national day, the Union Jack had been hoisted and within minutes, abruptly lowered again, to leave the Union flag floating in solitary splendour. Rumour flashed round the assembled company that General Hertzog, on his way to the ceremony, had refused to carry out his intention to be present at the parade so long as the Union Jack continued to fly. As if to point the implications of the situation, the ceremony concluded with the playing, not of God Save the King but of Die Stem van Suid-Afrika.

Reflecting the nature and the depth of the emotions which these occurrences as reported aroused, the Minister of the Interior,

Mr. Stuttaford, immediately tendered his resignation from the Cabinet to the Prime Minister. The Prime Minister felt impelled to offer an explanation of what had occurred which resulted in Mr. Stuttaford withdrawing his resignation. According to this, as subsequently elaborated in the House of Assembly by Mr. Pirow, under the terms of the agreement arrived at at the time of the flag controversy, the Union flag was the only flag to be flown on Defence property except at the Natal Command where the Union Jack and the new Union flag were to share the honours on all occasions. On this occasion, an officer of the Natal Command, in charge of the proceedings at Defence headquarters, had by mistake given the order for the hoisting of the Union Jack at the Union Day parade. Another officer, perceiving the mistake, hurriedly ordered the lowering of the flag. The rumour that the Prime Minister, on his way to the function, had said he would not put in an appearance if the Union Jack continued to fly was quite without foundation.

Turning to the subject of the anthem, Mr. Pirow went on to explain that it would have been most improper to play God Save the King on this occasion since that was purely a royal salute, and neither the King nor his representative, the Governor-General, was present. As for the playing of Die Stem, that had been done not as an anthem but as a slow march for which any other familiar tune would have been equally suitable.[1]

How deeply fraught with emotion the subject still was was evidenced by the critical questioning that Mr. Pirow had to face from his newer colleagues in his own Party in the course of this speech. Anxieties were clearly very deep, nor did the attitude of the official Opposition do anything to alleviate them. Encouraged by what had happened, the Malanites began to press their own case on the subject of anthems. Dr. Malan led the way with a motion calling upon the House to declare that no solution of the question of a national anthem would be satisfactory otherwise than on the basis of a single purely South African and officially recognised national anthem, and called upon the Government immediately to take the necessary steps to effect this. He further asked the House to express its disapproval of any policy, declaration, or action on the part of Ministers inconsistent with this as being a disparagement of South Africa's independent status and as affecting South Africa's national honour.

[1] Hansard, Vol. 32, Col. 359.

Having begun this first session of the new Parliament with this challenge to the sentiments of a large part of the white electorate, including many of the Government's own supporters, Dr. Malan ended it as the international situation moved towards the Munich crisis with an amendment to the Appropriation Bill calling upon the Government to give a guarantee that South Africa would not be drawn into any of Britain's wars.

While these two themes ran through the whole two months of the session, they did not preclude a continuing emphasis on the colour issue. On this front, the demands of the previous session were repeated—job reservation (not yet given this name), and the extension of the segregation policy to the Coloured population, while Mr. Strydom went on with his attacks on the Government's so-called indulgence of the Native population. In this he found a new, or recovered an old ally in Mr. J. J. Serfontein, later to become Minister of Social Welfare in Dr. Verwoerd's Cabinet. Whatever was illiberal and reactionary found strong support from this team. We ourselves provided them with one of their best occasions for display. This was on a motion by Mr. Molteno on the subject of the poll tax.

In the years immediately before the war, the country had suddenly become seriously concerned about the ravages of poverty and its accompanying disease of malnutrition. This was undoubtedly the reflection of a worldwide movement receiving considerable stimulus from the work of the World Food and Agricultural Organisation. In South Africa, where both poverty and malnutrition were dangerously widespread, it had plenty to stimulate it. While politicians of all parties were willing and anxious to exploit the emotional appeal of this cause where it affected the white electorate, there had been growing concern in commercial and industrial as well as administrative circles over the extent of these evils among the African population as endangering the country's labour supplies and reducing its productive capacity. This concern had expressed itself in increasing support among the general public for an agitation among the Africans themselves for some relief of their taxation burdens. There were, of course, plenty of people prepared to argue that a tax of £1 (R2) per head per annum, even when it fell on youths of eighteen years, was not excessive, but where prevailing wage rates left a grave gap between earnings and the cost of even the simplest living standard, with the burden of that cost largely inflated by high protection duties which are always regressive in action, the sympathetic support for some effort to secure a review of the situation encouraged my colleague to put up his motion asking the House to disapprove of any tax such as the Native General Tax, the Poll Tax, which could only be paid at the expense of the taxpayer's barest necessities of life and resulted in imprisonment for failure to pay, and to ask the Government to abolish it forthwith.

In the circumstances of the session, the subject got less time than it deserved, but enough to draw an amendment from Mr. Strydom, seconded by Mr. Serfontein; this was that 'the native policy of this country should be (a) in the direction of the native population depending for its education and other development upon its own taxation and other contributions and (b) with a view to encouraging natives to perform farm labour and to remain on the farms and combating the influx into the cities, differentiation in favour of the farm labourer should be made between the tax paid respectively by native farm labourers and other natives'.[1]

Speaking to this amendment, Mr. Strydom remarked that 'the tendency is more and more being exhibited of spending more and more Government money in favour and on behalf of the natives'. He hastened to add in regard to the second part of his amendment, lest anyone should have any doubt about it, that he wanted it to be clear that he was not advocating a reduction in native taxation. Mr. Serfontein, in terms which were to become disagreeably familiar to us over the succeeding years, began his supporting speech by stating explicitly that what was needed was not reduction but increase in taxation. What had been done for natives in recent years in improving their conditions was gradually placing them in a better position than that of the poor Whites, he maintained, and he declared that he was opposed to an increase of expenditure on natives 'at the cost of Europeans'.

In the time available, only three other speakers succeeded in getting into the debate, all members of the United Party—Mr. Louw Steytler, father of the present Leader of the Progressive Party, Mr. J. J. Wentzel, now in the ranks of the Nationalists, and Mr. J. L. V. Liebenberg who, like Mr. Wentzel, followed General Hertzog in 1939 and subsequently also joined the Nationalists by way of Mr. Havenga's Afrikaner Party.

Mr. Steytler put up the proposition, which at that time had a

[1] Hansard, Vol. 32, Col. 1310 *et seq.*

measure of popularity among the farming community, that farm labourers should be exempt from the poll tax as getting little out of it by way of education or other services to which a portion of the tax was by law applied. Messrs. Wentzel and Liebenberg suggested that nothing should be done until a recently appointed committee of enquiry into the reasons for the prevailing farm labour shortage should report.

The whole debate, albeit brief, served to confirm the narrowness of the ground on which we as Native representatives had to build our hopes of any liberal approach in respect of Native affairs. At the same time, there were new evidences that the Government was being driven along the segregationist path to a degree that must more and more confirm the official Opposition's position. It was being generally rumoured that plans were being made to transfer Native education from the Provinces to the central government, where it would be administered not by the Department of Education but by the Department of Native Affairs. This had been made a live issue by the Native Affairs Commission—under the pressure and inspiration of Mr. Heaton Nicholls. A convinced segregationist, Mr. Nicholls was persuaded that the control of the African population by the Native Affairs Department was the appropriate line of development in terms of the Government's declared policy. This was a direct challenge to our approach, and with the support of my colleagues, I took the earliest opportunity to state our opposition to any proposal to give the Department of Native Affairs an over-riding control over the African population, which meant in effect the growth of a state within a state.

For the rest, our main drive was for an improvement in the economic position of the people whom we represented. I urged the Government to abandon the position taken up by Mr. Pirow in the previous session and to give a lead to private employers by improving the position of its own non-White workers. Mr. Molteno put the spotlight on the depressing effect of the wide use of convict labour in the private sector of the economy. While my plea addressed to the Minister of Native Affairs, then Mr. Henry Fagan, later Chief Justice of the Union, passed unanswered, General Smuts, to whom as Minister of Justice Mr. Molteno's case was made, gave us our first experience of that generally warm liberal response which was to characterise all his dealings with us. He expressed his dislike of the convict labour system and the hope that it might be possible at least to reduce it. Today, after more than a quarter of a century, it is still firmly rooted in South African practice, with so much else that seemed to have little place in a modern society, and which we fondly hoped soon to see relegated to the limbo of the past where such things appeared clearly to belong.

7

Pre-War Stresses and Strains: Segregation Demands Spreading

Our first long ordinary session—our only one before the war and under the original United Party—confirmed all the trends which our earliest experiences had revealed. Its effect on me, as I explained to my constituents in my following series of report-back meetings, was to leave me depressed and anxious about the future. The small Nationalist Party was steadily revealing itself as a compact and determined team whose pressures the large and increasingly amorphous Government Party seemed incapable of resisting. All these pressures were in directions that ran counter to all I believed sound and right for South Africa, and we ourselves, as representatives of the African people, were unable to make any effective impression on the situation.

This depressing session was opened by the Governor-General, Sir Patrick Duncan, at the beginning of February 1939 on a highly hopeful note in regard to both external and internal affairs. The international situation had eased, we were told, and the celebration of the centenary of the Trek, which had recently reached its climax, had given striking proof of the 'solidarity which has already been achieved by the people, and a good augury for its united future'.[1] How much of this was wishful thinking, was almost immediately exposed by notice of motion by the Leader of the Opposition specifically calling for the recognition of Die Stem as the one and only national anthem.

It did not need this to revive all the tensions of the previous session. That had already been done in the recess by an adventure of the Minister of Lands, General Kemp, one of the Hertzogite stalwarts in the Cabinet, in the capacity of acting Minister of Defence during the absence overseas of Mr. Pirow. At one of the final events of the centenary celebrations, in a fit of enthusiasm begotten of the occasion, he had suddenly announced that the site of the Defence Force headquarters, inherited from the British

[1] Hansard, Vol. 33, Col. 3.

Government and hitherto known as Roberts Heights after General Lord Roberts, would in future be known as Voortrekkerhoogte. This unexpected and apparently unplanned gesture was, according to report, greeted with tumultuous applause by those present, mainly Afrikaners, but as news of it filtered through to the general public, it revived all the alarms of the English-speaking members of the Government Party. The Government attempted to allay the agitation which followed by another compromise in terms of which the actual defence headquarters would go by the new name while the old name should continue at the post office and the radio station. This concession, which scarcely achieved its proclaimed intention so far as the English-speaking public were concerned, inevitably became another fighting point with the Nationalist Opposition, and the accusation that again Afrikaner sentiment was being sacrificed on the altar of political expediency was to become the subject of more long and acrimonious debates.

Feelings were still running high over these emotional issues when, in the beginning of March, Hitler walked into Czechoslovakia and the war clouds began to gather again in earnest. This immediately gave fresh point to arguments in which the implicit and essential factor was whether, in the event of war, South Africa should go with Britain and the Commonwealth or stand aside and carve out its own destiny alone. Both sides of the House were now deeply anxious about the decision which the Government would make if and when an open break should take place on the international front. The Nationalists were determined that South Africa should have nothing to do with 'Britain's wars'. The South African Party element in the United Party and all the non-Nationalist Oppositions were clearly equally determined to maintain the commonwealth connection, whatever the powers implicit in the Constitution.

The uncertain element in the situation was General Hertzog himself and his old Nationalist followers in the United Party, and on them the Malanites concentrated their pressures, persistently challenging them to stand by what, they claimed, were the old Nationalist policies and the essential South African way of life, which meant neutrality in international affairs and colour bar politics at home. In an increasingly tense atmosphere, Dr. Malan brought this programme again before the House in the budget debate in an amendment which covered the old ground of the need for an effective segregation policy 'on economic, industrial and political as well as social and residential lines'[1] as the cure for poor Whiteism and unemployment and the protection of the White race, and, in a speech which dealt primarily with foreign affairs, called for a clear statement of policy from the Government as to its intention should war eventuate.

The pressure was not without its effect. On the following day, March 23rd 1939, the Prime Minister rose to reply to the challenges which had been made to him specifically. On the question of neutrality he had, he said, nothing to add to previous declarations. If and when a situation arose on the international front which concerned South Africa, Parliament itself would immediately be called upon to decide what course should be pursued. On the colour issue, however, he proceeded to make a statement of major importance covering every field on which the Opposition had called for action.[2] The method of its presentation implied that the Government would not yield to pressure but would stand on the traditional South African policy of keeping the Coloured population with the Whites. But as the programme developed, it more and more appeared to me that whatever the language used, we were witnessing the launching on its way of what could and probably would become a full-scale segregation of the Coloured people that would differ from the African pattern only in the absence of any territorial basis to give it a semblance of justification. Very soon there were to be evidences that to the Coloured people themselves it had the same appearance.

Arranging his case under the headings which Dr. Malan had specified, he began with an unequivocal declaration that so far as political status was concerned, the Coloured people would not be deprived of their existing political rights and the Government would resist any proposal to change their franchise in a manner that would diminish those rights—a phrase that was to assume a special significance later. On the subject of economic status—the Coloured people 'would not by reason of race or colour be debarred from engaging in any form of industrial occupation or employment but the Government would endeavour to ensure that the working conditions of employment would accord with the Government's social policy'. In this regard, the Prime Minister took his stand on

[1] Hansard, Vol. 33, Col. 2140.
[2] Hansard, Vol. 33, Col. 2228 *et seq.*

the claim that neither White nor Coloured desired social intercourse
and that social separation was accepted by both as the definite and
settled policy of the country. In the circumstances, he said, wherever
social or economic conditions conflicting with this policy of social
separation were found to exist, the Government would do its best
to remedy such conditions; but it would always try to do so in a
manner that would avoid causing ill-feeling or a sense of grievance,
and 'would involve no greater discrimination than the necessities of
the case required'. The question was how to achieve this. Already
a good deal had been done to provide separate housing estates and
it was the Government's policy to go ahead with this. But, he added
significantly, in terms which had a sinister ring in my ears, legislation would be necessary to carry out this policy. 'Local authorities are at present not equipped with proper powers to provide for
the establishment of separate European and non-European townships; while servitudes on property limiting the right of occupation
either to Europeans or non-Europeans have frequently been imposed, with very satisfactory results, by private owners when cutting
up their estates for sale, our common law does not allow public
bodies to impose such a condition. It is proposed to introduce
legislation which will rectify this position.' This legislation would
empower public bodies when selling or letting land or buildings to
impose conditions limiting the ownership or occupation to either
European or non-European. It would also empower townships
boards to require the imposition of such conditions by way of
servitude when land was sub-divided.

On the basis of this policy, General Hertzog announced that the
Government looked forward to the time when most of the Coloured
community would be living happily and contentedly in their own
villages, townships, or suburbs when 'it would be possible to make
them responsible for running their own affairs and services as far
as practicable'.

In industry, 'the policy of separating Europeans and non-Europeans wherever conditions are such that, but for such separation,
there may be social intermingling was already in force and was
being carried out with very willing co-operation on the part of all
concerned. This policy would continue to be applied administratively, but if, at any time, it was found necessary to introduce legislative measures in this regard, that would be done.'

So far as mixed marriages were concerned, that was the subject
F

of a commission of enquiry and could safely be left until the commission had reported.

While the Prime Minister's assurances in regard to the Coloured franchise seemed clear and unequivocal (we had yet to learn the interpretation that could be put upon the word 'diminish') it was impossible, for me at least, and I should have thought for anybody familiar with the course of Native policy over the preceding years, not to be seriously concerned at the threat to property rights implicit in the proposed legislation. That was, in our experience, the beginning of a road that must in the end reduce the political status of the Coloured people. What, in fact, would have happened if circumstances had not intervened to prevent the implementation of this part of the programme it is impossible to say. I have reason to believe that the programme had never been before the Party Caucus;[1] but if it had been, it is problematical whether the members would have seen in it the dangers which to me seemed almost self-evident. General Smuts was reported a few days later as having given the Coloured people the assurance at a public meeting in Cape Town that so long as he was in the Cabinet there would be no interference with their rights, but in view of his own Party's record, it is doubtful whether, so long as the political position of the Coloured people was guaranteed, he would at that time have made an issue of this matter of property rights to which our experiences lent so great a significance. Indeed the Minister of the Interior, Mr. Stuttaford, himself a representative of a Cape constituency and a follower of Smuts, already had a bill in draft under which, if 75 per cent of the property owners in an area decided that they wished the area to be entirely White, the local authority should proceed to make provision accordingly—what Dr. Malan referred to as his 75 per cent approach.

A week later, events took place which were to show that this matter of the rights of the Coloured people was rapidly advancing beyond the stage of academic discussion, to assume immediate political importance. At the very moment at which General Smuts was delivering the speech in which he gave his assurances to the Coloured people, a procession of Coloured people was converging on Parliament carrying banners protesting against any and all attempts to apply the segregation policy to them.

This was the aftermath of a mammoth meeting on the Grand

[1] I gathered this from a talk with Mr. J. H. Hofmeyr after the change of government in September 1939 to which subsequent reference is made. See p. 102.

Parade[1] to protest not only against Nationalist policies but, as Dr. Malan was to underline later, against the Government itself for its attitude to the Coloured people. The meeting had passed off without any untoward incidents, as General Smuts, in his capacity of Minister of Justice, was subsequently to emphasise. The procession was no part of the plan of the meeting but was, it appeared, a spontaneous reaction to the emotions engendered by the meeting and the situation out of which the meeting had arisen. Unfortunately it sparked off a clash between the police and the Coloured people that spread far beyond the precincts of Parliament. In its course, four policemen were injured, two of them seriously, but many more civilians were, it was subsequently claimed, the innocent victims of irresponsible police action.

In the light of latter-day circumstances and events, the episode and the debates to which it gave rise have more than an historical interest. When the House met the following day, the leader of the Opposition asked for and was granted its adjournment on a matter of urgent national importance to discuss the happenings of the previous evening. Dr. Malan immediately launched an attack on General Smuts as Minister of Justice for his failure to ban the meeting out of which the demonstration had developed or to control the demonstration which, it was contended, had automatically turned into a riot. The terms of the attack were that (i) a serious riot had occurred in Cape Town amongst other places also near and at the Houses of Parliament, in which Europeans were molested and attacked and seriously injured and damage done to property; (ii) the rioters were under the leadership, amongst others, of a number of Europeans with communist tendencies; (iii) no adequate measures were taken to prevent the disturbances; and (iv) the necessity of taking immediate steps to put an end to communist agitation and to protect life and property adequately.

The case which Dr. Malan proceeded to make was amply covered by this motion, but the terms in which he made it seemed to confirm my worst fears of the implications of the Prime Minister's statement of the previous week. Stressing his contention that trouble between Europeans and non-Europeans was the greatest danger facing South Africa, he claimed in significant terms that the demonstration of the previous evening had been aimed not only at the Opposition but also at the Government. 'It was a

[1] A traditional place for public meetings of protest in Cape Town.

meeting of protest against the segregation policy, not only against this side of the House but clearly, as appeared from the speeches, also against the segregation policy which was announced a few days ago by the Prime Minister and the Minister of the Interior,' he said. '. . . I point out to you that when the segregation policy was adopted, or was brought forward by this side of the House, but especially when it was also accepted in principle by the Minister of the Interior on behalf of the Government *and was agreed to, as was stated a few days ago by the Prime Minister* (my italics), the Communists became more active than ever and that they are making use of the opportunity to stampede the non-Europeans against the Europeans on a large scale.'

Ignoring the references to the Prime Minister's speech as interpreted by Dr. Malan and the Opposition, General Smuts defended himself against the accusation of having neglected his duty in regard to the demonstration.[1] This he did in a speech which reflected a broadly tolerant approach to politics in this complicated country which now seems to belong to another era. True, it seemed that there had been some 12,000 people at the meeting on the Parade, he said, but there had been no reason to expect trouble there; nor had there been any trouble. There were, he believed, twelve policemen present, not four as Dr. Malan claimed. The heads of the police had themselves been there and had seen no grounds for augmenting the force. 'We do not want to make an unnecessary display of force on such an occasion unless there is necessity for it,'[2] he remarked. When the situation changed, which was after the meeting was all over and this procession to the Houses of Parliament took place, it was clear that the criminal element in the population was exploiting the situation. The police had then been called out in force and had been armed, but, he added, 'it was in no case necessary to make any use of the arms'. He then turned the attack. 'There was also a political agitation going on against the Coloured population which put the people into a state of panic and fear, and that, of course, has a reflex.' Leaving that issue there, he went on to say that law and order of course would have to be maintained. They had now been warned of the danger and would be more wideawake in the future. He concluded with an appeal to the House not to continue the debate but to wait until the noise and dust of the

[1] Hansard, Vol. 33, Cols. 2487–90.
[2] Hansard, Vol. 33, Col. 2498 *et seq.*

previous evening's events had subsided when the whole episode might be seen in perspective. Then it might be possible to take a more constructive approach to the situation.

It was an appeal which went unheard, and for the rest of the day the Nationalists continued to repeat their case with little or no variation, in between the claims of the other minority groups to be heard on what was still a very exceptional event in our political life. Mr. Madeley, the Leader of the Labour Party, felt that the Minister of the Interior should not be frightened by the events of the previous evening into abandoning his Bill for residential segregation of the Coloured people. Any withdrawal on that front would simply be interpreted as weakness and would give encouragement to more kicking over the traces. At the same time he did not like the official Opposition's proposals to curb free speech. 'The Coloured people have as much right to meet and discuss their grievances,' he declared, 'as Europeans have': and added 'and I want to say to my friends here' (the Nationalist Party), 'more in sorrow than in anger, that the only difference between the action of our Coloured people last night and that of the Nationalist Party is that the Nationalist Party is a little bit cleverer and stops at words while the other people go on to deeds'.[1] Mr. Marwick, now Parliamentary leader of the Dominion Party since Colonel Stallard's failure to hold his seat in the previous election, felt that the Government should call off all talk of Coloured segregation which was really the cause of all the trouble.[2]

This was our first experience of an adjournment of this kind, and while we were all taken by surprise, I felt impelled to state my own view of the case and what I imagined would be that of my colleagues if we had had an opportunity to discuss the matter. I expressed my confidence in the contention of the Minister of Justice that there had been no justification for banning the meeting. On the strength of information which I myself had had of what had taken place I also felt, however, that the Government had been remiss in one regard. 'It is impossible,' I said, 'to have sat in this House for even the short time I have sat in it without realising the trend today of party propaganda in this country.' I had listened for three sessions now to continuous attacks on the Coloured population by the official Opposition. In the days when segregation of the Native population

[1] Hansard, Vol. 33, Col. 2495 *et seq.*
[2] Hansard, Vol. 33, Col. 2518 *et seq.*

had been the immediate issue, they, like other parties, had been loud in their insistence that the Coloured people belonged on the White side of the colour line and should remain there. Recently, however, the focus had changed and there had been a determined onslaught on the position of the Coloured people, and the Coloured people had reacted as we might have expected them to react, in panic, as the Minister of Justice had said. If the Government, three months ago, had made a definite statement that they would not be a party to segregating the Coloured population, these unfortunate happenings would not have taken place.

Dr. Malan challenged me here with the interjection: 'They did say they would not segregate. That was before the election'—the implication being a pre-election appeal to the Coloured voter. I could only reply that, to my knowledge, there had never been as explicit a statement of policy as the situation seemed to call for.[1] In any case, since the election many things had happened to suggest that if the Nationalist Party were sufficiently vocal and insistent, the United Party would yield to its pressure and modify its policy accordingly, a circumstance which had undermined the confidence of the Coloured community.

Apart from this interruption by the leader of the Opposition there was no reaction to my intervention from Nationalist ranks. There was however a significant response from that same Mr. Liebenberg who subsequently joined the Nationalist Party.[2] In the course of a speech in support of the Government to which he still belonged, he had two significant pieces of advice to offer to his own leaders. One was that the time had come when there should be proper control over the influx of Coloured people into the towns. Farmers, he said, were having to go farther and farther afield for labour for their vineyards, while these Coloured people came into Cape Town and stayed there to swell the ranks of the unemployed and the criminal. His second piece of advice was that the police ought to be armed 'properly', even with firearms, because 'we must enable them to protect their lives'.

He also felt the necessity to address some remarks to me. He wanted to tell me, he said, that it depended on the way in which the Natives and Coloured people in our country were addressed, and on what representations were made to them what the relationship

[1] Hansard, Vol. 33, Col. 2514.
[2] See p. 75.

would be between them and the Europeans. If there were Europeans among us who made the Coloured people understand that their rights were being trodden underfoot then one could understand that a spirit of resistance would be set up amongst them. Indeed we could then expect that the Natives also would start resisting. 'But when we make matters clear to them, just as they actually are,' he declared, 'then I believe that we shall find much reasonableness amongst those sections of the non-European population'.[1]

Mr. Liebenberg then went on to elaborate what he apparently regarded as 'things as they actually are'. He said. 'My experience is that the greatest justice should be maintained towards the non-European population. But at the same time, we must let them understand that the white man has come to South Africa to rule, and the white man is not going to allow that right, which is his prerogative, to be taken away from him by any other section of the population.'

Whether indeed such an explanation was likely to stimulate that reasonableness for which he hoped, I was entitled to doubt. The important thing was that Mr. Liebenberg's views obviously found considerable support in the ranks of his own Party.

The subject of the riots and all the surrounding circumstances took on a new life and developed some new aspects on the vote for the Department of Justice when my colleague, Mr. Molteno, asked the Minister, General Smuts, for an enquiry into all the happenings on the evening of the demonstration. The ground of his request was a number of affidavits in his possession from Coloured people who maintained that they had been unjustifiably attacked by the police. The Nationalists strongly opposed the suggestion of an enquiry and again challenged General Smuts for failing to ban the meeting on the Parade under provisions introduced in 1930 into the Riotous Assemblies Act by the old Nationalist Party Government. These provisions empowered the Minister of Justice to take direct action to prohibit meetings likely to cause ill feeling between Europeans and non-Europeans. Dr. Malan and his followers demanded that the Parade meetings should be prohibited altogether and that the police should be regularly armed.

In reply General Smuts, while he did not accede to Mr. Molteno's request, contended that these Parade meetings did not, as the Opposition claimed, fall into the category which the amendment to the Riotous Assemblies Act had been intended to cover and that

[1] Hansard, Vol. 33, Col. 2517 *et seq.*

therefore he could not on this occasion legitimately use the powers that Act provided. 'The procedure which we are following is that I must be advised by the local authority, and I keep to that procedure,' he said. 'I am not going on my own account to say that when a meeting is being held anywhere, it is going to be a riotous assembly and that I prohibit it. That would give the Minister power to prohibit any meeting without any limitation'—a prospect he obviously considered highly dangerous in itself and contrary to the spirit of our society.

In reply to two other speakers he said: 'They have referred to the meetings on the Parade. But these things have been going on for years, and for generations, and no one takes them seriously. If we are to take steps in connection with all these speeches, then we will never get to an end of the matter.'

Later, to Mr. Haywood, Nationalist Party member for Bloemfontein (South), he said: 'The hon. member must not forget that the meetings which are being held are meetings which were intended to protest against the so-called segregation policy. . . . They wanted to protest against the proposals of the Opposition, or the Government, in connection with the separation of the coloureds from whites in the towns. No one could suspect that that meeting of protest would result in hostility between coloured people and Europeans.' 'They are meetings about a purely political matter, the matter of separate residential areas and the separation of coloured persons and white persons, and they do not necessarily coincide with hostility between one section and the other.'[1]

On the subject of arming the police, his reply has also a special interest today. 'The local officer judges the circumstances and sees that the police are armed when it is necessary,' he said. 'It is very seldom necessary for the police to be fully armed. That is the law, that is the practice and it works well. There may be cases where something happens owing to a policeman not having been properly armed, but the Committee can see that there is just as much danger connected with it in allowing a policeman to go about armed on every occasion because he may possibly make unnecessary use of his arms.'[2]

So he resisted all the pressures brought to bear on him to curb

[1] Hansard, Vol. 34, Col. 2835 et seq.
[2] One of the first actions of the Malan Government after its victory in 1948 was to arm the police.

freedom of expression, and, by implication at least, remained committed to the maintenance of the position of the Coloured people and thus against any extension of the field of segregation. But before the end of the session a further crisis had arisen which was to make it uncertain whether he could or would try to maintain this position as a general proposition. It arose over legislation in respect of Asiatic land and trading rights in the Transvaal—the first of the pegging Acts which were to bring South Africa and General Smuts himself into the dock at U.N.O.

On the Witwatersrand, these rights were supposedly limited and controlled under a Gold Law dating from 1908 which denied Coloured persons rights of occupation in the declared mining areas. The law however had been extensively evaded and, over the years, Asians had acquired considerable vested interests in property and trading licenses. From time to time, attempts had been made to sort out and regularise the position, leading eventually in 1932 to legislation under which it was agreed that, while generally the prohibition of Asian and Coloured occupation in the mining areas should continue, in some areas even within the range of the Gold Law vested rights should be recognised. To decide which rights should be brought within this provision, a Commission was appointed under the chairmanship of Mr. Justice Feetham of Ulster boundary fame. In 1935, this Commission had reported. In its report it not only gave its considered reply to this specific reference; it went further and recommended the principle of the right of ownership of land to Asian and Coloured persons in areas set aside for them as distinct from individual stands, but it proposed that all these adjustments should be subject to the passing of resolutions by both Houses of Parliament. All this had been embodied in legislation in 1936, but so far no resolutions to implement it had been passed by Parliament. In the dying days of our second session, the brief post-election session of August–September 1938, the Minister of the Interior, Mr. Stuttaford, had indeed introduced a proposition in this regard in the House of Assembly to which, he informed the House, he had the agreement of the Opposition; but it had been hurriedly withdrawn when a new member of the Government Party objected to it, and the Government had fallen back on an extension of earlier legislation designed to hold the situation while the Commission was pursuing its enquiries. The new member who thus held the House and his own Party to ransom was Mr. B. J. Schoeman, then in his first session as the representative of the working-class Johannesburg constituency of Fordsburg. He became Minister of Labour in the Nationalist Cabinet in 1948 and graduated from there to the senior portfolio of Transport, which he still holds. He is also now (1968) Leader of the House of Assembly.

With the interim legislation now again due to expire in the near future, the Minister of the Interior introduced an Asiatic (Transvaal) Land and Trading Bill designed to do two things, one already familiar, one entirely new. It proposed to extend the interim legislation in respect of the Gold Law areas for another two years but it then went on to peg the position of the Asians over the whole of the Transvaal Province in respect of occupation and trading licences where hitherto no legal differentiation on racial grounds had applied.

The Bill brought an erstwhile Cabinet Minister, Mr. J.H. Hofmeyr, and a front bencher, Mr. Leslie Blackwell, into conflict with their own Government and ended in their expulsion from the Party caucus.

On the Bill, Messrs. Hofmeyr and Blackwell, while accepting the first part of the Bill as all that seemed possible at the time, objected to the second part as involving potential segregation of the Asiatic population. My colleagues and I objected to both sections of the Bill, the first as being an unnecessary prolongation of an unhealthy situation and the second as prejudicing the existing rights of Asiatics outside the Gold Law area. The Nationalists led by Dr. Malan, now encouraged by Mr. Schoeman's stand of the previous year, moved to refer the Bill to select committee with instructions to bring up a comprehensive measure dealing with residential separation of Whites and non-Whites, a proposition involving a wide extension of the area of segregation in terms of their declared policy.

In the debates which followed on the various stages of the Bill, members of the Opposition from Dr. Malan downwards challenged the Government to fulfil its promise 'to introduce segregation measures not only with regard to the Asiatics but also between Europeans and non-Europeans'.[1] Mr. Strydom declared he was very glad that 'owing to our actions we have up to the present succeeded in bringing about that even the Minister of the Interior himself is prepared, as he said, to come forward with segregation

[1] Hansard, Vol. 34, Cols. 4055-6.

proposals which will include to a small extent residential segregation'.[1] Referring specifically to the 75 per cent measure, he went on to say that it would be necessary to do more than that.

In reply, the Minister of Lands, Senator Conroy, said, 'We, as Transvalers, will support the Minister of the Interior on this Bill, and I give him the assurance that we will have proper legislation next year to put an end to the Indian question, and to the Colour question.'[2] All of which suggests that General Smuts' attitude was not likely to win the day within his own party circle—that we, like the Coloureds, were justified in feeling extremely anxious about the future.

One other topic exercised an influence during this session, out of all proportion to its intrinsic importance. This was a bill to regulate the trade of electrical wiremen. While such a measure might have been expected to get the attention due to a piece of incidental industrial legislation, in fact it achieved a special degree of notoriety as the beginning of Nationalist practice to demand the application of the principle of job reservation. The Party moved that the trade of electrical wiremen should be reserved for white Union nationals, and determinedly held up the progress of the Bill with a repetition of this demand at every possible stage. The Minister of Labour, Mr. Harry Lawrence, with more resistance than his colleague, Mr. Stuttaford, had shown, while paying lip service to the white labour policy on which both the major parties found common ground, refused a demand which would have thrown a number of Coloured workers out of employment. We were to become very familiar with the demand that offices and jobs were to be reserved for Union nationals of European descent and not all United Party ministers, even later when the Hertzogites had hived off in the war, were to show an adequate capacity to resist.

As all these pressures developed, the Native Representatives were more and more faced with the problem of tactics. What course could they pursue in the midst of this party struggle that could promise any return for the people they represented?

Reviewing the situation soon after the outbreak of the war, I wrote as follows:[3]

'The first representatives of the Africans were confronted with

[1] Hansard, Vol. 34, Col. 4087.
[2] Hansard, Vol. 34, Col. 4095.
[3] Political Representation of Africans in the Union. New Africa Pamphlets No. 4. S.A. Institute of Race Relations.

a problem in tactics which was peculiarly complex. What course could they pursue that was not fraught with danger to the cause they were committed to serve? Their easiest and simplest line, undoubtedly, would have been to be unprovocatively critical of the Government when African issues were at stake, and for the rest, to vote with and for the Government as less dangerous than the Opposition to the future well-being and the aspirations of their constituents. This was a course which commended itself to that quite considerable body of philanthropic opinion which had for years been uneasy about the direction which Native policy was taking, and which had offered a stout resistance to the progress of that policy, but which had never worked out in detail either the character or the price of an alternative policy which would have for its positive and declared objective what alone could give the African what he wanted, a real democracy in South Africa. It would also have had the virtue, for what it is worth, of being to some extent understandable by the rank and file of the Government Party, whose general attitude to criticism of their leaders and their policy was reinforced by the assumption that members occupying seats created by General Hertzog owed the General an obligation to support him, and who were completely puzzled and extremely critical of the failure of these members to recognise and fulfil this obligation.

'But to us who had to carry the responsibility of using these seats, and the platform they provided, to express the thoughts and aspirations of the Africans, it did not seem possible to take this comparatively easy course. It appeared to us that something more was demanded of us than the mere propagation of a cause in a way which would not seriously disturb or annoy anyone. The only justifiable use of three seats in a House of 153 Members, 150 of whom had come to regard the segregation policy as the settled, and agreed, and unchangeable policy of the country, at least by people who had consistently opposed this type of representation as contrary to democratic justice, appeared to be to use them as a platform from which to attempt to loosen the foundations of this acceptance by the suggestion that the segregation policy was, in fact, neither the only one nor the best one for South Africa. And this, in our opinion, could not be done by docility and accommodation but only by reasoned argument, proven fact, and above all, by independence, which alone could give the rest a value. As a consequence, the line we chose was that of using every issue directly involving Africans to propound the democratic as distinct from the segregationist or essentially Nazi policy, reinforcing the argument as far as possible with illustrations of the failure of the latter policy to provide even European South Africa with the security and well-being that were its objectives; while, where voting issues were involved, we endeavoured to treat each on its merits, supporting in general neither one party nor another, but whatever side represented the more liberal or the less reactionary policy.

'This was anything but an easy line to follow. It necessitated that continual vigilance from which the caucus system and the rigid party machine have rescued the majority of Parliamentarians, with marked loss to the standard of Parliamentary government. It also brought criticism from a wide diversity of directions, the Opposition accusing us of merely being Government supporters, while the Government back-benchers were loud in their insistence that we always voted with the Opposition. But it had the merit of focussing on us and our opinions more attention than our numbers or our voting value appeared to warrant.'

Following this line, we in the House of Assembly continued to press our demand for a constructive approach to African poverty as distressing in itself and dangerous to the whole community. We urged on every occasion the need for the Government to give a lead in its own service. And whenever occasion offered, we argued the general case for a new, non-segregationist approach to Native policy that would of itself check the attack on Coloured and Asian rights. Following that line, I put up a private members' motion calling for the recognition of African trade unions and the extension of the right of collective bargaining to African workers which our Industrial Conciliation Act denied them. Together we again stressed the case against the growing tendency to build the Native Affairs Department into a state within a state, this having become a newly critical issue by the explicit announcement in the budget of the Government's intention to hand over all the proceeds of the Native poll tax to the Department of Native Affairs together with the responsibility for Native education and all Native services and development.

Finally on the general front, including the legislative front, we supported or endeavoured ourselves to initiate on each occasion what appeared to us to constitute the democratic line. It was an

approach which on more than one occasion brought us into conflict
with Government and official Opposition alike, as in the case of the
Asiatic Land and Trading Bill.

It is only fair, however, to acknowledge that the picture was
not all entirely dark, although the practical gains were few enough.
In a bill to improve the administration of the Poll Tax, commend-
ably designed to keep defaulters out of gaol as far as possible, Mr.
Havenga, as the Minister in charge of the Bill, accepted an amendment proposed by me that under the stop order system which the
Bill initiated, no amount could be deducted from the employee's
earnings that would leave him with less than enough to meet the
cost of the basic needs of his family—the principle of the garnishee
order. Admittedly the concession was a tribute to social logic
rather than to reality, since if conscientiously applied, with prevailing African wage rates what they were, it must have cut at the
roots of the whole poll tax system. But its acceptance by Mr. Havenga,
together with his decision to put £50,000 (R100,000) on loan account
for African school buildings on the strength, he said, of earlier
representations by me, and his polite defence of his inability to meet
some of our other demands on the ground that he simply could
not find the money, gave a little encouragement to us to feel that
our arguments might yet make some impression. They were at any
rate the reflection of a humane approach to opposition which we
can only now look back on with nostalgia.

8

Effect of the War on the Political Set-up

By the end of the 1939 session of Parliament, there were many indications that the strains in the United Party were mounting rapidly. Mr. Hofmeyr, regarded as General Smuts' right-hand man, had already found himself at loggerheads with the Prime Minister and his friends on two issues which he regarded as of major importance and was out of the Cabinet and out of the party caucus, taking with him one of his colleagues on each occasion. General Smuts was obviously an increasingly uneasy and unhappy partner in the alliance.

My feeling about this was greatly strengthened by a conversation which took place between the General and myself one dreary evening late in the session. The typical Cape winter weather outside seemed appropriately to reflect the depressing atmosphere in the debating chamber where the Nationalist team were hammering at the obvious chinks in the Prime Minister's armour in the hope of effecting the split that seemed imminent. Tired of the spectacle, I was reading in the members' lounge when I was joined by General Smuts who had been wandering library-wards clearly under the same impulse of escape. Already I was aware that, consciously or sub-consciously, the deputy Prime Minister was counting his resources, estimating his potential strength, as the Prime Minister, I thought, with advancing age and ill-health, was feeling the estrangement from his old colleagues and a strong pull back towards them.

The conversation as I remember it drifted almost immediately to Native policy. In this field, I expressed a fear that the emphasis which some of our anthropologists were laying on traditional cultures rather than on the needs for adaptation to changing circumstances was politically dangerous as offering a basis and a philosophy for the policy of segregation. I was gratified to have my view endorsed by the deputy Prime Minister, with an implied criticism of the whole policy which he was to voice publicly a couple of years later. From there, the conversation drifted to the post-election blunders which had strained relations between the two sections of the Government Party. Referring particularly to

95

the events of the previous May, 1938, why, I asked, when the Party had had such a sweeping victory, was it necessary to create these unfortunate situations and throw away so much confidence and goodwill? General Smuts sighed and shook his head. Why indeed? he asked. Whatever hopes had inspired his entry into fusion showed all the signs of wearing thin.

Thus there seemed good reason to feel that the existing position could not last. The question was, on what occasion and along what line would the split come? I and those whose interests were mine naturally hoped that whatever the occasion, it would end in a repudiation of the reactionary line on colour, the abandonment of the policy of segregation and the discriminatory principle on which it was founded. All our efforts, naturally, were bent in this direction. Even before the session was over, I had approached Mr. Hofmeyr to form a new party, with a racially liberal programme, promising him at least a team of informed propagandists to support him. In the recess itself a number of us, who had for a few years been working on this plan, organised a meeting in the Carlton Hotel in Johannesburg with Mr. Hofmeyr and Mr. Leslie Blackwell as the target for another attempt in this direction. The meeting itself was well attended and encouraging and the case we had to make was obviously not without its effect on Mr. Hofmeyr who was the chief focus of our pressure. But behind everything were the gathering war clouds which dictated the immediate decision; if by September war had not eventuated, we would meet again to consider the possibilities.

With that we had to be content; and in the beginning of September, Parliament was again in session, primarily to deal with the Senate which was due to terminate in the near future, but in fact to meet the challenge of the war. In mid-August, someone had discovered, and realised the implications of the fact, that the upper chamber was due to expire on September 5th and that, as the law then stood, it could not be reconstituted before October. This meant in effect that for some weeks our bi-cameral system would be in abeyance over what might prove to be a critical period in international affairs. It was therefore decided forthwith to summon a brief session of Parliament to extend the life of the Senate until new elections should be completed. But when this special session opened on the morning of Saturday, September 2nd, it found the issue of the life of the Senate of secondary importance. Hitler had already launched his attack on Poland, and a declaration of war by Britain and France seemed only a matter of hours. The situation about which there had been so much argument, and anxiety, in the preceding session was shaping up rapidly; and there were already signs that it might prove the final blow to the United Party as we had known it.

General Hertzog had been repetitively emphatic that if and when war should break out in Europe, Parliament would decide what course of action South Africa should pursue. Here, it seemed, was the challenge; and here, fortuitously, was Parliament in session to meet it.[1] What would it decide? And what would the effect of its decision be on the domestic political situation? These were the anxious preoccupations of members of all groups in Parliament when, after a tense week-end in which Britain and France had declared their intention to fight, the House reassembled on the morning of September 4th to hear what lead the Government had to offer in this critical situation.

When the position of the Senate had by common consent been expeditiously regularised to guarantee the continuing functioning of the legislature, General Hertzog proceeded to set the stage for what was to be probably the most momentous session in our Parliamentary history.[2] Obviously under great emotional strain, he announced to an anxiously waiting House and country that on the issue of war or peace which the week-end events in Europe had precipitated, the Government was split in two—and would hence-forth be split.[3] In extended meetings over the week-end—of which the country had been generally aware—he had been unable to carry his Cabinet with him in his determination to declare South Africa's neutrality in the forthcoming struggle. Reading from a prepared statement, he proceeded to set out his view that South Africa should maintain its existing relations with the various belligerent countries while standing by its contractual obligations with Britain or any other member of the British Commonwealth—including the use of the naval base at Simonstown—and denying

[1] Colonel Deneys Reitz in his book *No Outspan* (p. 237) argues that General Hertzog had promised to consult Parliament if he decided to go to war but had given no promise of consultation if he decided not to go to war. The fortuitous meeting of Parliament faced him with the obligation of consultation in any case.
[2] For the impression it made on old-established Parliamentarians see Deneys Reitz, *No Outspan*; Heaton Nicholls, *South Africa in My Time*; B. K. Long, *In Smuts' Camp*; Leslie Blackwell, *Farewell to Parliament*.
[3] Hansard, Vol. 36, Col. 18 *et seq.*

G

to anyone the right to use Union territory for the purpose of doing anything which might impair these obligations in any way.

From this point, he went on to expound his view that not only should South Africa not participate in a war against Germany but that the war itself was an attack on Hitler for justifiable efforts on his part to undo the wrongs done to Germany after the previous war, efforts with which he himself could sympathise deeply in view of his own and his people's experience of defeat and the humiliations that accompanied it.

In the highly strained and emotional atmosphere generated on both sides of the House by this speech, General Smuts rose to state his own position, and implicitly to mark out the path of separation which it inevitably involved. Illuminating much that had gone before, he said that never in all the years of political collaboration between him and the Prime Minister had he made a serious point of differences on small issues. 'I have always been prepared to give way,' he declared, 'to hold the peace and to see that the young life of this nation is given a chance, and for the people to have the opportunity to grow together. Today we have come to the point where I have to call a halt and I have to adopt a different attitude; and I do so because I am in my very soul convinced that we are up against most vital issues for the present and the future of this country.' He proceeded to state his belief that in international law there is no middle course, no 'modified neutrality' such as General Hertzog had proposed for South Africa. In war, you are either a friend or an enemy. For himself, he had no doubt where South Africa's obligations lay and what their implications. She must stand by and with her associates within the Commonwealth, and that meant being in the war with them.

While it was not generally known that General Hertzog had met Dr. Malan over the week-end and that an agreement had been reached between them on General Hertzog's proposed stand for neutrality, it was early realised that the leader of the Opposition and his following would find much common ground in the position that General Hertzog had taken up. The general presumption of a countervailing attitude on the part of the smaller groups, Dominion, Labour and the Native Representatives was soon confirmed by their spokesmen—Mr. Molteno speaking for the Native Representatives in this regard. However since General Hertzog had not called the caucus of the Government Party together, the balance of

forces in the major and determining group in the House was still
undefined when a day-long debate on the opposing points of view
presented by the two leading figures in the House and the country
concluded and the most fateful—and most dramatic—decision in
the Parliamentary history of South Africa was called. With the
resultant count of eighty votes for General Smuts and sixty-seven for
General Hertzog, Parliament gave its decision for our participation
in the war. It also confirmed and established the split in the United
Party. All at once the whole political scene was changed. With his
majority of thirteen votes, it was clear that General Smuts would
replace General Hertzog as Prime Minister. It seemed equally clear
that General Hertzog and his followers would rejoin their old
colleagues.

What was this change going to mean to us? We had voted with
General Smuts on the issue of war or neutrality. The new Government was to be a coalition government into which General Smuts
had immediately gathered the other two minorities whose votes
had helped to put him into office, the Dominionites and the Labour
Party. The Leader of each of these Parties was given a seat in the
Cabinet and the parties themselves were thus committed to common
action over the widest possible field. All of which raised pertinently
the question of what we should do.

I myself had not the slightest doubt as to what our course should
be. We were by our votes committed to support the new Government in its major task, which was to see the war through. In the
circumstances, some of my colleagues, several of whom had been,
and some still were, members of the United Party although not
of its Parliamentary caucus, were drawn to a course similar to
that of the other minorities. Such a course had obvious attractions,
but I could not see my way to adopt it. I explained the situation
thus to my constituents:[1]

'The policy of the representatives of the Africans since their
election has been that they should remain independent of all
parties. The question now arises whether or not we should join
General Smuts' party: I and my colleagues agreed that we should
consult our electors and that none of us would take any action
without informing the others. Now our position is this: while we
agree with the Government's policy in regard to the war, there are
many other fronts on which we would find it difficult to stand with

[1] Reported *Umlindi we Nyanga* (The Monthly Watchman), October 16th, 1939.

the Government, particularly in regard to Native policy. I think we should make it perfectly clear that, while giving the Government full and loyal support in regard to the prosecution of the war, and doing nothing to endanger its position, we do not agree with all its policy, and I at least want to be free to say so when we are affected. Our votes were not asked for; we gave them of our own accord and doing so did not involve us in any undertaking to join the Smuts party. We should be free to express our opinions so far as expression of them does not put the Government in danger of being defeated, for none of us wants to see the Nationalist Party succeed the present Government. At the same time, I do not think it would be disloyal to suggest that this is a good time to get the Government to listen of some of the things we feel should be done.'

It might be asked, why should it have seemed to me impossible to do what the Labour and Dominion Parties had done? Could it not also be argued that they too had planks in their programmes that normally separated them from the United Party? Was not the argument against coalition as strong for them as for us?

While I felt at the time that Labour and Dominion would probably have done better to do what we did to retain their independence and to play the part of friendly critics of the Government, there were in fact no essential grounds for their maintaining independence such as operated in our case. In fact, developing circumstances were making both parties as we had known them redundant, as time has shown. The Dominion Party had in fact lost its whole *raison d'être* when South Africa went into the war. It had come into existence on the principle of the solidarity of what constituted the British Commonwealth and once General Smuts was back in the saddle with his international outlook and attachment to that Commonwealth, the party gradually but effectively faded out of existence.

As for Labour, the function which had given it its earlier appeal, that was the defence of white labour and the promotion of the interests of that group, had already passed to the two major parties. Both these parties were now at pains to woo the votes which had originally supported the Labour Party and both were in a much stronger position to produce the promised benefits. Indeed, from this time on, the Labour Party remained in Parliament only by the grace of the United Party whose leader, General Smuts, could apparently never forget the pact between Labour and Nationalist

which had defeated him in 1924. He did not wish to see any repetition of that situation—however unlikely a contingency in the
circumstances then developing in the country.

Not all my colleagues were as convinced as I was of the wisdom
of our maintaining an independent course. One person however
was fully satisfied with it, and that effectively decided the issue.
That was General Smuts himself. This he made abundantly clear to
us when, soon after the conclusion of the brief, critical session
which put the reins of office in his hands, we went as a group to
Pretoria to see him, in effect to discuss our future relationship
with him and his Government. In the meeting we had together
before our interview, the subject of this relationship was still a
matter for discussion between ourselves. When we concluded our
discussion, only one thing had been settled, that was that I intended
to tell the Prime Minister that I was not joining his party. Very
early in the interview, I proceeded to do this. General Smuts'
relief at this declaration ('Oh no, my dear, of course not') could
not fail to have its effect on my colleagues. His old allies—and his
old opponents—alike were already attacking him violently for his
new alliance with 'jingoes' and 'imperialists', and accusing him
of betraying Afrikanerdom in order to stay in the British train; he
did not wish to have to face the further accusation of being in office
by the votes of the 'kaffir members'[1] as we were quite commonly
called. In the issue, while relations between the Native Representatives and the Government became somewhat more benign under
the new dispensation, the group remained both officially and practically independent.

At intervals over the years, I have wondered whether I and
others like me were in fact as wise as I believed at the time in the
course of consistent political independence which we pursued.
Could we, having a specific direction, a political philosophy to
reinforce it and some appreciation of the practicalities of politics,
possibly have done better, exercised a more effective influence from
inside the less illiberal of the major parties in this earlier and, at
this time, more fluid period in the Party political position? The
determining factor in practice would appear to be implicit in my
inability to define even the Smuts United Party in other than
negative terms on the colour front. Even now I can scarcely imagine
that association with declared segregationists like Colonel Stallard

[1] Generally in the Afrikaans version—*Kafferlede*.

and Mr. Madeley, and scarcely less specific segregationists like some of General Smuts' own Party members in his Cabinet, to say nothing of his less prominent followers, could have been more fruitful or less frustrating than continuous opposition. And any such association must have meant an open surrender of our platform that could only have seemed a concession to expediency.

All this was indeed implicit in a talk I had with Mr. Hofmeyr immediately after the war vote when he returned not only to the Party but to the Cabinet, and that in its senior portfolio of Finance. In response to my fervently expressed hope that the new Government might take what I regarded as a more sane and safe line on colour issues, he responded with the comment—'You must remember (in regard to the Party) they are the same people. I think the best we can promise you is that they won't do bad things. We can't promise you that they will do good things.'

While I had to agree with his estimate of the position, there was one change I thought might improve the prospect. That was the removal of Mr. Heaton Nicholls from the Parliamentary front. In response to Mr. Hofmeyr's query as to where I thought the Government might put him, I suggested that it might find it useful to promote him to a diplomatic post.

Mr. Nicholls, a Natal farmer, was the most pronounced and the most effective segregationist in the United Party. A dynamic personality and a speaker of considerable ability and force, he had since the formation of the United Party entertained hopes of Cabinet rank. His strong views on the imperial connection, however (like those of Mr. Leslie Blackwell), and on such emotional issues as flags and anthems, had not endeared him to General Hertzog and had made him something of a liability to General Smuts. His devotion and ability, however, called for some reward and with that curious failure to correlate persons and policies which is one of the puzzles of so much of General Smuts' career, he was given a seat on the Native Affairs Commission.[1] This meant in effect that he was put in a position to press the application of a policy in this most important field which, as he himself tells in his book, had been continually at variance with that of General Smuts in the years of its formulation. From this office he had in fact, over the preceding four years, bent all his energies to the implementation of the segre-

[1] Vide *South Africa in My Time*, G. Heaton Nicholls, p. 270. 'I was opposed nearly every day to Smuts on the Native Bills Select Committee.'

gation policy. In particular he had pressed for that Bantuisation of Native education which we and all our African constituents viewed with so much alarm, while in general he argued strongly and worked consistently for that strengthening of the Department of Native Affairs which we condemned as the policy of a state within the state, a proposition which appealed strongly to the Nationalist element both inside and outside the Government Party. While I felt that Mr. Nicholls' reputation as an expert on Native Affairs had suffered somewhat from our advent on the Parliamentary scene, there was no doubt in my mind that, with the continuance of the general ignorance, indifference and prejudice within the Party in regard to Native Affairs, it would be an advantage to our cause if he could be promoted to a sphere in which his dynamic energy could be used on other fronts.

In hoping for this, I had one great factor in my favour. In the tense and crucial 'war' debate, he had made an almost disastrous speech in which he had accused General Hertzog of misleading the United Party over the years and in effect warning that if South Africa did not go into the war with Britain, there would be civil war in South Africa. I can still feel the shock of that speech to people like us who were not even on the fringes of the party fight. It must have struck panic into the hearts of those who were inside that tense ring—as indeed it did.

Particularly must this have been the case with General Smuts, who was at pains to maintain that South Africa was taking that independent decision which had been the common ground between himself and General Hertzog, and doing his best to establish the contention that for South Africa this was to be a defensive struggle. In the circumstances, there was little doubt that the feelings of the heads of the new Government towards Mr. Nicholls were not going to be very warm, and it seemed that if an elevation could be found that would remove the danger of the repetition of speeches likely to exacerbate the 'tribal' feeling that the situation had inevitably and unfortunately engendered, it would probably be welcomed. Hence my suggestion to Mr. Hofmeyr.

I have no reason to suppose that my views influenced the course of events in this regard in any way. I can only state that within two months, Mr. Nicholls had been promoted to the calmer atmosphere of the Senate. From there he graduated first to the Administratorship of his own Province, Natal, in 1942, and in 1944 he became the

Union's High Commissioner in London. I may say that if my representations did in fact have anything to do with a progress which took Mr. Nicholls out of the line of succession to the Cabinet, all unknowing he got his revenge a few years later by blocking my apparently pending membership of the experts' committee on indigenous labour of the International Labour Organisation, an office I should have been as gratified to hold as he no doubt would have appreciated Cabinet rank. It was, as I remember, in 1943 that I received a letter from Mr. Benson, Director of the Non-European (Indigenous) labour section of the I.L.O. In it, he informed me that the Organisation, having been disrupted by the outbreak of war, was getting back into working shape again from its wartime headquarters in Canada. In the circumstances, it was re-establishing its committee of experts on indigenous labour and he wished to know whether I would accept a seat on this committee if it were offered to me.

To a politician whose views made opposition practically inevitable, the prospect of any constructive co-operative job had naturally an attraction all its own. This one had a very particular attraction for me. Not only did it hold the promise of an opportunity to develop an interest in labour problems which I had always entertained; it offered the possibility of an opportunity to contribute something to the solution of the special problems of labour in a multi-racial society with which I had been much concerned over a long period.

In making the suggestion that I might be asked to join this committee, Mr. Benson made it clear that, in terms of the Constitution of the International Labour Organisation, no invitation could be extended to any one to serve on such a committee who was not *persona grata* to his or her own government. He was happy to tell me, he said, that I had been recommended by the South African High Commissioner in London. At that moment, the officer in question was Colonel Deneys Reitz. Alas, before the proposition could be brought to fruition, Colonel Reitz died. He was succeeded by Mr. Heaton Nicholls, whose views on Native policy, including Native labour, differed as fundamentally from mine as they apparently did from those of General Smuts and Colonel Reitz himself. Some years later I gathered from Mr. Benson, then on a visit to South Africa, that Mr. Nicholls had not regarded my views with the same tolerance that had actuated Colonel Reitz's recommendation. I was not surprised at that; there was in fact no meeting point in Mr. Nicholls' views and mine on the matter of Native policy, save the desire which I believe we both entertained to do our best for our country in the light of our own firmly held beliefs as to what that should be and how it could be achieved.

9

The Smuts Regime—The Reckoning

It is difficult if not impossible to imagine any adequate compensation for a world war. Looking back, however, it is clear that, for South Africa, the second world war years were not only years of anxiety, strife and tribulation, although there was plenty of all of these; they were also years of opportunity, a breathing space, a time for laying new foundations on which might be built a better, a more rational society than that which was in fact being shaped under the pressure of a determined Nationalist minority. As I have suggested, there can be little doubt that even if the war had not eventuated, the United Party would have split. Much, all too much in my opinion, has been made of the happy fruits of fusion. To anyone on the fringes of the political scene in the years immediately before the war, as I was, the strains in the Party were more apparent than the accommodations, and these were clearly growing more threatening, with what seemed an almost irresistible call of the blood on the part of the old Nationalist element in the Party. True, its members had sought to justify their acceptance of fusion by claiming that they had put the greater loyalty above the less, but the continuous challenge by their old colleagues to their Afrikaner sentiment found them uneasy and aggressive in their new alliance.

Thus all the evidence suggested that the line of cleavage when cleavage should come, would result in a re-assembling of the Nationalist forces with a new emphasis on their common ties and their exclusive attitudes. With this re-assembling achieved, the attainment of political control would only have been a matter of time, making the emergence of any more comprehensive ideal than that which the Malanites had chosen dependent on some unpredictable accident.

That unpredictable accident, in this case the war, was to precipitate the split and to condition it—and war tends to be a forcing ground of change on many fronts. In this instance, it set in motion changes on the economic and social fronts that were to prove practically revolutionary in dimension. Even in the years before

106

the outbreak of the war, the main socio-economic feature of the South African situation had been the process of urbanisation of all the country's racial groups. Something in the nature of an industrial revolution had already taken place in the course of the first world war. Later, we experienced a new tempo of economic and social development with the phenomenal prosperity which followed our emergence from the gold standard crisis. All this was to be given a fresh impetus on a quite colossal scale by the demands of the new world conflagration.

It is true, from the beginning, the townward flow of population consequent upon the industrialisation process had been misunderstood by one important section of the population and all too little understood by others. To the Nationalists the process of Afrikaner urbanisation was in the nature of a tragedy—a weakening both of the economic position and the cultural quality of Afrikanerdom, and the continuing cry was back to the land. The townward movement of Africans they regarded as equally disastrous, although for different reasons. Here, according to Nationalist thinking, blacks were invading white preserves, getting mixed up socially with whites and competing economically with those unfortunate Europeans who, under pressure of circumstances, were being forced to abandon their legitimate heritage on the soil. Hence the contingent demand for barriers to African migration townward and for colour bars in the industrial field.

But while the unprecedented scale of urban development after 1939 aggravated all the old problems of our changing life and created new ones, the nature of the war itself seemed to call for new approaches to all the problems of social living and a new evaluation of social and political practices. A war against Hitlerism and totalitarianism had perforce to be justified to those called upon to make the sacrifices it demanded. The virtue of the alternative had to be established. In the circumstances, that was in effect the ability of a democratic society to provide not only the wherewithal for its members to live but the freedom to give both work and life their savour, ideas that were to find their formulation first in the Atlantic Charter with its emphasis on freedom from want and the fear of want, and later in the Declaration of Human Rights with its challenge to any and all discriminatory policies and practices.

The question was, what were these concepts of democratic

obligation to mean in practice and how were they to be achieved? These were very practical questions in a world round which the echoes of the great depression still reverberated ominously and in which the racist doctrines of Nazism had provided a philosophical foundation for discriminatory practices. In the early days of the war, the British Government offered a significant lead on both fronts. It appointed a committee under the chairmanship of Sir William (later Lord) Beveridge to produce a blue print for full employment in a free society to meet the claims on the home front;[1] and even as this was getting under way, it issued a declaration on colonial policy. In reply to the accusation that Britain was in the war to defend her imperial position, this set out the intention to develop all dependent territories in their own interests and with the assistance of all the financial support the mother country could supply.

Inspired by the same impulse which produced these developments, the Smuts Government in the first months of the war appointed a commission to investigate the industrial and agricultural requirements of this country under the Chairmanship of Dr. H. J. van Eck. This commission brought in its final report before the end of 1941.[2] It was for us a highly encouraging document. It endorsed our case that, to provide stable and reasonably remunerative employment for everybody, it was imperative that the fullest use should be made of all our resources, including our human resources. This meant in effect that all the people of all races must be encouraged to function more effectively as both producers and consumers, which meant in the circumstances of South Africa the removal of artificial barriers to the acquisition and use of skills. It challenged the idea of the competitive relationship of racial groups which inspired white labour and colour bar policies and stressed the interdependence of all the groups in our developing society.

It also significantly found that the level of consuming capacity of the African population was so low that the African community could not begin to be effective either as producers or consumers unless and until some drastic treatment was applied to it. Indeed, it considered their situation too serious both from a human and a national point of view to wait upon the progressive effects of a

[1] Vide *Full Employment in a Free Society*. A report by William H. Beveridge, Geo. Allen & Unwin Ltd, 1944.
[2] U.G. 33 of 1940, U.G. 49 of 1940 and U.G. 40 of 1941.

policy of increasing wages, and urged an immediate policy of food price subsidisation to meet its most urgent needs.

Following upon this comprehensive enquiry came a whole series of particular enquiries all of which were either specially concerned with African affairs, such as the enquiry into the conditions of urban Africans presided over by the then Secretary for Native Affairs, Dr. Douglas Smit, and an enquiry into the wage rates of African workers on the mines, or more general enquiries which included the Africans, as for instance the enquiry into the treatment of miners' phthisis and the levels of compensation of the victims of this occupational disease. Working alongside all these was a permanent Social and Economic Planning Council which, established in 1941, again under the Chairmanship of Dr. van Eck, over the years provided authoritative reports and recommendations over a wide range of national problems. That range included the whole field of social security which was considered from the standpoint of the needs of all the racial groups in the country. Between them these enquiries touched upon all the main aspects of African life in our rapidly changing society, while point was finally laid on the essential controlling factors in this situation in the appointment in 1946 of the Commission under the chairmanship of Mr. Henry Fagan, erstwhile Minister of Native Affairs in the Hertzog Government, later to become the Chief Justice of the Appellate Division of the Supreme Court, to enquire into the operation of the laws governing the lives of the African population and to make recommendations in regard to their amendment in the light of changed and changing conditions.[1]

Each and all of these enquiries established from their own angle the individual poverty and the national ineffectiveness of our African population, subjected to restrictions and controls based on the assumption that their rights and needs were subordinate to those of the rest of the community. Most of them, as a result of their investigations, queried at least by implication, while the Fagan Commission specifically rejected, the idea which the segregation policy had sought to establish, that the African population did not form part of the permanent urban population of the country. More and more consistently the country was being faced by the argument that if South Africa was to meet the needs and claims of the most privileged of its citizens, it must release the energies of,

[1] See p. 191 for full text of Terms of Reference of this Commission.

and provide opportunities for, all its members—and that, in doing this, it would only be fulfilling the obligation of its democratic profession.

Even without the awakening social conscience which the mere fact of war tends to stimulate, such a weight of authority could not fail to have its effect on the thinking of the public, and there was increasing evidence that in fact it was making an impression. As against the migrant labour system on which the segregationists took their stand, organised commerce and industry on the one hand and agricultural associations on the other began to talk in favour of a stabilised labour force in which permanence of employment would encourage skill, which in its turn would justify those rising standards of wages which were being increasingly recognised as essential if the ravages of poverty were to be arrested and the tempo of industrial development was to be maintained, that is, for both humanitarian and economic reasons. And as a corollary to such a stabilised labour policy, the proposition was quite widely canvassed that the Native reserves should be organised and developed to become the homes of full-time agriculturalists whose improved standards of production would save both the land and the people and help appropriately to swell the national income.

With all these developments in mind, I felt justified, when addressing a group of business men in India in 1946, in claiming that we, that is, people of my political colour, had won our battle on the philosophical level. I had to admit that the political battle had still to be won—that is, that what had since Union become increasingly the general pattern of race relations in the country, and the legislative framework that supported it, had still to be revised and made to fit the new thinking. This was the need with which my colleagues and I were still at that date contending. Encouraged by the extent to which public enquiry supported our argument, and the apparently growing sympathy in the country itself for our case, we continued—it seemed to ourselves, and perhaps more to those who had to listen to us—unremittingly to press for a revision of policy that would bring national practice into line with our views of what it should be. As Parliament and the electorate began to be preoccupied with the specific shape of the post-war society in prospect of returning peace, and with the problems of demobilisation, we pressed the urgent need of change to provide the expanding economic activity and national income necessary for a successful fulfilment of wartime promises to the country at large. In the House of Assembly in 1943, I moved:

'That in view of recent happenings in Johannesburg, on the Reef and in Pretoria [a reference to a series of riots about which I have something to say in another context], this House urges the Government to undertake an immediate revision of the Native policy of the country in order to bring it into line with industrial development, the needs and aspirations of the Native population and the principles of the Atlantic Charter, to which this country has subscribed.'[1]

The following year, Mr. Molteno called specifically for the abolition of the pass laws. Again in 1945, we endeavoured to focus attention on the problems of the reserves and of the large army of African farm labourers whose conditions of service left them no alternative to periodic incursions into the towns to earn the cash to meet even the costs of their modest standard of living—incursions depressive of the standards of permanently urbanised labour and inimical to effective levels of productivity in both urban and rural employment. I moved in now familiar terms for a full review and revision of our Native land policy with a view to the effective use of the reserves as areas of land settlement, the improved productivity and standard of living of the farm labour population and the stabilisation of the whole African population. On any and all particular occasions when the ordinary business of Parliament provided the opportunity, we did our best to point the implications in practice of our case and thus to fill the gaps which these general debates inevitably left. In the Senate where rules of procedure offered ampler scope, the same programme was pursued indefatigably by our colleagues there.

Against this background of enquiry and discussion the practical record of the period is a curiously mixed one. It is a record of quite impressive gains in one direction, that of social services, of dangerous losses in another, that of personal freedom and democratic rights.

In South Africa as in other countries, the great depression had encouraged a demand for something in the nature of social security and the idea of the welfare state. In response to this, a modest range of Social Services designed to alleviate the harshest pressures of modern life was already in existence when, in 1938, a Department of Social Welfare was established in recognition of public responsi-

[1] Hansard, Vol. 45, Col. 1642.

bility in that regard. When we went to Parliament, however, few of these services extended to Africans. In this field as in the field of labour, the assumption was that, for the African, the misfortunes of life—sickness, unemployment, aged poverty—were provided for by their 'homes' in the reserves—and if not there, then by the traditional African feeling of the family and the tribe under which all shared what they had with one another, an attractive characteristic, it was argued, that must not be undermined by public assistance. These assumptions and arguments were reinforced by the simple proposition that to provide social services for a population so large as our African population was beyond our means. As I wrote in 1942 on the subject of a post-war Native policy: 'Today old age pensions are denied to Africans because so many Africans need them. Tomorrow more will need them as the burden of aged poverty keeps the present working population poorer even than they need be. Today we make no provision for the treatment and training of invalid and handicapped African children because the population to which they belong is so large and these services would cost so much. Tomorrow the need will have got still further beyond our generosity and probably also beyond our means.' These services, and greater educational facilities, were the urgent demand of the Africans. In all meetings and at all levels, two requests were put forward by them—schools and old age pensions. By 1948, grants for invalidity and old age pensions had both been in operation for a few years, and while still only some 40 per cent of African children of school-going age were in school, and the amount spent was lamentably low in comparison with the need, African education had developed enormously, both in width and in depth. In the Cape Province, the most advanced part of the country in the matter of Native education, in 1937 when our first election took place, while there were old-established secondary schools in rural areas, thanks to early missionary effort, no urban area could boast such an amenity for Africans. By 1948, when the Smuts regime came to an end, there was an African secondary school in most large towns and in many of the small towns as well. At the University level the Native University College of Fort Hare was well on the way to full University status; the Universities of Cape Town, Johannesburg and Natal were accommodating more and more African students, and the plans for a Medical School for non-Europeans in Durban were well advanced. In contrast to the practice of the pre-war years, wherever a new service was provided, with rare exceptions it gathered in the African. Admittedly it was often on a very narrow level, as in the case of old age pensions, which provided £1 (R2·00) per month in cities,[1] 15s. (R1·50) in villages and 10s. (R1·00) in rural areas. But this was more than a gesture in all the circumstances and one of which, I felt, we could justly be proud.

In the industrial field also, there were gains. In Workmen's Compensation, the level of compensation for African workers in the case of injury was doubled over the period, as was the level of compensation for the victims of miners' phthisis under the legislation applying to the mining industry. It is true, we failed to achieve the extension to African workers of the principle of continuing benefits, that is a pension, in the case of permanent disability, in spite of strong support by the Commission of Enquiry into Miners' Phthisis for the case we made to them, and a strong recommendation for the adoption of our proposals. That position is still unchanged and without the special interest of representatives of Africans to press it, it is likely to remain so.

In the field of employment, there were also gains to record. From the beginning of the new regime, under General Smuts' own instructions, efforts were made to meet the case we had continuously made that the Government should put its own house in order and set an example to outside employers in the matter of conditions of African employment. Both on the railways and in the general civil service, progressive improvements in rates of pay for African employees were made, and in respect of the railways, Mr. Sturrock, who proved ever sympathetic and helpful in this regard, early instituted a quite remarkable pensions scheme for the casual labourers in his department, specially designed to bring in the African employees in the service who, by administrative tradition and practice, generally fell—and still fall—into that category.

It is interesting if not encouraging to record that, in considering the case submitted to it in respect of the general civil service, the civil service commission which is responsible for recommendations in the field of government employment found that the prevailing

---

[1] Over the years these rates were gradually raised as the rates for other groups were raised until in 1965, the rate for cities was R47·40 per annum, R41·40 for villages and R35·50 for rural areas. In that year, these rates were made uniform at R44·40 per annum. This involved a reduction in the city rate justified by the then Minister of Finance in Dr. Verwoerd's Government as intended to discourage the African drift to urban areas.
Hansard Vol. 14 Col. 3327.

level of wages of African labourers in the service was so low that it would need a large advance indeed to bring it to any reasonable level. Such an advance the Government would find difficult—or at least uncomfortable—to carry through in the face of the inevitable reaction of the Nationalist Opposition. In the circumstances it was decided to try to achieve the desired result by indirect means, of which a specially high cost-of-living allowance on the lowest wage rates was the principal one. This was to apply in all fields of Government employment including the railways. Alas, there would seem to be particular dangers in seeming to do good by stealth. Soon after the advent of the Malan Government in 1948, these special adjustments were discovered by the Nationalist member for Newcastle and exposed to his Government, and the House, as an anomaly due to inefficiency and racial prejudice in favour of Africans on the part of the previous Government, and they promptly disappeared without any counterbalancing adjustments in wage rates. The energetic young member who thus early succeeded in re-depressing the rates of the lowest-paid servants of the Government has since moved up, via the Native Affairs Commission and a junior ministerial post, to the position of Minister of Bantu Education and Indian Affairs in the Verwoerd Government.[1]

In the last years of the Smuts regime, an Unemployment Insurance Act covered African industrial workers as well as all others.[2]

Thus again in India in 1946, I could legitimately and sincerely claim that the Union of South Africa had indeed achieved a level of social service for all groups in its population that had no parallel in any country approximating our racial character, that is, with a large emerging population still only partially industrialised.

Yet South Africa was not a happy country. The Natives Representative Council which had begun its work hopefully in 1937 had reached a deadlock in its relations with the Government and South Africa was in the dock at U.N.O. on an accusation of denying democratic rights to its Asian population. Everywhere widening gaps appeared in the relations between Black and White, with increasing unrest and tension among the Africans.

The explanation of this unfortunate situation is to be found in the failure of the political system to keep pace with the other developments that were taking place among the African popu-

[1] He retired from office and from Parliament in 1968 on grounds of ill-health.
[2] Act 53 of 1946.

lation. Even before the outbreak of war the critical spirit was on the march. Asked in 1942 to outline a post-war Native policy for South Africa, I urged that what South Africa needed was not a post-war Native policy but a new Native policy to be adopted and put into operation at once. I wrote:[1] 'On the eve of the war, the disastrous social effects of post-Union Native policy in this country were abundantly apparent to anyone with the eye to see them. In a country of ten million people, with bounding revenues and industries developing with phenomenal rapidity, the chief characteristics of our society were poverty and wasting resources in the midst of plenty, the juxta-position now familiar from industrialised countries of a rising standard of living for many and a progressive physical deterioration of all those sections of the community unable to maintain that standard out of their earnings; the steady undermining under pressure of material necessity of family life and the moral standards which uphold it; and most significant of all, the steady spread upward, like a contagious disease, which it really is, of economic insecurity from the least privileged group to the very heart of the most privileged.' What the war did, I added, 'was to reveal the psychological background of this situation, the progressive refusal of the African population to believe in and give allegiance to a democratic principle that stopped short at the colour line. When South Africa declared war on Germany the most significant thing that happened in this country was not the formation of the Herenigde Party (the re-alliance of the Nationalists) with its anti-war, anti-British, Republican platform. That was to be expected. The most significant thing that happened was the reaction of the African population to the demands upon active loyalty which war always makes. With significantly few exceptions, the African people were simply not interested in the war. When pressed to define or to explain their attitude, they did so by a series of simple statements and questions which ran more or less like this. "You tell us this is a war in defence of democracy. What has such a war to do with us? What have we to defend?" or "Why should we fight your war?" or even directly, "If we go to fight this war, shall we get back the rights we have lost? Shall we get back the right to buy land? Shall we get back the franchise?" Very pertinent questions, it seemed to me, and in the light of what is happening today, particularly in the East, very significant questions for a state that claims to be democratic.'

[1] *Common Sense*, October 1942.

These statements of mine were based on actual experiences in a constituency tour in 1940, the dark year of Dunkirk; and my experiences were those of my colleague, Mr. Molteno, as he travelled his wide area. I drew up a report on our combined experiences which I asked Mr. Hofmeyr to submit to the Prime Minister. The immediate answer by General Smuts was that he was not surprised at this attitude of the Native population. He thought that we must remove as many of 'the pinpricks' as possible, and invited suggestions in that regard. This proved a task beyond our capacity, since the need went much deeper than pinpricks. What was needed in fact was a new attitude to the African population and a new appreciation of its place in the community.

There were encouraging evidences that the Prime Minister himself appreciated this. With Colonel Deneys Reitz at Native Affairs, we were early assured that, on the authority of the Prime Minister himself, the African would be brought within the scope of our Industrial Conciliation legislation—the proposal I had made unavailingly in 1939, that is, that they would be granted the rights of collective bargaining from which so far they had been excluded. And following on a report on the pass laws which Mr. Fagan as Minister of Native Affairs had initiated in 1939, Colonel Reitz declared that in his opinion there was no greater cause of strained relations between African and European than the pass laws, that he would issue instructions that no passes should be demanded except where there were obvious grounds for suspecting that crimes had been or were likely to be committed, and that he proposed to see the Prime Minister with a view to getting his support for the complete abolition of the pass system.

In 1942, General Smuts made a now famous speech on the occasion of the annual Conference of the Institute of Race Relations in Cape Town in which he said that segregation had fallen on evil days, that it had failed to do what it had been intended to do, which was to keep the Africans out of the towns, and that we should have to meet new situations with new ideas. In the years that followed, on one occasion after another, he stressed the need to recognise that in a changing society, no settlement of race relations could be as final as General Hertzog and his friends had claimed the 1936 settlement to be, and that in seeking the basis of a new and better accommodation, it was essential that such an accommodation should be mutually acceptable and should appeal to the outside world as just.

This indeed was a theme to which he constantly returned, insisting on the need to find new answers to what he regarded as new situations. On all occasions where he was personally called upon to reply to us, he consistently gave the 'liberal' response, always, it is true, in the most general terms but equally consistently in terms that encouraged the hope that the lines would be progressively drawn more clearly between the two major parties—certainly in terms that induced the Nationalists to accuse him of drawing more and more to our side.

Yet we came out of the war and faced the 1948 election with the area of African freedom not widened but signally contracted. Not only had Africans not been accorded rights of industrial organisation and of collective bargaining. Under War Emergency Regulations passed in 1943, and faithfully extended each year even after the conclusion of the war, all strikes of all Africans in all circumstances had become and remained illegal, while no machinery for negotiation and conciliation was provided save that the Minister of Labour might acknowledge that a condition calling for negotiation existed in an industry and might agree to appoint a conciliation board to consider it. Thus all effective bargaining power was denied to the rapidly expanding African labour force. At the same time, the pressures of the segregation policy as embodied in the Native Trust and Land Act of 1936 which had brought the Cape Province into its orbit, coupled with the demands of industry, were inducing a new tempo of movement townwards of the rural African population. This in its turn was creating new demands for housing which, with the outbreak of war, became increasingly difficult to meet, so that vast slums erupted in or around every urban area, large and small.

To meet this situation, a system of influx control was established and encouraged, a system by which work-seekers were compelled to obtain permits to be in urban areas and were turned out if they failed to find work within a specified limited time. This system involved a wide extension of the already bitterly resented pass system, particularly in the Cape Province where the system had not previously generally existed. Indeed latterly, the Cape came to suffer a special disability in this regard. Since the best wage rates for unskilled work—all that the shifting African population could hope for—prevailed in Cape Town and its environs, thanks to the presence of the Cape Coloured people with their higher standard of living, the tendency naturally was for the overflow from the eastern regions, the overcrowded reserves of the Transkei and the Ciskei, first to seek employment there. In response to the resultant congestion in these areas—in essence a shortage of housing and not of available work—African travellers from the Transkei and the Ciskei to the Western Cape were put under the necessity of producing to railway clerks authorisations to travel from local public authorities of the status of magistrates before travelling tickets would be issued to them. This was a system which affected—and afflicted—the African professor, teacher, doctor as well as the unskilled labourer, no matter what the urgency of his need to travel, and that in a province which before 1936 had enjoyed a Parliamentary system which enfranchised males of all races on a common roll, and maintained the civil liberties which supported such a system.

And when all those restrictions were imposed on a man's need and will to work, the need and the will remained, unassisted and all too often unmet, certainly on any effective or intelligent basis. In spite of a great deal of lip service to new ideas and ideals, and to the need to meet modern problems by modern methods, South Africa in 1948 was not only still carrying on the methods of the eighteenth century but extending their operation to new fields where they could only end in disaster. The effects and the tragedy of the failure to see, or seeing, to meet, the need for change are both clearly to be seen in the record of the Natives Representative Council. It is a record to which inadequate attention was paid at the time and has been all too little appreciated since. It is, alas, a record of lost opportunity for which, it would seem, we have not yet paid the full price. Before dealing with this area of our experience I feel that it is probably appropriate to consider some of the possible reasons for the failure which it represents in our national history.

10

The Failure of the Smuts Regime

Why did the Smuts regime, with all the Prime Minister's commitments on the international front, and all the encouraging omens on the home front with which it began its career, fail to set us in a new direction in South Africa which would have made it difficult, if not impossible, for us to turn our backs as we have done on the new world that was emerging? What is the key to the dichotomy of social concession and political retrogression that was to leave us so vulnerable to the powers of reaction which have led us along the unhappy and highly dangerous road we have since travelled?

The answer to all this is probably as complex as South Africa and Smuts himself. Fortuitous circumstances certainly played an important part. It was indeed unfortunate that, even as Colonel Reitz as Minister of Native Affairs was adumbrating a more modern and liberal approach to the administrative problems of our rapidly changing multi-racial society, a series of events occurred which gave a new impetus to all those fears and prejudices which are never far from the surface in South Africa and encouraged a wave of reaction in the country which undoubtedly frightened a government which had still to face its first appeal to the electorate after the war crisis of 1939.

The first of these was the outbreak of a whole series of strikes of African workers in the Transvaal and Natal, leading to riots and bloodshed in Pretoria and on the Natal collieries at Northfield. It is true, independent judicial enquiries immediately instituted by the Government, and conducted at the highest level, established as the cause of the strikes deep and long-standing grievances rendered explosive in the Pretoria case by indecision on the part of the 'Labour' Minister of Labour, Mr. Walter Madeley, in applying recommendations of his own Wage Board for improved rates of pay for unskilled workers, and bad management on the part of the administrative authorities as responsible for the bloodshed in both cases.

But while these facts were taking time to emerge, there was a rising agitation among the white electorate over the first of the so-called crime waves that were to afflict our society during and immediately after the war years. In the context of South African society, this was easily and glibly attributed to the Africans, whose phenomenal rate of urbanisation under the mounting pressure of rural poverty and mounting demands for labour, were producing these extensive slum conditions to which reference has already been made. While these shanty-towns were the miserable homes of thousands of legitimately employed, hard-working and law-abiding people, they also inevitably provided a shelter for many who were none of these things—enough to lend colour to the accusation that the responsibility for what seemed a growing state of lawlessness lay here. The result was not the heart-searching over obviously bad social conditions which our wartime professions might have justified us in hoping for, but a widespread demand for more and stronger controls over the lives and movements of the whole African population. Even before the riots in Pretoria, the Johannesburg City Council, together with the Johannesburg Publicity Association, had demanded an extended curfew for Africans, the removal of all African-driven cars from the streets after dark, including buses for African passengers, greater control of servants by employers, and the endorsement of Africans' work passes with any convictions against them, including of course convictions in respect of the wide range of statutory offences applying to Africans only which made it well-nigh impossible for them to avoid conflict with the law.

The unfortunate result of all this was not the promised concession of full trade union rights to Africans to provide legal machinery for the settlement of labour disputes as a means of avoiding a repetition of the strikes and their contingent dangers, but War Measure 145 with its complete embargo on all strikes by Africans; it was not the abolition or even the modification of the pass laws but the withdrawal of the instruction under which the administration of these laws had been relaxed, and their stringent re-application.

Reflecting the public mood which inspired these moves by the Government, the Conference of Cape municipalities rejected unanimously the request of the Natives Representative Council for representation on municipal Councils (which the Council asserted was more important even than representation in Parliament as being nearer to the day-to-day lives of the people). In doing so, they set an example in this regard to the other Provinces which they were not slow to follow.

Thus the impulse begotten of Colonel Reitz's attitude came to nothing. Colonel Reitz himself left for London in 1943 to become South Africa's High Commissioner there, and thereafter the segregation policy, and the administrative controls by which alone it could function so long as it assumed that Africans had no abiding place outside Native reserves, pursued its relentless course to crisis. At the very beginning of his term of office, which lasted for the rest of the life of the Smuts Government, Colonel Reitz's successor, Major van der Byl, took his stand on this policy, as indeed he was entitled to do. It was, after all, the official policy of the Government, as General Smuts himself declared from time to time in response to Nationalist challenges, even while he asserted that it could not be regarded as immutable but would have to be adapted to changing circumstances.

No doubt the position was a difficult one for a conscientious and loyal member of his Party, with little experience in the important field of Native Affairs in which he was suddenly called upon to exercise a controlling interest and to acquire his first ministerial experience. Nor did our persistent efforts to exploit the Prime Minister's qualifying statements, in an effort to deflect administrative practice into more modern channels, make it any easier for him. Indeed in the very first months of his tenure of his new office, he was called upon to take up a position in this regard. Following upon a private motion moved from our benches, calling for a full review and reform of our Native policy to bring it into line with the needs and demands of a modern society—a motion inspired by the Prime Minister's then recent speech on the failure of the segregation policy —he complained privately to me later that it was unfair of me to face him with this wide challenge when he had not had time to get to grips with the ramifications of his large Department.

Undoubtedly a major proposition of this kind was bound to make great demands on any new Minister, whatever his previous knowledge and experience. In all the circumstances, it was not surprising that his response to our case was a firm declaration of faith in the official policy. At the time, I was inclined to regret my action in moving so comprehensive a challenge to a new Minister, inevitably forcing him to take up an attitude he might find difficult later to modify—as we were encouraged to hope he might wish to do. Some five years later, however, in almost the last Parliamentary session of the Smuts Government in 1947, when the Natives Representative Council's crisis was already one of our major preoccupations, in reply to an outstanding speech in the Senate by the Senator for my constituency, Senator Malcomess, Major van der Byl could only reaffirm his first declaration in the most emphatic terms, and again with obvious justification; segregation was still the official policy of the United Party which he had done and was doing his best to apply.

Senator Malcomess had accused the Minister of failing to make the Government realise the implications of the situation that had developed in the country, and particularly in the Natives Representative Council, and the seriousness of it. In every sphere of life, Senator Malcomess declared, the African people were subject to discrimination. What, he asked, was the Minister doing to protect the rights of the Africans? Speaking in New York the previous year, the Prime Minister had said that loss of faith and economic maladjustment must lead to trouble. Did the Prime Minister know, or had the Minister of Native Affairs told him, that eight million people of his country had lost their faith, that they were restless and that the spirit of non-co-operation with Europeans was growing? 'The honourable Minister knows,' he added, 'that the eyes of the world are on us. The colour bar runs through our Government, it runs through our churches, it runs through our public bodies. It is the essence of our faith and it is the essence of our actions.'[1]

No doubt the Minister would in any case have found these criticisms a great trial of spirit, particularly coming as they did from an old member of his own Party, and at a moment when he was facing accusations from the official Opposition of inability to handle the crisis in the Council and of having had to call in the acting Prime Minister to deal with the situation. The peculiar dualism of the position—the inevitable inner conflict between the principles of the official policy, with the machinery which its implementation demanded, and the Prime Minister's repeated references to the need for change—gave him a peculiarly difficult situation to handle, and undoubtedly was imposing a great strain upon him, conditioning his reply. Resentfully he declared, in terms already all too familiar from less responsible quarters, that the agitation among the Africans was the work of communists who were stirring up the people for their own advantage. Even the Parliamentary Representatives were not free from blame in this regard. He deprecated strongly

[1] Senate Hansard, 1947, Vol. 1, Cols. 920–1.

what he claimed was the tendency of these representatives to convey to the Native people the impression that the Government was ignoring them. Taking up the challenge to the Government's policy, he again took his stand on the 1936 settlement, and as if to prove to appreciative Opposition benches (who, as I noted at the time, were always ready to praise him as one of themselves) that there had been no backsliding, he gave the assurance that the term 'African' (then coming into use by choice of the people themselves) was not used by his Department which kept strictly to the word 'Native'.

Clearly the critical factor in this situation was the Prime Minister himself. Where did he stand in it? To what extent was he aware of, and party to, the administrative developments in terms of his Party's official policy which were leading to such serious conflict between white and black? Where and when did he seek advice? Or give direction?

Even as I was recording for African readers the argument between Senator Malcomess and the Minister of Native Affairs, I noted that General Smuts had readily agreed to meet a deputation composed of the Cape representatives of Africans in the two Houses of Parliament, to whom had been committed the duty of presenting to him a resolution of the Cape African National Congress that read:

'The Executive Committee of the Cape African National Congress deplores the present break in the relations between the Government and the Natives Representative Council and desires to call upon the Government to take immediate steps to end the deadlock.'

I could report further that in the discussion that took place, it was clear that the Prime Minister was much concerned about the widening gap between the Natives Representative Council and the Government, and that there were grounds for believing that he would himself make a move to bridge it.

This he did in tentative proposals to reform and develop the Council which, alas, reached no effective point before the fateful election of 1948 which was to wrest the reins of government from his control and to place them in the hands of people with far other views as to the needs of the situation.

General Smuts' reception of us on this occasion was typical of all his relations with us throughout the period of his office. I cannot remember any occasion on which he did not accede to a request from us as a group, or from any of us, to see him, nor can I remember any occasion on which we were not given the most sympathetic hearing for our case, even when he did not see his way to accept and take action on it. Typical also, perhaps, was the fact that on this occasion, when a vital aspect of Native policy was at issue, his Minister of Native Affairs was not present at the interview.

My first and my last interviews with him as Prime Minister were, I believe, particularly characteristic of him. One of the very few personal talks I had with him in my earliest days in Parliament, that was in the old United Party days, occurred on one of the rare occasions when he stopped in the lobby to converse for a moment, obviously exploring the extent of his own support in the event of a rupture between himself and General Hertzog. Very much pre-occupied with the case my colleague, Mr. Molteno, and I had been trying to make for improvement in the position of the African workers on the railways and in Government service generally, I took advantage of the occasion to try to enlist his sympathy for it. He immediately began to talk of 'the real need' of the Native as being food, and told us how impressed he had been with that need in his East African campaign in the first world war. Improved nutrition and improved health were the basic needs of all Native communities in Africa, he considered. The relation between these needs and wages seemed to me obvious, but he continued to take evasive action on that point, and left me with the feeling that there was little chance of getting him to take more than a passing academic interest in this matter if he could be induced to remember it at all. I was all the more surprised and, naturally, considerably impressed when, on the occasion of our meeting as a group with him in Pretoria when he had become Prime Minister, after I had relieved his mind about the relationship which was likely to subsist between us, he turned to me and said, 'Have you seen the Minister of Railways yet?' To my surprised response that we had not done so, he suggested that it might be a good thing to do. Naturally we were not slow to take the hint. We forthwith sought an interview with the new Minister, Mr. Sturrock, from which derived that friendly association the fruitful results of which I have already recorded. Those years saw the quite considerable improvements I have already noted in the position of all the non-Europeans employed by the Department of Railways.

It was at this time also that reference was given to the Public Service Commission to see what could be done to bring the earnings of Africans in the Government service into some closer relationship with their needs.

My final interview was one which I had sought personally in the course of the 1947 session, when the Natives Representative Council crisis was already nearly a year old. I wrote him a note saying that, being much concerned about the growing gap between the Government and the African population, I would appreciate an opportunity to discuss the situation with him. Immediately on receipt of my note he sent his secretary, Mr. Henry Cooper, to invite me to meet him there and then, and we sat down for an hour's talk, in the course of which we covered the whole field of policy and administration. My theme was the need to govern rather than to control the African population, to recognise the modern character of our state and to help the African people to make their essential accommodations to it. I pressed the need for not only allowing but helping Africans to acquire and use skill, and the advantages of replacing pass laws with their penal sanctions by modern methods of bringing workers and jobs together. I told him we had supported his Labour Department's legislation for Registration for Employment because it provided constructive machinery for this purpose as against the negative, destructive effect of the pass laws and an equally negative system of influx control which seemed to regard the willing and needy African worker as an enemy of society. He had not registered on this piece of legislation, and went off to his bookshelf to see it for himself.

He listened to what I had to say with his usual consideration and then asked, 'But isn't it votes they want?' I said I didn't think so at that stage. I was convinced that if the pressures of the pass laws were replaced by genuine effort to provide better economic opportunity, and if the leaders of the people were drawn into consultation on this and other efforts to improve the standard of living of the people, we would get possibly ten years in which to prepare the country for the political changes that should and must come. I did not believe that in the then state of public opinion it would be possible to get the necessary support for any worthwhile change in the existing political set-up as it affected the African people—a case which no doubt his experience of the hostility even among his own supporters to his effort to give a modest group representation to the Indian Community fully confirmed. The change which Mr. Hofmeyr had then recently adumbrated, by which each non-White racial group should come to represent itself in Parliament, was as unlikely as any we might have proposed to find an easy passage to the Statute book. Nor was it one that roused any enthusiasm in us, since it retained the communal franchise, although we could not condemn it since it involved the disappearance of one colour bar, that which deprived non-Europeans of the right to sit in Parliament. Indeed I considered that any major legislative change in the field of Native policy would be extremely difficult without a dynamic preliminary propaganda campaign, but I argued that no such challenge to prejudice was necessary to improve the position of the Africans and with it the relationship of black and white. So much of the law as it stood was permissive, allowing a wide range of administrative action within which the whole character of the policy could be remoulded in practice. This, I argued, made it possible to substitute a modern approach to the problems our rapid industrialisation had produced for the frontier mentality habit of control which was our substitute for sound economic practice and new political thinking.

This conversation was interrupted by the ringing of division bells, but it concluded with a request from the Prime Minister for a memorandum covering the field of our discussion which I was happy to prepare for him.

Some months later, in the final session before the 1948 election, I found myself covering much the same ground in the House of Assembly when the Government came forward with a Bill to extend the life of the War Measures Act and the regulations framed under it. These included not only War Measure 145, with its denial to Africans of legal rights of collective bargaining, but also the restriction on the movements of Africans from the Transkei and the Ciskei to Cape Town and the Western Cape in search of work. I insisted again that what was needed in a modern industrial state like ours was not to put people in gaol for failing to find work, but to establish machinery to help them into employment; it was not to prevent people seeking employment in the area where wage rates were best, but to level up basic wage rates over the country to encourage a more even flow of labour in process of urbanisation; and of course again I urged improved wages, not only to meet the needs of the workers but in the interests of the country as a whole.

I was gratified to hear the Prime Minister, in his reply to the debate,[1] tell the House that he had discussed this matter with me,

[1] Hansard, Vol. 63, Col. 3474 *et seq.*

and that he believed I was right in my analysis of the needs of the situation. We would have to do what I suggested, he said; we would have to learn to handle the problems of our new society in this way. In extenuation of his own legislative proposition, he considered that this learning process would take time. He argued that the urban situation had developed so rapidly and was still so new to us that we had not been able to catch up with it in our thinking.

I was naturally encouraged by this recognition of our case, even while privately I deprecated the suggestion that our problems were so new. Had they not been developing over the preceding half century, and developing with particular speed in and after World War I? There is no doubt, however, that it was taking the scale of population movement in the thirties, accentuated by the phenomenal war-time development of industry in the second world war period, to make white South Africans begin to realise the fact of change. Any conception of how to deal with it had still to overcome the blinding influence of the colour factor. And as the record shows, what lead there was on the political front in this regard was as yet tentative, uncertain, even confused. This was all the more important —and unfortunate—in that progressively throughout the whole period, but with ever increasing insistence as the war drew to a close and another election loomed ahead, the whole issue of colour was coming to occupy a dominant position on the political stage, thanks mainly to an Opposition that was neither tentative nor uncertain in its approach.

From the beginning for the Nationalists, whatever their vicissitudes and divisions, of which there were many in the early days of the war period, there was one rallying point—colour. On this they were consistent, and continuously insistent in their demand for segregation the ramifications of which, in terms of their policy, tended to grow with the years. Here it is interesting to note that even against their old Hertzogite friends returned to the fold the Malanites, who were and were to remain the hard core of the re-united party, were to make no concessions in this regard. As I have recorded, in the pre-war session of 1939, in reply to Nationalist demands, General Hertzog had taken his stand firmly against any derogation of the political rights of the Coloured people. Yet in 1940, in the first session after the opening of the war, with General Hertzog officially in the leadership of the re-united forces, Dr. Malan put up a motion calling for the removal of the Coloured voters from the common voters' roll. The motion was moved, but never came to a vote, so we have no knowledge as to what General Hertzog and his friends would have done about it in the last resort. It is possible that they had been led to accept the proposition Mr. Havenga was later to accept, that a separate roll did not represent a derogation of rights.

Before that 1940 session was over, a new programme had been shaped in which the re-united party was pledged to reduce the rights of the Native Representatives in Parliament so that never again should they be able to interfere in matters vital to the White people of the country. Later, as it became impossible to agree as to what did or did not affect Africans only which, it was argued, was the appropriate and only appropriate area of activity for Native Representatives, and as the Representatives themselves had constituted themselves the protagonists of a democratic system to include all sections of the population, Dr. Malan, speaking for his party, declared that, having only a nuisance value, they should be removed at least from the House of Assembly.

In the meantime the recruitment of Coloured and African troops, even though unarmed, became a constant point of attack from the Malanite benches as a menace to white civilisation; as indeed was everything that seemed to suggest that the Coloured and African populations were to be accepted as part of the South African community. Already every move on the part of the Government to extend the widening field of social services to Africans had been the source of acrimonious debate the emotional content of which mounted steeply after 1942, when the speech from the throne announced the intention of the Government 'to make plans for the Native population both rural and urban'[1] to 'participate in the enhanced well-being which it is desired to secure for the community as a whole'. In 1943 when, in accordance with this declaration, the Government included African school children in a school-feeding scheme, and the Minister of Finance excluded third class railway fares from the general rise for which that year's budget provided, the House was treated to a whole series of violent opposing speeches led by Mr. Serfontein, who had great pleasure in stigmatising the budget as a coffee-coloured budget. The following year, when the Government included Africans in the provisions for old age pensions and invalidity grants, Mr. Strydom became almost apoplectic in

[1] Hansard, Vol. 43, Col. 6.

his denunciations of the waste of the white man's money; and in 1945, when his Party moved to delete the vote for the feeding of African school children, he had much to say about the disastrous effects of this service on the farm labour position.

This was a theme that was to be elaborated both then and later by those members of the official Opposition who vied with Mr. Strydom in his reactionary attitude to any concession to Africans. Indeed in 1946, when Mr. Serfontein and others got going on a vote of £10,000 (R20,000) for victory celebrations among the Africans in the reserves, sneeringly referred to by Mr. Serfontein as the Farthing Feasts, even some of their own people seemed a little ashamed of a performance which I wrote of at the time as a particularly unpleasant and degrading exhibition of illiberality. At any rate, Mr. Paul Sauer felt impelled to enter the debate to explain that what his Party objected to was not the spending of a 'miserable £10,000' on a victory celebration but the spending of anything in this way when the people were starving and crying out for food and were given none. It was an explanation which sounded less than sincere against the background of a renewed attack on the school-feeding scheme not only as an iniquitous waste of the white man's money but as undermining such limited willingness to work as the Native population could be forced to show. As I wrote it, seemed that boys were leaving the farms and going to school, 'simply to gorge themselves on the food recklessly supplied to the pupils—at the princely cost of twopence per day'.[1]

By 1945, it was already clear that colour politics were to dominate the next election due in 1948. Throughout the Parliamentary session of that year, colour was Dr. Malan's main subject of debate. On the budget and again on the Prime Minister's vote he pressed the policy of his Party, which was now emphatically the removal of the Coloured voters from the common roll and our disappearance from the House of Assembly. In response to a renewed demand to know where the Prime Minister stood in this matter of segregation, General Smuts took his stand on the 1936 settlement, but as a starting point from which to go forward. He again argued that since that settlement had been made, a great change had come over the country, creating new problems and situations which General Hertzog could not have foreseen and for which his policy made no provision. He was in favour of dealing with those on a

[1] See *The Union Review*, March 1946, p. 25.

I

basis which would not shock the feelings of people outside or public opinion in this country, and which would not give rise to a feeling of injustice in the hearts of the Coloured person or the Native.

He would however give one assurance to the Leader of the Opposition, and that was that his Party would not depart from 'the principle of white supremacy based on apartheid, separation in the social field'[1]—an announcement that evoked considerable Opposition applause.

Another year was to add a further plank to the Nationalist platform. In the 1946 session of Parliament, General Smuts introduced that Asiatic Land Tenure and Indian Representation Bill which was to spark off so many troubles, both for him and for South Africa. This embodied two propositions, the curtailment of the property rights of Indians in Natal and the Transvaal and what he himself called a quid pro quo in the form of communal franchise rights to the Asians on the model of the Africans' representation in Parliament. It was highly acceptable to the majority of all parties in Parliament in respect of the first of these and equally objectionable to even the majority of his own party in respect of the second which the Nationalists determined to repeal whenever opportunity should offer to do so. His followers were in fact only induced to vote for the franchise clauses by the force of the Prime Minister's own personality. Driven to concede the attack on property rights to the prejudices of his Natal supporters (English), his determination to impose upon them the grant of even meagre political rights to the Asian community was undoubtedly the measure of his desire to keep South Africa in the current of Western thoughts and values. It was a measure which unfortunately neither the people to whom it was conceded nor the world outside regarded as adequate to its purpose. The Asians at home would have none of it, and at the United Nations Organisation, which he had done so much to initiate, he was roundly condemned for illiberalism. It was an experience which shocked him deeply.

He explained to a South African public incensed at the attacks upon its policies and practices that much of the criticism he had had to meet was ill-informed, based on ignorance of the complexities of South African life. At the same time, as I wrote soon after his return, 'he has courageously made it equally clear that he has himself found it difficult, and in some cases well-nigh impossible to

[1] Hansard, Vol. 52, Col. 3407.

defend South Africa's approach to colour issues. He has warned his country that it must take stock of the position and be prepared to weed out whatever runs counter to the essential principles of democratic living. He has told us that he himself could not meet a number of specific charges levelled against our policies and practices. Most prominent among these was the industrial colour bar and the housing position. Housing was one of the most acute problems in the world today, he said. Everyone abroad knew of South Africa's housing problem. They knew that the Native people suffered even more from inadequate housing than did the Europeans. 'They also knew,' he added, 'that we are not allowed to train Natives to build their own houses in their own locations. That was flung at me in London and in New York. What could I as Prime Minister answer? Nothing, because it is a fact.'—a reference to the failure of his Department of Labour down to that point to get agreement on this matter with the white artisans in the building trades.

Equally unanswerable, and even more serious, he felt, was the accusation that we in South Africa tend to judge all men by the colour of their skins. There is too much of a tendency in South Africa to look at a man's skin and judge him by that, he declared. 'A man is not the same because he has the same skin as another man. We have in South Africa Natives, Coloureds and Indians. They are not all the same because they have the same skin.' We have seriously to consider whether we are not going too far in that respect, he warned. 'Why treat all with a skin of a different colour on the same level, which is the level of the lowest?' he asked. 'A man with a different colour skin with qualities of leadership, high training and education should not be accorded the position which is the lowest level of his colour.'[1]

Summing up the situation as I saw it at that moment, I concluded that 'In all the circumstances, although we are undoubtedly facing a year of acrimonious and unpleasant argument on non-European and particularly on African Native issues, there are more signs of the possibility of intelligent and fruitful change in this dangerous and contentious field than we have seen for many years.' In the months that followed, fears and hopes tended to chase one another as the Opposition insistently demanded an elaboration of the Government's intentions, which they contended were clearly to move away from the segregation policy. Under this

[1] *Umteteli wa Bantu*, January 13th, 1947.

pressure these took on a shadowy form with the final formulation awaiting the report of the Fagan Commission, which in effect meant waiting until after the election. In October 1947, a newsletter emanating from the United Party office on the subject of Native policy did indeed accept the fact of integration of the African people into the general life of the community and, with it, the permanence of the African in the urban areas. It also declared against industrial colour bars and the insecurity in respect of their homes in the towns which was a major affliction from which the Africans suffered. At the same time, however, separation within the common society had already spread to a wide range of amenities on the hopeful assumption of separate but equal, which was to prove illusory; and it seemed to be making new and, to any liberal, sinister advances in a variety of directions. The Prime Minister himself announced his belief that it was unfortunate that Coloureds and Europeans had come together in trade unions, and as time was to reveal, the Railway Department was preparing boards to reserve carriages 'for whites only' on the Cape suburban railway, a concession to a repetitive Nationalist demand which had hitherto been successfully resisted, it seemed on principle. Unfortunately it was a demand which found an echo in the hearts of some Transvaal members of the United Party itself.

Altogether, it was a confused and confusing situation in which a basic difference of approach between the two sides of the political field was struggling into existence, the idea of one society which must provide opportunities on all fronts for all groups against the exclusive sectional separatist approach of isolationist Afrikaner nationalism. There was even an incipient recognition of the fact that this acceptance of the idea of one society must make new administrative methods essential, but so far without any practical results. The Prime Minister could tell his own supporters that there would have to be a new Native policy in South Africa; but to tell them no more than this, even while his own Government seemed to be making concessions to what the Opposition claimed to be the South African way of life, was scarcely to arm them effectively for a vital election in which this very issue was to predominate.

It is easy to blame Smuts for his failure in this regard; and undoubtedly he must carry the responsibility for the degree and the extent of his preoccupation elsewhere, particularly in the latter years of his office, which left him little or no time to keep up with the demands of the domestic situation. As Selope Thema, one of the outstanding figures of the Natives Representative Council, once somewhat bitterly declared, the Prime Minister was busy building peace in the world, whereas what we needed was that he should build peace here where he lived. The Prime Minister might have argued that, while he was engaged in the important business of trying to build peace in the world, the affairs of the country were in good hands—and he was indeed to claim to us on more than one occasion that they were in good liberal hands. I felt on experience entitled to query the grounds of his confidence in this regard. With one exception, in the later years, it would indeed have been difficult to find among the people around him anyone capable of advising and directing him in so important a matter. It was not in his character and temper to choose such people or, choosing them, to encourage them to exercise the dynamic which the occasion called for. Decisions when taken were his decisions, and in all the circumstances, at least so far as Native Affairs were concerned, these were taken at crisis moments, since it was only when events in this field reached crisis proportions that they forced themselves, or were forced, into the forefront of his life. As I have suggested, to us who stood outside his Party it was difficult often to see the grounds of his most important appointments; and as early as 1943 I wrote that his cabinet was freely and publicly described as the weakest the history of Union had thrown up.[1] It was a view that seemed to have penetrated to his own hearth. Talking to Mrs. Hofmeyr, mother of J. H. Hofmeyr, one day in the lobby some two or three years later I remarked that her son must be feeling the pressure of work very seriously. He was at that time acting Prime Minister, as he did on the frequent occasions when General Smuts was out of the country, and already it had been reported that his health was causing anxiety. 'Indeed,' she said, 'he is very tired. Everything falls on him. Even when he is half unconscious they come to him for decisions. And what do you think of this?' she added. 'The other day when we were visiting at Irene (General Smuts' home), Ou Ma (Mrs. Smuts) said to him, "Jantje, I hear your Cabinet is so bad. Why don't you do something about it?" ' To my query as to what he could reply to that, she said 'What could he say? "It's what the Ou Baas (General Smuts) left me," he said. "What can I do about it?" '

[1] *Umteteli wa Bantu*, August 21st, 1943.

But if Mr. Hofmeyr could not change the composition of the Cabinet, as an acclaimed liberal and Smuts' successor elect, could he not have helped to plot a clearer course for the Party at that crucial juncture that might have given it a fighting line to hold? Could he not have met the changing circumstances with a plan of action that would have given the rank and file of the Party some feeling of confidence, the necessary conviction that they were on a purposeful road forward even though it might be a long one? Then, as now, the economic argument was all in favour of abandonment of the old courses and, as I have suggested, in the course of the trying war years, a great deal of anxious goodwill had come into being to offer moral support for such a move.

I believe two factors militated against this. The first of these was the enormous burden of both administrative and political work which seemed to fall to his lot, not only during the critical years of the war, but in the years that followed. He had indeed an almost phenomenal capacity for work, but there is no doubt that it was often taxed to its limit in the service of his country. It seemed indeed that over those years he pinned the whole machinery of government together and kept it moving.

It could not be surprising if so much immediate demand left little time for the thought and opportunity for the discussion which planning for the future of a country must entail. But although a liberal in the Cape tradition and faced, as we all were, with the challenge of this period in our history, at no time did Mr. Hofmeyr evince any general political philosophy that would have enabled him to appreciate, and urged him to try to meet the needs of the developing situation, to blaze a new trail in South African thought and practice. His handling of the Natives Representative Council crisis, which was one of the situations which fell to him as acting Prime Minister, and of which I shall have something to say elsewhere, is almost startling evidence of this. In the homily which he delivered to the hopeful and expectant Councillors, he failed to touch any of the essentials of the situation, as he failed to establish any contact with the Councillors themselves. This was in line with his failure throughout his political life, to gather round him those who would have been happy to find in him a leader under whose banner they might help to guide South Africa into more modern ways. In this regard we who, from outside the Government Party, had looked from time to time to him for a name and a personality to give body and substance to the liberal spirit definitely growing in the country, were not the only disappointed ones. In the same category fell members of his own Party, among them the young men in whose advent to Parliament in 1943 I had seen grounds for encouragement and hope. Among them were those who were prepared to find in him, with his established and authoritative position, a source of strength to which they might harness their own idealism. His response to any moves in this direction, I am reliably informed, was to discourage anything in the nature of a following that might suggest the growth of a group spirit within the Party.

Whether in the circumstances of the case, in a Party with the dichotomous origin of the United Party, this was a sound tactic to pursue is not to be judged from the outside. However, one tactic he pursued which I was, and am still, convinced was completely unsound. With the Government's massive administrative duties to meet, aggravated enormously by the dual-capital system, as leader of the House he was always understandably anxious to get the session to as speedy a conclusion as possible. But when this led to his closing down the debate on his own side of the House while practically every member of a more and more cohesive Opposition fighting force poured forth his Party's line on colour, which they did on every conceivable occasion, it seemed to me a very bad tactic indeed. There was no doubt that Mr. Hofmeyr, in any debate in his charge, could present all the answers and present them all usually superlatively well. However, in a country as politically conscious as South Africa, where current practices and ways of life made ignorance the handmaiden of prejudice, to allow reiteration of the Opposition's case, without immediate and equally repetitive answer from the other side, seemed to me conspicuous folly. On more than one occasion I suggested this to him. I had as little success as had the members of his own Party in changing his belief in the virtue of his own course. Unlike most Party men, he seemed to prefer to fight the Opposition alone. Certainly he would appear to have consulted no one when he made his statement about the inevitability of non-Europeans representing themselves in Parliament, a statement which challenged the deepest prejudices of the Official Opposition and of many of his own side. It was to cost the Government—and Sir De Villiers Graaff, offering himself for the first time to the electorate—the seat, which was then at issue in a by-election, and to begin those attacks on him personally that were to make his own Party saddle him with the responsibility for the débâcle in the general election in the following year.

Whatever the relative importance of these factors in the developing political situation on the eve of the fateful 1948 election, the essential fact would seem to be that, under pressure of events both at home and abroad, Smuts was more and more convinced of the need for a change in colour policy, but he had not yet come to any clear decision in his own mind as to the real nature—or extent— of the change that the circumstances of the case needed and called for. It was a situation which left his Party as a whole in a state of flux that made it extremely vulnerable to Nationalist attack. His failure to appreciate this seems to have derived from a miscalculation of the time factor in the situation. Curiously certain of victory in this election as he had been anxiously doubtful about the result in 1943, and taking his stand on the wisdom of meeting the problems of society as they developed—the pragmatic approach— he clearly counted on time to see how things would shape—and time to enable him to carry his people with him along the path which all his thought and emotion seemed to indicate as his eventual choice.

In this context, 'his people' undoubtedly meant more than his Party, and herein surely is to be sought the key to his failure to move more rapidly to a more definite position. Speaking at Port Elizabeth after the 1943 election,[1] he said the question of the Native African weighed profoundly with him. He did not think that we would succeed in our efforts for the future of South Africa unless we came to grips with that question and he did not think that we would succeed as a united European South Africa unless we could justify our consciences in our relation between Black and White. But he thought the first step for us was to unite our European people. In 1908, as a young man at the National Convention, he had taken the line that the question of the position of the African should be put to a suspense account, that the uniting of European South Africa should come first. He still regarded this as the primary challenge to statesmanship in this country. Surely it was this conviction which gave his course in the field of colour policy, with its highly explosive content, such a shifting appearance. In the face of Nationalist repetitive insistence on the essential difference implicit

[1] See *Umteteli wa Bantu*, July 2nd, 1943.

in colour, and their persistent demand for the maintenance of what they had come to claim as the traditional South African way of life, his concessions to the principle of separation in practice, even while taking his stand on the demands and obligations of a common society, begin to fall into place. He must not frighten 'his people', hurry them along an unfamiliar path. He must give them time to get accustomed to the new ideas beginning to operate in the world. In all of this he thought that he, certainly his Party, had the requisite time at their disposal.

This interpretation of events as we knew them would seem to be confirmed by a brief talk I had with him after the election. I felt it incumbent on me at the beginning of the post-election session in 1948 to call on him to express my very sincere regret at, and my deep concern over, his defeat. Obviously deeply hurt and shaken by a defeat that had involved his own seat as well as his office, he shook his head sadly and said, 'Alas, I am too liberal for my people.' It was an explanation of the course events had taken that I did not find easy to accept then, although our later history would seem to confirm it. I respectfully said I could not believe that that was the essence of the case. Indeed, I was convinced that what he had offered, which from my standpoint was modest enough, should have been very generally acceptable wherever there was any appreciation of the forces at work in our society. The difficulty as I saw it was that the young men of the Party (and I might have said, even more the old men) had not been trained to argue the case. A purely reactionary case such as that of the Nationalists called for nothing more than appeals to emotion and prejudice. A case which had to appeal to reason and faith made great demands on its advocates—indeed, involved a technique that South Africa had still to learn.

The shock of defeat and the pressures of opposition were to begin the learning process. Even then it was to prove tragically slow.

PART II

The Natives Representative Council Launched

The brief history of the Natives Representative Council serves to point both the possibilities and the disappointments of the wartime period. It is impossible to read its record without being almost oppressed by the tragedy of the failure of those years. It is a record in which two things stand out conspicuously—the high level of African development in South Africa as compared with any other African community in Africa; and, in spite of already accumulated grievances and frustrations, how little it would have taken to establish a co-operative relationship with both the leaders and the mass of the African people that could have encouraged and, I believe, would have produced a stratification of South African society on economic and not on racial lines. Had this happened, not only would the subsequent history of South Africa have been a different and a happier one; the history of the whole of Africa, and indeed of the world, would have been different and happier. The continuing emphasis by South Africa on colour as a basic essential difference with, in the circumstances, the suggestion of a difference in human value, has bedevilled the relations of White and non-White everywhere in this generation, with disastrous results at every point and on every level.

The composition of the first Council, and indeed of all the Councils, of which there were only three, was itself an earnest of good intention on the part of the Africans, the intention to try out honestly and sincerely machinery to which the African people had been strongly opposed as involving the policy of segregation which they consistently repudiated. It had been claimed by the sponsors of that policy that, although conceived in the interest of whites, and with the intention of securing permanent white domination in South Africa, it was the only policy that held any hope for blacks. Could it indeed be made to serve this dual purpose? Without much conviction, but in the belief that if it could be shown to be unequal to this task and unacceptable in itself, in the best tradition of government by discussion and consent, it might yield place to something better, leading figures among the African people, with the backing of the people themselves, decided to accept the responsibility of exploring the possibilities which the system offered.

Most of the elected members were old-established, widely known and highly respected leaders of the African people. Many of them had taken an active part in the prolonged fight against the abolition of the old Cape franchise and the policy that that involved. All were men of ability, some of them—like Dr. John Dube, Mr. Selope Thema, Mr. R. H. Godlo, men of very marked ability, and some considerable experience.

Dr. Dube, the founder and head of a large school for boys in Natal, had been the first president of the African National Congress. Of him, when his service to the Council was terminated by death on February 11th, 1946, the Chief Native Commissioner of his Province, Major Liefeldt, moving a vote of condolence, had an impressive list of achievements to record. In addition to his services to African education, he had founded the newspaper *Ilanga lase Natal*, which is still the foremost medium of African opinion in Natal province. Mr. Liefeldt added, 'Dr. Dube took a leading part in public affairs and his advice was welcomed not only by his own people but by Government and all sections of the population of the Union.'

The climax of Dr. Dube's career was reached when the University of South Africa, then a federal University including all the University institutions in the country with the exception of the young Universities of Cape Town, Stellenbosch and Witwatersrand, decided, as a gesture of inter-racial goodwill, to confer upon him the honorary degree of Doctor of Philosophy, 'the first of such awards to a Native of this country'.

Selope Thema, a forceful speaker with a singularly clear, logical and independent mind, was the first editor of a paper for Africans established in Johannesburg in the middle 1930's, the *Bantu World*. Messrs. R. H. Godlo[1] and Mack Jabavu were also journalists, the latter the editor of a paper founded by his father, Tengo Jabavu, himself one of the earliest and most remarkable of the African leaders under the freer system which the old Cape Colony threw up. The remaining eight elected members were mainly teachers and small farmers.

For the four nominated members, the Government had chosen the more prominent and important chiefs. These included Chief

[1] Editor of *Umlindi we Nyanga*, published by Baker, King & Co., East London. Mr. Lex King gave me invaluable assistance in my first election.

Mshiyeni, the acting paramount chief of the Zulus, and Chief Victor Poto, the paramount chief of the Eastern Pondos, today one of the key figures in the Transkei.

At the second election in 1943 Professor Z. K. Matthews, professor of Law and Native Administration at the University College of Fort Hare, took the place of Mr. Jabavu whose health was failing rapidly, and Mr. Paul Mosaka, a successful businessman and, down to his day, regarded as the most brilliant student Fort Hare had had, became the urban representative of the Transvaal-Orange Free State constituency. Mr. A. W. G. Champion, from Natal, was an old campaigner of the early days of African trade unionism. At the final round, in 1948, Mr. Champion was joined by another old stalwart of early trade union days, Mr. Selby Msimang,[1] while Chief Albert Luthuli began establishing his now long list of records by being the first and only chief to enter the Council by popular election.

This impressive assembly, conspicuously representative of the emerging African population, was launched on its way in December 1937, even before the newly-elected Parliamentary representatives had taken their seats in Parliament, and on the whole, auspiciously, it seemed. General Smuts, as deputy Prime Minister, performed the opening ceremony in place of General Hertzog who was prevented from attending by indisposition. With typically skilful omission of any reference to the policy from which the Council derived, to which he had himself been consistently opposed in principle, he sought to link the Council with the more constructive developments in the past history of Native administration. Reviewing the progress of local government machinery in Native areas from Rhodes' Glen Grey Act of 1894 to the establishment of the United Transkeian Territories General Council in 1930, he commended this 'national' Council as the logical outcome and culmination of these developments. With a passing reference to the provision of 'separate representation in Parliament of Native interests throughout the Union', he gave status to the members of this first Council by declaring: 'This Natives Representative Council has been instituted as a constitutional body advisory to Government and Parliament, through which elected Native representatives are enabled to represent the views and interests of their constituents to the Government

[1] Was banned in 1965—presumably as a member of the Liberal Party. Has since had his ban removed.

and to Parliament.' In thus calling on the Native people of South Africa to advise and assist constitutionally in the task of their own government, Parliament had taken 'a far-reaching step in advance'. He added, 'It is the earnest wish of us all that through wisdom and moderation, and in the statesmanlike use of the new opportunities, this notable advance may be fully justified and become a landmark in the happier relations between the European and Native peoples of this land.'[1]

More typical of the general political atmosphere and of the anxieties behind the launching of the Council (the 'Purified' Nationalists were strongly opposed to it) was the speech of Mr. Piet Grobler, the Minister of Native Affairs and friend of General Hertzog. Speaking in Afrikaans, which few of the Councillors could understand, Mr. Grobler felt compelled to link with his welcome and good wishes a serious if friendly warning to the members of the new body not to over-estimate their own powers and not to be misled by irresponsible people into making unreasonable demands. 'I don't want you to be under any wrong impression as to the powers which have been entrusted to the Council. The Parliament of the Union remains the highest legislative authority in the Union and the function of your deliberations will be to bring your ideas and propositions regarding Native Affairs to the attention of Parliament and the Government, who will then consider them in relation to the general interest and policy of the country. Not for a moment,' he added, 'will I detract from the importance of your proceedings, since I don't doubt that they will produce worthy and competent service within the framework of a policy that will provide abiding benefit to both sections of our common life; but I want to guard you from any disappointment in your first session if I should perhaps give you the impression that there was no likelihood that the Government would differ from your proposals and resolutions.' The already familiar advice followed: 'My advice to you is, be moderate and reasonable in your resolutions, for the more reasonable your requests, the greater the possibility that the Government will meet your wishes.'

In thanking the speakers on behalf of the Council, Dr. Dube significantly laid his emphasis on the Council's sense of the responsi-

[1] After the first session of the Council, the verbatim records of the meetings of the Council were limitedly circulated in roneo form only. Copies of these records are now rare. All references in this section are to this record kindly made available to me by the University of Cape Town.

bility that their own people had placed upon them, and expressed the hope that they 'might justify the hopes and aspirations of the souls of the black people of South Africa'. Following him, Chief Poto assured the Government of the desire of the Native people to be continuingly loyal to the Government. He also expressed the great shame and distress of the whole African population at an unfortunate episode which had recently taken place at Vereeniging, when several policemen had lost their lives in a fracas with the local African population which had arisen in the course of a police raid in search of liquor and passes, one of the first but, alas, not one of the last of such episodes.

Thus sped on its way, the Council settled down to the business of exploring the nature and the range of the task allotted to it. For those who had framed the legislation to which it owed its existence this was no less—and no more—than to advise on and assist in the application of that legislation and the policy it embodied. It is doubtful whether any of the African Councillors saw the situation in quite those sharply defined terms, or, seeing it thus, would have been prepared to accept it. The experience of this first session was to go a long way towards clarifying the issue, as it was at least to foreshadow the difficulties such an interpretation would have to surmount if it was to achieve any practical result.

At the moment, however, hopes were high and omens good. Here were freely elected Africans called on by Government both to hear and be heard on their own affairs, meeting in a Council which, as one Councillor expressed it, 'had been put on a very elevated plane right from the outset' by the attendance of the deputy Prime Minister and the Minister of Native Affairs at their opening function; meeting also, as the same Councillor noted, within the precincts of the Pretoria City Hall 'where I believe no black man has ever set foot before'. In the face of such gestures of goodwill, assuredly the Africans were on their mettle to conduct themselves responsibly and thus to justify and to guarantee the success of this new venture.

In this optimistic atmosphere, and in the presence of a considerable gallery of Africans and Europeans, the Chairman[1] proceeded to lay before the Council the Trust account, the Government's estimate of revenue and expenditure for the ensuing year. This covered not only the provision to be made for all services for Africans, including education; it included also the Government's plans

[1] Mr. (later Dr.) Douglas Smit.

K

for the acquisition and development of what one of the Native Affairs Commissioners, Mr. Heaton Nicholls, referred to later as the African estate, the land that was to be the foundation of, as it was to be the justification for, the policy of segregation.

Just as this was the first time that the Government had drawn its black subjects into a regular constitutional relationship and was seeing them in a capacity other than that of an unenfranchised opposition, so was it the first time that an African representative body was being initiated into the activities, the plans and the intentions of Government from the inside. So far as services were concerned, the effect was quite other than might have been expected considering the clamant demands which mounting poverty had inspired over the preceding years. The Chairman, setting a wise and useful precedent, called in senior civil servants from all the main departments of Government, including the chief administrative officers of the Provinces in the fields of education and health which were under Provincial control, to place before the Councillors their efforts, their hopes and their ambitions for the people whom they were called upon to serve. As they proceeded with their task, those who had come to complain found themselves deeply impressed by the obvious good will of all these officers, and ended with expressions of sympathy for them over the magnitude of the task with which they had to contend with such inadequate resources. Indeed, when the session came to an end, even so critical a politician as Selope Thema, supporting a vote of thanks to the Chairman, could say: 'It has been an eye-opener to me to have heard of some of the things that have been done in Native development, things of which I have never heard. When the officers of the Department were reading or telling us what they were doing, I wondered why such information was never given before. We did not know of the things done by the Native Affairs Department. Some of us had begun to think that the N.A.D. was an instrument of oppression, just because perhaps we did not know of these activities that had been put into operation; but I think that from now on, this spirit of friendliness, and of co-operation, will be carried out; and, I think, our Native Commissioners must have had their eyes opened. Perhaps in the past, they thought that educated Natives were mad people and therefore men who should not come near their offices, but I am sure that in future they will consult us on this and that matter.'

The officials for their part were agreeably surprised at the moderate tone of the Council. Sir Edward Thornton, Chief Medical Officer of the Union, having reviewed the rather bleak scene of African health, and listened to the comments from the floor on a subject on which the Councillors obviously felt very deeply, was moved to associate himself with the appreciation expressed by the Chairman of 'the extreme moderation' with which their views had been expressed. 'I came here prepared, I candidly admit, for rather a hot morning,' he said, and he clearly felt that the grounds of his expectation were fairly solid.

But if this first session saw a new confidence established between the administration and the representatives of the African people, wherever the business of the session touched even the fringes of policy, significant differences of approach at once made themselves apparent, to suggest that the ground for co-operation, as distinct from comment, might prove dangerously shallow.

The first evidence of this appeared early in the session on the subject of the control of Native education. By the Act of Union, all education other than higher education had been committed to the Provinces. In 1925, however, as the process of centralising and uniformalising Native policy and administration began to get under way under the first Hertzog Government, the right to tax Africans was withdrawn from the Provincial authorities and the financing of Native education was taken over by the central Government, to be linked to and to advance with the proceeds of the Native general tax, the poll tax. In the meantime, however, administration remained with the Provinces. As the anomalies of divided financial and administrative control began to emerge, and as the outlines of the segregation policy began to harden, the argument had arisen that the administration of this service should also be shifted to the central authority, while the more convinced segregationist urged that the relevant department for the control of such a service was not the Union Department of Education but the Department of Native Affairs as the Department responsible for the administration of the country's Native policy. With the legislative acceptance of the Hertzog policy, this had become a live issue, as had the whole subject of Native education. The Government had therefore appointed an inter-departmental Committee to consider and advise on this matter. Its terms of reference had been drawn widely enough to cover every aspect of this increasingly important service, including both content and control. This Committee had recently reported and had recommended the taking over of the administration of Native education by the central Government, but advised that the Department to which responsibility should be committed should be Education and not Native Affairs —that is, that the service should be regarded as essentially an educational one and not a political one.

Almost contemporaneously, the Native Affairs Commission issued a comprehensive survey of the character and the implications of the segregation policy as embodied in the recent legalisation. They had come down forcefully in favour of centralised control of Native education through the Department of Native Affairs. The report was obviously inspired by, as it was mainly composed by, Mr. Heaton Nicholls, who had been appointed to the Commission in 1935 with a mandate, he believed,[1] 'to carry out the policy' which he had consistently advocated throughout the lengthy period of its struggle towards the statute book.

With the issue thus in the balance, the Chairman now asked the Councillors for their views on the matter. Immediately they took the stand that was to be that of the whole African population so long as it remained free to express its views on this subject. This was an emphatic no to any suggestion of placing their education under any control that was not explicitly educational, a suggestion which implied, where it was not explicitly stated, that education for the African might and should be something other than that provided for other sections of the community, and designed to keep him 'in his place' in that community. In particularly forceful terms, Councillor Thema repudiated any such suggestion on two grounds. The first was that the segregation policy was not really a policy of segregation; it was only a policy of residential separation, under which black and white would continue to live together within one state and under the control of the economic and social forces which ruled the lives of all sections of the community. But even if it had been a policy of complete segregation—'the real logic of the policy' —the need of the Africans was still 'to know and understand and capture Western methods, Western know-how', and that meant Western type education.

The advocates of segregation had always been strongly vocal on the rights of Africans to develop in their own way—'on their own lines' was the current phrase. Councillor Thema proceeded to put

[1] *South Africa in My Time*, p. 326.

the African's reply to this argument in pungent form. 'Where,' he asked, 'is the race that has developed along its own lines? Along what lines were the English developing when the Romans went to England, or the Germans before the Romans went to Germany, or the Dutch before the Romans went there? Even the Romans got their civilisation from somebody else. Can anybody say: "These are my ideas. I am developing along my own lines"? Nobody can say that.'

Referring then directly to the Native Affairs Commission's report, he went on: 'What we are asked is that we must develop in such a way that we must not become competitors to the white man.' Pointing to the Native Affairs Commission's report, he said: 'I do think that if we read this report, we will find that this report actually wants to keep us in a state where it will be impossible for us to develop . . .' He concluded: 'We think there is no education which belongs to a certain race. How can we remain stationary, how can we not be Europeanised in a European Africa?'

In reply to this speech, Mr. Heaton Nicholls, who with the other members of the Native Affairs Commission was present at the meeting, felt called upon to defend not only the case which the Commission had made, but the way in which it had been made, since their report had already been the subject of considerable public argument and attack, in which it had been contended that it had been couched in provocative language and had departed from the usual type of governmental report. On the point of content, he argued that for the mass of the African people in their then condition, special type education was an essential, and he claimed that with control of the service by the Native Affairs Department the Council itself could achieve a controlling position in regard to it. This was an argument of which the Councillors were later to seek elucidation —unsuccessfully. On the subject of the form and method of the publication of the Commission's views, Mr. Nicholls explained that the Native Affairs Commission was not a departmental committee. It was, he said, a political commission specially appointed to consider matters of policy.

This explanation of the position of the Commission was later to have wide repercussions in the Council. The immediate response of the Councillors to Mr. Nicholls' speech was to thank him for it and to state that the Council were entirely unconvinced by it on the main issue of the control of Native education. On this subject there were no doubts and no two minds among the Councillors. Rural members and urban members, well educated and less well educated, thought alike on this. Education for them was education, and any attempt to divorce Native education from the ordinary channels of educational administration was only another trick of a privileged society to keep the African down, to build up a state within a state which should shut him off from all the means of advance in a modern world.

On the other basically important subject raised by the estimates, that of land, the Chairman's need was not for advice but for co-operation. Detailing the Department's plans to improve agriculture by acquiring land to relieve the pressure on the existing reserves—that 7,250,000 morgen of land promised in 1936 to implement the territorial side of the segregation policy (and still in 1967 1,545,632 morgen short of the total)[1]—he made two appeals to the Councillors for their assistance. One was to help to persuade the rural people to curtail their stock in order to reduce the pressure on the land as the essential condition of improvement; the second was to discourage people from moving townwards unless they were absolutely assured of work—this to enable the Government to implement that facet of the segregation policy which aimed at limiting the urban African population to the labour needs of the whites.

While the Council, in warm terms, expressed its appreciation of what the Department was doing to improve the use of land, its answer to these two specific appeals was significant. To the first, it laid very pertinent emphasis on the proved and admitted over-population of the reserves, which suggested that the first need was not so much a reduction in the already very low average stock holding of the rural family as an increase in the amount of land available. The only alternative to that surely was more jobs, and where were jobs to be found if not in the towns? Here was the answer not only to the Chairman's appeal in respect of the land position; it was the curtain raiser to a discussion on the recently passed amendment to the Urban Areas Act in which it had been sought to round off the segregation policy by abolishing the right of Africans to buy land in these areas, and to strengthen the provisions designed to control and to curb the movement to the towns which had already been written into the law at intervals since its inception in 1923. What was to happen to people if they could not

[1] See note 1, p. 19.

go to the towns for jobs, and to those who, having become accustomed to town life and probably now completely divorced from all rural ties, were apparently to be turned out of the town when they were no longer willing or able to serve Europeans? For the 1937 Amendment to the law was not only to make it more difficult for Africans to enter urban areas but to underline the principle that these areas were 'white' areas in which Africans should only have the status of temporary sojourners with no rights of permanent domicile.

Thus when the Chairman sought advice from the Council on how best to apply the terms of the new law, he found himself faced with questions rather than answers. To these questions, the Councillors had to be content with the Chairman's assurance that established African residents could not be turned out of the towns in terms of the law unless and until he could find land on which to settle them.[1] He added the assurance that people would not be turned out so long as they were performing any reasonable service even to their own people contingent on the presence of an urban African population. On the other hand, the Chairman himself had to accept, at least by implication, that the Councillors were either unable or unwilling to assist in the administration of a policy that seemed to make no practical provision for the needs of their people.

While Government business continued throughout the session to occupy the bulk of the time of the Council, private members' motions were woven into the agenda at what seemed relevant and appropriate points. These, revealing in themselves, served to illumine the general exploratory character of the session, to point the major preoccupations of the African people, and to accentuate the pressures which lay behind the relationship of the Government and the African population.

The pass laws early took their place in the list of subjects to which the Government's attention was directed as long overdue for reconsideration. In surprisingly moderate style considering the agitations to which these laws had repeatedly given rise, Councillor Thema moved that 'in view of the fact that the Pass Laws prevent Africans from earning wages in accordance with their skill and efficiency, the Council urges the abolition of these laws or alternatively for their modification along the lines recommended by the Pass Commission of 1919, namely that the present pass system should

[1] A condition which has since been successfully modified in the law in spite of the extension of segregation into apartheid.

be abolished and substituted by a lifelong document for the purpose
of identification only'.

Seconding the motion, Councillor Godlo could say, 'I have never
lived in the Transvaal. All my life has been spent in the Cape Colony
where the Pass Laws do not operate' (How soon this was to change),
'and from what I have seen as a visitor mostly in the Transvaal, I
have come to the conclusion that these passes have not served their
purpose. Instead of being a protection to anyone they are hardening
the hearts of those who are affected.'

Without a great deal of discussion, and without any heat, this
motion was carried unanimously. Not so another significant
motion also emanating from Councillor Thema. This called for the
reform of the Native Affairs Commission.[1] It read:

'That in accordance with the policy of differentiation as laid
down in the Representation of Natives Act, 1936, this Council
is of the opinion that members of the Native Affairs Commission
should not be Europeans who represent European interests in
the House of Assembly and in the Senate, but men free from
Party Politics and who will thus be in a position to give an
impartial and disinterested advice to the Government on Native
Affairs.

Further, that the time has come when Africans should be included in the personnel of the Commission so as to ensure the
confidence of the Native people in the Native Affairs Commission.'

In introducing this motion, Councillor Thema was at pains to
explain that he was not activated by any motive against any
particular person. He supported his proposition with the general
argument that, when the Representation of Natives Act was under
discussion in Parliament, the removal of the Africans from the
Cape voters' roll had been repeatedly defended on the ground that
those elected on the basis of that roll 'do not actually represent
Native interests because they had the white man in the same
constituency to consider'. He went on: 'I think I will be well

[1] This critical attitude of the Africans to the Native Affairs Commission largely
stemmed from Mr. Heaton Nicholls' drive on the segregation policy and the
pamphlets which, under his inspiration, set out the practical implications of the
policy as he saw them. See African Studies, Witwatersrand University Press.
Vol. 26, No 2, 1937 for reprint of the original pamphlet under title—Racial
Separation: a view taken in 1936.

understood when I say that this same argument can be and should be applied in respect of the constitution of the Native Affairs Commission . . . I think this Council should really make Parliament understand that we want in this Commission men who are not interested in any constituency, who do not participate in the debates in Parliament, who will not be actuated or swayed by the feeling that here they have the interests of the white people to safeguard. Personally I am against this division of the people,' he added, 'but this having been forced upon us, I think we have to follow it to its logical conclusion. We do not feel it is right that in respect of the Native Affairs Commission, the members should be members who are political members, representing a European constituency. They should be Europeans who do not represent Europeans, or they may be Europeans who represent us in the House of Assembly or in the Senate, or may be Europeans who do not represent anybody, that is, Europeans who have no obligations to other people.' He then pressed for the appointment of an African to the Commission as a guarantee to his own people.

The fate of the motion has an interest of its own. It was seconded by Councillor Godlo, who 'like my friend Mr. Thema, never believed that the separation of the two races politically and in other directions will do either the European or the Bantu any good', but since Parliament in its wisdom had decided in favour of such separation, he felt it was essential that the Commission should be reorganised so that 'it should be able to make its representations without fear or favour based on the facts that have been placed before them'.

Councillor Jabavu, also the product of an urban environment, supported the motion on the specific ground that the Commission had 'given the green light' to the Government in the previous session of Parliament to go on with a Native Laws Amendment Act strengthening the segregation provisions of the Urban Areas legislation[1] 'although they were supposed to represent our feelings and our feelings were diametrically opposed to those of the Commission at that time'. It was a complaint he and others were to return to at intervals in the following sessions.

Councillor Mapikela, representing the urban vote in the Free State-Transvaal constituency, reminded the Council of Mr. Heaton

---

[1] Native Laws Amendment Act 46 of 1937. This amendment was carried while the first elections under the Representation of Natives Act were still in progress.

Nicholls' statement in his speech defending the approach of the
Native Affairs Commission to the control of Native education, to
the effect that the Commission was no departmental Committee but
'a political Commission specially appointed to consider matters of
policy'. He reckoned that a man could not serve two masters.
Councillor R. G. Baloyi, also a product of urban surroundings, was
strongly of the same opinion.

But the rural members would have nothing to do with the motion,
and that for two reasons. In spite of the reiterated disclaimers of
the supporters of the motion that there was no intention to reflect
on anyone, enough had been said in earlier debates to give them
an uneasy feeling that the motion was in fact one of no-confidence
in the dominant influence in the Commission, Mr. Heaton Nicholls,
and their instincts of courtesy, not yet blunted by political experience,
shied away from that. But they were further influenced by the sincere and determined efforts of the Commission to meet the demands
of a new and important duty imposed on them since the passage of
the 1936 Land and Trust Act. This was to get the consent of European farmers to release and sell for Native settlement the land
essential for the implementation of the bargain which the policy
ostensibly involved. It was to prove no simple assignment. It has
always been easy to get a South African electorate to vote for
segregation, separation, apartheid, call it what you will; it has not
yet proved possible to get it to implement even the all too modest
provision made in 1936 for a policy that was in fact still merely
one of residential separation. In pursuance of its duty in this regard,
the members of the Commission had travelled round the country, and
Dr. Dube, who had made it his business to accompany them through
his own constituency of Natal and Zululand, could testify to the
difficulties 'these honourable gentlemen appointed by the Government' had had to face and the demands they had made upon their
own people to fulfil their side of the bargain. With all this in mind,
he urged Councillor Thema to withdraw his motion as 'beginning
to bring about racial feeling between whites and blacks in this
country'. To him it seemed that 'whereas Government has given us
one finger, this resolution seems to be taking the whole hand . . .
Before we are able to walk this resolution is urging us to run'. The
furthest he would go with the supporters of the resolution was to
say to the Government that 'it would please the Native people if
one member of our race was included in the composition of the

Commission'. And that was as far as any rural member would go, with Chief Josiah Moshesh feeling that even that was too much to ask. Chief Mshiyeni confessed himself deeply shocked at the whole proposition, and also begged Councillor Thema to withdraw it. But Thema preferred defeat to withdrawal, and the motion was lost by nine votes to seven.

For the rest, the session was notable for the general preoccupation of the Councillors with the daily pressures of life on their people. Recurring emphases were laid on the difficulties Africans experienced in their efforts to earn a living. Councillors from all areas and all groups were not slow to put a finger on the poverty that caused ill-health and created the need for the social services so grudgingly supplied by a Parliament dominated by white fears of black competition or by the desire for cheap labour or both. Chief Mshiyeni found himself voicing the common feeling of the Council in his request that the Government should hold an enquiry into the level of wages paid in urban employment. Nor could anyone complain of the spirit in which this and all other matters presented to the Council were approached when Councillor Thema, with the support of all his colleagues, could move that 'this Council, while agreeing to the prevention of the influx of Natives from the rural areas, urges the Government to improve the economic conditions of the reserves and those of farm labourers so as to induce the people to remain on the land'.

There is little doubt that the mere opportunity to state their side of the case on levels they had never reached before relaxed tension in people who had for so long been not politically inarticulate, but articulate beyond the range of Governmental attention, and the Council terminated its first session in the hopeful and firm belief that it had come into being, as one member expressed it, as a third chamber of the legislature, not only to be heard but to be listened to. Here indeed were grounds for encouragement and for hope.

The Natives Representative Council and the War: Democracy or Segregation?

The Council's second session, a short post-general election session in November 1938, broke little new ground. True, there had been little response from Government quarters to the record of the first session's discussion and requests, but that could be attributed to the distractions of the first fusion election, which had given the Government little time to consider the working of its new constitutional machinery rather than to Mr. Strydom's noisy attacks on the Council's proceedings.[1] So the Council went through the session perfunctorily repeating a good deal of its previous record. When it met again in November 1939, it found itself addressing a new Government involved in a war already acclaimed as a fight for democracy against the recent trends towards dictatorship. What if anything this was to mean in the field of Native policy in South Africa was a question that had as yet scarcely even been formulated. There was a new Minister of Native Affairs, Colonel Deneys Reitz, but he had not yet had time to make any impact on the conciousness of the Council or the people. He was not even available to meet the Council, being on a mission overseas. To his deputy, the Minister without Portfolio, Major Piet van der Byl, who came to open the session in his name, the two chiefs, Mshiyeni and Poto, moved a vote of thanks for his presence and address in speeches which were confined to expressions of loyalty implicitly endorsing our vote in Parliament in support of our entry into the war. Thereafter the Council settled down to what was already becoming the traditional pattern of business, the consideration of the estimates of expenditure, interspaced with appropriately timed private motions. The only immediate evidence of the change in the political situation was the inevitable warning, as senior officials gave their reports on work in hand, particularly in respect of land, that with a war to finance, hopes for the continuance of that work must not be too high.

[1] Noted on pp. 66–67.

As the session went on, however, it became obvious that the implications of the segregation policy as adopted by Parliament in 1936 were beginning to be clarified, and the anomalous position of the Natives Representative Council, as a body called upon to co-operate in the application of a policy it had never accepted, to emerge. Two debates were particularly revealing in this regard. The first of these took place on a renewed attempt by Selope Thema to get a vote in favour of the abolition or reform of the Native Affairs Commission, the second on 'edictal' legislation.

By this time, of five members of the Native Affairs Commission, one only was not a member of Parliament, and of the four Parliamentary members, two were now members of the Opposition,[1] having gone out of the Government with General Hertzog. The fact that neither these two gentlemen nor anyone else had apparently seen any reason for their resigning their membership of the Commission might legitimately have suggested that Mr. Hofmeyr's analysis of the situation[2] was somewhat optimistic, and that in the field of Native policy no one in authority was yet aware of any essential conflict between a fight for democracy and the pursuit of a policy of race relations openly designed to protect the position of a privileged minority.

All the members of the Commission were present to hear Councillor Thema move that:

'The Council respectfully urges that, as the Commission was declared by one of its members at a meeting of this Council to be a political body, it no longer serves the purpose contemplated in the Native Affairs Act of 1920; that this Council is now in existence and the Commissiom should either be abolished or re-modelled to enable it to co-operate more closely with the Council and to include in its personnel direct representatives of this Council.'

The ensuing debate, which showed a new degree of acrimony among the supporters of the motion, tended to come back to the point that there were now two sources of advice open to the Government and that, as things were, these were unlikely to find any substantial measure of agreement. In the circumstances, the Com-

[1] Mr. Tom Naudé and General Conroy. Noted on p. 33.
[2] See p. 102.

missioners, being appointed by the Government, were bound to be the more acceptable, as well as having the more immediate access to the sources of authority. 'If the advice which we give here is not agreeable to the Native Affairs Commission, then whose advice will the Government take?' Councillor Thema asked, and added, 'And I say that since it is a Political Body the Native Affairs Commission will not agree with us.' As evidence supporting this view he instanced the fact that the Pass Laws, to which all Africans were bitterly opposed, were extending their ramifications. 'Instead of the Pass Laws being modified, they are actually being increased under our various new Acts. I say that if the Native Affairs Commission had been doing its duty—the duty of advising Government on the grievances of theNatives—none of our new Acts would have included these pass law provisions.'

Particular point was given to this contention by the recent closing of Cape Town to Africans seeking work except under special permit, the beginning of the policy of imposed influx control in terms of the 1937 amendments to the Urban Areas Act. Referring to this, Councillor Thema went on to say: 'It is because some of the members of this Commission are members of political parties that they will in the natural course of things always advise against our wishes. Let me give you an instance. What happened at Cape Town? I understand that the City Council of Cape Town did not want to enforce certain regulations debarring our people from going to Cape Town. The Native Affairs Commission, without investigating matters in Cape Town, and without obtaining the views of the Native people of Cape Town, advised that Cape Town should be an area in which Natives should not be allowed to enter without first obtaining permission.'

This 'closing' of Cape Town by Government decree, which meant the first serious extension of the pass system to the Cape Province, had reopened what was by this time almost an old wound in the hearts of the urban Africans, namely the determined passage of the 1937 Amending Act while the Council and the Parliamentary representation were still in process of coming into existence but were not yet functioning, and that on the advice of and with the concurrence of the Native Affairs Commission. This was a case that had been made in earlier sessions, and again a few days previously in this session when Mr. Heaton Nicholls, again acting as spokesman for the Commission, had felt impelled to reply to the implied accusation of bad faith on the part of the Government and its advisers. He found in the Commission's attitude and action, for which he was no doubt primarily responsible, nothing illogical or dishonest. In his view, the Council had been created to work within the framework of the Hertzog policy, and under that policy this control of the townward movement of Africans was basic. This, he argued, should be recognised and accepted by the representatives of the Africans as the condition of their political existence. On any other basis, they were simply beating the air.

As for the passage of the Act in question before the formal operation of the Council, he commended as generous the Commission's advice to the Government to let the House of Assembly pass the Bill in the 1937 session and then to hold it over for consideration by the Council, whose proposed amendments could be considered by the Senate when the first elected representatives of the whole country would be present to argue them.

Councillor Godlo, supporting Councillor Thema's move to have the Commission abolished, or at least modified in personnel, was not slow to point the emptiness of a proposed concession which put the principle of the measure beyond the reach of the Council; and Councillor Jabavu returned to an old accusation that it was in fact the support of the Native Affairs Commission that had defeated the concentrated efforts of the Africans to have the Bill, with its wide extension of the segregation policy in the urban areas, delayed until the Council and the Native Representatives in Parliament should be in a position to express the African point of view.

The desire for land, however, and the absence of the pressures which were increasingly complicating the lives of the townspeople, kept the rural representatives conservatively to the line they had chosen on the previous occasion, and the vote again went against the motion in the same proportion of nine to seven.

On the other hand, a unanimous vote went in favour of what might be regarded as almost a contingent motion moved by the Eastern Province urban member, Councillor Xiniwe. This was to the effect that 'The Council, which is a statutory body, created as a link between the African people on the one hand, and Parliament and Government on the other, registers its protest against the practice hitherto followed by the Native Affairs Commission in recommending draft proclamations and other legislative measures affecting Natives without these having first been submitted to this Council for consideration. The Council would like it brought before the notice of the Hon. the Minister of Native Affairs who is the chairman of the Native Affairs Commission that in the opinion of this Council the practice is tantamount to a breach of an undertaking solemnly given that no draft legislation affecting the African peoples of the Union would be translated into law without the views and feelings of our people thereon having been ascertained, and obtained through this Council. It is further pointed out that the operation of some of the proclamations has introduced various forms of Pass systems of a most irritating nature in urban areas and what is more several towns in the Union have been closed to our people as fields of labour. The Council views this as unprecedented and immoral in that this policy operates against our people only and that it prevents our people from freely earning a livelihood for their families in any centres they choose within their own homeland, and it compels them to give their labour as forced and cheap labour to the European farming community. The Council earnestly and respectfully re-quests that the whole method of legislating for our people be reviewed and all sources of irritation and pinpricks of our already harassed people be removed.'

The Chairman objected to the use of the word 'immoral', which the mover immediately withdrew out of regard for the Chairman himself.

There followed a comprehensive and patient explanation from the Chair of the two fields of 'edictal' legislation which the motion covered, that in which laws could in fact be made for Native reserves without previous reference to Parliament,[1] and regulations framed, under Act of Parliament. The explanation was designed to justify both these procedures on the grounds of administrative efficiency; but explanation and justification alike failed to impress the Council, and the motion went on record as the considered opin-ion of the Councill as a whole. The rural members, while they failed, as Councillor Thema said, to appreciate the pressures of the segre-gation laws on the urban population, were quite familiar with proclamations that sought to establish stock limitation, to limit the collection of wood and to regulate all the other activities of their daily lives, and automatically took a stand against all such legis-lative powers.

On the whole, however, as the Chairman was not slow to acknow-ledge and commend, the Council generally attempted to meet each

[1] In terms of the Native Administration Act, Act 38 of 1927.

proposition that came before it on its merits and to deal responsibly with it. This was curiously demonstrated in the final days of the session on a motion by Councillor Godlo. This read: 'That in view of the growing menace of unprovoked aggression by some of the great powers of Europe, which threatens the integrity of every country in the world, the Council requests the Union Parliament to consider the advisability of amending the Defence Act of 1912 so as to open the door to all loyal South Africans, irrespective of race or colour, to take part in any sphere of hostilities for the defence of their common country.'

Intending only to stake a claim for his people to share in the burdens of national defence, he found himself accused by his own colleagues of going right out of his province, to embarrass the Government and cause trouble for them, with two of the townspeople, Jabavu and Mapikela, leading the attack. Indeed Councillor Jabavu was insistent that 'as a subject race', the Africans should be content to be led by the Government and remain quiet until told what to do. And, on that note, the motion was thrown out.

Indeed the spirit of the whole meeting was one of accommodation. While the rough edges which basic differences in outlook and policy were bound to produce were still being blunted by the personal quality of the officials, the new dynamic which had undoubtedly been put into the administration by the establishment of the Native Trust, and the encouragement which came of a representation which, certainly on the Parliamentary front, enjoyed a very considerable and sympathetic publicity, were generating a hope of better things to come.

All this was reflected in the closing speeches of thanks to the Chairman. Councillor Sakwe of the Transkei, who had been selected by his colleagues to perform this office, feeling under the necessity to refer to the vote on the Defence Act motion, said it had seemed almost to divide the Council. He explained that the rejection of the motion was due to a wish not to dictate to the Government and must not be interpreted as any failure in loyalty. Quite the contrary: 'We have done our little bit in the way of considering the matters that were placed before us, and should there be any noticeable mistake in our deliberations, we wish to assure you that there was not the slightest idea of making any destructive criticism, but our object is always that we should offer constructive criticism if we are making any.' And in so saying, he clearly spoke for all his colleagues.

L

3

The Natives Representative Council: A New Council

The first Council concluded its final session in November 1941 with everyone immediately associated with it congratulating it on the fine example it had set of a spirit of goodwill and co-operation, 'through which alone our ideals can be achieved', to use Colonel Deneys Reitz's words in his opening address to the session. But while the will to co-operate was still conspicuous, the feeling that things were not moving as rapidly as they should in a direction which would make co-operation easy and effective was already beginning to make itself felt. There was indeed a growing sense of isolation, of what Councillor Godlo was later to refer to as intellectual segregation, which led him to compare the Council to a toy telephone with no connection anywhere.

This had been pertinently if politely reflected in the speeches of Councillors Godlo and Thema in reply to the Minister's address at the opening of the 1940 session. This was, unfortunately, another occasion on which the Minister was unable to be present in person, his speech being read to the Council by the Chairman. Proposing the customary vote of thanks to the Minister in his absence, Councillor Godlo expressed the Council's appreciation of the appointment of the Deputy Prime Minister as Minister of Native Affairs 'as showing the importance of this Department in the State'. He proceeded then to take up the statement in the Minister's address that 'the prosperity and well-being of every section of the population is dependent on the prosperity and well-being of all other sections and that it is therefore in the interests of each of us to ensure that everyone is happy and prosperous'. Unfortunately, he said, 'and I am not saying that with any intention of criticising those in authority, there has been no clear indication that the Government is proceeding along that path which will make every section of the country happy and prosperous'. Following him, Councillor Thema elaborated. 'The Minister has mentioned the fact that the authorities are impressed by the loyalty shown by the Native people. We

have been loyal and we are still loyal, but we want to know whether
the white people of South Africa realise the importance of that
loyalty and whether they think that because we are loyal we are
happy. . . . I want the white people to realise that although we
are deeply loyal, we are deeply hurt by the hardships that are
inflicted on us and by the disabilities that are imposed on us. . . . I
think it is in the interest of the white people of this country that this
loyalty should not be undermined by these oppressive laws'—a
reference to the pass laws against which the Minister had already
spoken strongly in public.

He added pertinently: 'We are accustomed to hear that our resolutions will be considered by the authorities. We come here every
year and we hear about our cause. Someone said that sympathy without relief is like mustard without meat. So we think that this sympathy should be translated into action some day.' In conclusion,
he remarked:

'The Minister himself has said that the Council has been established as an experiment and that he wanted us to show that we could
make use of what has been given us, and make this really a useful
body in the life of South Africa. I also want to say to him that the
success of this Council depends on the action which the Government
will take with regard to its resolutions.'

At that point, however, the situation was not without its en-
couragements, for the Councillors as for us in Parliament. Prominent
among these was the personality and approach of the Minister
himself, to which I have already referred. These had commended
themselves highly to people like Councillor Thema who was much
impressed, as we were, with Colonel Reitz's public statements on the
pass laws, and his obvious wish that the country's practices might
be brought into line with its wartime pretensions. This, with a report
on the pass laws by the one non-political member of the Native
Affairs Commission, a highly respected ex-chief Magistrate of the
Transkei, Mr. J. Mould Young, advocating abolition in favour of one
identity certificate, gave new hope of an early change for the better
in this regard, a change which by its very nature must involve a re-
direction of policy. It is true, the Native Affairs Commission had
again come under fire in the course of the session, and a good deal
was heard of government by decree since, without consultation
with the Council, meetings of more than ten persons had, by proclamation, been put under ban in Natal and the Transvaal unless

authorised by a Magistrate—this as a wartime measure to control
Nazi propaganda. Yet the session ended with three cheers for the
Chairman, who had been responsible for the proclamation, who
represented the Government, and whose business it was to see that
the Government's policies and laws should be effectively applied.
He had assured the Council that the rights and privileges of
Councillors to meet and address their constituents would not be
affected by the proclamation, and the Minister had agreed in the
Parliamentary session, when Senator Edgar Brookes had called his
attention to the earlier debate in the Council on this subject, that
in future, proclamations to be issued under the Government's
special powers of legislating for Native areas should be submitted to
the Council for its prior consideration.[1]

Indeed over the last two years of this first Council's life, the factors
which had given us grounds for encouragement, reinforced by the
progressively happy relations between the Chairman and the
members of the Council, had made the Council itself more attractive
to people who had tended to stand aloof on the first round. Thus, the
second Council opened in 1942 with the feeling among the Councillors and their supporters that, while the Council itself could not be
accepted as permanent in its then existing shape and constitutional
position, there seemed solid ground for believing that circumstances
were paving the way for something better in which a truly co-operative relationship between Black and White, between Government
and people, would be achieved. As already noted,[2] the Minister
had not only announced his belief that the pass laws should go but
had declared his intention to move in that direction, as he had
announced Government support for the recognition of African
trade unions with rights of collective bargaining. This latter was a
development which even the rural members had come to feel quite
strongly about in view of the difficulties which their constituents,
forced into the labour market as migrant workers by economic
pressure, were finding in making a living.

The new Council's first session was opened by Colonel Reitz in
person on December 7th, 1942, in what seemed particularly propitious circumstances—a Council greatly strengthened in debating
power by the addition of Professor Z. K. Matthews and Mr. Paul
Mosaka. The Atlantic Charter had just been released, by which the

[1] Senate Hansard, 14/2/40. Cols. 375, 382.
[2] See p. 116.

allies committed themselves to work for a world free from want and the fear of want. The Chairman of the Council had been put in charge of the enquiry into the needs of the urban Africans to which I have already referred,[1] and he had publicly stated that the colour bar laws would have to go. Here were new grounds for both Councillors and Parliamentary representatives to feel that not only was an acceptable objective, recognising the rights and claims of all persons, irrespective of race, achieving recognition but that the path to it was being effectively plotted. There were of course plenty of grounds for anxiety. The situation was still one of promise rather than performance, and the promise was largely implicit rather than exact; and there was an uneasy feeling that, with the pressure of events, and preoccupations with other fronts, together with release from anxiety as the tide of war turned in a more favourable direction for us, essential change might be unduly delayed.

Again the key to the mood of the Councillors, and the people whom they represented, is to be found in the replies to the Minister's opening address. Welcoming the new Council and commending to it the spirit of its predecessor, Colonel Reitz declared that he looked upon the problem of Race Relations between the African (*sic*) and the European as the biggest problem the country had to face. He then proceeded to talk of trusteeship, the new word coming into use in political circles, and remarked, 'European opinion, I am confident, is moving gradually, more quickly in recent years than ever before, towards a fuller realisation of what is implicit in our assumption of trusteeship for the Native people, and there are many good friends of the African races who are doing their best to foster and hasten this movement.'

But the inevitable warning followed: 'There is, however, still a great deal of fear and prejudice to overcome, and we must walk warily to avoid antagonising public opinion and arousing uncompromising forces of reaction.' It was essential, he said, to carry the Europeans with us. To do this, we must adapt our ideals to existing conditions so that they are educative and formative and do not lead to excesses of expression or conduct.

The Council had again put up Dr. Dube to reply to the address. This he did in a speech which I made it my business to see that members of Parliament should hear by quoting it at length in the House of Assembly in the following Parliamentary session. Address-

[1] See p. 109.

ing the Minister, he said: 'We fully appreciate what you say about overcoming fear and prejudice in the public mind on both sides of the colour line. We on our side do not forget that the ruling race needs a great deal of education before it can understand the African people and their difficulties. We must be patient, without yielding at all on the fundamental rights of our people. It is this lack of understanding on the part of our rulers that is our greatest difficulty because it prevents them from seeing us as we really are.' He added: 'We may not approach matters as white people do, but that is also true of other races and people—Chinese, Japanese. Who would dare speak of the Chinese as a "child race"?' He then went on to commend the Minister's statement that all who care for the welfare of the African people must go 'all out' for certain fundamental things. 'For, if the Government and we can agree as to what the fundamental things are, then nothing can stop us from getting them.' This led directly to the subject of the Atlantic Charter, and he proceeded to pose those questions that were to re-appear throughout the session. 'What does it mean for us?' and he asked pertinently, laying his finger on the sorest spots created by a segregation policy conceived in the interest of one section of the population, 'Does freedom from oppression mean that no white man dare hit me or my wife or my child, that no policeman dare break into my house at night and drive out my wife naked and break up my furniture? Does it mean that the abominable pass laws will be destroyed for ever? Does it mean that my people shall be respected when they move in public places, on the railways, in Native Commissioners' offices, and elsewhere? For at present there are many forms of oppression and many degrees of it.'

The Council was to come back to all this on a motion subsequently put up by Councillor Mosaka, whose reputation as something of an *enfant terrible* had preceded him. The motion was to the effect that the Minister should come and explain the implications of the Charter to the Council. Speaking on the motion, which the debate had widened to take in the doctrine of trusteeship, Councillor Thema, with his recognised capacity for going to the root of the matter, challenged the existing set-up in the country. 'Here, educated and uneducated, civilised and uncivilised are all grouped together. If that is going to continue, we do not see how this policy of Trusteeship will work. The Minister has rightly said that the majority of our people do not understand the conditions of civilised life. Now what is the intention of the state with regard to these people? Are they going to be left in that condition? And then the few others who have advanced will be told that they must go slowly because they leave behind these illiterate masses of people.'

He then gave this warning:

'I want to say that friction between white and black will not come from our side—it will not be the result, if it does come, of our being extremists, but the cause will be that the Europeans are not prepared to recognise us as citizens of South Africa. They want to restrict us in many respects, and if these restrictions can be removed, and if other laws restricting us can be done away with, there will be peace and harmony and co-operation in this country.'

Then with that generosity and will to accommodate which had characterised all the past discussions of the Council, he added, 'We know that you personally (the Chairman) would do these things if you had your way, and we know that if the Minister had his way, some of these laws would have been abolished here now.' He also, however, urged the Government to speak out now as to its plans for the future so that the people might have a chance to work out the implications, and he counselled wisely, 'Don't leave these things to be decided after the war because then they will not be done—as after the last one. If South Africa is going to play its part in the civilisation of this continent, the time has come for her to put her own house in order. We must civilise and advance this country and we must help the continent of Africa to go ahead.'

The session was a short one; it followed too closely upon the election for the members, particularly the new ones, to have had time to collect their thoughts. It was therefore agreed to adjourn and to re-assemble in the early part of the following year, 1943. A significant request that this meeting might take place in Cape Town, where Parliament would be in session, was not granted, a decision which was accepted out of consideration for the Chairman who argued that his staff and his records were all in Pretoria and that the process of removal to Cape Town would impose too great a burden on his administrative resources. But when the adjourned session opened in May 1943, Councillor Godlo, who had put up the proposition of a Cape Town meeting, came forward with the proposal that the Minister of Native Affairs should attend the Council, and that the other Ministers should come from time to time to explain to the Council the policy of their Departments. In the course of the discussions which followed, we began to hear more of the claim that was taking shape that the business of the Council was to advise the Government and not the Native Affairs Department; that in fact its purpose and function were primarily political and not administrative.

Equally significant was a crop of proposed amendments to the Representation of Natives Act. Many of these were undoubtedly the reflection of recent election experiences, but the range went much further than attempts to effect the most obviously necessary changes in an electoral system that had no precedent and had proved cumbersome in practice. Writing about it at the time, I noted that the members of the Council were disappointed at their failure to get nearer to the legislature of the country. This was made abundantly clear in the discussion on one of the motions moved on the opening day of the session. That was a motion by Councillor Sakwe from the Transkei asking the Government to consider seriously the question of erecting a building for the Natives Representative Council compatible with the dignity of this Council in the administrative capital of the Union of South Africa. The motion was opposed by Councillors Godlo, Matthews and Champion on the two-fold ground that the African people did not accept as permanent the principle of separate representation for Africans reflected in the existence of the Council and that, while the Council did continue to exist, it should not be tied always to meet in Pretoria, 'away from the scene of legislative action'. There was an uneasy feeling abroad among the members of the Council that their voices were not getting beyond the precincts of the Native Affairs Department and that, in general, the Council was not proving the effective organ for informing the Government of the will of the people that it had been claimed it was to be.

The uneasiness, I noted, was reflected in a number of the motions dealing with the constitution and the methods of working of the Council. Among these was the one by Councillor Godlo noted above, calling for a closer link with the Minister of Native Affairs and with the Cabinet generally. Councillors Moroka and Mosaka both had motions on the order paper asking for a change in the Chairmanship of the Council, the first evidence of a sense of the anomaly of a civil service chairmanship of a political body. Councillor Mosaka asked that the Secretary for Native Affairs and the Chief Native

THE FIRST NATIVES REPRESENTATIVE COUNCIL

This photograph was taken in 1937 on the occasion of the opening of the first meeting by General Smuts. From left to right:

Front Row: *Mr. A. L. Barrett, Chief Native Commissioner, Ciskei; Mr. Piet Grobler, Minister of Native Affairs; Mr. D. L. Smit, Chairman of the Council and Secretary of Native Affairs; Mr. H. C. Lugg, Chief Native Commissioner, Natal.*

Second Row: *Mr. E. W. Lowe, Chief Native Commissioner, Northern Areas; Mr. B. W. Martin, Director of Native Labour; Col. W. R. Collins; Messrs. J. Mould Young and C. Heaton Nicholls, members of the Native Affairs Commission.*

Third Row: *Mr. R. Fyfe King, Chief Magistrate, Transkei; Mr. T. F. Coertze (Secretary) and Mr. Carl Faye (Zulu Translator).*

Fourth Row: *Council Members: B. B. Xiniwe; A. M. Jabavu; G. Makapan; T. Mapikela; S. Mankuroane; Dr. J. Dube; Mshiyeni ka Dinizulu; W. W. Ndhlovu; A. Mbelle (translator); M. Monareng (translator).*

Back Row: *Council Members: E. Qamata; J. Moshesh; C. Sakwe; V. Poto; R. V. Selope Thema; R. H. Godlo; R. G. Baloyi and M. Molife (translator).*

MR. R. H. GODLO

MR. SELOPE THEMA

Some prominent African political personalities
who served on the Natives Representative Council

MR. A. W. G. CHAMPION

PROFESSOR Z. K. MATHEWS

MR. PAUL MOSAKA   DR. JAMES MOROKA

Other prominent members of the Natives Representative Council

DR. ALBERT LUTHULI

WALTER STANFORD   MRS. BALLINGER   LEE WARDEN

The last three native representatives in the House of Assembly, entering the House during the last session of Parliament before the abolition of native representation.
May 21st, 1960

Commissioners should be members of the Council in an advisory capacity only, while Councillors Thema and Matthews proposed that the African membership of the Council should be increased to make the Council more representative of the people at large.

But the Councillors were not only concerned with the Council. They were concerned also, and indeed particularly, with the whole constitutional position created by the 1936 Act. All the inadequacies and failures of that Act from the African point of view were reflected in these motions. Councillors Thema, Matthews and Xiniwe had all given notice of motions asking for increased representation in all the representative institutions of Government, the Assembly, the Senate and the Provincial Councils. Councillor Xiniwe asked for the immediate extension of the franchise to the Orange Free State, Transvaal and Natal, and Councillor Godlo that it should be extended to women also. Councillors Moroka, Mosaka and Mabude all attacked the system of communal voting for the Senate and the Natives Representative Council. It was a system which had caused widespread dissatisfaction in the recent elections, and there was a general demand for its abolition in favour of a system of individual responsibility for the vote. This, I and others hoped the Government would consider favourably before the next election which was due in 1947.[1]

All these motions were referred to a Select Committee which was to function in the recess and report back to the next session of the Council, and the Council settled down to a lengthy discussion of the report of the inter-departmental committee of enquiry into the conditions in urban areas over which their chairman had presided. This report, just released, had established all the contentions of the Councillors and of all interested and informed parties as to the extreme poverty and generally depressed condition of the urban African population, the complete inability of the people to meet the costs of even the simplest standards of decent living on the prevailing rates of wages in the jobs open to them, and the impossibility of their bettering their own position in the circumstances governing their lives.

With this confirmation from so responsible a quarter of one of the most insistent cases the Council had made repeatedly since its inception, Councillors Godlo and Sakwe, that is, town and country representatives, together put up a motion on the need for Govern-

[1] Eventually it took place in 1948, without any of the changes suggested.

ment's attention to the 'abject poverty of the Reserves'. When the Chairman expressed his sympathy with this proposition, the Councillors seemed justified in feeling that they were getting somewhere at last.

In the meantime, they were much disturbed by the Government's decision to send Colonel Reitz to London as High Commissioner, involving another change of Minister. While the Council was concerned about the loss of a Minister on whom they had pinned high hopes, they also deprecated the change simply as change. Over the short period of its existence, the Council had already had three Ministers[1] to deal with.

As if to counter the impression that the Government was less concerned with Native Affairs than it should be, Mr. Hofmeyr, then acting Prime Minister, came to open the following session in December of that year, 1943. In doing so, he made it clear that he was in fact representing the Prime Minister, although he was also deputising for the new Minister, Major van der Byl, who was visiting the northern battlefields and making acquaintance with the Africans there. The address which he had prepared for the occasion was clearly designed to show the Council that the Government was deeply concerned to promote their interests in spite of all the other claims on its attention and resources. He reviewed the progress of the work of the Native Affairs Department in the rural areas where, in spite of the hampering effects of war conditions and the absence of many of the Department's technical officers, the Department had still, he claimed, managed to keep services going and in some cases had carried out new projects. In this connection, he stressed the necessity for increased production in the country generally if we were to attain that better life which we all hoped for after the war. That increased production must come from Africans as well as from Europeans, he urged, and to this end, he offered to the Council and, through the Council, to the whole rural African population the advice to love their land. 'Love your land as you love what is dearest to you,' he said. 'Love your land more than your cattle. Do all that you can to conserve your soil—prevent it from carrying too heavy a burden.'

In the urban areas, as in the rural areas, Mr. Hofmeyr thought the Africans had grounds for encouragement in Government activities. Here he emphasised the increased concern for improved

[1] Mr. Piet Grobler, Mr. Henry Fagan, Colonel Deneys Reitz.

housing, and he certainly caught the special interest and attention of the Councillors by the statement that 'the question of greater security of tenure for African town dwellers has been receiving a great deal of attention of late. It will, I think, be acclaimed as a valuable forward step that Government funds are now being made available through local authorities by means of which satisfactory houses can be built or acquired by approved residents[1] and that, wherever possible, the Department of Native Affairs is urging local authorities to encourage this type of housing to augment the sub-economic dwellings which can only be leased.'

On the topic of education the Minister had also some important things to say. Indeed here he made two unexpected and very significant announcements. The first of these was that 'it must now be clear to everyone that a stage has been reached when Parliament cannot be expected to go on providing increasing amounts of money while Native education continues to fall under the Provincial Administrations. The whole question of the control of Native education must therefore . . . come up for urgent consideration.' He then proceeded to state his own conviction that the aims and method of Native education were also due for review. In this connection he remarked, 'I have never accepted the policy of the development of the African "on his own lines" in so far as that was merely a cloak for keeping him in what is regarded as being his place, a place of stagnation and servility. But I have also never believed that the African should develop simply as an inferior type of European. There is, as I have said, too much of value in his tradition and heritage for that. And that is true also in relation to education. There should be something distinctive also about the aims and methods of education for the African, especially the rural African, but it is to the African himself that we must chiefly look to determine what that distinctive element should be; he must decide what features of his indigenous culture should be preserved.'

Mr. Hofmeyr has always been regarded by the world in general, and by most of South Africa in particular, as the great liberal of my generation. Writing on this speech at the time for the African reader, I noted that Mr. Hofmeyr had certainly put his finger on the major issues of present-day African life and, in his treatment of them all, had certainly given the Council plenty of food for thought.

[1] In fact this scheme never got off the ground before the change of government in 1948.

That the result of that thought was not complete agreement with what he had had to say was at once apparent from the customary speeches of thanks, on this occasion from Professor Matthews and Dr. Moroka.

In his speech Councillor Matthews expressed himself as puzzled, as were many others who attended the opening ceremony, by Mr. Hofmeyr's reference to 'an inferior type of European' as the fate which he appeared to consider awaited the African unless his educational system was planned on some basis which would preserve something of his indigenous culture. As an African, Professor Matthews assured Mr. Hofmeyr that he and his people were proud of their cultural heritage and had no intention of letting it be lost; that they would not become either 'imitation Europeans' or 'inferior types of Europeans'. As an educationist, however, he politely but firmly challenged the Minister's contention that this was a matter of a different type of education for Africans from that given to other sections of the community. After years of educational work, he said, he had yet to discover what aim and method African education required as distinct from that of any other group; even for rural Africans, whose need is surely that of any other rural group, namely that of becoming good farmers.

He added significantly, 'The danger which I see, a danger which we are running, is that of going off into this blind alley of African civilisation and not marching together with the rest of the peoples of the world towards a world civilisation. . . . We are not satisfied to be a drag on the progress of the people of this country, and we should like to be put into the position where we shall have all the means of obtaining knowledge, skill and the techniques necessary for their application.' He welcomed Mr. Hofmeyr's statement that the new world order was to be for Africans as well as for Europeans; and he expressed his gratitude that 'at last the question of security of tenure for Africans in urban areas is going to receive attention', although he noted rather anxiously that there was nothing in the amending Bill coming before the Council on that subject.

The matter of freehold rights and security of tenure in urban areas had been repeatedly brought up in the Council. It had been pressed with particular insistence in the previous session of the Council, together with requests for representation of Africans on municipal councils which, as the Councillors had argued before and were to argue more forcefully in the future, really controlled the lives of the urban African population.[1] The Government had referred the suggestion of local representation to the United Municipal Associations for their comment, but had, so far as the Councillors knew, done nothing about this matter of property rights in the urban areas. The fact that the municipal Councils had not so far turned down the suggestion of African representation—even by Europeans, which the Councillors were willing to accept—suggested that the Government was indeed moving towards a departure from the rigid principles of the segregation policy. Had not the Prime Minister himself said in the previous year that the policy had failed to do what it had set out to do—that was, to keep the Africans out of the towns—and that some new thinking would have to be done in this matter? Was that new thinking really on its way?

In seconding the vote of thanks, Dr. Moroka, himself domiciled in Native reserve, confined himself to Mr. Hofmeyr's advice to the rural Africans to love their land. He assured the Minister that no people loved their land more than the African does; but he pointed out that land was simply not available for a large proportion of those desiring it, while for those who had an established claim to land, the restricted amount available under the terms of the Government's policy was leading to so serious a curtailment of the size of allotments that it was difficult to see how the Minister's further advice 'to prevent it from carrying too heavy a burden' could be effectively pursued.

Thus the Council seized the opportunity to put before the acting Prime Minister, and the accepted liberal in the Cabinet, the weaknesses of the segregation policy as it had revealed itself from the African side, and the essential departure from it implicit in the Minister's own statement that the new world was to be for Africans as well as for everybody else in the country.

This session produced the report of the Recess Committee on proposed constitutional changes. While this got lost subsequently in the growing preoccupation with immediate political problems, it has a significance of its own as reflecting what leading Africans were prepared to accept as the framework of hoped-for post-war change. Accepting the principle of the 1936 Representation of

[1] This is now (1968) largely changed or changing as successive Nationalist Governments have extended their control over the administration of urban African townships.

Natives Act, it proposed the extension of the House of Assembly and Provincial Council representation to the other Provinces and the increase of the Senate representation by the additional two seats for which the Act provided (in fact, the plan which the United Party was later to propose). As for the Natives Representative Council itself, it proposed an increase in African members to 60, of whom 12 were to be nominated and 48 elected.

Surprisingly enough, it did not support the proposals that the Secretary for Native Affairs or an official should not be chairman of the Council, curiously missing the constitutional significance of this situation which Dr. Verwoerd was not slow to seize upon when he decided to abolish the Council.[1]

While conservatively rejecting the proposal that women should be enfranchised, the Committee made what appeared to the Council the revolutionary proposition that the franchise for all seats, Parliamentary, Provincial Council, and the Natives Representative Council itself, should be the adult male vote—the first appearance of the one man, one vote proposition. The ground of this proposition was the obvious failure of the highly complicated and vulnerable system of election by electoral colleges from which both the Council and the Senate representation had suffered. Since, in any case, and in all cases, the number of seats was to be defined by law and independent of the number of voters, there seemed no justification for either a qualified vote or an electoral college system. But its application to the Assembly seats clearly startled some of the Councillors themselves, and they played safe, as usual, asking for time for the people to consider so new and revolutionary a proposition.

---

[1] He was to argue that the Council, in talking politics, had obviously stepped outside its field, since its chairman was a civil servant and therefore the Council could not be a political body. See p. 210n.

4

The Natives Representative Council: *The Crisis*

Looking back over the history of the Council, the 1943 session with its adjourned meeting in August 1944 stands out as critical. It did indeed end on the customary note of more than polite appreciation of the Chairman and his conduct of the Council's business, but throughout the proceedings there were recurring evidences of that mounting tension which was destined within two years to find the Council practically on strike against the Government over its failure to adjust its political practice to the principles to which its spokesmen continuously paid lip service. Implicit in the replies to Mr. Hofmeyr's opening address was doubt about the extent to which the representatives of the African electorate and the spokesmen of the White electorate, even the most reputedly sympathetic towards and understanding of African claims and aspirations, were seeing the way ahead in the same terms. As has been said, Councillor Matthews, while welcoming the Minister's statement that the Government was pressing for the release of urban areas for African private ownership, was concerned about the absence of prospective legislative provision for such recognition of the domiciliary claims of completely urbanised families which this proposition implied. In fact, no new legislation was necessary for this purpose; all that was needed to proceed along these lines was the will to act in terms of a permissive clause in the existing Urban Areas legislation. But a Government dependent on the white voters who controlled municipal Councils was anxious to carry the local authorities with it. The Councillors were subsequently informed that the Department was engaged in negotiating with this end in view.

But what the proposed new law did contain was a clause empowering the local authorities to control any areas within their jurisdiction which should be released for African ownership by regulations of the type which applied to the ordinary municipal Native township. It was a provision to which the Council took particular exception as being a derogation of both property and

175

personal rights. Nor were they moved to modify their opposition to it by the Chairman's explanation that this provision was the only condition on which the municipalities would agree to the opening of such areas. It was in fact on this condition that the Department was at that moment negotiating with the Johannesburg City Council for an area to be opened for purchase by Africans.

It was in this 1943 session of the Council, and initially on this question of the position and the rights of Africans in the urban areas, that a positive challenge to the segregation policy began to take shape from the African side. According to the now established practice of the Council, the proposed amending legislation under which the urban areas situation was raised, was referred to a Select Committee of the Council for its consideration and report. The outcome was a quite remarkable document that, for general quality and political maturity, would have done credit to any legislative Assembly. Its preamble is, alas, still so pertinent that it deserves to be quoted in full. It read:

1. The Natives Urban Areas Act as amended from time to time is one of the corner stones of Union Native policy. The whole of urban Native Administration in the Union is based upon the principles underlying this Act, which affect directly and vitally the interests of a growing section of the Native population, a section which is the spearhead of the industrialisation and Europeanisation of the African people in Southern Africa.

For that reason, the principles underlying this Act are deserving of the closest scrutiny in the interests of both white and black.

2. In order to understand the principles referred to above it is necessary to remind ourselves of the circumstances under which the original Act came into being and the problems with which it purported to deal.

Twenty years ago, when the original Act was passed, South Africa had become aware of the situation which had been created in the urban areas:

(i) by the Mining Industry;
(ii) by the concomitant industrialisation of the country, which was accelerated by the 1914–18 war;
(iii) by the application of the Natives Land Act of 1913, designed primarily to increase the flow of cheap Native labour into the industrial centres.

These facts, taken collectively, gave rise to a considerable urban native population.

The uncontrolled and unplanned ingress of Natives into towns created slum conditions and social evils which were thrown into high relief by the 1918 Influenza Epidemic. That outbreak demonstrated the fact that disease knows no colour bar and forced the legislature to take immediate steps to deal with the situation of Natives congregated in haphazard fashion both in European residential areas and in the then existing Native locations. In these circumstances, it is clear that the Act was an emergency measure designed to deal with pathological and abnormal social conditions. The Act as passed in 1923 dealt with

(a) the conditions of residence for Natives in or near urban areas;
(b) the better administration of Native Affairs in urban areas;
(c) the registration and control of contracts of service;
(d) the regulation of the ingress of Natives into, and their residence in the urban areas;
(e) the restriction and regulation by licence of possession of kaffir beer.

A perusal of the Act shows that the legislature had not yet made up its mind as to the future place of the African in the new South African Industrial Economy. This is indicated, among other things, by the types of accommodation which the Act empowered local authorities to provide for urban Natives, viz.:

(i) Native hostels.
(ii) Native locations.
(iii) Native villages.

The cardinal feature of these types of accommodation was that the African was only allowed to occupy them under conditions which guaranteed their insecurity.

The African was regarded as a temporary sojourner in the urban areas whose permanent interests lay elsewhere, namely in the Reserves. The industrialists, influenced by the labour policy of the mines, favoured migratory labour. . . .

3. Since the passing of the Act in 1923 South Africa has had time to see the process of the industrialisation of the country take its natural course and consequently to envisage more clearly than was possible then the direction which urban and in fact the whole of Native policy ought to take. During this period industry has steadily grown and become an important and permanent feature

M

of the South African economic life ¡and the African has likewise
become a permanent and integral part of the industrial structure
of the country.

> (i) Whereas twenty years ago, the urban Native problem was
> primarily a problem of Native males, today it has become a
> problem of family life—men, women and children with all
> that implies for such fuller social life (schools, churches,
> social amenities etc.).
>
> (ii) The emergence of an industrially conscious working class
> among Africans is evidenced by the growth of Native trade
> unions.

This implies the existence of a population dependent upon wage
earning, upon regularity of employment and the development of
increased skill and of the aptitudes and attitudes of urban Europeans.

The needs and requirements of this type of population cannot be
met by the emergency character of the legislation of 1923. The
restrictive measures have become irksome, the conditions of residence create a sense of frustration and insecurity and the impression
of at once being wanted and unwanted in the urban area make the
Africans live under a smarting sense if grievance and resentment.

This situation demands the orientation of urban Native policy
in order to bring it more into line with the realities of today.

According to the best informed opinions the future economic
development of South Africa lies in the direction of greater industrialisation (see Van Eck Report), a process which must speed up
the townward drift of black and white alike.

4. The recognition of the permanent character of the urban native
population implies

> (i) the right to participate in the local self-government granted
> to urban local authorities;
>
> (ii) the right to possess and own a home in the urban area;
>
> (iii) the right to come and go (freedom of movement);
>
> (iv) the right to sell one's labour to the highest bidder (freedom
> of contract);
>
> (v) the right to inviolability of one's home (the right to be and
> to feel safe in one's home);
>
> (vi) the right to self-expression (freedom of speech, assembly
> and action).

5. The outstanding feature of the amending Bill under considera-

tion is the negation of these elementary human rights, which are basic to any system which pretends to provide a minimum of social security.

Your Committee is shocked that when the African people are looking forward hopefully to the reconstruction period in which these rights would be recognised, the legislature should continue to frame oppressive laws such as the present bill in which elementary human rights are denied.

The only justification that can be adduced for the application of the principle of residential segregation which underlies the Urban Areas Act is that the African people shall, within the areas set aside for their occupation, be given residential security, and the right to develop along lines of their own choosing. The granting of the right to urban local authorities to legislate for Africans in urban areas should carry with it as a necessary and inescapable condition the right of direct representation of the African people on the governing body of that local authority; otherwise segregation becomes an instrument for the oppression of the people discriminated against.

Your Committee feels that the legislature should seize the earliest opportunity for overhauling the Urban Areas Act in order to bring it into line with the changed and changing conditions of the African people in the urban areas, rather than to continue to tinker with this vast problem in the manner indicated in the Bill under consideration.

There followed then a detailed consideration of the proposed measure, in which all its basic principles were repudiated by the Councillors. None the less the Bill was duly passed by Parliament in its 1944 session, with minor concessions only to the African point of view, none of them touching the essential issue at stake, which was whether the process of African urbanisation then going on at an increased and almost phenomenal tempo under pressure of African need and wartime demands, should be recognised as a natural, even if not a desirable, phenomenon, and its problems met with corresponding consideration for the needs and rights of the defenceless immigrating population. It was therefore with a rising sense of frustration that the Council met in adjourned session in August 1944. Its mood was reflected not only in expressions of disappointment that its views had received so little consideration, but in a number of challenging resolutions. These began with a unanimously supported proposal initiated by two of the Transkei representatives, Councillors Mabude and Sakwe, that the Representation of Natives Act should be amended to provide that the Minister of Native Affairs should be elected from the Parliamentary Representatives of the African people.

This was followed by a series of questions and debates on two topics which were clearly more and more engaging the attention and involving the emotions of the Councillors. The first of these was the question of the resumption of the Government's plans for the rehabilitation and development of the reserves somewhat violently interrupted by the outbreak of war, with particular emphasis now on the place which the Government visualised for the reserves in their general scheme of post-war reconstruction. The second was the continued application to the African population of administrative law and 'edictal' legislation. The course of the discussions on these topics was to reveal a new awareness of their common interests on the part of town and country members that was to express itself before the end of the session in a unanimous vote in favour of the abolition of the Native Affairs Commission.

The question of the future of the reserves was set on its way by the Minister himself when he made his first appearance at the Council and delivered his first address to it on August 14th, a few days after the opening of the adjourned session. After reference to recent developments in the field of social welfare, which included the extension by the 1944 session of Parliament of old age pensions and disability grants to Africans, the Minister came to the main theme of his address which was the intention of the Department of Native Affairs to go ahead with the reclamation scheme which had perforce to be largely put in cold storage when the war broke out.

In the war years, unfortunately, there had been a continued process of deterioration and overcrowding in the reserves, he said. This was leading to many evils which had to be prevented if the future of the Native people was to be preserved. With the end of the war now in sight, he felt that a bolder policy than had been proposed in this regard should now be planned. With the help of the Department's technical staff a scheme which would be put before the Council had been drawn up for the reclamation of all the Native areas in the country. It was proposed to appoint planning committees of experts to survey each location or reserve and to undertake the necessary planning so that when the materials and staff became available, the actual work could be commenced without delay. His special message to the Councillors was an appeal for their help in forwarding all these plans. 'The trouble is,' he said, 'that among our rural people very few are far-sighted enough to support measures of soil conservation, limitation of stocks, regulation of grazing areas and forest preservation.' Yet without the co-operation and goodwill of those whom it was the Government's intention to assist, there was no hope of success in that regard.

The Council listened with its customary politeness but on the routine vote of thanks to the Minister for his presence and his address, Councillor Msomi from Natal made no attempt to hide his disappointment and, he claimed, that of the Council generally, at the course which events had been taking over the preceding years and at the continued absence of any comprehensive plan for welding the African population into the common life of the country. They had looked forward to the Minister's visit hoping that such a visit would have the effect of curing many of their ills and grievances. 'They had thought and hoped,' he said, 'that apart from touching on the policy of contemplated improvements which were to be effected in Native reserves and also on improvements which had been effected in regard to Native education and social reform, the Minister would also touch on the Government's policy on actual legislation in this country.' He went on, 'We are very anxious to have an explanation of how the Government intends improving the legislation affecting the Africans in such a manner that we may look forward to the post-war reconstruction plans in the hope of being freed from fear, freed from want and freed from other disabilities.'

He then seized the opportunity to get directly to the Minister some of the things that were occupying the attention of the Council at that moment. People were being turned out of the towns under the segregation policy. Where were they to go? And what about the rural African population outside the reserves where all the land belonged to European farmers? They were largely placed in the hands of these farmers. Some policy should be devised by which a larger percentage of that population could be enabled to live on those private farms under satisfactory conditions.[1] He would like

---

[1] The Minister's visit came in the middle of a debate on a motion introduced by Councillor Thema calling for the extension of the Wage Act to cover farming which, with domestic service, was specifically excluded from its range.

to see a commission appointed to enquire into the conditions of people working on the farms 'with a view to establishing our African people permanently on the land'. And something should be done to assist the African landowner where he existed. It was always argued that land in the possession of Native people was simply allowed to deteriorate. Great opportunities were given to European farmers to improve their land but little or nothing was done for the African farmer.

When the detailed plans for the rehabilitation of the reserves came up for discussion with the Department's technical officers, the attitude of the Council was one of caution dictated by the continuing failure of the Government to define the character and the standard of the life which it visualised for the population of the reserves. There had been no effective reply yet to its pertinent questions as to whether the reserves were to become the homes of fulltime farmers; and if so, what was to become of those who would have to be turned off the land to provide the consolidation or holdings necessary for even the most modest economic standard fof the average family? This led back inevitably to the principle of the Urban Areas Act and the insecurity of the position of the urban African population which it created.

The issue of the powers of arbitrary government of Native areas, which included the power of the Governor-General—in effect, the administration—to banish individuals from their homes without trial if their influence was regarded as inimical to peace and good government—was initially raised by Professor Matthews. His motion in this regard was inspired by the recent use of these powers on more than one occasion against too insistent critics of the administration. It called for the repeal of the provision in the law under which these powers operated, or at least amendment to provide for trial and conviction in open court.

The debate which followed had the effect of leading Councillor Xiniwe, another of the Cape representatives, to move for a Committee of the Council to review the whole Act from which these powers derived, the Native Administration Act of 1927, and to propose a general amendment to it. At a later stage in the proceedings, Councillor Champion from Natal moved for a judicial enquiry into the workings of the Natal Native Code upon which the Native Administration Act had been built and from which the powers at issue in Councillor Matthews' motion mainly derived.

The debates which ensued on these motions have a particular interest in the light of the subsequent course of events in South Africa.[1] Introducing his motion, Councillor Matthews said he had been told that the power which he sought to have withdrawn or at least modified was useful for dealing with individuals who were causing trouble in a particular area. He held no brief for agitators. He thought that the agitation of people was a bad thing, that it was a bad thing to cause disaffection between the people and the public authorities. He considered that any person who was guilty of such action should be severely punished. At the same time, ordinary common justice demanded that a person charged with an offence should be given an opportunity of a fair trial. Here we had a situation under which an individual might be deported for an offence of which he might perhaps have no knowledge whatsoever. Pointing the implication, he said he felt that as the section in the law stood, 'all those of us who have to do with public work among the African people stand in very grave danger of having reports made about us based on completely incorrect information, and this information being used to have these orders made'.

Turning to the argument put up in Parliament in support of these that they were based on Native law, that in the past, Paramount Chiefs had had this power of removal of persons from one place to another, he challenged the validity of this contention. Where such tyrannical powers had been used, it had been a departure from traditional practice for which the tyrants themselves, from Chaka downwards, had suffered.

But even if these powers had in truth been based on Native Law, that did not make them consistent with the circumstances and the condition of the people today. He felt that the existence and the use of this power of removal without trial to get rid of so-called troublesome people was not calculated to increase the confidence of the people in the Government, particularly in the circumstances of South African life where so much was decided without consultation with the Africans. It had been reported in the press that chiefs in the Northern Transvaal had asked for the greater use of these powers. He did not feel that a man who had to rely on a power like this was fit to govern a tribe.

---

[1] In 1956, the application of these powers and the whole system of administrative law embodied in the 1927 Act was extended to cover the whole African population, urban as well as rural. See pp. 344–5.

Supporting the motion—as all those who spoke did—Councillor Thema returned to the argument that these powers of deportation derived from Native Law, that the Paramount Chiefs in the past had had such tyrannical powers. He and his colleagues had always submitted and still submitted that that was not correct. This power had been introduced into the Natal Native Code on the model of Chaka's practice. 'We all agree that Chaka was a great warrior,' he said. '. . . In fact he was a genius and perhaps we are proud that he belonged to our race, but like any other tyrant, even in Europe, he went too far.' That was the way of a tyrant. Tyranny always went to extremes—'even in civilised Europe today that was the difficulty'. But we in South Africa are told that 'we must still have something that was laid down in the laws of the tyrants. This law is not dissimilar to the laws which Hitler is imposing in Europe.

Turning to Councillor Matthews' remarks on agitators and agitation, he did not think Councillor Matthews meant just what he had said. He thought they all held a brief for the agitators who stood for right and justice for their (African) race. The only way we could do away with the agitators was by having laws which were just, laws with which the people could comply. He felt strongly that the Africans who had shed their blood in the war in defence of freedom and justice had a right to demand that the system which prevailed in this country should not be allowed to continue. Could they say that people governed under these powers of arbitrary removal were a free people? 'If we criticise our rulers we are liable to be deported, our people are liable to be deprived of the services of men who can assist them.'

One aspect of the law under discussion which he found particularly offensive was that it applied to Africans only. There was no similar law for Indians or for Coloureds or for Europeans. Were there not agitators among them? Indeed there were. At that very moment there were agitators among the white people who were even upsetting the Government, yet they were not dealt with in this way. Carried along by his strong emotion in regard to this matter, he decided that it was useless to ask for the amendment of the offending section of the law because it would not be done, so the Council might as well ask for the repeal of the whole Act 'so that the authorities will know that we are dead against such ways of dealing with our people'. He wound up with 'all we are asking is that we should be dealt with and treated as human beings', a sentiment which the Council endorsed wholeheartedly.

Throughout this debate and the debates on the contingent motions introduced by Councillors Xiniwe and Champion, these two themes recurred insistently, that powers of arbitrary removal were not part of traditional tribal practice and that inherent in them in a changing society was a grave danger to all Africans engaged in political activities. That these powers had no place in the organisation and life of a country fighting a war against dictatorship was repetitively underlined.

In the generally critical atmosphere which these debates reflected, Councillor Champion called for the repeal of the 1913 Land Act, the foundation of post-Union Native policy, and the 1932 Native Service Contract Act which had bound the whole family of an African farm worker to his employer where the contract of service included the right to put up huts on the farm for their housing—as it had perforce to do where no other right to a home existed under the conditions of the segregation policy. This he claimed should be done 'in recognition of the distinguished and meritorious services of our boys serving with the Union forces in North Africa and Italy and as a gesture of the Government's will and intention to extend to the African the benefits to accrue under the system of social security and freedom from fear and want, these laws having in their application caused untold misery and in effect reduced our people to a condition of economic slavery'. Councillor Mosaka proposed to round off this motion by an addendum calling for the repeal of all discriminatory laws 'which curtail the rights of Africans to buy, own, rent or lease land, as well as laws which restrict the rights of contract, and include specially the Native Trust and Land Act'.

After a lengthy debate on the insecurities and hardships created by the denial to Africans of legal rights of domicile outside Native reserve, in which the emotions of the Councillors were clearly deeply involved, the motion was carried unanimously, to be followed by a motion by Councillor Godlo formally calling upon the Government to abandon the segregation policy in the interest of the country as a whole. The policy was not one of separation but of discrimination, he declared, a policy of domination of one part of the population by another, a policy of exploitation of the black man by the white man. Its effect was to make the African feel inferior and to

make him resentful of his position. So long as it was maintained
black and white could never work harmoniously for the rebuilding
of South Africa after the war. They would never be able to see eye
to eye about its occupying its rightful place among the nations of
the world.

Seconding the motion, Councillor Matthews warned that among
the generation growing up under the pressure of the policy, mistrust
and suspicion were growing strongly. That was why some Europeans quite rightly thought that the older generation was much
better to deal with; they were less resentful. The reason for that was
that they had grown up under conditions when this policy was not
so widely practised. 'Our fathers lived under conditions when they
could be friends with the Europeans, but the kind of legislation
in this country since 1910 has been such as to drive the African and
the European people into two antagonistic groups through this
policy of segregation, and the generation which is coming after
us, the generation which has never known anything different from
the one under which we live today, is shot through with this spirit
of mistrust and suspicion.'

The Council was unanimous on all this also.

Thus by the end of the session, both generally and particularly
the whole segregation policy stood condemned by the African
representatives as having failed to establish its claim to serve the
interest of their section of the population. Yet the session ended
with a special vote of thanks to the Chairman 'for the distinction
and tact' with which he had guided their discussions, and added
that if they had made any mistakes, he should correct them.

5

The Natives Representative Council Challenges Government

When the eighth session of the Council opened in November 1945, the war had come to an end and the Minister had much to say in his opening address about the Government's and the public's appreciation of the part the Africans had played in it. 'The war effort of the Native people, especially the gallantry in the field that has resulted in many awards for bravery, has undoubtedly made a deep impression upon the national mind,' Major van der Byl declared. He instanced as evidence of this 'the movement started among our European soldiers up north to establish a war memorial fund with the main purpose of providing better health services for the Native people', for which purpose £10,000 (R20,000) had already been subscribed by each European soldier contributing two days' pay.[1] For the rest, his speech followed the usual line, noting the increased amount of money for social services and the intention of the Government to push ahead with the rehabilitation of the reserves, and wound up with the customary appeal for the support of the Councillors. Conspicuous by its absence was any reference to the basic questions raised in every session since the inception of the Council, and raised in the last two sessions in so comprehensive and specific a form. It was and is difficult to believe that the records of the Council were ever read at the highest level where they should have been a priority claim on time and attention; surely if they had been read, they could not have failed so lamentably to make any impact on the minds of Government spokesmen.

In the customary vote of thanks, Councillor Moroka again remarked that 'It is not often that we have the Minister with us on our deliberations and when opportunity offers as it does now, we are all very keen to say a few words which ordinarily we would like to say, and we sometimes do say, but we always have the feeling

[1] I was proud to be nominated as one of the first trustees of this fund, and of the National War Memorial Health Foundation which it inaugurated, a quite remarkable gesture to the implications of the war and a dedication to the causes it had claimed to defend.

187

that they never reach the right quarters.' He went on, 'It is one of the purposes of this Council to advise the Government, but I always feel that we are advising the administrative officials who have been charged with carrying out a policy for which they themselves are not responsible.' He then expressed the hope that health services were not going to be 'the only major aspect of the new order in which we are going to share as the result of our participation in the war. 'I think the time has come,' he said, 'for a revision of the whole Native policy of the country.' He stated his belief that 'the new spirit which is partially symbolised in the National War Memorial could find a greater and better expression in a change in Native policy so that the Native might become an integral part of the life of South Africa'.

But on the whole, both this speech and that of Councillor Godlo who supported the vote, were surprisingly moderate and un-challenging, particularly in view of the major issue of the session, which was the recently promulgated regulation affecting the move-ment of Africans from the Transkei and the Ciskei to the Cape, significantly issued without any reference to the Council in spite of Colonel Reitz's assurances,[1] and establishing a new and drastic pass law in the Cape Province. So strongly indeed did the Council feel about this development that Councillor Godlo, in the name of the whole Council, asked that the Prime Minister be approached to receive a deputation of the Parliamentary Representatives of the Africans and the Councillors so that they might put before him this whole matter of the pass laws. The Africans throughout the country were in a state of agitation about it, he said. A National Anti-Pass campaign had been launched and, said Councillor Matthews, following him, 'As you know, Mr. Chairman, protest meetings are being arranged all over the country and it is only natural that they (the people generally) should ask us as their leaders, "Why did you agree to such regulations?" And local authori-ties are to run these regulations. That also is a departure from past practice on which we should have been consulted.'

Councillor Mosaka, speaking to the motion, said the Africans regarded the pass laws as enemy No. 1, and he for one had been very disappointed at the absence of any reference to this vital issue in the opening speech of the Minister. 'We had expected something big, something spectacular,' he said. 'We expected a statement from the Minister something to this effect: "You people have fought for

[1] See p. 164.

peace and freedom and as a gesture of the new era which has set
in we have now decided to abolish all passes and do away with this
system." Well, instead of that, the Government goes in the diametrically opposite direction. Instead of abolishing passes it says "We
are going to extend the Pass system". We have been objecting
during the war period to this steady encroachment on the liberties
of the African people—and what are they getting? The transfer of
the administration of these laws to the local authorities just at a
time when they were asking for their abolition.' Yet the Africans were
entirely unrepresented on these bodies 'and I say that the amount of
tyranny you allow on the local councils does not justify, does not
warrant your transferring what is already an oppressive measure to
a body or to bodies which are only too ready to apply oppression
even without their having the powers you want to give them'.

To Thema, to whom 'this is a matter which touches my heart and
makes my blood boil', the failure of the Government to meet the
Africans on this matter was taking on the dimensions of a crisis
situation. To all the other warnings he had issued from time to
time on this matter he now added this: 'The time is coming when
we shall have to preach Africa for the Africans . . . It will come if
the white people persist in the attitude which they are adopting.'
He concluded with the challenge which I have already noted in
another context:[1] 'As a statesman of world fame he' (the Prime
Minister) 'has spoken of peace. Well, we want him to create peace
in South Africa, the country in which he lives.'

In the adjourned session of the previous year, 1944, a request had
been made that the Prime Minister should come and address the
Council. In reply to a question as to what had happened to that
request, the acting chairman replied that it had been put to the
Prime Minister and had indeed been raised again with him a few
days previously by the Minister of Native Affairs and the Secretary
and he had said he was not yet ready to address the Council.

It was against this background that the Council was summoned to
Cape Town for the one session of its history to be held there. It was
a special session occasioned by the belated discovery that certain
measures before Parliament then in session had not been put before
the Council as required by law. Among the measures in question
was a further amendment of the Urban Areas legislation to meet
some of the administrative implications of the transfer of control

[1] See p. 133.

of the influx restriction provisions to the local authorities, which Councillor Mosaka found so unacceptable. They were highly technical provisions dealing with the apportionment of the registration fees for permitted immigrants—what Councillor Matthews stigmatised as sharing the swag. In the meantime, the Prime Minister had finally refused the request to meet the Council.

The Councillors found none of the interest in Government circles in their doings which they had hoped for from a meeting in Cape Town. On the other hand, the Opposition was obviously increasingly gratified at the way things were going, at the growing tension between the Council and the Government with its effect on the tone of the Councillors. Indeed, Councillor Thema felt so strongly about the failure of the Council to make any real impact on the political situation and so incensed by the continuing build-up of restrictive legislation that, in spite of concessions to African workers in regard to both silicosis and unemployment benefits included in the comprehensive amending measure they had been called together to consider, he was all for rejecting the whole Bill. He was indeed only persuaded to agree to consider the measure on the ground that there were provisions in the Bill for exemptions from the operation of the restrictive provisions of the existing law that would mean a great deal to quite a number of people; but he was induced to accept the argument with the greatest reluctance and made it clear that he was rapidly reaching the conviction that only mounting pressure leading to the inevitable explosion would really bring the white people to a realisation of the dangers of the course they were pursuing.

Nor was he alone in this. Indeed, the Councillors as a whole without any exception took a very serious view of the Government's continuing disregard of their representations. They took the occasion to repeat the preamble to their report on the 1943 Urban Areas Amendment Bill, with the now almost traditional result that the Bill went on to the statute book as if they had never spoken.

This was in April 1946. When the ninth session of the Council opened in Pretoria a few months later on August 14th, it seemed as if the crisis had indeed arrived. Some thousands of the Witwatersrand mining industry's African contract labour force had gone on strike a few days previously, the seemingly inevitable shots had been fired, with the loss of a number of African lives, Johannesburg was restless and anxious about the situation, with the press hinting

broadly that this was no ordinary strike but the result of the machinations of agitators with dangerous political objectives. With this
as backdrop, the Council met, no longer in the Pretoria City Hall
but in the cramped conditions of a Labour Department conference
room for which the acting chairman felt compelled to apologise,
as he did for the absence of the official Chairman, the Secretary for
Native Affairs, who was importantly engaged elsewhere. He then
announced what in other circumstances should have been a subject
for hope and even for congratulation—the appointment by the
Government of a commission to enquire into

(a) the operation of the laws in force in the Union relating to Natives in or near urban areas and in areas where Natives are
congregated for industrial purposes other than mining;

(b) the operation of the Native Pass Laws and any laws requiring
the production by Natives of documents of identification;

(c) the employment in Mines and other industries of migrant
labour; its economic and social effect upon the lives of the
people concerned, and the future policy to be followed in
regard thereto:

and to draft such legislation as might be necessary to give effect to
its recommendations.

In fact, the Government had at last appointed a commission to
enquire into all the matters which the Council had repeatedly
challenged so far without result, and had put it under the chairmanship of an eminent and respected judge who had himself been
a Minister of Native Affairs. This was the Fagan Commission to
which reference has already been made.

With a reference to the fact that history was being made as they
gathered there—at the Peace Conference sitting at that moment—
and welcoming Chief Luthuli, who had just come to the Council as
the result of a by-election occasioned by the death of Dr. Dube, the
acting chairman hopefully turned to the routine business of the day.

By this time, Mr. Douglas Smit was no longer Chairman of the
Council. That forceful personality, who had helped to mould the
shape of the Council over all its earlier years and had dominated
the Department of Native Affairs for considerably longer, had retired
in the previous year, leaving the field and the responsibilities in
new and as yet inexperienced hands, at what was to prove the most
difficult and most dangerous period in its history. At that particu-

[1] See p. 109.

lar moment, thanks to the Cabinet's own handling of what was a serious situation, the Chairman himself, Dr. G. Mears, was not even present to meet the impact of the mood in which the Council received an opening address that contained no reference to what was uppermost in all the members' minds—the trouble on the mines. Without even acknowledging the appointment of the Fagan Commission, probably because the Council was convinced that it was merely a delaying action on the part of the Government, Councillor Mosaka immediately rose to challenge the gap in the Chairman's address and tabled a series of questions on the strike situation. He followed this at once by another series relating to recent serious disturbances at one of the oldest and largest schools for Africans, Lovedale, ending not only in the closing of the institution but in the appearance in court of many of the students on charges of public violence.

From that moment, the temperature of the meeting rose. The Chairman had little to tell on the subject of the mine strike except that a Cabinet Committee was meeting at that moment, with the Secretary for Native Affairs in attendance. The situation was, he said, in a fluid state which made any precise statement impossible. He would refer to the Secretary for Native Affairs the Council's particular question as to whether any negotiations had been entered into with the Mineworkers' Union, an unrecognised though not illegal body which had been very active over the preceding year or two.

On the subject of the trouble at Lovedale—obviously only contingently serious so far as the Council was concerned, although serious enough in itself—there was also little specific information to be given—certainly little of an encouraging kind.

The reaction of the Council might not have been unexpected. The idea of a Cabinet Sub-Committee on the subject of the mine strike did not create any sense of confidence. 'We hold the Government responsible for the shooting which has taken place, because, according to the newspaper reports, the shooting took place on advice from Pretoria. . . . We would be more satisfied if our African representatives, our Representatives of the Africans in Parliament, were consulted in this matter, if members of this Council were also consulted about the negotiations which the Government is setting afoot. We do not think that justice can be done if a Cabinet Sub-Committee is merely going to meet by itself and is going to make decisions in regard to this whole matter. We want to be consulted on this question.' These words of Councillor Mosaka's were only the preliminaries to a series of speeches in which the feelings of the members became progressively heated until Councillor Godlo announced that with things as they were, he could not apply his mind to the agenda of the meeting. Challenged then by Councillor Champion to move the adjournment, he found himself moving that 'we do not proceed with the items on the Agenda until such time as we have been given a full statement in reply to those questions raised by Councillor Mosaka, because those questions represent the voice of the Council as a body'.

Thus, without previous intention, and unorganised, the Council had come to a deadlock. It is true, the Chairman refused the motion and the Council found itself for the moment involved in the current business of the session. But by the time it returned to the Council chamber after the lunchtime break, the course had been shaped. A lunchtime caucus concerned to arrange the order of business for the rest of the meeting, part now of the established practice, decided to put certain motions ahead of everything— and these, together with one by Councillor Mosaka again on the mine strike, ended with inevitable logic in one moved by Dr. Moroka that 'This Council, having since its inception brought to the notice of the Government the reactionary character of Union Native policy of segregation in all its ramifications, deprecates the Government's post-war continuation of a policy of Fascism which is the antithesis and negation of the letter and spirit of the Atlantic Charter and the United Nations Charter.

'The Council therefore, in protest against this breach of faith towards the African people in particular and the cause of world freedom in general, resolves to adjourn this session, and calls upon the Government forthwith to abolish all discriminatory legislation affecting non-Europeans in this country.'

Thereafter followed a series of bitter speeches reviewing the history of the Council and its failure to influence government policy, ending with one by the rural member, Councillor Sakwe, from the Transkei, calling attention to the fact that 'we had no caucus before we came here (to this session), yet we have motions that all point the same way.'

'This fact that our motions all have the same object in view, and are similar to each other in spirit, must have conveyed to you the

N

fact that the Africans throughout the Union are unanimous, that they feel alike in regard to the treatment that is meted out to them. . . . There is a great unanimity among them on this subject. . . . We demand the fruits of victory, of that victory which we helped to win.'

And with that the Councillors went home to await the Government's response to the position which they had now taken up.

It came almost three months later—in November 1946. With ample time for serious consideration of all the implications of the situation, and with so much at stake, it was awaited with anxious hopes in all responsible quarters.

On November 20th, the Councillors met, with the Native Affairs Commission in attendance and most of their Parliamentary colleagues in the public gallery to hear what the spokesman of the Government had to say. With Mr. J. H. Hofmeyr, Acting Prime Minister, in that capacity, there seemed every reason for optimism. Had not Professor Matthews, on the earlier occasion when Mr. Hofmeyr addressed the Council, told him that the Africans had named him Ntembu, meaning 'Our Hope'?

The opening sentences of his speech came as something of a shock to all of us. Announcing that the Council's resolutions had been brought to the Government's notice and that he as Acting Prime Minister was present to give the Government's reply, he said:

'I must commence by saying that we have noted with regret and surprise the violent and exaggerated statements which were made in support of the resolution—statements which were in many respects not in accord with the standard of responsibility to be expected from a body like this Council.'

The resolution itself, he added, asked for the abandonment forthwith of all discriminatory legislation affecting non-Europeans in this country. It should be clear to the Council that it would not be practicable to accede to this request if account was to be taken, not only of the process of adjustment that was taking place between the different peoples living in the Union, but also of the interests of the Native people themselves. 'Many of the differential provisions in the existing laws to which exception is taken were in fact enacted to protect Native interests, and if they were indiscriminately to be removed those interests could not but suffer.'

In illustration of this last claim Mr. Hofmeyr proceeded to deal with the land position, to emphasise that land in African occupation or ownership under the terms of the Land Acts was not open to purchase by other than Africans, which alone secured it against European competition—the familiar argument which was to be used by all parties in justification of the segregation policy.

Thereafter he applied himself, 'at the risk of repeating what has been said on other occasions', to summarising briefly the action taken during the last decade, including the difficult war period, to improve the position of the Native people and to give them a greater share in the assets and the income of the country as a whole and to fit them to play—especially in their own sphere of possession and influence—an effective part in the country's activities.

In this connection, he stressed—as an ex-Minister of Education and Minister of Finance with responsibility for the financing of that and other services—the increasing provision for African education and the widening scope of this service.

From reference to the development of plans for African medical training it was a short step to health services which may have justified him in putting in the forefront of social services, pre-institutional care for lepers and mentally afflicted persons, and free treatment for sufferers from infectious diseases. From there, such positive health services as clinics, better housing and the relief of distress in old age and invalidity, the whole gamut of social services to which we have already referred were traversed by the Minister, ending with a brief reference to the resumption of the purchase of land.

Under the heading of economic matters, brief reference was made to the repeated demand of the Council for the recognition of African trade unions, to which the mine strike had given particular point. The Government had indeed intended to introduce legislation on this subject in the preceding session of Parliament, but 'unforeseen difficulties made it impossible to proceed in the matter'. The Government however intended to go ahead with this legislation in the near future. It could not, however, provide for recognition of a trade union for Native mine workers. For them some other channel of representation would be provided.

But although African trade unions had no statutory basis, they had received quite considerable *de facto* recognition which had helped the Wage Board to advance considerably the wage levels of the workers.

The Minister ended his review with the claim that all these

benefits, 'being given freely and in many cases without any specific request having been made, speak for themselves. They should be regarded', he considered, 'as an earnest of the Government's general attitude of good will to the Native people, as a proof of its desire for their advancement; and as an answer to the resolution passed by the Council and the speeches made in support thereof'.

On behalf of the Council, Chief Poto politely thanked the Acting Prime Minister for his presence, and remarked, 'We know that you have various calls in different directions, but we feel that we have as much claim on your presence in our midst from time to time as any other section in the community,' while Councillor Thema, speaking in support of the vote of thanks, repeated his recurring contention, 'We cannot live in South Africa as masters and servants, but we can live here as partners because this country belongs to you as it belongs to us.'

Thereafter, without either the Minister or the Councillors referring to the one constructive move of the Government on the policy front, the appointment of the Fagan Commission—a curious omission on the Minister's part—the Council adjourned to consider the Government's answer. They continued to adjourn for several days, putting all business, other than a brief examination of the education estimates, in cold storage until they should be able to decide to what extent Mr. Hofmeyr's statement gave them any hope for the future. On November 26th they declared their readiness to give their considered estimate of the value of what he had said to them. Reviewing the circumstances which had led to the situation which the Acting Prime Minister had come to deal with, Councillor Matthews on behalf of the Council presented the result of their deliberations, of which the essence was the Council's sense of disappointment with the statement made by the representative of the Government. 'To us it seemed to be merely an apologia for the *status quo*, apparently oblivious of the progressive forces at work not only in the world in general but even in South Africa itself. The statement makes no attempt to deal with some of the burning questions of the day such as the Pass Laws, the colour bar in industry, the political rights of the non-Europeans in the Union, etc., and in effect it raises no hopes for the future as far as the African people are concerned.'

After reviewing the Minister's review, Professor Matthews continued, 'The burden of our resolution is not affected by minor concessions granted or denied in this or that aspect of African life. We are more concerned with questions of principle and policy. The benefits to which the Minister has made such detailed reference do not affect the fundamentals of the policy of white domination in a country the population of which is 80 per cent non-white. The permanent subordination of the bulk of the population to a minority, however well-intentioned, is a policy to which we cannot subscribe. The denial of the right of direct representation in governing bodies such as municipal councils, provincial Councils and Parliament, and the establishment for Africans of differential institutions with purely advisory functions is part of the system for the preservation of white supremacy in South Africa. In our view the time has come for South Africa to abandon this policy under which it will never be possible to harmonise the legitimate interests of the different racial groups represented in this country. It is our intention to continue to work for the ultimate achievement of this result by all means at our disposal.'

In the circumstances, the Council moved

1. That the accompanying statement embodying the comments of the Council on the Acting Prime Minister's speech be communicated to the Government.

2. That the Government be asked to reconsider its statement of policy in the light of the principles set out in the Council's memorandum.

3. That pending the receipt of a more reassuring reply from the Government, the proceedings of this session of the Council be suspended—the Councillors remaining in Pretoria to await such reply.

The following morning the Government's reply was forthcoming, which was that 'the Government finds itself unable to vary its decision'. It added, possibly hopefully, 'The Council has rendered a contribution of great value to the progress which has so far been made. It is most desirable that, in the interests of the Native people themselves, the Council should continue to play its part in the promotion of their further advancement. The Government looks to the Council for its continued co-operation.'

Was the Government genuinely hopeful that this sweetening of the pill would really beguile the Council? If so, it was doomed to disappointment. The Council's reply was cogently put in a further and final resolution: 'That this Council, having carefully considered the further reply of the Acting Prime Minister, finds itself unable to discover in his statement any disposition on the part of the Government to undertake a revision of its Native policy in order to bring it into line with the changing conditions of African life.

'Since its inception this Council has loyally co-operated with the Government, and would continue to do so as long as it is not expected either expressly, or by implication, to sacrifice in the process the legitimate rights and interests of the African people.

'In the circumstances, this Council feels compelled to adjourn the session in order to make it possible for Councillors to make fully known to the African people the nature and contents of the Acting Prime Minister's statement.

'The Council makes a further appeal to the Government to undertake such revision of its Native policy with a view to making possible co-operation between white and black in this country.'

With this last gesture, what was to prove the last meeting of the Council during the Smuts regime came to an end. In making it known, the Councillors had endeavoured to show that they did not wish this to be the parting of the ways, that they still hoped for a change of heart and a change of direction on the part of the Government that would pave the way for that happier relationship between black and white the need for which General Smuts had himself spoken of at the opening of the Council's first session.

At first it looked as if this might yet eventuate when the Prime Minister, who had been out of the country when the crisis arose, decided to summon six of the members of the Council to meet him to discuss the situation informally and to consider what might be done to heal the breach. With the African people in general strongly backing the Councillors on their stand and already beginning to talk of the boycott of all elections beginning with those for the Urban Advisory Boards which were imminent, and with the Nationalist Party now calling loudly and insistently for the abolition of the Council as simply a platform for agitators, this was a gesture of some considerable importance. The question was, how far was he likely to go?

The Prime Minister himself, when he met the group he had selected, said he had no final plan to offer, but he suggested the possibility of an enlarged Council under an African chairman of the Council's own choosing and the addition to its consultative powers of a share in the special legislative and administrative powers which the

Government exercised in Native areas. He further suggested a closer link up of the Council with the urban townships through elected local boards and a strengthened and statutory national conference of such boards to speak authoritatively for the growing urban population.

He made it clear that these suggestions were purely tentative, 'a bone to chew on', he called it, but gave those who had come to meet him to understand that he planned to meet the full Council to discuss the whole situation.

The deputation received the proposals with caution. They were suspicious of any schemes that could fit into the segregation pattern, and there was no doubt that this one as it stood could do so. So much would depend on the spirit and the intention of its application and the political philosophy on which it should be based in practice. As it stood, the scheme—if it could justifiably yet be called that, but it was all the Council had to go on—had all the appearances of a purely administrative approach, leaving the fundamentals of the situation unchanged—rights of movement and of contract both in regard to property and to work, and the whole foundation upon which the pass laws rested. When by November the Prime Minister had not fulfilled his promise of meeting the full Council, the Councillors met in conference themselves and issued a statement on the position as they saw it.[1]

Referring to the fact that the Prime Minister had not so far met the Council, they felt justified in attributing his reluctance in this regard to a desire on his part to await the election of a new Council, due early in 1948, in the hope that its members would be 'more amenable to Government control and guidance' than those who had been responsible for the deadlock then existing between the Council and the Government.

As for the proposals themselves, they appreciated that these were tentative in form and substance and might ultimately be drastically altered, but their very tentative nature made any decision on the Council's part difficult. As they stood, they gave no guarantee of an intention on the part of the Government to go to the root of the trouble which had caused the deadlock, that was the need for a new approach to Native policy which would recognise the interdependence of black and white, and open the door to citizenship to the African people.

The proposals, they declared, were entirely consonant with the

[1] *Umteteli wa Bantu*, November 15th, 1947.

familiar policy of separation, a policy which engendered a spirit of hostility and racial bitterness between black and white, as against that of mutual co-operation in the interests of both sections of the community. What was required, both to heal the breach between the Council and the Government and to restore the confidence of the Native people, was, they said, a policy that would give the people a sense of security; a policy which was flexible and could readily be adapted to changing conditions and varying circumstances; in fact, a policy which recognised that Natives were citizens of this country and not things apart.

They showed that they still did not despair of achieving a workable adjustment by calling upon the African electorate to return to the Council in the forthcoming election people who would steadily pursue the policy to which the members of the existing Council were now committed, until its aims and objects had been fully achieved. In other words, they themselves repudiated the policy of boycott.

It may be asked, where did the Parliamentary representatives stand in all this? From the beginning, we endeavoured to keep in close touch with the Council. We were concerned, however, that they and not we should make the decisions on which they should act. We attended their sessions regularly as an unofficial gallery, prepared to offer ourselves for consultation wherever that should be invited, but by common consent, resisting the temptation to press it. Between sessions, I imagine we all pursued the same policy of endeavouring to keep in touch with those members who represented our own constituencies. I personally made it my business to send Government papers to those who lived in my area and with whom I was regularly in contact as I travelled my wide constituency. But I imagine we all had the same attitude to the Council, that while we had gone to election on what we regarded as the sound policy for South Africa and not on a sectional or emotional approach to Africans and African rights as such, it was only right that Africans, denied the right under the laws to speak for themselves, should be allowed and encouraged, so far as we were concerned, to exercise complete freedom of decision in regard to the shape they would choose for our common society. How often their attitude was more moderate and accommodating than we ourselves would have expected, or we ourselves, as white South Africans, would have taken up, is written on the pages of Hansard.

It follows from this that when the crisis in the affairs of the Council came in 1946, we were unprepared for it—at least in point of time. Immediately thereafter, I, as the by then announced leader of the first group of Native Representatives, and as domiciled in Johannesburg, endeavoured to get the Councillors together before they scattered throughout the country. The purpose of this was to see whether we could arrange a meeting between the Parliamentary representatives and the Councillors so that they would either consider with us, or, as I knew my colleagues would acknowledge to be their right, to tell us what their plans and intentions were. Those whom I was able to assemble at the house of Dr. A. B. Xuma,[1] however, were much too excited and, indeed, much too taken by surprise themselves to be able to make any plans on either count. When they met and adjourned for the second time I was on a private visit to India; but immediately on my return I again endeavoured to organise a meeting at some convenient centre where we might again consider the future together. In this I had no success either. A group of individuals, we had neither organisation nor funds to meet the contingencies which were arising and, with the Prime Minister in negotiating mood, time seemed at least not hostile—a misjudgment we shared with the most of South Africa.

So far as my own responsibility in the situation was concerned, there seemed little more that I could do than I had already done or was trying to do. So far as the Prime Minister's proposals were concerned, which were now the focal point of the situation, I had always held, as I still hold the view that there is nothing essentially wrong in differential machinery in the field of local government: on the contrary, there is much to be said for it where it is framed to offer opportunity to communities to take an active and constructive part in the conduct of their affairs, and so to learn the responsibilities of government within the democratic system. Thus while I deprecated as strongly as the Councillors could do the absence from the Prime Minister's proposals of any recognition of the real defects of the segregation policy, the denial of basic rights to the African people, when I was invited to open the Advisory Boards Conference in Springs in December 1947, I made this approach clear by urging the Conference, of which one of my Councillor constituents, Mr. Godlo, was Chairman, to accept any powers offered to it which might increase its own experience, and thus strengthen and develop its own competence to demand and to make further advance.

[1] Then President of the African National Congress.

Implicit in this attitude was of course complete repudiation of any suggestion of political boycott. I have always felt that any voice in the affairs of the nation is better than none, particularly in circumstances such as ours in South Africa, where it has been very easy for unenfranchised communities to be forgotten. Probably, ultimately it will be seen that the greatest weakness of segregation policies is the extent to which it prevents the various groups in the nation from knowing and learning to understand something of their neighbours. I ventured to suggest this when, in the stormy days when the Asiatic Land Tenure Bill was paving the way to our unhappy position at the United Nations, I was invited to open the meeting of the Indian National Congress in Cape Town. I urged the Congress to take and use the limited communal franchise which General Smuts had offered as a *quid pro quo* when, under pressure from his Natal supporters, he reluctantly agreed to limit their property rights. It was not popular advice, as I expected, and it was not accepted. Had the Indian community accepted it, and had they used the power given to them at the succeeding election, Dr. Malan's majority of five in the House of Assembly would have been reduced to two, while in the Senate, even one additional anti-Nationalist vote must have made the position quite untenable. One of Dr. Malan's first actions as Prime Minister was to remove the provisions in regard to these seats from the statute book.

In due course, the new Council was elected. It presented almost entirely the same appearances as its predecessor, its members still the same in generation and outlook, still hoping for a peaceful accommodation that would set South Africa on a path which would do away with tensions and allow people a rest from politics. But now the white electorate was absorbed in its own impending election. There were no thoughts and no time to spare for anything else, even among a Government party complacently certain of victory, and even though the main issue was Native policy. In May the general election took place, the generally unexpected happened, and the reins of government passed to people committed not to accommodation but to abolition. The Nationalist Party had always been against the Natives Representative Council, some because they were sure it could only become the home of 'agitators',[1] others,

[1] How often had Councillors, including the conservative rural members, even in United Party days, asked: 'Why should we be called agitators when we only put forward the needs and views of our people?'

like Mr. Strydom, because in addition, it would bring the African tribes together into one nation which would be a menace to and a disaster for 'white civilisation'. The history of the Council had strengthened both reliefs, and with every move in the deadlock, even before the election, the Party's demand for its abolition had been becoming ever louder and more insistent. Here at last the situation was in their hands. Would the responsibilities of office change their attitude? With one figure waiting in the wings, the issue was never in doubt.

6

The End of the Natives Representative Council

The final events in the process of demise of the Council are revealing in respect of both parties involved. While the Nationalists came to office in May 1948, it was not until January 1949 that the Council was again called together. The occasion, as explained by the Chairman, Mr. Gordon Mears, Secretary for Native Affairs in succession to Dr. Douglas Smit,[1] was the result of his own representations to the Minister of the desirability of calling the Council together to fulfil the letter of the law, since the Government was planning legislation directly affecting the African people. The Minister, Dr. Jansen, later Governor-General of the Union, agreed to the summons, but himself refused to attend the meeting and authorised the Chairman to explain the reason for his absence. It was quite simply that in view of the Council's past attitude 'it would', he said, 'serve no good purpose for me to address you'.

The Chairman thereupon delivered what purported to be the rest of the message committed to him. 'The Government will at all times be prepared to consider any reasonable and practical suggestions as to the manner in which better co-operation between white and black can be made possible, but Councillors must know that no government could abolish all discriminatory legislation, and that such a course is quite impracticable. Further, the assessment by the Councillors themselves of the value of this machinery for the representation of Natives fully accords with the views of the Government. As it is only an advisory body and has no executive powers, it has apparently created a sense of frustration in the minds of the Councillors themselves. The determination to suspend action has now lasted two years, and during that period of suspension it cannot be said that the interests of the Native people have suffered thereby, and its permanent abolition would therefore be no serious loss.'

---

[1] Dr. Smit in the meantime had become a member of the Native Affairs Commission as well as a United Party member of Parliament. It had been General Smuts' intention to make him Minister of Native Affairs in his next Cabinet.

There then appeared for the first time the extraordinary accusation against the Council by the new Government which was to become the final justification for its abolition.

'It is questionable whether the Council has ever presented the real needs of the Natives. Matters affecting the everyday affairs of the bulk of the population, particularly the rural population scattered over all parts of the Union, are so divergent that they have received relatively little attention; on the other hand the Council turned its mind to politics, and in a demand for political equality insisted on the removal of all distinctions between blacks and whites: these distinctions include matters of policy which are of a protective nature for Natives such as the Native Land Laws and Liquor, to mention only two.'[1]

It was then made clear to the Council that General Smuts' plans were quite unacceptable to the new Government—that indeed Dr. Malan and his Cabinet had quite other ideas for both rural and urban areas, and for the African population as a whole. With the general statement that the Representative Council was after all an experiment, it was stated that, the experiment having failed, 'it is the Government's duty to find some other and more effective connecting link between it and the Native people. This the Government is determined to do in the interests of the Natives themselves as well as those of the Union as a whole.'

As the Chairman expected, the Council, having heard and considered this statement, could find nothing to encourage it to resume its statutory functions. On the contrary, after consideration it moved:

'That this Council, having considered the Address delivered by the Secretary for Native Affairs, deprecates what, in its opinion, amounts to a dereliction of duty on the part of the Minister of Native Affairs—namely, his failure to place before the newly elected Council the new Government's policy of apartheid.

---

[1] It may be appropriate here to notice that the one discriminatory law that the Nationalist Government has found it appropriate to remove—and that since we left Parliament—is the embargo on their right to buy liquor; this in spite of the contention put forward by the Secretary for Native Affairs on this occasion, presumably in the name of the Minister, that 'the demoralisation which would follow upon the unrestrained acquisition of spirituous liquors is something which every thinking individual would wish to avert'. It is worth recording that the Council had made signally little effort to get this particular discrimination removed, nor does it seem ever to have been under much pressure to do so. On the one occasion when it was proposed, the majority voted against it.

'In the circumstances, this Council finds itself unable to proceed with the Agenda of the session until the Government has, through a Minister of the Crown, laid before Council, for its consideration and report, the full details of its Native policy and its relevant Native programme, and especially its own proposals to provide the so-called more effective connecting link between it, the Government, and the Native peoples.' This motion was carried unanimously after a series of acrimonious speeches which were not calculated to build bridges between themselves and the new Government. Naturally the Councillors were amazed at the accusation of having indulged in political activities—and even more amazed, as anyone with their record in mind was entitled to be, at the accusation that they had ignored the day-to-day interests of their people.

But while they still agreed that the Council in its present form provided no effective machinery for consultation between the Government and the African population, they claimed that the Government's plans for better machinery should be placed before them for their consideration as the freely elected representatives of the African community. 'We are in honour bound,' said Councillor Mosaka, 'not to leave it to Government unilaterally to decide on the nature of this new institution without consulting us, the elected and accredited leaders of our people. The Government of this county is responsible to the European electorate, and until we have a Government elected on the basis of a common franchise, any instrument or institution intended for use by the African people must be the subject of consultative negotiations between the Government on the one hand and the accredited leaders of the African people on the other hand, unless indeed your Government is prepared to depart from the elementary democratic principle of rule by consent to rule by force.'

With more logic in terms of the existing South African situation, he went on '. . . the Natives Representative Council was offered to the African people as part of a bargain, in prolonged negotiations between the Hertzog Government and the leaders of the African people in 1936. The Natives Representative Council represented the *quid pro quo* for the loss of the Cape Native franchise. It was an unfair bargain in as much as it is now admitted even by the present Government that the Natives Representative Council experiment is a failure. To abolish it, therefore, without providing a fair and adequate substitute would be to defraud the African people and to do an injustice to those who, like General Hertzog, felt that this compromise was an act of good faith. Our duty as a Council is to see to it that the bargain shall be honoured.'

With that, the Council again adjourned—on January 5th—to await the next development in the contest between them and a Government which was unlikely to endorse either the spirit or the letter of the Chairman's concluding remarks:

'I feel it is incumbent on me . . . to express my appreciation of some of these excellent speeches to which we have listened during the course of the day, which were marked by clearness, forcefulness and yet, at the same time, by restraint and moderation, and at times almost an objectiveness which is rather remarkable in dealing with such a human subject and one so vital to the interest which we all have at heart.'

When this episode took place, the Native Affairs Commission had already begun to acquire an essentially Nationalist complexion. Mr. Serfontein had come to join its ranks, together with the Nationalist Senator, Senator Spies.[1]

When the next episode occurred, some more significant changes had taken place in the *dramatis personae*. Dr. Jansen had gone to Government House as Governor-General, and his place at Native Affairs had been taken by Dr. Verwoerd; and while Dr. Mears had retired from the office of Secretary for Native Affairs, Dr. Eiselen had been brought from the University of Pretoria into the Public Service in this senior office, since it was felt necessary to have a Secretary for Native Affairs whose views were in accord with those of the governing party.

On this occasion, the Minister did come in person to explain to the Council the grounds on which he proposed to abolish it. In a long and elaborate speech, covering a variety of topics in addition to apartheid, he set out his reasons for supporting a policy of separation—the essential one being that Whites in South Africa would never relinquish political control: hence an intermixed society could only mean conflict in which all would suffer, but in which the black people must inevitably suffer more that the Whites. The prob-

[1] Just as the Nationalist Party has had no place for an open press, its newspapers being essentially and exclusively party organs, so it has had little time or place for multi-party committees or commissions. I early found myself out of the two offices which I had enjoyed for some years under a more tolerant regime—as consumers' representative on the Maize Control Board and as Vice-President and Government appointed member of the Nursing Council.

lem admittedly was to divide a society now already so inter-mixed
—'The facts are that just more than one-third of the native population, of the Bantu population, does live in its own areas, or in
areas the white man can say should fully become its own by the
gradual withdrawal of the white man as he is no longer needed by
the black man. . . . Slightly more than one-third . . . lives in our
rural areas, either in locations adjoining villages or on farms, and
something less than one-third of the Native population lives in
European areas. These,' he added, 'are facts which no policy can
get away from and which no policy tries to get away from, in spite
of the fact that it has sometimes been said that the policy of apartheid
does not recognise this fact.'

He then proceeded to explain what he felt should be done in
respect of each group. For the reserves, in accordance with the
experience of other countries, those people who lived on the land
must live on economic units 'on which a family would survive and
earn and become prosperous'—a policy which seems to have got
lost in the mists since then. And the others—those for whom a policy
of economic holdings could not provide? For them there should be
village and urban development. 'That means, in the first instance,
the development of certain industries' with which the Government
must assist. But these industries need not necessarily be in the Native
areas. From there it was a short step to the idea of the encouragement
of border industries, which was to become one of the main escape
features of the Verwoerd policy.

For the rural areas—where Mr. Strydom had always maintained
that apartheid already existed since the only relationship subsisting
there between black and white was that of servant and master—
Dr. Verwoerd's exposition of the Party's intentions was, to say the
least of it, cloudy and vague. Apartheid in the platteland did not
offer many difficulties, he said, in effect endorsing Mr. Strydom's
view. Yet one-third of the Native population lived there. For them
he had two propositions to offer. For those who lived in the village
locations—where in fact no farm labourer had or has a right under
our laws to live—the Native must be encouraged to carry his own
burdens. 'Mostly the European villages build these locations and
have to look after sanitary arrangements. Therefore they must
retain supervisory powers. The greater executive power the Native
inhabitants can wield with success, however, the more we will be
satisfied—but it must be with success. They must not say "we must

rule but you must foot the bill".' To anyone with any knowledge or experience of South African villages, this is one of Dr. Verwoerd's many ideas that seemed to have no connection with reality.

For the rest, where the rural Natives had lost contact with tribal organisation, that contact must be restored. 'Also among the Natives living in the rural areas can tribal self-government increase,' he declared.

As for the cities, 'the European cities in the European areas', while many of the Bantu then in these areas would be drawn off as the reserves developed, many would remain. Here he enunciated the Group areas principle: 'Just as I want to have the situation that the Bantu must live apart from the Whites, so I want to separate the Indian from the Bantu and the Coloured from both.' For the Bantu, he went on to explain, apartheid intended that in each Native township, the Native should be able to do most things for himself. This meant that in each such township, there should be Native shops, Native clerks, Native preachers. There the Native should even be able to rule himself by means of Village Management Boards or whatever their organisation may be. . . . 'There he should be able to serve his own people and serve them well, since he comes into daily contact with the everyday needs and interests of his people.' Here he arrived at a topic which was to engage him much over the years. 'The mistake that many leaders of the Bantu make is to think only in terms of the highest superstructure of politics. Within this sphere they seek their own personal ambition, and forget that 99 per cent of their people do not have these ambitions . . . Their ambitions and their difficulties are concerned with their homes and their work, their children's future, and the necessity of being given opportunities to make a better livelihood.' This brought him to the subject of education. Here he announced another favourite idea with which we were to become extremely familiar. 'We are not against education which makes a man a worker in the service of his own nation, and we believe that what the Bantu needs more than anything else today is vocational training in many ways. There is one very clear provision and that is that when he is educated he may not use that education to slip out of the company of his fellow Bantu and try to go among the white men and use the knowledge there.'

Having thus set out, with that clarity of exposition which Dr. Verwoerd regularly claimed but which was often very difficult for others to discern, what the policy of apartheid meant, and having

o

again advised the Councillors not to pursue their personal ambitions but to serve their people, he then informed the Council that these were matters of 'high politics' which could not be discussed with him in this Council, nor indeed with one another in the Council.[1] He had indeed himself done what was not right in this matter, he said, but that was to meet the recurring requests of the Councillors themselves and 'not being a member of your Council, it was possible for me to do so'. He proposed now to depart, but he undertook to make himself available at any time during the session when the Councillors, not as Councillors but as leaders of their people, might come and talk over any and all of the matters he had raised.

'I think,' he said, 'I have now fulfilled my duty in addressing you, but I grant you the further opportunity of carrying out your desires and meet me if you want to discuss these other matters which cannot be discussed usefully here.'

With this amazing interpretation of the law—but with the instinct of the skilful politician for putting his finger on the weakness of the Council's composition—the chairmanship of a civil servant, the new Minister of Native Affairs introduced the African population, and the white electorate, to the purpose and his indomitable will to pursue it which was to carry him to the Premiership and to enable him, in a highly conservative country, to put across his most revolutionary propositions.

With the Council's record in mind, its reaction was logical and not unexpected. As usual, it was reflected in the speeches of thanks to the Minister for his address. Proposing the vote, Councillor Matthews said, 'The Minister believes and his supporters are entitled to believe that apartheid is the answer to our problem in this country. I do not quarrel with anyone believing that, but I say that as long as a policy is a unilateral policy, conceived, worked out and applied by one section of the population, it will not meet the needs of all sections of the population'; and he asked the Minister to convey that idea of theirs to the Government, to the supporters of the Government and to the European people generally. Referring then to the combined effort that had built up this country, he added, 'We would like you to try and see if your Government will not also consider the views of other sections of the population

---

[1] 'These matters cannot be discussed under the chairmanship of an official. Therefore, these matters should not be discussed in the course of the session of your Council.' See note, p. 174.

with regard to the future of this country as seriously as you want us to consider the policy of the Government.'

Councillor Thema, who seconded the motion, was characteristically more emphatic. The Minister had come to them and had told them about apartheid. It did not seem to him very different from the policy of segregation as they had known it. What the Africans wanted, if there was going to be apartheid, was that they —black and white—should come to an agreement together. 'But if the Minister and his Party are going to tell us where we are to live, well, we just cannot accept that.' There had been apartheid in the beginning, but the white man had come and claimed the land of the blacks. 'Now is it fair,' he said, 'that when this country is beautiful as it is now, when together we have made it what it is, we should be told "You have no right to be here, you should live somewhere else"?'

He then explained his idea of apartheid. If there were to be apartheid, 'what we want is a division of this land into two States in which the Africans will make their own laws'. And then he warned again of awakening Africa. 'The bigger clash is coming. The people living in other parts of Africa, the Arabs, are not white people; the people in Egypt, in Morocco, in Palestine and so on, are not white people. They live all over and they are not going to agree to the white domination of this country.' But he added, still hoping, 'So we have to help to find a policy to which we can all agree. . . . We want to live in this country as partners, not as one man being the master and the other a servant.'

From that point the ultimate fate of the session was not in doubt. The only question was how it would be arrived at. That was soon decided. To the issues which had already divided the Council and the Government the Minister had added a new and over-riding one—the right of the Council to discuss policy. It was soon the focal point of discussion, with the Chairman showing what was no doubt an instructed attitude in the matter. When the Minister had withdrawn and the Council re-assembled for work, to the Chairman's proposal that it should now proceed with its agenda which included the seemingly now inevitable amendment to the Urban Areas Act, Councillor Godlo immediately moved that the Council adjourn for the day so that its members might first of all study the implications of the Minister's speech. The Chairman said he was willing to allow the adjournment but that the Councillors should realise that the speech had been made to them not as Councillors but as leaders. 'So tomorrow when we meet, and after you have had time to study the words contained in the Minister's speech, you will meet here again as a Council, but your study of his speech you will make as political leaders, and you will come to decisions as regards what you would like to do with that speech not as Councillors but as leaders of the Native people. So that it will not really promote the work of this Council, which has been in abeyance for a long time, if you were to insist on discussing these matters here.'

A new tone in the Council, indeed, and a new approach which took for the Councillors sinister shape when they were informed that, in considering the Bills placed before them in terms of the law, they should be clear that 'the principle of the Bill is something of high politics and does not fall within the purview of the members of the Council'.

Thus things stood at the close of the first day. When the session resumed on the following day, the Chairman, who had been in consultation with the Minister in the interval, was ready, armed with two new moves. One was a message from the Minister himself to elucidate the implications of his use of the word political in his speech of the previous day. The message deserves to be quoted in full— since any intelligible summary must fail to do justice to it. It read: 'Do not let words or interpretation of words lead to unnecessary misunderstandings. Deal with ideas and facts. Now, I understand that the word "politics" has given you reason to feel worried. It may mean much or little. It is sometimes used to describe absolutely everything connected with the affairs of State and it is sometimes misused just to describe mudslinging or dishonesty in connection with the conduct of public affairs. From the context of my address it should be quite clear that I only do not wish the Council to spend its time in useless—to it and to the Bantu people—discussion of party political differences which should be fought out elsewhere, or of general principles of higher politics which might have led, or could lead, nowhere or can lead to disruption as they did before. Therefore I insisted that the agenda should be systematically dealt with as it is based on the provisions of the law. Naturally I could not have intended that when the discussion of a Bill is part of the agenda, nothing political in some ordinary sense may be mentioned. In so far as all legislation and all budgeting deals with the affairs of State, the discussions could all be called political. It would be foolish to make your work impossible by denying the right of full and unfettered discussion of such a Bill or any item on the budget. The Chairman must naturally see to it that discussion is to the point. It therefore seems to me unnecessary to waste any further time on defining words or meanings, but that the right thing to do would be to test what is intended by proceeding with the agenda systematically and finding out in actual practice if unjustifiable curtailment of debate takes place. I am sure that if, just as in Parliament' (of which, incidentally, the Minister had at that time himself a very brief experience), 'you submit to the discipline of the Order Paper, you will find that your apparent difficulties vanish.'

Here emerged the Chairman's second move. This was the reading out to the Council of a regulation under which 'the order of business at any meeting of Council, subsequent to the confirmation of the Minutes, shall be in the discretion of the Chairman.'

The regulation was not a new one; it was in fact of long standing but it had been so little used that the Councillors were not even aware of its existence. The reference to it now had too obvious an implication to be missed. The Councillors were not to be allowed to make the Minister's speech a subject of debate, and by this means apply themselves to policy as they had done during recent years.

But the Councillors were not to be muzzled by these means. They refused to appoint committees to deal with the Bills and the Estimates, and when, at the instance of one of the official members, taking his tone from the Chair, the Bills were submitted to Committee of the whole Council, they countered by breaking the quorum.

When they met again on the following morning, the Chairman was again met by a motion which he stigmatised as a further attempt to get behind his ruling. Mr. Msimang—a new member who had expressed his desire to do his duty in the Council, had submitted the following:

'That this Council, on a matter of urgent public importance, suspend the order for the day (the amending of Urban Areas) to consider the Minister's speech, especially in view of the fact that the Bills submitted for the consideration of the Council are based on the policy of apartheid discussed by the Minister in this address.'

Having refused the motion, the Chairman told the Council that he had been informed that the Council wished a small deputation

to see the Minister in regard to differences of opinion between the
Councillors and himself as Chairman on the conduct of this session.
He had placed this request before the Minister and the Minister
had indicated that he was always prepared 'at any time' to see a
deputation of the Council on any matter 'provided that this is a
functioning Council'. 'So', he argued, 'it would be quite in order
for the Council to send a deputation to the Minister at a later stage
when some progress had been made with the work of the Council,
to discuss such matters with him as they might deem to be of urgent
importance.'

'You will realise,' he said, 'that one thing which he does not wish
to happen is that the Council should be adjourned in order to
make it possible for this deputation to be sent. He wants a deputation from a Council which fulfils its functions, and not from a
Council which fails to do so.'

This naturally led to further argument, in which the point was
pertinently made by Councillor Godlo that there was no deadlock
in the Council, merely a difference of opinion on procedure, and
on what were the vital interests of the African people and what were
not. Councillor Mosaka elaborated the Council's point of view:

'We say it is not for the Minister or yourself to determine which
are the real interests and which are not. . . . The Minister has not
retracted that statement (re politics), but he has merely sent in an
explanatory statement indicating that it will be within our rights
to discuss political matters, but only if they are incidental to the
discussions of legislative matters or budgetary matters, if they arise
in the course of a discussion; but real matters of interest, matters
which you determine to be matters of real interest, are we allowed
to discuss them? . . . Now if you feel that we can only deal with
administrative matters, then we are not going to be faced with that
line of action just because it suits you—we are not going to agree to
a lowering of our status, because that is what it would amount to.'
Whereupon Mr. Msimang submitted a further motion:

'That this Council stand adjourned to enable the Council to
move the Courts of Law to obtain a Mandamus or Declaration of
Rights in that the matter of the Minister's speech was placed on the
agenda on the resolution of the Council in January 1949 and that
therefore the consideration thereof by the Council is not in the
discretion of the Chairman.'

And here finally deadlock was reached. The Chairman, having

again endeavoured to refuse the adjournment, decided to adjourn for five minutes to consult (whom?). He came back prepared to accept the motion provided the mover would put in *sine die*. Which he did—and the Council adjourned, never to meet again.

According to the official record, Councillor Moroka had given notice of the following motion which could not be considered prior to the adjournment:

'That this Council rejects the ban on political discussions clearly enunciated in the speech of the Minister of Native Affairs and in his supplementary statement to the Council. Council reaffirms its determination to exercise its unrestricted rights to discuss all matters, political and otherwise, affecting the interests of the African people.'

In 1952, the Council ceased to exist in terms of the Bantu Authorities Act, the first but typical victim of strong-arm politics, of an attitude and a mood which were something new in our experience, and for which nothing in our past had really prepared us, but of the implications and significance of which we were to learn much in the years that followed.

PART III

The Afrikanerisation of South Africa

I

Malanite Victory

The first ten years of African representation had been a period of continuous hard work, both inside and outside Parliament. It had been a period full of anxieties and discouragements, but it had not been without its hopes and consolations to keep us going. It had given us some grounds for believing that South Africa was moving, albeit slowly, and possibly too slowly, in what we regarded as the right direction. With the progressive acceptance by General Smuts himself of the interdependence of all our populations, involving the repudiation of the implications of a segregation policy, the stage seemed set for a new approach to both the social and the political problems which our changing society was inevitably throwing up. And however reluctant the more conservative members of the governing party might be to face the implications as we sought to propound them, we could at least feel that we were making our case to people who talked the same language, and to whom our differences were no greater than those between conservatives and liberals within a party system. We were indeed accepted by the Government as a legitimate part of the political organisation of the country, meeting the demands of our office to the best of our ability. Altogether there was enough to make us feel that the democratic spirit was sufficiently deeply rooted to produce in the long run the sort of society we believed to be not only sound, but essential for the peace and well-being of the country and in harmony with the world around us.

As I have endeavoured to show, however, even in the war and immediate post-war years, even as the country as a whole seemed gradually to be accommodating itself both to the implications of our own economic advance and the movement of world opinion, the official Opposition had consistently turned its face to the past. In spite of changing times and circumstances, they demanded the maintenance of what they claimed to be the traditional way of life of the country, ways which had lost, or were in process of losing, any *raison d'être* they might ever have had. Throughout their period of opposition, but particularly after the Hertzog-Smuts split on the war, they had indeed many points of attack on the Government, but more and more, every road led eventually to the matter of colour.

At first the demand was simply for the strict application of the Hertzog policy of segregation of Africans. This they claimed they had a right to expect of the Smuts Government since it had been part of the Government which had given the policy its legislative form in 1936. This amounted in effect to a check on the process of African urbanisation which Dr. Malan and Mr. Strydom were both to argue later, if applied in the beginning, could have kept South Africa safely 'white', on the basis of a migrant labour system which would have prevented the Africans from putting down roots anywhere outside Native reserves. However, as the apparently irresistible forces of an industrialisation, which the Nationalists themselves, in other contexts, proudly claimed to have initiated and encouraged in their first period of office, brought more and more Africans to the cities and created ever more interdependence, the range of the demand widened to cover all contacts, social and political, and that not only between white and black but between all racial groups.

As the first post-war election drew near, this programme naturally assumed an increasingly immediate importance. Everywhere, wartime governments were falling. Suppose, however unlikely, the Smuts Government should suffer the same fate, what could it mean in a modern industrial state with its practical demands, and in a modern world where the doctrine of human rights was beginning to assume considerable political importance? And what sort of a philosophy could the apostles of such a programme claim to support it?

The issue was pertinently raised in the brief pre-election session, when Dr. Malan challenged the Smuts Government in a no-confidence motion which called specifically for the repeal of the Indian franchise instituted in 1946, and the abolition both of our representation in the House of Assembly and of the Natives Representative Council.[1] He supported his case laboriously with what were already old and threadbare arguments. The Indians, he said, did not want the representation that they had been offered: in fact, they had already repudiated it. So far as the Africans were concerned, they had always chosen representatives who had consistently refused to stick to their own last, Native Affairs, but had constituted themselves the champions of all colour groups, including the Indians,

[1] Hansard, Vol. 62, Col. 62 *et seq.*

thus making themselves a focus of all coloured discontents. In any case, he contended significantly, neither group should be represented in a House where only 'national' interests should find a voice, and that through people elected to serve those interests. Arguing by implication that African interests were not national but sectional, he claimed that the right place for their voice to be heard was in the Senate, and then only when matters affecting them were under discussion. Asians were a foreign element, and should not be represented in Parliament at all.

As for the Natives Representative Council, he had always held that it would become the happy hunting ground of agitators, which was, he claimed, exactly what it had become. Nay, more than that, it had become, as it was clearly bound to become, the centre of communist activity in this country and thus a danger to the whole peace and security of the land—an absurd and unfounded accusation which the whole record of the Council belied.

With a buoyancy of spirit apparently begotten of the complete confidence in an easy victory with which he appeared to be approaching this fateful election, General Smuts replied immediately.[1] Indian representation could not be said to be a failure, since the Act constituting it had not yet been applied. As for the representation of Natives, both in the House of Assembly and in the Natives Representative Council, the Leader of the Opposition wanted to take these away also. 'Let me describe them as the two ewe lambs that were given in exchange for the deletion of the natives from the common voters' roll.' To take these away, would be a breach of faith, he maintained. It would be a step that would have the most far-reaching consequences in the relations of the races. It might indeed be the final estrangement between black and white in the country. It was a proposition which he could not accept. 'Let us do our duty', he concluded. 'Let us go ahead on the road on which we find ourselves, and do not let us take away rights and act in an unChristian-like manner.'

Following this lead, the Minister of Native Affairs, Major van der Byl, attacked what he called the hollowness of the Nationalist cry of apartheid, if apartheid was indeed to be interpreted as separation. He propounded the argument that was later to become very familiar, that if it had so far been found impossible to acquire the land to fulfil the limited purposes and promises of the 1936 legislation, how

[1] Hansard, Vol. 62, Col. 62 *et seq.*

was a foundation to be provided for the hiving off of the whole African population?

An angry interruption from Mr. Strydom of Waterberg that the policy contemplated no such separation formed the immediate background against which I had to state our case as Native Representatives in regard to the Opposition's programme for an alternative Government.

In spite of General Smuts' optimism, like many other people I felt that there were in fact many forces making for a change in government. These ranged from petty grievances about the absence of white bread, more serious grievances about bad distribution of goods in short supply, and many other difficulties which had been cheerfully accepted in the darker days of the war, but had become increasingly irksome as the tide turned and the pressures relaxed—all aggravated by the exceptional unpopularity of the Cabinet, to which I have already referred. One thing, however, seemed to me to militate against change. That was the sectional character of the official Opposition and the nature of the programme it proposed to present to the electorate. Consisting entirely of Afrikaners, and deriving its support mainly from Afrikaans-speaking farmers, its colour policy, which was clearly to be the focal point of its appeal, seemed designed to provide its own supporters with cheap labour kept 'in its place', rather than to encourage that industrial development on which the comfort and well-being of the whole community, including the farmers, hinged; while its oft-declared republican objective, as it had been elaborated and canvassed throughout the war years, could not fail to alarm everyone not himself bred in the Voortrekker tradition and prepared to identify himself with Afrikaner Nationalist ideas and ambitions. Altogether it seemed to me that the country, even with all its dissatisfactions, could not entrust its future to a party the outlook of which was so limited and exclusive, so tribal, both economically and politically. I certainly hoped it would not do so for the sake of the people I represented. So far as I could see, Nationalist policy, however dressed up from time to time as concerned to protect the black man's culture as well as that of the white man, had in reality nothing to offer the Africans but the status of a migrant labour force with the culture of the compound and the back yard, a danger to themselves and to everybody else.

As I made this case, I sincerely hoped that the electorate would in fact see the implications of the Nationalists' programme and approach as I saw them, and reject the Party as not only unequal to the needs of our stage of development, but as a positive danger to it. I hoped this particularly since, although I still did not see a Malanite victory as other than a temporary aberration, delaying the already belated adjustment of South African thinking and practice to the demands of twentieth century developments, as I watched the Party in operation, I had come to believe that it could not survive another defeat—a consummation greatly to be desired, as paving the way to what was so often canvassed in political circles, a party division on economic and not on 'racial' lines.

My hopes were doomed to disappointment. The country did accept the Malanites, not warmly but in sufficient numbers to put the reins of government into their hands. True, the margin between victory and defeat was very narrow. Under a constitutional provision which allows a variation in the numerical value of constituencies of 15 per cent above or 15 per cent below the average, with some 42 per cent of the votes cast, the combination of Malanite Nationalists and Mr. Havenga's Afrikaner Party (which, after complete Parliamentary extinction in 1943, came to life again for this election), succeeded in getting a majority of five seats in the House of Assembly over the combined forces of United Party, Labour and Native Representatives.

In the Senate, their position was more precarious—indeed, so precarious as to seem quite untenable. Thanks to the resignation of one of our small team, Mr. Hymie Basner, the Nationalist ranks could muster a majority of one, which, with the presiding officer's vote neutralised by his office, necessitated his casting vote to carry any proposition until such time as our elections, due in the latter part of the year, should fill the vacancy. When that occurred it seemed as if stalemate must ensue. This was a situation which was to be of considerable importance to me.

Thus, while my prognostications of the effects upon the party of defeat were not to be put to the test, it looked as if that attributed to Mr. Hofmeyr would not be fulfilled. He was reported as having said that if the Nationalists once got into office, they would not be got out again. In the following few months, it seemed as if they could not survive. Yet, in 1966, they won their fifth victory with an overwhelming majority; and who would now be rash enough to prophesy when they will sustain their first defeat? Mr. Hofmeyr might not have been a very good political tactician, but he knew a good deal about his own people. Even as my husband's return to the Senate in the end of 1948 to fill the vacant Orange Free State-Transvaal seat in the Senate made the Government's position in that Chamber seemingly impossible, there were rumours of an impending defection from the United Party ranks, and the new session had scarcely begun when one of General Smuts' old supporters, Senator J. W. van H. Brink,[1] found himself irresistibly drawn to the winning side.

A little earlier, Mr. Karl Rood, a United Party front bencher in the House of Assembly, who in the last years of the Smuts Government had shown signs of appreciating the needs of developing industry, into which he had been very successfully drawn, was suddenly overwhelmed with the menace to white civilisation of a policy of integration, and went out of Parliament altogether, giving the new Government its first positive encouragement in the winning of the ensuing by-election[2] in Vereeniging on May 18th, 1949, by Dr. J. H. Loock, formerly a member of the United Party. The occasion of this victory, otherwise naturally a matter of considerable disappointment to the non-Nationalist side of the House, provided me with one of the few moments of complete satisfaction I experienced in the course of my Parliamentary life, enhanced by the Government's alarm and consternation. On the day the victory was announced, the vote of the Minister of Native Affairs was under discussion—on which I had moved the reduction of the Minister's salary on the ground of his incompetence as Minister in this important field. When the moment came for me to call a division on this proposal the count found the Government defeated by 57 votes to 53. The result was a flurry and an adjournment of the debate. A few minutes later, a group of Government supporters, led by Mr. Schoeman, Minister of Labour, walked into the House with a very sheepish air. They had been celebrating their electoral victory. In their own defence, they claimed that the division bells had not rung in the Whips' room where they had foregathered. The next day, there were what seemed hours long testing of division bells before Parlia-

[1] Resigned on March 22nd, 1949, to be succeeded by Nationalist Mr. P. W. Joyut on May 9th, 1949.
[2] In 1949, the Government legislated to incorporate South West Africa in the Union. The South West Africa Amendment Act of that year gave the Europeans in South West Africa six seats in the House of Assembly. It also provided for a nominated member in the Senate. In 1950, the Nationalist Party of South West Africa which was, and is, affiliated to the Nationalist Party in South Africa, won all six Assembly seats which they have held ever since.

ment re-assembled. In due course, the Minister's salary was re-voted with the appropriate majority, and the one and only defeat of the Nationalist Government in Parliament since 1948 passed into the realms of history. This was, however, still in the future. For us at that moment, the question was, what would the advent of a Nationalist Government mean for us—even a temporary one? As for one that could fulfil Mr. Hofmeyr's prognostications, what would that face us with? Here, as at the beginning of our political adventure, the first year was to decide the pattern and dictate the terms for us. But not only for us. The course of history was amply to prove that all South African politics are Native affairs. In the last resort, by our attitude to our African population, the whole shape of our lives was to be determined.

P

2

The Colour of Nationalism

There is no doubt that the election result came as a great shock to the majority of the electorate—and the majority of the people. Now in the saddle, however insecurely, was what General Smuts was to describe as a uni-racial party, an Afrikaner-Nationalist group committed, by continuous and insistent propaganda over the years, to the establishment of a republic that would bear their stamp. It would be a republic where white supremacy would be rescued from the menace of black numbers and saved from the machinations of communists and jingoes. Now, what this programme would mean in practice was immediate and insistent. The question was anxiously canvassed both in private and in public. Would the new Government try to establish its republic at once? Dr. Malan had always said there must be substantial support for such a move, and no one could yet claim that the new Government had that. But what about apartheid—the main slogan of the election? What in fact did this mean? Separation? What more separation than already existed was now possible that would not destroy the whole fabric of South African life? Had not the Fagan Commission recently established the fact that 60 per cent of the African population was outside Native reserve—that it had no domicile in Native area, and was thus entirely dependent on employment in so-called white area to live? And was not expanding industry, on which alone the possibility of maintaining white standards depended, itself dependent on this progressively urbanised immigrant labour force? In other words, the interdependence of black and white was one of obvious mutual advantage. Surely to interfere with it would be to loosen the roots of 'white' civilisation itself.

These were facts which increasing acquaintance with the responsibilities of government must surely bring home to the most conservative of the country's new rulers. And in the acquisition of the relevant and essential information on which to base their policy in practice they were going to be assisted by a new research organisation, the first of its kind on their side of the political line, the South African Bureau of Racial Affairs—SABRA[1]—now in process of forma-

[1] Suid-Afrikaanse Buro vir Rasse-aangeleenthede.

tion. This was to be the counterpart in the Afrikaner-Nationalist
field of the Institute of Race Relations which had been in operation
since 1929; the counterpart and something more, for the new
organisation, in addition to its research intention, was to have a
specific political purpose, namely 'to propagate a healthy race
policy'. Clearly, if not technically aligned to the governing party, it
was obviously designed to provide the Party itself with a research
arm—a valuable component of any party organisation which I had
fruitlessly urged upon General Smuts as particularly important and
indeed invaluable in a complex country such as ours, where social
prejudice and political discrimination made it practically impossible
for those with whom power lies to know how the rest of the community lives.

Unlike the Institute of Race Relations, SABRA was to be an
organisation of whites only; yet as it got under way and began to
probe the facts of the situation, it must surely lead to a modification
at least of the more extreme attitudes to colour that could and did
thrive in opposition.

Gradually the continuing belief in the essential logic of the party
system as discouraging violent change began to assert itself, and the
argument that the new Government should be given a chance began
to circulate in both political and commercial circles. Dr. Malan's
first pronouncements in his new capacity of Prime Minister seemed
designed both to encourage and to exploit this attitude. In a broadcast address to the nation a day or two after the final results of the
election were known, he thanked those who had voted for him for
their support and their confidence. To those whose votes had gone to
the other side, he gave the assurance that they would not find him
and his government 'as bad as they had been painted'. He declared
the intention of his Party to take a 'broad national outlook' on all the
country's problems and to 'aim at justice and fair play all round'.

To the non-Europeans, he addressed a special message, of particular interest to us. He assured them that the new Government
would also serve their interests to the best of its ability. Apartheid,
he said, was not the caricature it had often been represented to be.
On the contrary, for the non-Europeans, it meant 'a large measure
of independence with the growth of their self-reliance, self-respect
and at the same time, the creation of greater opportunities for free
development in conformity with their own character and capacity'.[1]

[1] Quoted, *Umteteli wa Bantu*, June 12th, 1948.

On the back of these conciliatory if somewhat vague pronouncements, he went off to Pretoria to organise his cabinet. Some ten days
later he returned to Cape Town—in high spirits, the contemporary
press noted. At first he had seemed rather overwhelmed by the
prospect of the responsibility which had so suddenly and unexpectedly descended upon him. The intervening days had already apparently accustomed him to the idea and the feel of power. He now
announced to his friends—and to the country—that he had chosen
a best-man team, disregarding personal or provincial preferences,
and that he had high hopes of securing for his Government that
support and co-operation from those who had opposed him that was
essential if his small majority was to be enlarged to efficiency strength.
And again he had a special message for the non-Europeans. The
days when people spoke of racialism were past, he declared. 'We
shall get the co-operation of the various races. There will be no discrimination against any section. We have a policy in regard to the
non-Europeans, but this involves no oppression or removal of any of
their rights.' With repetitive emphasis, he went on, 'We shall protect
them against oppression and bring about good relationships between
them and the European population.'[1]

It was just two years later that Dr. Verwoerd, then newly elevated
to the position of Minister of Native Affairs, declared that words
must be understood to mean what the speaker meant them to mean.
Looking back on these first days of the Nationalist regime, it seems
to me that the era of subjective language interpretation, which was
to prove one of our greatest problems in this period in our history,
and to complicate enormously the burden of these years for people
like us, whose only weapons were argument and propaganda, had
already begun.

On the very morning of the day on which Dr. Malan gave these
renewed assurances to an anxiously listening public, there came the
startling announcement of the release of a notorious character,
Robey Leibbrandt, and four others who had been serving varying
terms of imprisonment for high treason and acts of sabotage committed during the war. To a public among whom the memories and
the losses of the colossal struggle in which we had been so recently
involved were still fresh wounds, the Minister of Justice, Mr. C. R.
Swart, explained that this action had been taken out of 'a deep
desire of the new Government to relieve the people of the Union of

[1] *Umteteli wa Bantu*, June 19th, 1948

the strain of the war years and to endeavour to end all the un-
pleasantness and rancour that flowed from it'.[1] In the course of the
next few weeks, other members of the Cabinet felt impelled to give
some indication of the line they would follow through their own
departments in pursuit of the attractive objective of happy inter-
racial adjustment on which Dr. Malan had been so insistent.

Mr. Ben Schoeman, the new Minister of Labour, announced that
the Government would not proceed with the Bill drafted by the
previous Government to give recognition to African trade unions
and foreshadowed an intention to bring to an end any and all
association of whites and non-whites in trade unions. He would
introduce an amendment to the Unemployment Insurance Act
which had been put on the statute book in 1946.[2] At that moment,
I was technically a member of a Parliamentary Commission on the
subject of this Act. The Act itself had been passed without a colour
bar, but the inclusion of the African worker within its scope, which
we as Africans' representatives had naturally welcomed, had caused
considerable unfavourable reaction, and that not only from Nationalist quarters. The result had been the appointment of a select
Committee, which became a Commission in the Parliamentary
recess. It seemed that the Minister had already decided what his
line of action would be in this regard without waiting for the
Commission's report—my first, but not my last experience of the
attitude of the new dispensation towards Commissions, even those of
its own initiation.

Mr. Schoeman went on to announce that the scheme eventually
initiated by the previous Government with the consent of the
European building workers, to train African artisans to build houses
for Africans, would be discontinued. He was later to expand and
explain this announcement with a further statement to the effect
that the intention was to discontinue the scheme where it threatened
to create competition for white artisans.

He rounded off this pre-sessional declaration of his plans by withdrawing an invitation issued by the previous Government to the
International Labour Organisation to visit South Africa and see its
labour situation for itself.

The Minister of Defence, Mr. Erasmus, announced his intention
to tighten up the country's defence system, particularly in respect of

[1] *Umteteli wa Bantu*, June 19th, 1948.
[2] Act 53 of 1946.

military training on the platteland, the rural areas of the country, 'in view of the possibility of an internal threat in the event of war', a threat which he seemed to anticipate would arise from underground communist activities.

He also declared his intention to explore the British Government's policy in regard to the arming and military training of Africans in its African territories. If their intention was to embark upon this, it seemed he would endeavour by friendly negotiations to induce them to change their minds. As for South Africa itself, the Native Military Corps which had seen service through the war would be disbanded. There would be no military training for non-Europeans in South Africa.

In his turn, Mr. Paul Sauer, as Minister of Railways, declared that mixed travel on trains would cease. Since such travel did not exist except in the Cape Town area, this meant in effect the separation of White and non-White on the Cape suburban railway service, which these groups had shared both profitably and peacefully since the first South African train had been flagged on its way from Cape Town to Wellington; and forthwith the long demanded notice boards[1] 'Whites only' appeared on the privileged sections of these trains. Plans were also announced for the provision of separate approaches to trains, which had not so far existed. These would prevent contact between the two sections of the population even at that point.

Under the direction of the Minister of Posts and Telegraphs, post offices began to sprout whole forests of partitions at counters which up to then had served all races alike; this as a preliminary to the provision of more complete separation which would perforce take some time to achieve.

To round off this picture of the impending shape of things to come, the Minister of Native Affairs, Dr. Jansen, for many years Speaker of the House of Assembly, later Governor-General of the Union, announced the determination of the Government to check and control the townward movement of the African population. He followed this with a message of his own to the Africans. In this he too echoed the Prime Minister's assurance that the Government would do all in its power to bring about conditions under which Black and White might be able to live happily and 'in safety' together, but he warned the Africans that they would be expected to assist in this regard. This

[1] Already prepared under the Smuts regime. See p. 132.

they could do, he suggested, by preventing more people from going with their families to the urban areas where, he contended, there was overcrowding, and 'by seeing that the won't works and the evil doers did not remain in their midst', a theme he was to return to at intervals. As I noted at the time, he did not offer any suggestion as to how either of these things was to be accomplished with the existing pressure of a growing population on the land resources of the community, and the destructive effect of the legislative controls which, even then, prevented the growth of stable and responsible cohesive African communities. Nor did he seem to see anything illogical in continuing his message with the advice to the people to love and care for the soil, advice which wound up with the proposition that 'the population of any reserve that has been rehabilitated will have to be limited as far as possible to its reasonable carrying capacity'. What, in terms of his Government's policy, was to happen to those whom the process of limitation should displace was not the Minister's preoccupation at that moment.

This, with all the other implications of ministerial pre-sessional activity, would no doubt be explained and placed in perspective when Parliament met.

3

What is Apartheid?
The Constitutional Issue Raised

The first session of the new Parliament met on August 6th, 1948, just three months after the election. The customary brief post-election session, its essential business was to present and pass a budget which had been prepared but not introduced by Mr. Hofmeyr in the pre-election session. Understandably, a new Government could scarcely have had time to frame much in the way of legislation, even if it had been more prepared for its own victory than this one was. But the speech from the throne, while noting that there would be no legislation of 'a radical character' in the important field of Native Affairs that session, gave the assurance that by the following session, whatever legislation should prove necessary to the Government's purpose would be ready.

But if the session was to be brief and, legislatively, more or less passive, it was to prove of the first importance as setting the tone and the direction of all that was to follow. The new Government could legitimately claim that it had won the election on the cry of apartheid. True, it had had other planks in its platform of high emotional appeal to sections of the electorate. As I have noted, it had promised that if returned to office it would save 'White' South Africa not only from a rising black flood but also from the menace of communism—much the same thing, they argued, in the context of South African society—and from jingoes, the people who, with a divided loyalty, had dragged South Africa into two world wars at the coat tails of Britain. But while these latter objectives were to play their part in the unfolding drama which this new dispensation was to initiate, the first and essential, and indeed basic issue was that of race relations; and race relations were apartheid, from which all else was to derive.

The stage was set in the earliest days of the session when General Smuts, as leader of the Opposition, took the first available opportunity to ask what was to become the recurring question—what is apartheid? What was this thing that had 'raised such a hubbub in

232

the country in recent months'?[1] So far as he could see, it was only a slogan, a catchword, 'by which it was proposed to catch the vote of the country', something 'wrapped in a mass of misrepresentations such as we have never had in our political life in this country before'. But there was no policy. He reckoned it was not even meant to be a policy—only an intention 'to befuddle the public mind and confuse the public to make them vote blindfold over the most important and far-reaching and dangerous issue in this country'. Surely now, with the responsibilities of office on their shoulders, the leaders of the Nationalist Party owed it to the public to explain what they really meant by this word apartheid, still a new word in our political vocabulary. Was it to be a policy of sending the natives back to the reserves? That was at least understandable. But there were two things to make it absurd. First, where was the land to come from? 'All I know is that it is impossible even to carry out the modicum of expropriation which is involved in the Hertzog scheme of segregation. Whether you go to the Transvaal or Natal or anywhere else, you find the farmers of the country, the landowners of the country, say: "Are we going to part with our heritage? Are we going to sell the land of our fathers? We shall not." '[2]

Secondly, if you were to send the 'natives' back to the reserves on a basis which would give them 'a fair chance', doing 'our fair duty towards them', you would have to establish industries to provide them with the means of livelihood. Then what was the industrial future of this country going to be, 'when industries start in the locations, in the reserves, huge industries based on cheap native labour', what was to happen to white South Africa, to white industrial South Africa?

As against such a policy, he proceeded to make a declaration of his own policy, 'affirmed after careful enquiry by the Fagan Commission'. That was 'to go on developing tentatively very much on the lines on which we have been developing hitherto'. The Native must come more and more into the white areas. 'The Native is not confined merely to the reserves at his home, but he is part and parcel of industrial South Africa.' That, he added, 'is what has happened so far, and nothing can alter it.'

[1] Hansard, Vol. 64, Col. 200 *et seq.*
[2] Mr. A. H. Vosloo, Deputy Minister of Bantu Development, opening the 1967 Conference of SABRA on the subject of consolidation of the Bantu homelands, said that among other difficulties in this regard was the reluctance of White landowners to give up farms that had been in the possession of their families for generations or which they had spent a lifetime in developing.

This situation, he admitted, provided its own problems—many of them. But they must be faced and solved. It raised all sorts of difficult questions. 'You are taking the barbarian now into your system. It means education; it means housing; it means health—all those great social problems which afflict us not only in our white society but also in this larger set-up of Black and White South Africa.' And within the system, the native must not only be 'shaped into an economic instrument'; he must also be 'trained to look after his own affairs, a problem of government' which he was to elaborate later as meaning in effect that development of local government designed to meet local conditions and circumstances, of which he had seen the Natives Representative Council as an integral part.

From this starting point, he moved a comprehensive amendment in which, among other things, he called upon the Government to indicate clearly what its intentions were in respect of the policy of apartheid as affecting the Native and Coloured peoples, more especially in respect of their political and economic position, and to give an assurance that their existing political rights would not be tampered with.

This final paragraph had implications which he had not touched upon in his speech, but which subsequent events were to show were very much in his mind, implications that went beyond the social and even the political effects of a policy of racial separation to the attitude of the new Government to the Constitution itself and the principles upon which it had been founded. For years past, as I have indicated, the Nationalists had indeed been demanding not only social and economic separation of the Coloured people but political separation also. More recently they had determined upon the abolition of Native representation from the House of Assembly. These points in their programme were important in themselves as affecting the character of our multi-racial state; but they had a further significance involving the attitude of the new Government to the contract of Union under which these threatened rights existed. In terms of the Act of Union which enshrined that contract, these rights were protected against reduction by an entrenchment necessitating a two-thirds majority of both Houses of Parliament sitting in joint session. The query behind General Smuts' reference to tampering with these rights was, would the Government, with its slender majority, attempt to side-step this entrenchment, which incidentally also safeguarded the position of the two official languages? How far would they go in their determination to stamp their own pattern on the South African state now in their control?

The Prime Minister's reply to the challenge thus thrown out to him was to bring this issue into the very forefront of the political stage and the subsequent proceedings of the session established the profound importance of what was involved.

Rising immediately after General Smuts' speech to meet the challenge of his old political enemy, Dr. Malan announced,[1] in the uncompromising tones we had grown accustomed to from him and his party in Opposition, that to clear the decks he would make plain at once what apartheid was not. It was not political rights for Indians. So, even if the Government was not ready with any other measures for this first session, it would undo what General Smuts had done in 1946—it would repeal the franchise clauses of the Asiatic Land Tenure Act. And to show that this was not an isolated move but part of a general plan, he could give the assurance that his Government would not go on with General Smuts' proposal for the reform of the Natives Representative Council. 'No Parliament for the natives alongside this Parliament for Europeans,'[1] he declared. Also, no representation of Natives in the House of Assembly. His Party's policy was to abolish that representation—in favour of something better which he vaguely defined as 'institutions for them in their own reserves which will enable them to have a large measure of self-government and which will enable them at the same time to retain their own national character'.

This led him to the subject of the Coloured franchise. Here he announced that it was not the intention of his Government to deprive the Coloured people of representation in Parliament, but to give them representation 'through a better system than we have at present . . . and that is to give them representation just as the Natives have it now'.

From the political implications of apartheid, he turned to education. Here he declared his and his Party's determination to extend the field of separation from the schools, where it already operated, to the universities. A stop must be put to the entry of non-White students to the established 'White' universities, and separate institutions of higher education would be provided for those who were in a position to use them.

He wound up with the emphatic statement that it was not the

[1] Hansard, Vol. 64, Col. 213 *et seq.*

policy of his Party 'to eliminate all the Natives who are at present in the European area and who come here to work'. The new Government were not going to send them all to their reserves. That, he declared, was a caricature of their policy, designed to spread uncertainty and alarms in all economic spheres. And there he left this all-important topic of apartheid, saying that the members of his Cabinet would fill in the details of the policy each as it affected his own department.

The new Prime Minister had prefaced his reply to the Opposition challenge with the pronouncement that apartheid was both negative and positive. He had himself chosen to begin with the negative side —with what apartheid was not. When he ended, anything that might be regarded as positive, in the sense of constructively in favour of the non-white populations, was conspicuous by its absence, unless he regarded as falling into this category his promise of new institutions of higher education for non-whites, itself coupled with the shadow of the exclusion of all non-white students from our existing universities with their comparatively long history and extensive facilities which no new institution could hope to emulate for a very long time. Throughout, he had been at pains to stress the political aspects of his case, which General Smuts had continually rejected when they had been canvassed from the Nationalist benches in pre-election days. While the constitutional implications of this situation were to emerge before the end of the session, they were, to me at least, academic in view of the Government's weakness in numbers. At that moment, the essential concern for a representative of Africans was to discover if possible what benefits the apartheid policy could hold for the people we represented to justify the claim that Dr. Malan himself had been so insistent about, that apartheid was not oppression.

So far, all that we had seen and heard seemed, like Dr. Malan's own speech, to be essentially negative in character—a process of taking away what had been given or promised in the previous years, an extension of that retreat from democracy that we had hoped to see reversed. It was an impression which the budget itself was to strengthen. Introduced by Mr. Havenga, in a long speech warning of the dangers of mounting extravagance in public spending, it ended by conceding both increased social pensions and remission of taxation, but neither for the people we represented, the poorest section of the population. This was a striking departure from the practice of the preceding years, at least in the matter of social pensions. Coupled with a marked decrease in the previous allocations for services for Africans, it could not fail to stimulate our anxieties. What did all this portend? Was it just a matter of saving at the expense of the least politically powerful group in the country, or was it a matter of general policy?

In an effort to focus some attention on this aspect of the situation, I moved a further amendment[1] to the motion to go into committee of supply, calling for the inclusion of the Africans in the proposed scheme for improving social pensions for white and coloured persons for plans to check the spread and counter the ravages of poverty among the African population, and to build up the economic and social levels of that section of the people in the interests of the whole community. Within this framework, I took up Dr. Malan's insistent claim that apartheid was not oppression, and argued that oppression, like apartheid, could be either positive or negative. It could either be the subjecting of people to laws and administrative restrictions that ground them down and kept them on the lowest economic and social level, or it could be simply neglect. It seemed to me that in apartheid, from what we had already seen and heard of it, including the Prime Minister's statement on this matter, and as reflected in the budget, we were faced with both these forms of oppression. Anything we had so far been shown of Nationalist policy seemed only an extension of that segregation which had proved a thin disguise for a cheap labour policy imposed upon a politically powerless community. As for the budget, that was oppression by neglect. In other words, so far apartheid seemed only loss for the African population. I expressed the hope that the Minister of Native Affairs would be able to give us a less discouraging, less depressing picture of his Party's policy in operation.

With this and other pressures upon him to fill the gaps in the picture left by his leader, in due course Dr. Jansen applied himself to an elaboration of his Party's intentions.[2] His starting point was the firm determination of the Government to do all in its power to ensure the safety of the white race in South Africa. At the same time, it would do all in its power to bring about conditions under which the native people would have the opportunity of developing their own national life 'according to their own genius and character'.

[1] Hansard, Vol. 64, Col 252 et seq.
[2] Hansard, Vol. 64, Col. 599 et seq.

How this was all to be done, he admitted, had still to be worked out. Facts and statistics were lamentably few—a circumstance that, incidentally, we had been pressing upon the attention of both Parliament and public for years.[1] Until that gap should be filled, specific plans could not be formulated.

One thing however must be pursued at once—the control of the African townward drift, together with a check to the process of detribalisation which it had engendered. That was destructive from every point of view. The new Government would set itself to check not only the entry into towns but the efflux from the reserves. Among the African communities themselves, ethnic differences must be recognised and maintained, and the powers of the chiefs re-established and built up. Finally, a relationship must be established and maintained between the tribe at home in the reserve and its members on their (periodic) incursions into the towns.

To my query as to how the people were to live if their entry into the labour market was to be as rigidly controlled as this plan seemed to imply, Dr. Jansen's reply was that there was plenty of work on the farms. Had not the farmers long been crying out for labour? The towns, he maintained, had been drawing away labour from our two basic industries of farming and mining. That must be rectified. Dr. Jansen considered it could be done without adversely affecting secondary industry since, he declared, the towns were full of surplus labour—of those loafers and evil-doers of whom he had originally spoken. Pressed further as to the dangers to an expanding industrial economy of a policy of labour control, of what in effect seemed a policy of labour distribution, he declared his readiness to see the process of industrialisation checked if the price of its continued expansion was to be more and more African urbanisation with all the dangers he regaded as implicit in it.

'Now, talking about industry,' he declared, 'and the tremendous progress that has been made, I say this, that if industrialisation means that the European population of our cities is to be engulfed by natives, then I am not prepared to go on with industrialisation.'[2]

In the course of his speech, Dr. Jansen had a good deal to say about trusteeship and the responsibility of the trustee to 'protect the

[1] See my address to the South African Association for the Advancement of Science in 1944—'A Scientific Approach to the problem of post-war employment and the Non-European in South Africa'. Printed, *South African Journal of Science 1944*. Reprinted, *Rhodes Livingstone Institute Journal*, June 1945.
[2] Hansard, Vol. 64, Col. 606.

possessions and develop the potentialities of the ward'. This latter should include an education that would be 'on the right lines and will fit the Native for his future life in the country'. But the many services, pensions, unemployment insurance, feeding schemes and so on, had not only contributed greatly to the influx of Natives into urban areas but were, he believed, undermining the character of the people themselves. He had a brief word also to say on political rights as between trustee and ward, summed up in the assertion that the trustee was not called upon to give his ward a say in his, the trustee's, affairs. And so we were back on the political issue.

In spite of all their protestations, what did all this amount to other than a backward-looking policy designed to check the process of economic and social change on which the progress of all sections of the population depended? And for the African people whom we represented, what could it mean but a position of helotry?

While this discussion was proceeding, the possible implications and ramifications of the political aspects of apartheid, upon which Dr. Malan had concentrated, were beginning to take shape, inspiring anxious recollections of discussions on the continuing validity of the entrenchments in the Constitution following upon the passage of the Statute of Westminster designed by the British Parliament to underwrite the sovereignty of the British self-governing dominions in terms of the agreement reached at the Prime Minister's Conference in 1926. Unlike the other self-governing dominions, the South African Government of the day, General Hertzog's first Government, had had no reservations made in that Statute in respect of these special features of the South African Constitution. General Smuts, then the leader of the Opposition, had raised the possible legal implications of the omission on the occasion in 1931 of a resolution presented to Parliament by the Prime Minister, endorsing the proposed Statute. He had gone further, and had moved as an addendum to the resolution 'on the understanding that the proposed legislation will in no way derogate from the entrenched clauses of the South Africa Act'. This addendum had been accepted by General Hertzog and had been passed unanimously by the House. Among those who had not only voted for the resolution as amended, but had spoken strongly in support of the addendum, were two of the members of Dr. Malan's new Cabinet, Dr. Stals, Minister of Health and Education, and Mr. Swart, Minister of Justice. Dr. Conradie, become deputy Speaker of the House of Assembly and

Chairman of Committees, had also given his vocal support to the proposition. These speakers had indeed declared their conviction that the maintenance of these entrenchments was a matter touching the honour of South Africa.

In 1934, the question of the continuing validity of the entrenchments had again been raised in the debates on the Status Bill designed to regularise the constitutional position of South Africa in this new phase in commonwealth development. On this occasion, Dr. Jansen as Speaker of the House of Assembly, in reply to a question, had ruled that the entrenchments were still valid.

In 1936, for the third time, this issue had come before Parliament, and that in a very specific fashion, with the introduction of General Hertzog's Bill to abolish the Cape Native franchise and to establish the system under which we as Native Representatives held our seats. Again Speaker Jansen ruled the conditions of the entrenchment to be still operative, and General Hertzog accordingly summoned both Houses of Parliament in joint sitting to put the seal of a two-thirds majority on his Representation of Natives Act.

Subsequently what, in the circumstances of the day, could only be a delaying action by those who, outside Parliament, had continuously opposed this legislation, was taken in the Courts. There the validity of the Act was challenged. In the course of the argument in the case, Counsel for the complainants took the somewhat surprising point that the Status Act had in fact wiped out the entrenchment and that in consequence the Representation of Natives Act was invalid as having been passed by an irregular procedure. It was an argument to which obviously little weight could attach, since, if sound, it could have only a very modest delaying effect in respect of the Government's intention and in fact no attempt was made to pursue it seriously. In his judgment, however, the Chief Justice of the Appeal Court, the Hon. Mr. Justice Stratford, expressed the view that Parliament was no longer bound by the entrenchments, but that this did not invalidate the Act, since a fully sovereign Parliament might adopt any procedure it might choose for its purpose in any particular case. This view, which was to be widely canvassed by Government spokesmen as the Appellate Division's judgment of 1937, was to exercise a profound influence on the course of events in the years that followed. In 1949, its shadow was just beginning to loom over the political scene.

While the question of the attitude of the Government to the

entrenchments was implicit in the discussion of General Smuts' amendment to the budget, it was raised specifically in the course of a debate on democratic rights and freedoms initiated by the leader of the Labour Party, Mr. John Christie. Speaking in that debate, Captain du Toit, a United Party front bencher representing a Cape constituency which included a considerable number of Coloured voters, took the occasion to ask Dr. Jansen if he stood by his rulings given as Speaker in 1931 and 1934, that the entrenchments were still valid in spite of the Statute of Westminster and the Status Act. In response to this question, Dr. Jansen took evasive action, stating that that matter could await the appropriate occasion for reply. This move on the Minister's part raised new alarms in the United Party ranks, inducing Mr. J. G. N. Strauss, destined to become the leader of the Party in succession to General Smuts, to press for an elucidation of the Government's attitude in the debate on the Prime Minister's vote. Dr. Jansen's reply to Captain du Toit's question, he said, had done nothing to allay the growing anxiety of the people outside about the attitude of the Government to the Constitution. He then reviewed the circumstances that had given rise to Dr. Jansen's rulings, and urged him to be specific about where he and his leader now stood in this matter.

No sooner had Mr. Strauss sat down than Mr. J. H. Conradie who was to occupy the Speaker's chair during the critical years that followed, rose to declare that not 1931 but 1934 was the determinant year in our constitutional history. The Status Act of that year had declared and established the status of the Union of South Africa in unequivocal terms. Quoting the terms of the Act, he argued that it had provided that the Union Parliament was supreme, having the power to repeal any enactment of the past, and was not bound by the provisions of any law of the United Kingdom unless it extended such provisions to the Union by its own authority; which in the matter of the entrenchments, it had not done.[1] Mr. Strauss countered by quoting Dr. Jansen's ruling on that very occasion, and concluded with a challenge to the Prime Minister to say where he himself stood on this question of the entrenchments 'as a member of the Government of the day in 1931 when this resolution was passed'.[2]

When he got up to reply to the points raised on his vote, Dr. Malan chose to ignore Mr. Strauss' questions. It was an ominous omission

[1] Hansard, Vol. 64, Col. 1301.
[2] Hansard, Vol. 64, Col. 1316.

in the opinion of my colleague, Mr. Molteno, which he was quick to point out.[1] Surely these were questions of the very first importance in view of the Government's declared intentions in respect of the representation of Africans in the House of Assembly. Focussing particular attention on Dr. Jansen's ruling in 1936 on the occasion of General Hertzog's Representation of Natives Bill, he stressed the further argument in favour of the continuing validity of the entrenchments that the new franchise had been re-entrenched by that Bill. What, he asked, could be the point of that if the view was held by the House at that time that the entrenchment was a dead letter? He then proceeded to argue what, with General Smuts' personal experience to back it, was to become one of the main planks in the Opposition's case: namely, that there would have been no Union without the entrenchment of the non-European vote, and that therefore there was a moral as well as a legal obligation to respect it.

Dr. Malan, when he rose again to speak, felt it incumbent upon him to make some response to these combined pressures. He did so, however, in markedly non-committal terms. Referring to Native representation only, he remarked that he did not think it was necessary to get engrossed in legal complexities when there was no Bill on this subject before the House. He went on, however, to say that Mr. Strauss had quoted authorities supporting his contention of the continuing validity of the entrenchment. He had seen a counter opinion of high authority. He gave the assurance, however, that 'if we decide to introduce a Bill of this nature, we will certainly not do so without having obtained the very best legal advice in this connection'.[2] As a corollary, however, he added his belief that 'a democratic people exercise sovereignty at all times, but that this does not give them the right to bind the people hard and fast at a later stage—as the people continue to enjoy their sovereignty—and thus prevent them from solving the problems that confront them'— another argument that was to become very familiar to us in the succeeding years.

Taking up the argument at this point, General Smuts, while noting that the Prime Minister had apparently not made up his mind yet as to his specific intentions in regard to the abolition of Native representation, challenged the view that 'this seems to be largely a legal issue which should be gone into by the best legal

---

[1] Hansard, Vol. 64, Col. 1340.
[2] Hansard, Vol. 64, Col. 1369.

authorities'. But while agreeing that an important legal issue was involved, he contended that the matter went further than that. He proceeded to review the history of Union and the origin of these provisions of the Act of Union from his own personal experience, to state his own firm conviction that unification would never have been achieved at the Convention if such a fundamental agreement had not been reached, 'removing this matter from the field of party politics'. He reinforced his argument by reference again to the events of 1931, 1934 and 1936. In regard to the attitude of Parliament in 1931 and 1934, he declared, 'In both cases our status was determined on that basis (of the continuing validity of the entrenchments). And in 1936, Parliament acted accordingly.' He proceeded to argue that if a change was desired now, it must either be by a two-thirds majority, or 'in a revolutionary manner by a referendum'. It would mean a constitutional revolution to depart from that ruling. 'If such a revolution must take place it must be a matter for the people to decide upon in such a manner that there can be no doubt.'[1]

To these arguments Dr. Malan made the then surprising reply— the sort of 'political' reply that became less surprising by mere repetition later—that General Smuts had overlooked the fact that a Select Committee (after long deliberation and the taking of evidence) had agreed that there should be no representation of Natives in the House of Assembly and that General Hertzog, as Prime Minister in 1936, had actually framed and introduced a Bill on these lines—a Bill which suffered shipwreck 'through the party political machinations of the Leader of the Opposition himself'. It was that accepted policy he now proposed to implement.

With what relevance and on what authority it is difficult to know, he went on to declare that the Leader of the Opposition had conveniently forgotten that 'at the National Convention, during the discussions at the time, it was assumed, although no two-thirds majority was laid down in that connection, that the franchises of the non-Europeans would not be extended to the North'. But what had he done in his Asiatic Land Tenure and Indian Representation Act of 1946? He himself had broken the understanding which was arrived at at that time (i.e. in 1909), 'and which had always been maintained since then'. Similarly, he had let it be known that he intended to create a native Parliament . . . a Parliament which

[1] Hansard, Vol. 64, Col. 1410 *et seq.*

would have jurisdiction not only in the native reserves but also in the European areas—a reference to General Smuts' proposal for the development of the Natives Representative Council and its linking up with the urban Advisory Boards system. Thus far had he deviated from the agreement of forty years ago, Dr. Malan argued, yet he wished now to tie the Government down to an agreement made forty years ago in very different circumstances. He went on: 'We now have a new generation and new circumstances, and solutions must be looked for in the light of today's circumstances. How,' he asked, 'could a generation of forty years ago have the right to bind us hand and foot so that we shall be prevented from realising the solution, from putting into effect the resolution which we want to carry into effect?' Getting carried along by his own argument, it seemed, he ended this speech with: 'I again emphasise that at any moment of its existence the people are sovereign, are their own masters.' He declared, however, that whatever steps the Government decided to take, 'we shall see that the people will give a clear and distinct verdict in regard to this matter'.[1]

Now thoroughly aroused to the implications of the situation, General Smuts returned to the attack on the Appropriation Bill[2] with an amendment calling specifically for an assurance from the Government that it would adhere strictly to the entrenchment provisions of the South Africa Act in respect of any proposals which it might submit for the abrogation or diminution of the existing political rights of the Native and Coloured people. This he did in a fighting speech in which he concentrated on what was to be his main point of attack—that whatever the Nationalist Party had put before the electorate in the general election, the constitutional implications had never even been suggested. 'We heard on every platform, in all directions, this question of apartheid discussed as a matter involving the future of South Africa. But that most fundamental aspect of it, that the carrying out of this policy may mean tampering with the Constitution and by-passing the entrenched clauses of the South Africa Act—that, as far as my memory goes, was never laid before the people', and he went on to state, what to me at least was fully justified, 'I think the people never realised what was on and what was at stake. Even here in this House, it seemed during the early part of the discussion that people did not realise that this was really

[1] Hansard, Vol. 64, Cols. 1418–19.
[2] Hansard, Vol. 65, Col. 2901. et seq.

the ultimate issue in this great question. It was only in the course of the debates that gradually this issue emerged, and once more confronted us with a situation very different from, far more serious I may say, than that of apartheid itself.' To this Dr. Malan in his final speech of the session was to repeat his statement that the Government would take the best legal advice on the question of the validity of the entrenchment. If it went in their favour, good and well. If it didn't, the people would have to be consulted about it. The public would in any case have the matter before them in the near future, in the election for the Provincial Councils due to be held in the beginning of the following year. And there this important matter rested for the time being.

One other episode of this initial session of the new Government deserves notice as providing a significant shadow of impending developments. This was the debate on that motion of the Leader of the Labour Party in which the question of the Constitution was first specifically raised. It was a motion which Dr. Malan resented bitterly. Reflecting a widespread anxiety as to what the Nationalists in office, this uni-racial government, would make of South Africa, begotten of years of Nationalist Party propaganda, Mr. Christie called upon the new Government to give an undertaking that it would in no way infringe such democratic rights and freedoms as were then enjoyed by the people of South Africa, and specified in particular the freedom of ministers of religion to teach whatever their consciences dictated, the freedom of workers to organise themselves and fully to control their own organisation, the freedom of the press to report news and to comment on that news, and the freedom of educational institutions from political influence.

Speaking to his motion,[1] Mr. Christie admitted that it was an unusual one in a country with a Parliamentary tradition. Much was said on party platforms and in the heat of party contests that was forgotten in the more sober and responsible atmosphere of day to day government. The assurances for which he was asking, however, did not arise out of the heat of party controversy but from the published programme of the new governing Party itself and, in some cases, from statements made by, or issued in the name of, the leader of the Party, now the Prime Minister of the country. Particularly concerned about the churches and the trade unions, he wished to know first of all what was involved in what he regarded as a warning—

[1] Hansard, Vol. 64, Col. 755 *et seq.*

nay, a threat—to the churches of a kind which had never in his experience of politics (which went back many years) been made by any democratic party or any democratic Parliament. In this connection he quoted a statement made by Dr. Malan on the eve of the election campaign which read, 'Churches and Societies which undermine the policy of apartheid and propagate doctrines foreign to the nation will be checked.' What was this process of checking to amount to? If the churches, or any of the churches, took the line that apartheid was wrong, as many of them did, surely they were entitled to place their opinions before their congregations and the public.

As for the trade unions, the printed programme of the Party stated the intention of the Party to establish a Labour Council which, among other things, would 'exercise effective control over the appointment of officials by, and the general activities of the trade union or workers' organisations'—another statement with an ominous ring.

Dr. Malan's reaction to the motion,[1] the other points of which were elaborated by the succeeding speaker, was itself interesting, and now of more than historical importance. He was exceedingly indignant at the suggestion that he and his Party were not democratic. What sort of democracy had the mover in mind? he asked. Was it that of his friends in Russia—the inevitable insinuation—or that of the Western world? He himself and his Party stood for Western-type democracy 'based on the rights and freedoms of the individual'. 'The individual has human rights,' he declared, 'and nothing should be allowed to infringe those rights.' These he specified as 'the right to live, of movement and of action, of freedom of thought and of conscience, of religion and the right to express himself and his opinions. He and his Party stood for all these things, including the right to call into being political parties and in that way 'to join issue in public life with others whose views differed from him'. Then what about this matter of the churches and apartheid? As the argument went on, it appeared that this was something different. The human rights to which Dr. Malan and his Party subscribed (besides obviously not applying to people of colour) did not include the right of people 'who undermine the principle of apartheid, who preach equality and who propagate foreign ideologies in South Africa'. But who were these people? They were the

[1] Hansard, Vol. 64, Col. 774 et seq.

Communists and the communistically minded people. They would certainly be checked. That was the policy of his Party. The years that followed were to elaborate for us the implications of this interpretation of human rights, and of democracy as interpreted by Afrikaner nationalism.

4

The Coloured Vote

These first few months of the new Government's office had already outlined the three strands that, against all our hopes of a widening democratic structure, seemed destined to make up the pattern of the Afrikaner Nationalist state—(1) a separation on a basis of race which, whatever its logic might demand in the end, was designed to establish and maintain 'white' supremacy within and over the whole community for at least as far as anyone could foresee, (2) a bending of the Constitution to this purpose, and (3) a spreading control—check Dr. Malan called it—upon political activity based on and inspired by the contrary objective of a multi-racial, truly democratic state. This was indeed to prove the emerging pattern within which our representation was to function for the rest of its brief existence. The time and the circumstances of the termination of that representation were the measure of the determination with which the objectives of apartheid were pursued.

Over the first few years, a protracted constitutional crisis was to dominate the scene, overshadowing the process of social change which the policy of apartheid progressively demanded. It was a crisis of the most profound importance as touching the nature of the state itself. A consideration of its record would therefore seem to be essential to any understanding of the factors and forces at work in the South African situation over these critical years.

As I have shown, the emphasis laid by Dr. Malan himself on the political aspect of apartheid early established a sharp dividing line between the two major parties which brought into the centre of the political stage the question of the validity or otherwise of the entrenched clauses in the Constitution which had been incorporated in the Act of Union for the protection of the language rights of both sections of the white population and the franchise rights of the non-whites in the old Cape Colony. For the moment, the argument on this point had come to rest precariously on the Prime Minister's declaration of his intention to obtain weighty legal opinion on the matter before taking further action on the non-European franchises on which the issue had been raised.

248

When the new session met in January 1949, the first long session of the new Government, this opinion was duly presented to the members of Parliament. Not unexpectedly, it supported in full the Government's point of view. Dr. Malan and his Party had been given the green light to go ahead. Yet the speech from the throne, precise on other aspects of the Government's plans to pursue apartheid, made no mention of any pending legislation on either the African or the Coloured franchise. Now that they had had some time to consider the demands of the situation, we were told, the Ministers would take the necessary steps, by means of legislation as well as by administrative measures, to give effect to their policy of segregation, and the framework began to appear in a Bill for national registration, obviously to be applied on a racial basis, and that Bill to prohibit mixed marriages which had long been one of the main planks in the Nationalist platform.

What did this silence on what had already become the focal point of discussion on the nature of apartheid mean? The answer clearly lay in another weakness in the position of the governing party which had been publicly revealed in the recess. This was the attitude of Mr. Havenga to both the questions which were now in issue—the objective of political apartheid and the method by which it was proposed to establish it. The new Government was a coalition governing with an all-over majority of five votes, but with the control of nine votes in Mr. Havenga's hands, and Mr. Havenga had let it be known in the recess that he was not happy about his colleagues' intentions in either of these regards: that in fact he could not see his way to going along with his new colleagues on either of them, and without his support, even a favourable legal opinion was useless to Dr. Malan and his followers.

Each of the two issues involved was bound to have a highly emotional content for Mr. Havenga. The Representation of Natives Act, which was the immediate target of Malanite policy, had been the work of his own beloved leader, General Hertzog. It had been carried through only after years of effort, reaching conclusion through the accident of fusion that had provided General Hertzog with the majority laid down in the Constitution. Was Mr. Havenga now to turn his back on all that for the sake of a Party which had fought that same leader for so many years, and which had broken him in the end? True, he himself had come back into politics through that same Party; but only when the other side had failed to offer him an accommodation which there were plenty of reasons for believing would have suited both his temper and his political attitudes better. Whatever the actual position in this regard, faced in these first months with problems which had obviously not been discussed at the time when his agreement with Dr. Malan and his Party had been entered into, he felt it incumbent upon him to explain to his own supporters when they met in conference at Brakpan in December of the election year, 1948, that, while he did not accept the Opposition's contention that the entrenchments in the Constitution remained legally binding, he could not be party to the dissolution of the 1936 settlement which our proposed abolition from the House of Assembly implied, unless there was at least a substantial majority to support it and to give any new settlement some guarantee of stability. He was to explain more fully later that he could not agree that Dr. Malan and his Party had got that substantial majority that would justify their claim to a mandate in this regard.

It was against this background, and clearly relying on the Government's inability to move so long as this dilemma was unresolved, that General Smuts returned to the attack in the first days of the 1949 session with a renewed demand for a guarantee that the Government would not 'abrogate and alter the existing Parliamentary rights of the Native and Coloured peoples without a direct and unmistakable mandate from the people of the Union and by a two-thirds Parliamentary majority as provided by the entrenched clauses of the Constitution',[1] and condemned the suggestion that the verdict of the people in the pending Provincial election should be used as a yardstick in respect of this national issue.

In the debate which followed, much of the already familiar ground was re-traversed, with, to us, a not very encouraging emphasis by both leaders on the wide area of common ground between the two major parties in the matter of social and residential separation, and even of white supremacy. This gave Dr. Malan a manœuvring position from which to put up a long amendment in favour of a joint commission of members of both Houses of Parliament which should take into consideration the officially declared Native policy 'if any' of the various Parliamentary parties, the commission to report back to the Government in a year. It was a proposition which suited Mr. Havenga; at least it solved his immediate problem; but

[1] Hansard, Vol. 66, Col. 60 *et seq.*

for the Opposition it was vitiated, as all Dr. Malan's moves of this
kind were to be, by the condition that it should be an instruction to
the Commission to consider the application in detail, particularly in
respect of the Native question, of the principle of separation *as
approved by the electorate*.[1] This too Mr. Havenga could accept—was he
not to explain to the British people over the B.B.C. the following
year that apartheid was only 'a modified form' of that segregation
which had always been the policy of the Hertzog Nationalists? But
to the official Opposition, not unjustifiably suspicious of the interpretation that might and no doubt would be put upon this phrase, it
was unacceptable as seeking to commit them to a rigid pattern for
the future which General Smuts had already explicitly rejected in
general and in respect of political rights in particular.

If the Opposition had had any doubts as to the measure of the tie
intended, of the strength of the strait jacket into which the proposed
Commission was to be put, these must have been dispelled by the
speech which the Minister of Lands, Mr. Strydom, contributed to
the discussion. This followed a second incursion into the debate by
the Leader of the Opposition to explain his attitude to the Prime
Minister's proposition. Expressing his approval of the idea of a joint
Parliamentary Commission that might get the difficult matter of
colour out of the forefront of politics, where much heat made reasonable consideration impossible, General Smuts said he could not
accept the Prime Minister's contention that 'the main question'
that was, the principle of separation, had been decided, and that
only the method of implementation remained to be considered. The
Native problem was no longer what it had been twenty years before,
when General Hertzog laid down the lines of his segregation policy,
he argued. Then it had been the question of land, the desire to avoid
interpenetration on that front. Now it was the problem the Fagan
Commission had investigated, 'the millions of Natives who cannot
be sent to locations and reserves'. 'We recognise them as part of the
permanent population residing on the platteland and in the cities.
They are detribalised; they no longer belong to the reserves.' All
that must be brought under consideration, he contended, otherwise
the Commission would simply be 'a farce'.[2]

From there he proceeded to raise the question of the entrenchment again, and to argue that the legal aspect of the position should

[1] My italics.
[2] Hansard, Vol. 66, Col. 280 *et seq.*

be subordinated to the moral and practical aspects. Claiming to take his stand with Mr. Havenga, he repudiated the accusation levelled at him by Dr. Malan of attempting to impose 'the dead hand of the past' upon the country by his insistence on the maintenance of the terms of the entrenchment. It was not a case of immutability, he said. The Native franchise could be changed if the situation really were so dangerous or the people believed it to be so.

Finally, he noted that the Prime Minister's proposition had made no reference to the Coloured franchise. He assumed that this meant that 'it was not the intention to meddle with those rights while the proposed enquiry was in progress'—in effect, that the Government was going to forget about that at least for the time being, in which case he would not pursue the matter. He then made way for his lieutenant, Mr. Strauss, to put up a proposition that was in effect the Prime Minister's proposals for a Commission shorn of the unacceptable condition, and with an addendum making any abrogation or alteration of Native franchise rights dependent on the fulfilment of the conditions of the entrenchment.

These moves brought Mr. Strydom tearing into the debate to make it clear that, whatever anyone else might want in the way of an accommodation in the developing political argument, he wanted no compromises. To him the whole proposition of a Commission, certainly one that the Opposition might accept, was merely a stalling tactic. There were in fact fundamental differences between the two sides of the House which obviously in his opinion made any Commission that should include representatives of both a fruitless and pointless adventure. The two Parties differed at the very beginning on a basic issue, their conceptions of the South African community. 'The Leader of the Opposition advances the same proposition that our nation consists of all colours. To him I would say, "If that is your nation, or has become your nation, very well, but it is not our nation." ' And, if his leader was reluctant to draw the Coloured vote into the argument at that moment, for reasons which were soon to be revealed, he had no such reluctance in doing so to substantiate his thesis in that regard. 'I shall tell you what our policy is,' he declared. 'The Coloureds who are on the common roll with the Europeans today must be separated and given separate representation and the Native representatives in this House must be eliminated. The Indians must be regarded as outsiders who cannot enjoy political rights in South Africa.' As for the entrenched clauses, which seemed to stand in the way of the realisation of this policy, Mr. Strydom's attitude was simple if its logic was not particularly clear. To the Leader of the Opposition, these clauses were sacred and binding. But he (General Smuts) denied that the electorate was bound by its decision in the last election. 'He says the electorate must remain free and unfettered. When it suits him, the electorate must remain free and unfettered; on the other hand, when it suits him, the electorate must be regarded as bound by clauses which a handful of liberalists got into the Constitution in 1909'[1]—Mr. Strydom's generally typical reference to the Cape delegation at the National Convention, which included such eminent figures as Mr. J. X. Merriman, Mr. J. W. Sauer and Mr. F. S. Malan.

It fell to my lot to follow Mr. Strydom in this debate. On a topic which so closely affected the people we represented it was impossible for me to give a silent vote. At the same time, the terms of the argument and the terms of the amendment alike seemed to leave little common ground anywhere on which a liberal might take a stand. The suggestion of considering the possible implications of the segregation policy, even without the Nationalist Party's condition of its acceptance, ran counter to all my own views of the appropriate direction our ideas and efforts should be taking. However, while putting this on record, I declared my intention of supporting Mr. Strauss' proposition, not for itself but for the speech with which the Leader of the Opposition had prefaced it, which again underlined his determination to repudiate the retrogressive implications of Nationalist policy.

In due course the Government's proposition was carried—to prove an empty gesture, since the Opposition continued to refuse the conditions of the proposed Commission.

Where did we go from there? The Government was saved from its immediate dilemma by the departure of Dr. Malan to the Conference of Commonwealth Prime Ministers. This was the important conference which was to see the emergence of a republican India accepted as a continuing member of the family circle—a development which promoted the republican issue for a brief period from the background position it had tended to occupy since the election to the middle of the stage. The occasion was mainly notable for another of Mr. Strydom's outbursts, which suggested that the

[1] Hansard, Vol. 66, Col. 297 *et seq.*

coalition was having its own difficulties to meet, that some of Dr. Malan's younger men were in more of a hurry than, in all the circumstances, was convenient to the leaders. Dr. Malan had returned from London much impressed with the working of the Commonwealth machine, to tell Parliament that while a republic was still the aim of his Party, the objective was not an urgent one, and in any case, there seemed obvious reasons why South Africa, even as a republic, should remain within the Commonwealth now that that was a possibility. Mr. Strydom no doubt startled his leader as much as he startled the Oppositions when he again launched into the debate to affirm and reaffirm the intention of the Party to move towards the republican objective as rapidly as circumstances would permit, and that a republic outside the Commonwealth.

For the moment it seemed as if this might prove a distraction from the colour issue. In answer to a question put to him before his departure to London, Dr. Malan had said one piece of legislation must be put through Parliament that session; that was the Coloured Franchise Bill. That matter had perforce now to be cleared up. Was that merely a piece of bravado? In all the circumstances, how could it be done? Again the Prime Minister was saved by his London visit. In reply to further questions by General Smuts himself, he said his time had been so fully occupied by his responsibilities in that connection that it had not been possible for him to devote the necessary personal attention to this matter. But lest there should be any suggestion of weakening (which the obvious stresses within the coalition ranks might suggest), he declared, 'I want to add that this measure, the contents of which have been before the voters in this country for a long time and on which two elections have been fought (a reference to the recently completed Provincial elections, which had not noticeably strengthened the Government ranks), will be introduced. The Government regards it as a mandate from the electors to do so. As far as I personally, and as far as my Party is concerned, we regard ourselves as compromised towards the voters with regard to this matter.'[1] He undertook to see that the Bill would be introduced at the earliest moment in the following session, when, he said, they hoped to be able to carry it.

Clearly Dr. Malan was banking on negotiating some agreement with his partner that would solve his problem within his own Party

[1] Hansard, Vol. 68, Col. 6366.

and enable him to make the challenge to the Opposition which Mr. Strydom and his friends obviously longed for. In this he was not successful. What the negotiations produced was an agreement between himself and Mr. Havenga in which he undertook to do nothing for one year in the matter of the Native and Coloured franchises, while Mr. Havenga declared that except on the matter of the franchise, he stood foursquare with his partner on the general policy of segregation.

Exploiting the consequent inability of the Prime Minister to carry through the threat to proceed with his Coloured Franchise Bill, when the new session met in January 1950, General Smuts opened the next phase in the argument—destined to be his last contribution to the discussion. This he did with a challenge to the Government to resign, as being unable to fulfil what it claimed to be its mandate from the electorate, the political segregation of the Africans and the Coloureds. Dr. Malan, no doubt feeling the burden both of his years and of his problems, seemed extremely reluctant to meet the challenge. For three days, his back-benchers skirmished on the outskirts of it, all anxious to talk, but on anything other than this particular topic, and when eventually he entered the debate, it was with one of the most ponderous speeches it had ever been my lot to listen to from him. Replying to a contention by General Smuts that race relations had deteriorated seriously and were continuing to deteriorate, he agreed that that was the case; and then, with that instinct for attack which had always been his strength, he proceeded to prove to his own satisfaction that the sole cause of all this was the Leader of the Opposition who had so consistently opposed the ideas and the ideals which had inspired and guided the whole progress of Afrikanerdom.

With various other deviations, he came in due course to the question of apartheid and the non-European franchise. Emphasising the fact that the agreement between him and Mr. Havenga in this regard was for one year only, he now proceeded to argue that in fact the political aspect of apartheid was a very small part of the whole system of apartheid.[1] What apartheid was really concerned about was the day to day contacts of the races. That was an open field in which the Government were very busy, and where already consider-

---

[1] Exactly the opposite of the case Dr. Verwoerd came to make as physical apartheid failed to materialise; and Mr. M. C. Botha as Minister of Bantu Administration and Development is making again in 1968 in the same situation. See pp. 331, 463, 466–7.

able progress had been made. To their earlier record of separation on trains and in post offices, their population register and their legislation against mixed marriages, had they not this session added a Group Areas Act providing for separate residential areas defined on a race basis, and an amendment to an Immorality Act of 1928 which extended the range of illegal extra-marital relations of whites with Africans to such relations with members of any non-White group?

Inevitably the most important and tensely awaited speech of this debate was Mr. Havenga's. So far in the history of this conflict of policies and principles, while he might be said to be the key figure, practically all we knew of his approach to the issues at stake was his Brakpan speech, a few words in support of it in the previous session of Parliament, and the joint statement which embodied the standstill agreement between himself and Dr. Malan. Uneasily aware that great pressures were being brought to bear upon him to accept the line which Dr. Malan had taken and which Mr. Strydom was clearly determined to see should not be retracted, all the Oppositions alike were concerned to get out into the open just what the debating points in the struggle for intra-party accommodation were.

He too seemed reluctant to yield to the repeated requests from Opposition benches to state his own case. Eventually, he did so as the debate was fading to its close.[1] He then proceeded to declare his acceptance of the policy of the Nationalist Party in regard to both Africans and Coloureds except in one respect: that was in the matter of political rights. Apartheid, he said, had always been the policy of the old Nationalist Party and of General Hertzog, although it had been called segregation. He had therefore no difficulty in supporting what the Malanite Nationalists proposed generally in that regard. But he had certain differences from them on the subject of the franchise. He then proceeded to reveal something of the course of the manœuvres that had been going on between the two groups within the Government ranks. In the previous year, he said, the difference had been over the declared intention of Dr. Malan and his followers to abolish the Native representation in the House of Assembly. This year, it was on their proposal to put the Cape Coloured voters on a separate voters' roll. He viewed with anxiety any tampering with the existing political rights of any group in the community. For himself, he did not approve of such tampering, and if it were to be

[1] Hansard, Vol. 70, Col. 356 *et seq.*

done at all, he considered that it should only be done by the votes of a substantial majority of the electorate—which he again showed he did not consider the Government Party to possess, even with his nine votes.

He further explained by implication that, while he would not regard the removal of the Coloured voters from the common roll as in itself an interference with the established political rights of the Coloured people (a statement which came as a considerable shock to some of us), any limitations such as Dr. Malan and his friends proposed to impose upon the European members who would represent the Coloured voters when they were so separated would, he considered, constitute such an interference, and as such he would not be party to it.

This was a reference to the proposal that the members who should represent the Coloureds should have no right to vote on matters of confidence, of war and peace, or indeed on any other major issue affecting Europeans. It had arisen out of our vote in favour of participation in the war and had been strongly reinforced by the experience of the new Government in the Senate, where it was having the utmost difficulty in carrying through its contentious legislation. Indeed, Mr. Strydom had already been very vocal on this subject— and very irate. In the no-confidence debate in the beginning of the 1949 session he had raged: 'The Native representatives must not have the power to frustrate a White Government or to overthrow it. Let us see what the position is today. The Senate, the Other Place, is in a position to throw out every measure introduced by this Government, a Government which represents White South Africa. Then they (the Opposition) talk about the will of the people. Can it be said that the will of the people is the decisive factor in the Other Place? The decisive factor there is not the will of the people but the will of the four Native Representatives. Can we tolerate a continuance of this state of affairs, where the representatives of Non-Europeans are able to say which laws can be enacted in South Africa and which laws cannot be enacted?'[1] Mr. Strydom's own reply to that question was already written into the programme of the Nationalist Party. It was this proposition which Mr. Havenga found it impossible to accept, much to Mr. Strydom's displeasure, if the report of a speech of his delivered to his constituents was a fair reflection of his attitude. There he was credited with saying that Mr.

[1] Hansard, Vol. 66, Col. 302.

R

Havenga's statement at Brakpan gave every reason for disappointment. The Nationalists had fought the election as allies. Because the
leader of the Afrikaner Party and his followers had stated that there
were no differences of principle between them and the Malanites,
certain seats had been allotted to them.

Having stated his position, Mr. Havenga went on to review the
suggestion of an all-party Commission. He strongly urged General
Smuts to reconsider his decision in that regard. Obviously in a
difficult position and under great pressure in this new alliance, he
was anxiously pursuing the one course that might offer him some
hope of escape.

General Smuts' reply was equally obviously designed to try to
encourage Mr. Havenga to maintain the stand he had taken.
Referring to Dr. Malan's argument that in going ahead with plans
to rehabilitate the reserves and to solve the housing problem, the
Government was pursuing apartheid, he said those were not subjects on which there was any difference of opinion between the
Parties. The real difference was on the political issue. It was on that
issue that the plan for an all-party Commission had broken down
the previous year. The Prime Minister had not been willing then to
give a guarantee that the provision in the Constitution for a two-
thirds majority of both Houses as the essential condition of any
change in the non-European franchise would be respected, and on
this General Smuts and his Party could not compromise.

5

Separate Representation of Voters Bill

The recess of 1950[1] saw a series of important developments for the
following session of Parliament to meet. In the death of General
Smuts, it removed one highly significant figure from the political
scene, while the promotion of Dr. Jansen to the position of Governor-
General opened the doors of the Cabinet and the House of Assembly
to the man who was progressively to move into a more dominating
position in the life of the country than any political figure since
Union—Dr. Hendrik Verwoerd. And that there had been much,
and much more successful manœuvring within the Government
ranks was reflected in the first item in the legislative programme
announced on the opening day of the 1951 session of Parliament on
January 19th in the speech from the throne—a Bill to give Separate
Representation to Coloured voters in Parliament. Somehow the
grounds of difference between Mr. Havenga and Dr. Malan had
been resolved so that the Government now found itself in a position
to challenge the Oppositions in regard to both the Coloured Vote
and the entrenchments in the Constitution—for it had already been
made clear that if the Government should put a Bill of this kind
through Parliament in the ordinary way, the official Opposition
would contest the validity of the measure in the courts.

With this situation shaping up, the session began in an atmosphere
of increasing tension that was both reflected in and heightened by
the very first move on the Parliamentary scene. This occurred even
before the official opening with its challenging announcement which
merely confirmed already prevalent report. When the lower House
assembled for preliminary business before proceeding to the Senate
for the formal opening of the session by the new Governor General,
it was faced with the choice of a new Speaker. Mr. Tom Naudé,
who had filled this office since the advent of the Nationalist
Government, had elected to abandon the Chair in favour of a seat
in the Cabinet.

The Government, with an extremely limited choice of members
with the legal training then generally regarded as the appropriate

[1] From June 25th, 1950 to January 19th, 1951.

qualification for the incumbent of this important office, nominated Mr. J. H. Conradie, a member of the Cape Provincial bar who had entered Parliament in 1938. The United Party, now under the leadership of Mr. Strauss, took the unusual step of putting up a counter nomination. They proposed Mr. A. Trollip, an old United Party member who had graduated from the Provincial Council to become Deputy Speaker and Chairman of Committees in the Smuts Government.[1] Mr. Strauss, speaking for his Party, justified this move on a number of grounds. Of these the most important was that Mr. Conradie had already declared his views on the validity of the entrenchment on various occasions and in the most emphatic terms. A further consideration of importance was that the Minister of Finance, Mr. Havenga, on whose views so much depended in this constitutional struggle, in reply to a challenge by Mr. Strauss himself on an earlier occasion that the removal of the Coloured voters from the common roll would involve a deprivation of rights, had replied that 'the Speaker will have to rule on that, and if he rules that it is so, I shall refuse to vote for such a measure'.[2]

Here was one of those unexpected situations in which minorities are called upon to make up their minds forthwith as to the best tactics and the right choice for themselves. Besides ourselves, on this occasion this meant the Labour Party. Facing the challenge, Mr. Christie, with a team of comparatively new members behind him, declared the intention of his Party to take no side in this argument. To me, the whole issue appeared closely related to the constitutional and political struggle in which my emotions, and the interests of my constituents, were very deeply engaged, and I felt it incumbent on me, therefore, to take a stand in the matter. Fortunately my two new colleagues[3] agreed with me, and I was able then to state a position in which we all concurred. The Prime Minister had expressed his indignation at the counter-nomination, which he stigmatised as making history in South Africa—but history on the downward path. I argued that it was because Parliament was making history that it was of the first importance that every member of the House should make up his mind on what seemed the major issues of the day. One of these major issues was who should sit in the Chair of the House. The matters that would come before Mr. Speaker were

[1] Mr. Trollip subsequently joined the Nationalist Party and became Minister of Labour under Dr. Verwoerd.
[2] Hansard, Vol. 74, Col. 9.
[3] Mr. W. Stuart, Transkei, and Mr. Sam Kahn, Cape Western.

of a fundamental nature affecting the whole basis of the Constitution. In the circumstances, it was most important that the incumbent of this office should be a man in whom all could have the most complete confidence. In this regard, apart from Mr. Trollip's experience as Deputy Speaker over several years, the deciding factor here was that the Government nominee had often and emphatically declared his own conviction in regard to these important subjects. Like Mr. Strauss, I did not wish to suggest that he could not divest himself of his opinions and achieve the objectivity and impartiality required by the position for which he was being nominated, but 'it is asking too much of an honourable member to establish that position in the Session before us and on the issue which is going to be the fundamental issue of the Session, and to convince the public that he has succeeded in that time in achieving that measure of objectivity which is essential to confidence'.[1]

Mr. Conradie was duly elected to an office which he was to hold through many vicissitudes, personal as well as public, for nearly ten years. Over those years he was to claim on more than one occasion to me personally that he had always treated me well—this without any reference to, and possibly even recollection of my opposition to his candidature. Certainly he appointed me to his Standing Rules and Orders Committee, which none of his predecessors would do— a committee consisting of the leaders and chief whips of all the parties which is responsible, with Mr. Speaker, for the conduct of the House. It was a concession to our existence as a statutory minority in Parliament which I much appreciated. It was undoubtedly a gesture of good will and good intention that managed to survive some quite considerable challenges from time to time on the floor of the House —for Mr. Conradie was not a strong disciplinarian, a circumstance which became both more conspicuous and more important as the gap between the two sides of the House widened and as the attitude and character of the governing side became more and more inflexible, bringing in its train serious deteriorations in relations. These developing circumstances affected us as Native Representatives particularly harshly since, as the smallest group in the House at any time, we were forced to accept the last seats on the Opposition benches. This brought us immediately into the vicinity of the tail end of the Government ranks, and farthest away from the Speaker's chair, where it was extremely easy for those who wished to do so to

[1] Hansard, Vol. 74, Col. 16.

carry on a barrage of interruptions that could amount to sabotage without the Speaker being fully aware of what was going on. And as tempers frayed with the prolonged constitutional fight, he seemed less willing to believe the nature and extent of the difficulties I, and others, in our corner of the House had to contend with from the sometimes younger, always less responsible members of the Government Party. One of the more uncomfortable experiences of a quite lengthy experience of Parliament which, in its later phase, threw up all too many difficult situations, was the occasion of a motion of censure on Mr. Conradie for his handling of the duties of his office in which the special difficulties with which I personally had to contend in the course of my duties were made a particular case by Mr. Harry Lawrence, Mr. Strauss' first lieutenant, and Mr. Hepple, Leader of the Labour Party, who was my neighbour for a number of years and who, during that time, was nearly as continuous a victim of these trying attentions as I was.

All this still lay in the future, one of the side products of the events that were just getting under way. The matter of immediate concern was the intention of the Government to go ahead with the removal of the Coloured voters from the common roll by way of simple Parliamentary majority, with Mr. Havenga's support and consent. Recess negotiations had borne fruit for Dr. Malan and his team in a new Malan-Havenga agreement. Since this was naturally to prove one of the main talking points in the struggle that was to follow, it may be appropriate, and useful, to deal with it as Mr. Havenga himself dealt with it in what was moving from the battle of the franchise to the battle of the Constitution. The House—and the galleries—certainly found it an absorbing story.

Before that stage was reached, however, the preliminary hurdle, already foreshadowed in the nomination for the office of Speaker, had to be surmounted. The Prime Minister's motion for leave to introduce the Bill in the House of Assembly was immediately followed by a call by the Leader of the Opposition for the Speaker's ruling on the legality of this motion. In a tense and highly strained atmosphere, Mr. Strauss presented a carefully prepared and closely reasoned case for the acceptance of the continuing validity of the entrenchment in the Constitution, necessitating the introduction of any measure such as that proposed by the Prime Minister in a joint sitting of both Houses of Parliament. It was a case that called for a fully considered reply, and the debate was accordingly adjourned to give the new Speaker the requisite time for the purpose. In due course, his decision, upholding the view of the Government in the matter, was presented to the House, supported by an imposing list of authorities who, over the years since the passage of the Statute of Westminster round which the whole argument turned, had taken a view contrary to that presented by Mr. Strauss, now Leader of the Opposition, on behalf of the Opposition. Mr. Conradie prefaced his argument with the statement that he was not in the position of a judge having to deliver a legal opinion, that his duty was to satisfy himself that any motion brought into the House was in order. He believed this one to be in order. One point that it had been suggested he might rule upon, however, he felt he was not called upon to decide; that was whether the proposed measure involved a derogation of the rights of the Coloured people. This clearly left Mr. Havenga with the responsibility for making up his own mind on this aspect of the case.

The legal point having been given against him, not unexpectedly in all the circumstances, the Leader of the Opposition proceeded to the political battle. Immediately taking the point that, while Mr. Speaker had ruled that the Bill might be introduced in the ordinary way, there was nothing to say that it must be introduced in this way, he proceeded to challenge the intention of the Bill as a subversion of the solemn compact of Union and a repudiation of pledges repeatedly given to the Coloured people, and the manner of its introduction as a betrayal of the solemn undertakings given on the occasion of the resolutions of both Houses in 1931. In the course of his speech he issued particular challenges to Mr. Havenga as having been party to both the promises that had been made by his leader, General Hertzog, to the Coloured people and to the acceptance of the continuing validity of the entrenchments evidenced in the procedure adopted by General Hertzog in 1936.

Much stirred by these challenges, as he always was by any suggestion of lack of integrity on his part, Mr. Havenga proceeded to make his case to a waiting House and country—for of all the personalities involved in this developing crisis, Mr. Havenga was not only one of the most significant politically, holding the balance of power in this tense situation; he was also probably the most respected, respected not only for his own probity but for his high standard of political and personal conduct, standards for which there is less and less place in extremist politics.

On his own showing, the Nationalist victory of 1948 had indeed found him unprepared for the problems he had immediately to meet. True, his allies had gone to election on the cry of abolishing the Native representation in the House of Assembly and generally tampering with the 1936 settlement in respect of the Native franchise; but it would appear that he had never regarded this as a matter of immediate moment. As General Smuts had continually contended, the question of the method of procedure had not been at issue at any point in the election. The unexpected victory, however, and the narrow majority which made it so very insecure, undoubtedly alike encouraged extremist demand in Dr. Malan's Party for immediate action in this regard which would have the advantage of getting rid of three hostile votes in the Assembly and curbing the activities of four members of the Senate.[1] Faced with this situation as soon as the new Government began to consider its first legislative programme, he took up the position which he reported to the Conference of his own Party at Brakpan in December of that (1948) election year.

This, as he explained, was the background to the 1949 session, when it had been a question of the Native franchise.[2] Later, he said, the question of the Coloured franchise was raised. On this he had told Dr. Malan that he saw nothing wrong in separate political rights for the Coloured people. He considered such a scheme might have some advantages for them. Here he would seem to have been swayed by the settlement General Hertzog had made on the Native franchise rather than by the promises made to the Coloured people. And he had been influenced, as so many on that side of the House had been, by unfortunate reflections on the use and abuse of the Coloured vote in a posthumously published book by Mr. B. K. Long, for many years editor of the *Cape Times* and, later, a United Party member of the House of Assembly.[3] But he had informed Dr. Malan that he could not accept the Nationalist Party's proposals in that regard, namely that the number of representatives of the Coloureds should be fixed as the representation of Natives had been fixed, that was without regard to the number of voters, and that the powers of

[1] Who at that moment practically held the balance of power in the upper chamber. cf. p. 222. See Mr. Strydom, quoted p. 257.
[2] Incidentally, his stand on this first round was in fact to have the effect of putting the question of the Native franchise into cold storage for the rest of Dr. Malan's time as Prime Minister and beyond.
[3] *In Smuts' Camp.*

these representatives should be limited. He also had objections to the suggestion that the proposed representation in the Cape Provincial Council should be confined, like the Parliamentary representation, to Europeans, the Coloured people having long had rights of election to both Provincial and municipal bodies in the Cape.[1] All these provisions he considered amounted to a derogation of rights, and as such he could not accept them. On the basis of their discussions on these points, he and Dr. Malan had issued their joint Statement in December 1949, in which they agreed upon the principle of separate representation of the Coloured people of the Cape Province in Parliament and in the Cape Provincial Council, but disagreed both on the permanent limitation of the numbers of the Coloured representatives 'as well as in respect of the necessity of observing the provisions known as the entrenched clauses in the South Africa Act as advocated by Mr. Havenga in his well-known Brakpan speech'. In the circumstances, 'since the Herenigde Nasionale Party' (Dr. Malan's Party) 'did not have at its disposal the majority necessary to pass the proposed legislation, there would be no legislation on that matter in 1950'. For the rest, the statement had declared that there was no difference between the two parties in the coalition on Colour policy generally, both alike being committed to a policy of apartheid, 'the old familiar policy of segregation'.[2]

Mr. Havenga went on from there to insist that he did not, never had and never would accept the proposition that the mere removal of the Coloureds from the common voters' roll would of itself constitute a derogation of their pre-existing rights. 'That would mean that such legislation was in conflict with clause 35 of the Act of Union', which, he implied, would put it out of court for him.

This carried his story down to 1950. Thereafter he had gone overseas—when he gave the broadcast on the B.B.C. to which reference has already been made,[3] in which he explained that apartheid was 'a modified form of segregation'—a statement the Opposition was to endeavour to build on later. On his return he had had further talks with Dr. Malan 'to discuss whether an agreement could be reached which would meet his demands'. Agreement had in fact been reached, and another joint statement had been issued, in which he and Dr. Malan 'expressed the candid opinion and conviction that

---

[1] He found it possible to accept this later.
[2] Hansard, Vol. 75, Col. 4491 et seq.
[3] P. 256.

no deprivation or diminution of political rights was involved and that therefore it would not be in conflict with clause 35 of the Constitution'. The result was this Bill now. It had then been said that he wished to hide behind the Speaker. That was not the case. He had his fixed opinion on the matter. But he had said that if the Opposition could get a ruling from Mr. Speaker that this legislation clashed with the provisions of the entrenched clauses, then he would not vote for it. Since the Speaker had not seen fit to rule on this matter, he had to rely on his own judgment and conviction and to consult his own conscience—which had all convinced him that the case was a good one and one he could support.

While it might be difficult to follow the logic of Mr Havenga's case—and he was to hear plenty of the arguments against it in the days that followed—it was easy to understand the pressures that had been brought to bear on him. Having a genuine dislike of any suggestion of reducing franchise rights, as he declared at the time of his Brakpan speech, and entertaining a great respect for Parliament and democratic procedures, he must always have been uneasy about the intentions of his colleagues of the Herenigde Party. There was this to be said for the point to which he had now come in agreement with them. He himself, I had reason to believe, considered that the representation provided by the Representation of Natives Act had been a great thing for the African electorate.[1] Certainly he always treated me with the courtesy and consideration he accorded to all his opponents. Both in my early days when he was Minister of Finance in the Hertzog Government, and in these later days of the Malan Government, he gave not only polite, but sympathetic and often practical consideration to any case I had to make to him. Indeed, on more than one occasion he declared that he made a point of hearing all I had to say on behalf of the people I was there to represent. While Dr. Malan could say that Native representation had only had a nuisance value, and rarely found time or occasion to reply to any case we might have to make, to Mr. Havenga we were members of Parliament with an important duty to fufil and, as such, were entitled to be treated with the respect which our office—and his— dictated. That at least was my personal experience.

If this was in fact his attitude to Native representation, a similar representation for Coloureds might indeed seem to him likely to serve them well. And he could now comfort himself with the reflec-

[1] See p. 289, Mr. Havenga's statement to me.

tion that he had both saved Native representation and had rescued the proposed Coloured representation—and Parliament—from the prospect of second-class members confined within the narrow limits that Mr. Strydom and his kind had planned for it.[1]

It has always seemed to me that if the major tragedy of our political history in my generation was the clash over the war which broke the old United Party along a 'racial' line, perhaps even more disastrous on the domestic front was the re-entry of Mr. Havenga on to the political stage through the Nationalists and not through the United Party. It may well be asked, was that ever a serious alternative? My firm belief is that on Mr. Havenga's side, it was a very serious alternative; the failure, I believe, was on the other side. An old political war horse, it was inevitable that he should want to come back into the field, and after General Hertzog's death, and particularly after the 1943 election which gave an overwhelming vote in favour of Parliament's decision in 1939 on our entry into the war, I have no doubt that he could and would gladly have re-entered the field on the basis of the people's decision, the *volkswil* of which we were to hear so much after the Nationalist victory in 1948. Being myself in opposition even in United Party days and always independent, I had little personal non-political contact with the members of the Government and therefore little knowledge of the inner workings of the Party; but my convictions in this regard are based on an extremely interesting conversation with Mr. Havenga himself. The occasion was an accidental meeting in the lounge of a Johannesburg hotel where I had gone to meet friends. The date as I remember it was sometime in 1944. I found it easy to establish friendly relations with one who, having been in an exalted position, was now nearer my own level in life. We exchanged a greeting and he made some politely encouraging remarks about my own Parliamentary progress which scarcely seemed to have begun when he left us. I then ventured to ask him what I knew many people were interested to know the answer to—when he was coming back to us, meaning, when was he returning to the Party he had left and to Parliament? His retort was immediate and, I felt, tinged with some not unnatural bitterness. 'Oh, they don't want me,' he said, referring to his former colleagues. I said I thought that was a very great pity, and had perforce to leave the matter there.

I had occasion some years later to tell this story to my friend, Mrs.

[1] Dr. Malan had made concessions to him on both the points at issue, see pp. 264-5.

Bertha Solomon, then representing the Johannesburg constituency
of Jeppe. She then told me that she had had much the same conversation with Mr. Havenga, who was Minister of Finance when she
entered Parliament in 1938. In due course she had repeated the
conversation to Mr. Hofmeyr and asked him why the leaders
of the Party did not get Mr. Havenga back with them. To
this Mr. Hofmeyr's reply was, 'Why should we? What has he to
give?'

If this was indeed the attitude of the old United Party leaders, it
reflected signally bad judgment on their part. I don't think either
General Smuts or Mr. Hofmeyr would have found it easy to make
an accommodation with General Hertzog's erstwhile lieutenant, and
neither proved good tacticians on the party political front. In due
course Mr. Havenga was to prove an equally bad tactician, surrendering the position of power which he held in a coalition by merging
his forces with his numerically much stronger ally, to become merely
one of the Party's Provincial leaders. It was a surrender that left him
no bargaining power when Dr. Malan decided to withdraw from
the Parliamentary scene, hoping to pass the reins of government into
his hands. The Premiership fell not to him but to Mr. Strydom,
leading him soon to follow Dr. Malan into retirement, a disappointed and disillusioned man, denied the final prize of political
life which I believe he would have used to try to reintegrate the
forces making for unity in South Africa: with what success against
those which seemed determined to drive in an opposite direction
it is now fruitless to speculate.

At that moment, he had been able to engineer an accommodation
with those forces over the matter of the Coloured vote which he felt
he could accept, and which had brought us to the point we had now
reached. How serious the implications were, and were to become,
was reflected in Dr. Malan's own contribution to this debate on the
motion for leave to introduce his Bill. The House, Dr. Malan said,
had now had the Speaker's ruling, with which he and his Party
agreed. The Opposition did not agree with it. They had said they
would contest it in the Courts. He considered that if they did not
agree with it, they should have challenged it in a substantive motion,
and presumably have accepted the decision of Parliament. It was a
proposition that would obviously have smoothed the way of the
Government. If the Opposition chose instead to go to the Courts,
and if by any chance the Courts should decide to declare an Act of

Parliament invalid, that, he said, would be a serious matter for Parliament and for the country. It would mean the undermining of Parliamentary sovereignty. It would mean that a judicial authority was assuming powers belonging exclusively to the legislature. He hoped no crisis of that kind would arise in the Union of South Africa, and concluded, 'I do not expect for a moment that it will happen.' And having thus disposed of 'the legal question', he proceeded to elaborate a case which had been made often before and would be made often again, that the Act of Union was an Act of an imperial Parliament containing conditions imposed upon South Africa from without at the inspiration of people who were strangers to South Africa in spirit if not in fact. He then went on to discuss the accusation that the removal of the Coloured voters from the common roll, on which they shared in the election of the members returned to the House of Assembly by the Cape Province, and their limitation to four special 'Coloured' constituencies, involved a derogation of rights for the Coloured voters. He repudiated the accusation with this surprising argument: 'Today the Coloured vote can in several constituencies be the deciding vote as between Europeans. That is all the Coloured people now have to give up.'[1] He went on to quote that statement of General Hertzog in regard to the political rights of the Coloured people, the terms of which had seemed to me at the time to hold dangerous possibilities, namely that 'the Government will resist any proposal to change their franchise in a manner that would diminish those rights'. Having persuaded Mr. Havenga that this Bill would not do this, he had naturally persuaded himself as well.

When the Bill was released to Parliament and the public, it appeared to have met both Mr. Havenga's demands. Its starting point was the establishment of two voters' rolls in place of the pre-existing common roll, one for Whites and one for Coloureds. It then provided for the division of the Cape Province into four constituencies each of which might return a European to the House of Assembly to represent the interests of the Coloured people. It further provided for one nominated Senator and two elective Provincial Councillors. All these 'Coloured' representatives (all by law Europeans) were to enjoy all the rights and privileges of other members of their respective bodies except for the limitation imposed upon us as Native Representatives of not voting for the elected Senators. It went on to

[1] Hansard, Vol. 75, Col. 4583 *et seq.*

include a complex provision under which the House of Assembly
Coloured representatives should at all times be maintained at the
same ratio of four to 150, the then number of members representing
white constituencies within the Union of South Africa, a somewhat
curious concession to Mr. Havenga's demand that it should not be
static as Native representation was. On the basis of these concessions,
the two Parties in the Government were prepared to go forward
together.

The later stages in the passage of the Bill through the two Houses
of Parliament were chiefly notable for the revelation of the pressures
the Government was prepared to exert to achieve its objective. It
had a mandate to fulfil, it claimed, and it was going to be loyal to
that mandate. And already we were learning that it would do what
it set out to do, no matter how extravagant and dangerous it might
appear to be, and no matter what the degree of opposition aroused in
its course. Indeed, opposition seemed simply the great challenge, to
be met in a progressively uncompromising spirit. This took the form
early of an extensive use of the closure and the guillotine, becoming
ever more extensive as the hardening of party differences made
adjustments of the time of debates by agreement ever more difficult.
Thus, when the protracted struggle over the introduction of the Bill
had been decided, the Oppositions found themselves faced with
imposed restrictions on the time of each of the stages of the Bill
which, worked out on the basis of numbers, was to provide us, as
representatives of the mass of the population, and vitally concerned
over the widening circle of colour discrimination, with some eighteen
minutes between us to state our case on the second reading of the
Bill. Since we no longer presented quite the united front to the rest
of the world which had characterised our first ten years, we agreed
to use a few minutes each simply to put our stand on record as
against the Government and what it stood for as represented in this
measure, drawing lots in good biblical style for the position of first
speaker.

While the Oppositions were bound to oppose the limitations imposed upon them, there was in fact little need for more protracted
discussion except as a demonstration of feeling, since it was now
clear that the final decision in the whole matter was to rest with the
Courts. So, using the time allowed it on the main issues in the Bill,
each group reiterated its opinion, in which the diminution of rights
bulked largely.

In due course, the Bill passed its third reading and emerged from the Senate to be signed by the Governor-General as a Statute of the Parliament of the Union of South Africa—and the next phase in the contest passed to the Courts on whose decision its further history—and ours—would depend.

6

The Constitutional Crisis: The High Court of Parliament

In the concluding days of the fight on the Separate Representation of Voters Bill, Mr. Strauss had challenged Dr. Malan to elaborate his statement that if the verdict of the Courts went against him in the case which the United Party seemed determined to take, the matter would be a serious one for Parliament and the country. What would he and his Party do in that eventuality? To this request he got no reply, and Parliament went into recess on June 22nd, 1951, in an atmosphere of uncertainty and anxiety reflected in mounting tension on both sides of the political line.

In the recess, two new developments took place, both of considerable political importance. The first of these was the emergence of the Torch Commando, a spontaneous coming together of ex-service men and women alarmed by the Prime Minister's statement and at the direction public affairs seemed to be taking under the Malan Government. It was a direction which seemed to threaten all that they had fought to defend. The purpose of the Commando was to focus specific attention on the dangers that seemed implicit in what it regarded as Dr. Malan's threats in the event of an unfavourable court decision, and to warn the Government against arbitrary and unconstitutional action. The second was that closing of the Government's ranks in the merging of Mr. Havenga's and Dr. Malan's forces to which reference has already been made. Dr. Malan's determination to unite, not the nation, but the Afrikaner people—the *volk*—the story of which he tells in his book *Afrikaner Volkseenheid en my ervaring op die pad daarheen*,[1] was beginning to bear fruit.

The immediate importance of these two events lay in the case then pending in the Appellate Division of the Supreme Court. On August 25th, 1951, application to test the validity of the Separate Representation of Voters Act had been filed with the registrar of the Cape Provincial Division of the Supreme Court in the name of four Coloured voters on the existing voters' roll. On October 25th, a

[1] Afrikaner Unity and my Experience on the way Thereto.

bench of three judges, the Judge-President, Mr. Justice J. E. de Villiers, Mr. Justice C. Newton Thompson and Mr. Justice G. Steyn, gave separate judgments dismissing the application on the ground that because of the decision of the Appellate Division in 1937, they were precluded from questioning the validity of an Act of Parliament. The Judge-President in giving his judgment, expressed doubt as to the correctness of the decision in 1937 but indicated that the Appellate Division alone could reconsider and possibly reverse that decision.

The appellants consequently lodged their appeal with the Appellate Division of the Supreme Court at Bloemfontein. The 1952 session of Parliament was already under way when the case came before a bench of five judges on February 20th.[1] On March 20th, the Chief Justice delivered his judgment to the Court in which he found in favour of the appellants' claim that the Separate Representation of Voters Act, 1946 of 1951, should be declared null and void and of no legal force or effect in that in passing it bicamerally in the ordinary way, Parliament had not complied with the provisions of the entrenched clauses in the Constitution. Having considered the question as to whether the final Court of Appeal should be prepared to reverse its own previous decisions and having come to the conclusion that it was bound to consider any reasons that might be advanced to show that any of these decisions was wrong, the Chief Justice proceeded to deal at length with the Government's case as it had been presented to the Court. This was the now familiar one that the entrenchments were no longer valid, having fallen away with the passage of the Statute of Westminster by the British Parliament and the Status Act by the Parliament of the Union of South Africa; alternatively that, if judgment should be found against it in this regard, the terms of the Separate Representation of Voters Act involved no discrimination or derogation of the rights of the Coloured people and thus did not fall within the ambit of the entrenchment.

Taking this latter point first, the question of the derogation of rights, against which the entrenchment had been designed to protect

[1] The bench consisted of the Chief Justice of the Union the Hon. A. v.d. S. Centlivres, Mr. Justice L. Greenberg, Mr. Justice O. D. Schreiner, Mr. Justice F. P. van den Heever and Mr. Justice O. H. Hoexter. The full bench consisted of six members, five of whom constituted a quorum. The sixth member, Mr. Justice Fagan, recused himself on this occasion as having been one of the judges on the bench in 1937.

S

the non-White voter, the Chief Justice noted that Council for the Government had contended that Act 46 of 1951 did not disqualify any voters from being registered on the ground of race or colour within the meaning of the entrenchment in Section 35 of the South Africa Act; it had merely altered the manner in which the House of Assembly should be constituted and constituencies demarcated. Leaving the qualifications for registration of voters untouched, it deprived no voter or potential voter of his right to be registered as a voter entitled to vote at the election of members of Parliament. Indeed so far as the Coloured people were concerned, the new law not only did not prejudice them but in fact it gave them more generous representation than they were strictly entitled to.

The Chief Justice found both these arguments unacceptable. Discounting as absurd any suggestion that the right which the entrenchment was designed to protect was merely that of 'physical registration without its consequences', he declared that, in fact, in removing whites and non-whites from the register and creating two new registers, one for Europeans and one for non-Europeans, there was no doubt in his mind that the Act disqualified both Europeans and non-Europeans from remaining on the register on the grounds of race or colour.

The argument in respect of the non-Europeans, that they were not prejudiced in that they were given more generous treatment than they were entitled to, he found to be illusory. The entrenchment in the Act of Union contained a guarantee of defined rights, not of their equivalents. The argument suggested that a spoliator might deprive me of my property with impunity if he was prepared to give something of equal or greater value in return.

Having thus found that the Act did involve a derogation of rights, the Chief Justice turned to the question of the continuing validity or otherwise of the entrenchments. Here the decision revolved round the contention that the Statute of Westminster had conceded to South Africa a sovereignty involving a revolutionary change in its constitution. Reviewing the history of the Statute, the Chief Justice recalled the procedure under which it had come to be passed. The Imperial Conference of 1926 had declared that the Dominions were autonomous countries within the British Empire, equal in status, in no way subordinate one to another in any aspect of their domestic or internal affairs, united by a common allegiance to the crown and freely associated as members of the British Commonwealth of

Nations. In 1929, a Conference on the operation of Dominion legislation and the merchant shipping legislation had drafted a Bill designed to give shape and content to what this declaration should mean in practice. Certain safeguards were introduced into the draft at the request of Canada, Australia and New Zealand in regard to certain parts of their constitutions. The report of that Conference however stated that similar considerations did not arise in respect of the Union of South Africa and the Irish Free State. The constitutions of both of these countries were framed on a unitary basis and both included complete legal powers of constitutional amendment. It was noted that in the case of South Africa, the exercise of these powers was conditioned only by the provisions of Section 152 of the South Africa Act, that was, by the entrenchments now at issue. The draft Bill was considered by the 1930 Imperial Conference which decided that resolutions from the Dominion Parliaments should be forwarded to the United Kingdom with a view to the enactment of the Bill. It was in conformity with this decision that the South African Parliament passed the resolution of 1931 which endorsed the lines of the Bill on the specific understanding (moved by General Smuts and accepted unanimously) that the proposed legislation should in no way derogate from the entrenched provisions of the South Africa Act, and in December 1931 the main provisions of the Statute became operative.

This review underlined the fact that the resolution of the South African Parliament in 1931 preceded the passage of the Statute of Westminster and gave South Africa's conditional endorsement to the proposal to enact it.

Against the contention put up by Counsel for the Government that no country emerging from the status of a colony into that of a Dominion within the framework of the British Constitution could be a sovereign state unless it had a sovereign Parliament functioning bicamerally in the same manner as the British Parliament, the Chief Justice could find no grounds for such a contention. He felt it would be surprising if the British Parliament, in enacting the Statute of Westminster which was agreed to by all the Dominions, had gone out of its way to change the constitution of a Dominion without a request from the Dominion concerned to do so. He had sought in vain for such a request from the Union of South Africa. On the contrary, the joint resolution of the two Houses of Parliament made it abundantly clear that the Union did not desire any amendment to its constitution and emphasised that the proposed Statute should in no way derogate from the entrenched clauses. He therefore could not accept that after the Statute of Westminster, South Africa found itself with a constitution radically altered. Nor could he agree that sovereignty was limited by the entrenchments. So far as the Status Act was concerned, it was agreed by both sides that it had in no way changed the position established by the Statute of Westminster.

There remained for consideration the question as to whether the earlier decision of the Appellate Division should be reversed. The Court had never decided that its judgments were final; and although it was reluctant to change them, there was a duty to do so where these seemed demonstrably wrong. Having come to a conclusion different from that reached in 1937, the Chief Justice felt it incumbent upon him to give a contrary verdict. He felt not merely justified but in duty bound to depart from the decision of that year. He felt justified in doing so by the circumstance that clearly the case had never been argued at that time. On that occasion, the whole case began at 10.5 a.m. and concluded at 11.25 a.m., a short argument which contrasted strangely with the argument on this occasion which had lasted six days and had seen a mass of material presented to the Court by Counsel on both sides.

Individually each of his colleagues on the bench endorsed his judgment in all respects.

On the day that the judgment was released, it was reported to the House of Assembly by Dr. Malan in terms that could not but revive and heighten every anxiety as to the nature and direction of the forces which were now in political control in the country. Dr. Malan's statement read as follows:[1]

'The judgment of the Appeal Court in the matter of the separate representation of voters which reverses its previous judgment of 1937, has created a constitutional position which cannot be accepted. Neither Parliament nor the people of South Africa will be prepared to acquiesce in a position where the legislative sovereignty of the lawfully and democratically elected representatives of the people is denied, and where an appointed judicial authority assumes the testing right, namely, the right to pass judgment on the exercise of its legislative powers by the elected representatives of the people— particularly since that judicial authority does not, or is not obliged to, act consistently.

[1] Hansard, Vol. 78, Cols. 3124–5.

'The situation which has now arisen, creates uncertainty and chaos, where certainty and order should exist. There are now two conflicting judgments of the Appeal Court in regard to a constitutional issue which is of the very greatest importance. So also, there is no certainty that a subsequent Court of Appeal may not perhaps reverse the latest decision, just as the present Appeal Court has reversed its previous decision of 1937. We will continue to drift on a sea of uncertainty, in connection with a matter in regard to which there should be certainty and finality. It is most undesirable that decisions of this kind should vary with a change in the composition of the Court, because this would certainly bring with it the danger of a "packed" Bench, as has happened in other countries.

'There is the further danger—which is no longer imaginary—that the prestige and authority of the highest Court is bound to suffer if it is called upon to adjudicate on political-constitutional questions of fundamental importance. No matter how carefully such a Court comports itself which sometimes demands an almost superhuman effort, it will be difficult for it to avoid altogether the appearance of prejudice, one way or another. It is not fair and right towards the Court to expose it to such a danger, particularly since its authority in general must necessarily be undermined thereby.

'It is thus clear that the situation which has now arisen is an intolerable one, and the Government would be grossly neglecting its duty towards the people and towards a democratically elected Parliament if steps are not taken to put an end to this confusing and dangerous situation. It is imperative that the legislative sovereignty of Parliament should be placed beyond any doubt, in order to ensure order and certainty. The Government will take the necessary steps to do its duty and will at the appropriate time announce such steps after the reasons for the judgment have been studied and considered.'

In effect, the adverse judgment of the Appellate Division had shifted the focal point of the struggle between the Oppositions and the Government from the question of franchises to the Constitution. On this issue Mr. Havenga, in any case no longer in a determining position of power, was to prove as emotionally committed as Dr. Malan himself or even as Mr. Strydom. How much that meant was immediately clear in a declaration by the four Provincial Leaders of the Party.[1] This followed on the heels of Dr. Malan's announcement

[1] Dr. Malan (Cape), Mr. Swart (O.F.S.), Mr. Strydom (Transvaal), Mr. Havenga (Natal). Statement released to the press on the evening of March 24th. See *Cape Times*, March 25th.

to Parliament, on the day after the publication of the judgment, that his Government was determined that the sovereignty of Parliament must be established, and the rule of the people recognised and fulfilled. It was significant both in terms and in tone. The essence of its message was contained in these words: 'The struggle for freedom . . . is being re-opened today. The United Party demands that the Union Parliament should not have complete control over its own laws . . . but that it shall remain subject to provisions contained in legislation by the British Parliament. The people of South Africa will not tolerate such a condition of constitutional slavery as that into which the United Party wants to thrust it. The properly elected Parliament, representing the people, will not tolerate it. This first statement by the chief Leader of the Nationalist Party (Dr. Malan) and his provincial leaders goes out as a war-cry and a message to all Nationalists and to all who support the Government. Stand together in this new phase of the struggle for freedom. That struggle will proceed to its conclusion. No compromise is possible on this question as stated. It is a clarion call to battle for the most sacred rights of a nation as it exercises them through Parliament. The action will be forceful and uncompromising.'

The story of the constitutional crisis which this declaration initiated is a record of the lengths to which the forces now in control were prepared to go to put their own stamp on the country, to make over South Africa in their own image of it. They were lengths which remained technically within the law. Were not Dr. Malan, under whom the process began, and his successor, Mr. Strydom, under whom it reached its climax, repeatedly to underline that, however forceful and uncompromising, they were strictly legal in their actions? But the ingenuity that was put into commission to bend the law to their will could not fail to have its effect on the character and position of Parliament itself.

It began that very session with the introduction of the High Court of Parliament Bill. This was a Bill designed, according to the Minister of the Interior, Dr. Dönges, in whose curious and contorted brain this fantastic measure was conceived, (a) to fill the gap created by the abolition of appeals to the Privy Council which had been one of the Government's first actions, (b) to resolve the uncertainty created by the conflicting judgments of 1937 and 1952 by the Appellate Division in the matter of the validity of the entrenchments in the Constitution, and (c) to meet the need to save the Appeal

Court, and indeed any of our Courts, from the merest suggestion of political interest which, it was claimed, any testing right must involve.[1]

While all these intentions were, in the context in which they were made, not only singularly unconvincing and unnecessary, the last had a peculiar air of cynicism in the light of the slighting and disparaging references which even senior members of the Government had not hesitated to make to the members of our highest Court. Of these, Mr. Sauer's 'six old men of Bloemfontein'[2] was only the most startling as coming from one who not only held high office in the Government, but who had long enjoyed an exceptional reputation as a Parliamentarian. It was possibly also the most revealing. Only less startling and revealing was the statement of another Cabinet Minister in the course of a debate in the House of Assembly, that the people of South Africa would in due course show the country that they were not prepared to be governed by five paid officials whether they were judges or not.[3] South Africa has always prided itself, and with justice, on the standard of its judiciary. To hear the highest Court in the land referred to in these derogatory terms by people in authority was not only a shattering experience in itself; it was a reflection of new and frightening values in our public life.

The amazing measure which was to satisfy non-existent needs in our constitutional make-up sought to make of Parliament itself sitting as a Court, the judge of its own actions, the final arbiter in the matter of legislative power where, in terms of the Constitution, that might be put in issue. This, it was argued, would be a much more democratic and therefore a more appropriate instrument, as being the voice of the people, freely elected by the people themselves, than 'a panel of appointed officers', however skilled in the law and competent in themselves. This body, Dr. Dönges informed the House, would be free, entirely free to make its decisions. It might even decide against Parliament as Parliament. Its decision would then be as final as if it upheld itself in its legislative capacity.

Already this sort of reasoning from Dr. Dönges, coupled as it was with curious analogies from the special function of the House of Lords within the British system, intended to prove the democratic

[1] Hansard, Vol. 78, Col. 4911 *et seq.*
[2] *Eastern Province Herald*, August 17th, 1952.
[3] Mr. Tom Naudé. Hansard, Vol. 78, Col. 3756.

nature of what was being proposed, was all too familiar, and none the less frustrating for that. But its influence, and the drive behind it, were all too sadly apparent in the attitude of Mr. Havenga. In his reply to the Budget debate[1] which took place on the eve of the introduction of the Bill, he set the tone of a new phase in the constitutional struggle. In one of the most excited and disjointed speeches of his unhappy association with the Malanites, he made another vain attempt to justify his support of policies and actions which ran counter to all the traditions and promises of his old leader, General Hertzog. Like his Cabinet colleagues, he repudiated the findings of the Appeal Court and challenged not only the right of the Judges, but their wisdom and intelligence in rejecting the statement of the 1937 Appeal Court that the Courts had no testing right under the Constitution. Ignoring, as Dr. Dönges and others had done, the facts of the case, the circumstance that the 1937 Court had not gone into the matter of the testing right since it was not vital to their decision in the case before them, he repeated the contention that the 1952 Court had not increased its stature by its own action in rejecting that finding. He returned with high emotion to his now oft-repeated charge that the present struggle was just another phase in the effort of the United Party and its predecessor, the old South African Party, to prevent South Africa achieving her complete freedom, and he warned the Oppositions that, if they went to the country on the cry of 'save the Constitution' with its entrenched clauses, the country would merely think that 'it wants to keep us like a baboon chained to a pole'. Thus he lent his support to the specious and absurd contention that the entrenchments in the Constitution were a check on our sovereignty and an evidence of our continued subjection to Britain from which we must break free.

On the nature of the Government's move to circumvent the judgment of the Appeal Court wild rumours had circulated for days before the Minister of the Interior released his Bill to Parliament and the country; but none of them were quite as wild or fantastic as the reality. It would indeed have been difficult for responsible people to anticipate the sort of proposition which the Bill contained if only because it would have been difficult for anybody bred in the Parliamentary tradition to conceive of such a travesty of Parliamentary precedent and practice. To secure to the Malanite Government a power to do what they wished to do with a semblance of constitu-

[1] Hansard, Vol. 78, Cols. 4031-2.

tional sanction, a new High Court of Parliament was to be constituted as a final court of appeal in constitutional cases; that was, in
respect of the non-European vote and the equality of the two official
languages. To this Court would be referred any judgment of the
existing Appeal Court which should disallow an Act of Parliament.

The Court was to consist of all members of both Houses of
Parliament, of whom fifty should constitute a quorum. It would
have the final say in regard to the validity of Acts of Parliament.
It would itself be fed by a judicial committee of ten members of
Parliament, of whom four should constitute a quorum. This Committee would review any judgment of the Appellate Division of the
Supreme Court which the Government wished to challenge, and
would recommend to the High Court of Parliament what should
be done in this matter.

Thus the power of any Government to evade the guarantees
entrenched in the Act of Union was to be placed in the first instance
in the hands of four politicians and finally in the hands of fifty
politicians. All of which meant in effect that a section of the ruling
party could force through any Act against the principle of the
Constitution. And thus, said Dr. Dönges and Mr. Havenga, the
will of the people would be recognised and maintained.

These fantastic proposals might be of the nature of comic opera.
They were, however, unfortunately extremely serious and dangerous
—not so much for what they themselves purported to do but for the
spirit that inspired them. They were proposals which flouted every
sane and responsible tradition of government and, as such, they
justified the rapidly growing fear that we were now in the hands of
people who would indeed stick at nothing to retain control of the
country and mould it to their own design.

The subsequent phases in this tragic struggle did nothing to dispel
these fears. So far as this Bill was concerned, its course through
Parliament was fairly rapid, even without the use of the guillotine,
since the Oppositions had agreed that there was nothing to be done
with it but, having stated their general case, to vote against it clause
by clause. This was the beginning of a tactic which was to be used a
good deal in the later phases of this protracted constitutional
struggle. I did not think it a good one generally; it could concede too
facile victories to the Government. But I felt it was appropriate on
this occasion, and it had the special virtue that it left the Government in the dark on the Opposition's case against the legality of the

Bill, which, it had been made clear, would also be challenged in the Courts.

As soon as the session was over, the Prime Minister submitted an appeal to the Judicial Committee of the new 'High Court' against the Appeal Court's verdict on the Separate Representation of Voters Act, and the Court was duly summoned to Pretoria to consider the inevitable recommendation of the Committee that that decision should be set aside. The Oppositions as a whole disregarded the summons, and left the field to the Government members. It was indeed tentatively suggested to me by the Leader of the Opposition that I might consider attending this curious session merely for the purpose of reportage, but I felt that in no circumstances could I lend any countenance to this incredible adventure, this trifling with the principles and the foundations of our political life. He readily understood and accepted my attitude, which was, after all, his own.

In the meantime, the validity of the new 'Court' was being challenged in the Cape Division of the Supreme Court. On August 27th, 1952, the High Court of Parliament declared the Separate Representation of Voters Act valid. Two days later, the Cape Division of the Supreme Court declared the High Court of Parliament Bill invalid as contravening the entrenched clauses of the Constitution. Some three months later, on November 14th, the Appeal Court confirmed this finding.

7

Manœuvre and Counter-Manœuvre

The Provincial leaders of the Government Party had declared their unshakable determination to establish the sovereignty of Parliament as they professed to understand it. The Government had sustained two defeats at the hands of the Courts in their efforts in this direction. What could they try now? The ex-Speaker of the House of Assembly, Mr Tom Naudé, now Minister of Posts and Telegraphs (to become in the course of the next few years President of the Senate), in a speech in the country on the eve of the new (1953) Parliamentary session, adumbrated some of the methods that might be resorted to. The Government might pack the Courts; or they might create another new Court. They might reconstitute the Senate to manufacture the majority supposedly necessary to carry their legislation. And already the suggestion of lowering the age for the European electorate from twenty-one to eighteen as a subsidiary assistance was being freely canvassed.[1] However, this was election year, and when Parliament met in January 1953, for the customary brief pre-election session, no attempt was made by the Government to carry the contest further at that moment—no doubt in the hope that the election itself would solve their problem for them. It did in fact improve their position, but it did not bring them within measurable distance of the two-thirds majority which the Constitution demanded. What it did do, however, was not only to give them the encouragement of considerably improved numbers of both votes and seats; the circumstances which surrounded it and followed it gave them reason to believe that the Opposition forces were tending to disintegrate, that the official Opposition, with its composite character, could be split if the right amount of pressure could be applied at the right points. Already Senator Heaton Nicholls had left the United Party to lead a Federal Party pledged to save Natal from the Afrikanerdom of the Malanites by either federation or secession, and there were signs that other members of the Party were suffering

[1] This was eventually established by law in the short post-election session of 1960 by the Electoral Law Amendment Act of that year. (Act 30 of 1958.) It became operative first in the referendum on the republican issue in October of that year.

from the frustration of opposition which the high tension of the past few years had seriously aggravated.

Counting on these forces as going his way, and making great play with his Party's determination always to act within the law, Dr. Malan declared his intention to reintroduce the Separate Representation of Voters Bill in a joint sitting of the two Houses of Parliament. The Bill would include some important amendments. He expressed the hope that on this occasion the official Opposition would allow a free vote on their side, as he would on his, this with the intention of exploiting what he believed was the common sentiment of South Africans in favour of apartheid. As he was to explain it himself on the second reading of the Bill,[1] now called the South Africa Act Amendment Bill, presented to the two Houses sitting together in July 1953 there had been, he believed, a considerable shifting of ground in the election, at any rate on the part of a section of the Opposition. 'I should like to point out that in my opinion, there are quite a few members of Parliament who on the merits of the matter are not against this legislation. Their objection was not based on the merits of separate representation . . . but they did not want to act unconstitutionally according to their conception.' And they were concerned about what they regarded as a threat to the principle of the equality of the two languages. The Government had taken these matters into careful consideration, and had brought this measure in in this way—that is, in joint session and with appropriate amendments designed to allay all anxieties in regard to the language position.

He then proceeded to explain the new features he was introducing in this Bill. These he felt should meet all the objections to the earlier measures. It was now the intention to remove the entrenchment of the non-European vote since that had proved a stumbling-block to essential change. But since there had been anxiety about the language situation which had shared the entrenchment—quite unnecessarily of course, but the Government wanted to remove all possible fears, however unfounded—that would be re-entrenched and the Courts would be given an explicit testing right in this regard. He hoped—and felt justified in hoping—that these proposals would meet all reasonable demands and provide the two-thirds majority to carry the measure in terms of the decision of the Appeal Court. He was well aware that there was a minority—such as the Native

[1] Joint Sitting 1953, Col. 34.

Representatives, and now the Labour Party—who could not be induced to accept any change in the existing situation; but that must just be recognised as out of line with 'the traditional policy of South Africa' to which the vast majority of the population subscribed.

Thus he launched his new measure on its way hopefully, and, as the course of the debate was to prove, not unjustifiably hopefully. At that point, however, the main interest of his speech for us was a surprising addition to the now familiar argument that if only the Coloured vote could be isolated, the fears of the Europeans would be allayed and peace and happiness would prevail. Reviewing again the political development of the country since Union, Dr. Malan claimed that much progress had already been made—presumably in this matter of establishing peace and happiness, and co-operation. He instanced first the abolition by his Government of the franchise granted to the Indians by General Smuts in 1946. He did not think that there was 'any important section' of the House who would like to see that situation restored. 'I think least of all the province of Natal would be anxious to see the Act of 1946 restored to the Statute Book,' he contended, effectively striking at the weakest spot in the Oppositions' armour.

He then went on, however, to add: 'We made a good deal of progress in lifting the colour question out of the party political arena by the legislation of 1936 in connection with the Natives. There is no desire really today on any side to do away with that Act. As far as that question is concerned therefore, there is no longer any strife.' Yet the Nationalist Party had gone to election in 1948 expressly on the cry of abolishing Native representation in the House of Assembly, and had only been prevented from doing this already by Mr. Havenga's intransigeance in the matter. And it had already abolished the Natives Representative Council which had formed an important part of the 1936 settlement. It seemed to us that political cynicism could scarcely go much further until Dr. Dönges began to handle the proposal to re-entrench the two official languages. With five years of argument behind him and us that Parliamentary sovereignty was scandalously shackled and the Courts exposed to political influence by the entrenchments in the Act of Union, he proceeded to explain to the House how we might shackle ourselves by the exercise of our own sovereignty. While the House generally was not taken in by either of these adventures in political manœuvring, and the emotions of the Opposition forces outside were only

more stirred, with tensions daily rising at the evidences of the
character of the forces which had got control of the political
machine, the dangers from within, on which Dr. Malan and his
friends were relying in this their crude shifting of ground began to
come to light. The speech of Mr. Bailey Bekker, the Transvaal
leader of the official Opposition, revealed the basis of their hopes.

It was already widely known that relations between Mr. Bekker
and the Leader of the United Party, Mr. Strauss, were considerably
strained, and it was increasingly suspected that Mr. Bekker was
being worked upon by the evil genius of the Party, Mr. Arthur
Barlow, whose capacity for mischief was to prove almost unlimited.
Himself, I believe, a sincere Conservative, Mr. Bekker showed all
the signs of being torn between a dislike of the attack on the Constitution and of any derogation of established rights, and the Trans-
vaaler's general feeling about colour which made this latter less
basic for him than his Party's attitude in the matter seemed to
demand. This was very much the sort of combination of emotions
that Dr. Malan had had to meet in Mr. Havenga, with the additional factor in Mr. Bekker's case of his dislike of his leader, coupled
with the effects of a second electoral defeat for his Party which so
often induces the belief that the majority must after all be right.

To our surprise, Mr. Strauss led off the debate from his side after
the Prime Minister's introduction of the Bill, with an amendment
calling for a joint Select Committee of both Houses of Parliament,
to which should be referred the business of exploring 'the best
method of settling the multi-racial problem of the Union, with due
regard to the necessity of securing the co-operation of the Cape
Coloured voters and the leaders of other responsible and moderate
non-European opinion, and the steps, if any, necessary to ensure the
validity of certain Acts of Parliament'. This last was a reference to a
suggestion now being circulated that, in the light of the 1952 judgment of the Appeal Court, other statutes passed by Parliament in
the ordinary way might also prove to be invalid as indirectly
reducing the value of the non-white vote—for example, the laws
enfranchising white women and establishing a uniform adult
franchise for white men and women while leaving the Coloured and
African vote subject to qualification.

To meet the inevitable challenge that this was a considerable
departure from his earlier attitude when he had rejected the Prime
Minister's proposition of a Select Committee, he argued that much

water had flowed under the bridge in the last year. Hadn't the Minister of Finance told the British people over the B.B.C. that apartheid was simply the traditional policy of segregation? If that was really so, let us put this whole colour question to a Select Committee again, and see if we could get to some co-operative basis for working out what would appear to be a common policy. Let us review our whole colour policy again and see whether we could find a *modus vivendi* that would even carry the co-operative effort of the Coloured people themselves. In any case, the Coloured people ought to be consulted. In the general election he himself had proposed a 'volkskongres', a congress of the people. The Select Committee could serve that purpose, and as the Government would have a majority on such a Committee, it had nothing to lose by accepting this proposition.

This change of approach on the part of the official Opposition lent weight to the rumour that the Party was indeed finding some difficulty in holding together. In the circumstances, in the ensuing debate, it became evident that one speech and one speech only was of interest to, and was tensely awaited by the Government, that of Mr. Bekker. While Mr. Bekker delayed his entry into the debate, the House was treated to two speeches from the Government side, highly significant as revealing some of the cross currents in the Government's own ranks. The first, from Dr. Dönges, sought to convince the Oppositions that in what the Government was now offering, there were broad grounds for an accommodation between them and the Government which they should be eager to accept. Following upon this came a violently aggressive speech by Dr. Verwoerd which was mainly notable for its early evidence of his determination to have no co-operation and no compromise if he could help it. With a tactic with which we were to become very familiar, he levelled at the Opposition, and particularly at the Leader of the Opposition, all the accusations which in the course of time he was to face himself, carrying the war—and war it was—relentlessly into the enemy's camp. It had been said by the Leader of the Opposition that when the Government introduced this Bill, they actually asked a favour of the Opposition, asked them for their support. That was not correct. What they were doing was offering an opportunity. It was a favour that the Government was granting by creating an opportunity for those who said that they were in favour of the preservation of white civilisation, to agree that the Coloured vote be dealt with as it had been suggested to deal with it. It gave them a chance to show their true colours and to co-operate. It was an opportunity being offered, not a favour being asked.[1] It was the sort of speech which led Mr. Bekker himself on another occasion to say, addressing himself to the Prime Minister and Mr. Havenga, that whenever there seemed any move on the part of the Government to reach a compromise with the Opposition, one had to ask, What does the Minister of Lands (Mr. Strydom) say? What does the Minister of Native Affairs say?

When Mr. Bailey Bekker eventually got up to speak, the Government was all ears—if the official Opposition was all anxiety. How wide was the crack in the United Party's ranks through which the Government hoped to drive to its appointed goal? Not quite wide enough yet, it seemed, for Mr. Bekker, though full of admiration for the Prime Minister and his sincerity in wishing to reach a compromise that would still give him his objective, was also full of admiration for the Leader of the Opposition and impressed with his willingness to find a starting point for co-operation. To what end? Mr. Bekker was not very explicit about this. But he was quite explicit about what were now being called the trimmings of the Bill—all the constitutional manœuvrings. Why had Dr. Malan included these? Why hadn't he just left the Constitution as it was and asked simply for the validation of the Separate Representation of Voters Act—a clear enough issue? Immediately the question came back: Would Mr. Bekker vote for that—which was, after all, all that was wanted at that moment. Mr. Bekker gave a fumbling reply, his leader would answer that question—which was both encouragement and discouragement to his friends on the Government benches. Mr. Bekker and those who felt as he did—or more or less felt as he did—were still inside the United Party; and the United Party would have no 'free' vote, as the Prime Minister termed it. This Mr. Strauss made plain in the next round of the debate, in which he stated his Party's determination to have nothing to do with any of the clauses of this Bill. And Mr. Bekker, again stressing his contention that the Prime Minister should have been content to bring in only that section of the Bill dealing with the validation of separate representation, declared he could not accept the Bill as it stood. He thought the Coloured people ought to be consulted about it. At the same time he made it clear that, like Mr. Havenga, he might find circumstances

[1] Joint Sitting 1953, Col. 213.

in which the separation of the Coloured voters would not offend his conscience.

For the rest, when the Bill had passed all its stages except the final and critical one, the third reading with its essential two-thirds majority, the two major Parties were still fencing for position, with the two small groups, ourselves and the Labour Party, skirmishing ineffectually on the sidelines, both backing with all our resources the decision of the official Opposition to reject the Bill, but viewing with anxiety any suggestion of the select committee procedure which, we were convinced, could have no constructive outcome; both anxious spectators of the shifts to which Dr. Malan and those around him were prepared to resort to achieve their end—of which the disintegration of the United Party was almost too obvious to need argument. As for myself, where I had been amazed indeed to hear Dr. Malan, in introducing the Bill, tell the House of his new view of the 1936 settlement under which we held our seats, I found it difficult to believe the evidence of my senses when he wound up the second reading debate by commending the proposed separate representation of the Coloured people on the strength of the proved value of our representation. 'In conclusion,' he said, 'I just want to say that this legislation before the House is decidedly in the interests of the Coloureds. For all these years, the Coloureds have had the franchise together with the Europeans, but their voice was not heard in this House. The Coloureds were dumb because not even the Party which had their support really represented them and pressed their interests. Separate representation was given to the Natives, and just compare the position of the Coloureds hitherto with that of the Natives. The voice of the Natives is heard here. They are not dumb. But the voice of the Coloureds is not heard. Give them separate representation. Let them elect their own representatives in their own constituencies to which they are entitled, and their interests will be pressed much more in this House and much more will really be done for them.'[1]

When a later stage of the Bill gave me an opportunity to comment on this argument, I could feelingly and with deep conviction say that it was one thing to be heard and another to be listened to. This drew from Mr. Havenga by way of interjection the question, 'What about the enormous progress that has been made by the Natives by what we have done for them in those years as a direct

[1] Joint Sitting 1953, Col. 237.

T

result of your voice being heard?' To which my reply was that undoubtedly there had been an enormous advance in the social position
of the African population, but a serious deterioration in their political position. I could have added with justice that the advance had
taken place in spite of, not because of, the Party to which he now
belonged, and there were already significant evidences of the insecure foundations on which it had been built.

At this stage, with the certainty that the Government would not
get the requisite majority to carry its amended Bill, the debate was
adjourned with a date for resumption nearly a month ahead.
Immediately speculation arose as to the purpose of this move. The
announcement of the adjournment came on the back of rumours
that individual members of the United Party had visited the Prime
Minister at Groote Schuur, the Prime Minister's residence, over the
week-end to explore the possibility of an accommodation between the
two major Parties on the issues raised by the Bill. In the circumstances, it was assumed that a certain weight was being given to
these manœuvres and that such an accommodation was now something more than a possibility. At the same time, there was an air of
uncertainty about the whole situation, since no one seemed to know
who was manœuvring and what was the nature of the manœuvres.
Thereafter the situation clarified slightly. After a lengthy United
Party caucus meeting it was announced that Mr. Strauss was sending a letter to Dr. Malan setting out the terms on which his Party
believed an understanding might be reached. There was no information for the public as to the nature of the terms. A general guess was
that they included the condition that the Coloured voters must
remain on the common roll, but that the present qualifications might
be revised to bring them more into line with present-day values. It
was also rumoured that such a proposition should be linked with the
continuance of the entrenchment of the Coloured and Native franchises and the recognition of the testing rights of the Courts.

The reaction of the Nationalist Party press to these developments
was interesting and significant. So long as there seemed no prospect
of any attempt to compromise or co-operate on the part of the United
Party, there was a tendency on the part of that press to argue that
the United Party could only be strengthened, not weakened, by
allowing its right wing to find its own accommodation with the
Government. However as soon as these moves for negotiation were
established and openly acknowledged, the emphasis was all on the

struggle which, it was claimed, the Party had had to keep together and to find a basis of negotiation which all would or could accept. It seemed, therefore, that the Nationalist Party was less concerned at that moment for an accommodation than for the disintegration of the United Party.

There was a suggestion which seemed more than a rumour, that the Nationalists themselves were facing strains between their extremists and their so-called moderates which might become dangerously aggravated by an accommodation with the official Opposition. A week later, while the ferment in regard to the Coloured franchise and the Constitutional issue was still going on in the lobbies and elsewhere outside the debating chamber, it seemed that inter-Party negotiations had broken down. At the same time, it was widely rumoured that there was a group of United Party members who would vote for the separation of the Coloured voters if that issue could be isolated and their right to exercise their own judgment were allowed them by their party caucus. In the end, the Joint Sitting was not resumed until mid-September. It met then without any accommodation having been reached, but with those whom the Government regarded as potential dissidents in the United Party still appealing to the Prime Minister for further negotiations, further consultation and the open door, and the Prime Minister himself complaining of the so-called use of the sjambok, and the threat of being called Quislings by the Leader of the Opposition to keep his team together and thus to deny the Government the prospect of the required majority, 'when we do not even need much more help to put apartheid into effect'.[1] Had not the electorate given them twenty-nine more seats in the House of Assembly?

In these circumstances it seemed doubtful whether the Government would put the Bill to the vote. When their intention to do so was established, the general tactic of the Opposition parties was to state briefly their unshakable opposition to the Bill and then let the vote speak for itself. Although doubtful of the wisdom of letting the Government get so highly contentious a measure disposed of so easily, we as Native Representatives decided to confine ourselves to a re-statement of our case against the proposed separate representation of Coloureds by pointing to the disastrous effects of the 1936 legislation. This legislation, we contended, had had the effect of kraaling the African and European population in separate and

[1] Joint Sitting 1953, Col. 350.

increasingly mutually hostile camps, and we urged the Prime Minister not to extend the scope of so dangerous a system.

The debate went more or less quietly according to a simple plan by which the Government allowed each Opposition group to state its case, while it sat silent and offered no comment, until an unexpected diversion from the Labour benches which startled the whole House, including the Labour Party itself, into a new state of tension. As the House waited for the Prime Minister to wind up the debate, Mr. Norman Eaton, Labour Member for Umlazi, Natal, rose and, to the consternation of his colleagues, expressed his personal anxiety for the future now that the Government would not get the majority required to pass the Bill. He asked the Prime Minister to introduce the original Bill only—namely, the Separate Representation of Voters Bill—in a joint sitting and refer it to a Select Committee before the second reading, that is, before the acceptance of its principle.

While the House held its breath over this proposal from the benches of a Party which had time and again declared its complete hostility to the proposal to segregate the Coloured people politically, Mr. Sauer, Minister of Transport, and probably the most subtle Parliamentary manager the South African Parliament has produced, rose to ask the United Party how it would act if this interesting proposal was accepted. Since it was well known that many members of the United Party were now sympathetic to the principle of the Separate Representation of Voters Bill, although they would not accept the Bill then before the Joint Sitting with its wider ramifications, the moment was obviously a difficult one for them, particularly as the Party Leader himself had asked for a Select Committee at the second reading of the Bill. But the Minister had somewhat overcalled his hand in trying this tactic to divide the Opposition. In asking the question, he had also asked whether the Party would bind itself beforehand to accept the decision of such a Select Committee. Sir De Villiers Graaff, replying for the United Party, said no party had ever bound itself beforehand to the finding of either a Committee or a Commission, least of all the Nationalist Party, and he challenged the *bona fides* of the Government in putting up Mr. Sauer to explore the possibilities of consultation on this purely hypothetical basis which sought to get the Opposition to commit itself while the Government was offering nothing positive.

The Prime Minister thereupon closed the debate in what was for him an exceptionally short speech. It was also an exceptionally angry speech, in which he warned the Oppositions that the Government would now pursue other courses to achieve its end, for achieve its ends it would. And already the new course had been embarked upon. Two days later, the Minister of Justice introduced a Bill to reconstitute the Appellate Division of the Supreme Court with a view to creating a division to deal solely with constitutional matters.

This move in itself could not resolve the Government's difficulty in getting the Separate Representation of Voters Bill accepted as law. A fortnight later, on September 29th, on the day after the second reading of the Appellate Division Bill was to have been read, the Government announced a further Joint Sitting to meet on October 1st. On that day, the Prime Minister moved for leave to introduce a Bill to validate and amend the Separate Representation of Voters Act of 1951. He again justified this move on the ground that there were indications that 'there were certain members who on the merits of the matter, were in favour of the separate representation of Coloured people', so he proposed to give them their chance in that regard by removing all the so-called 'trimmings' which had been introduced into the South Africa Act Amendment Bill. He proposed to refer the Bill to Select Committee before the second reading, the proposition put up by Mr. Eaton.

What had brought about this change in approach in that short space of time? Undoubtedly the most important event was the widening split in the United Party ranks. Already known as the four rebels, Messrs. Bailey Bekker, Abraham Jonker, Blaar Coetzee and Frank Waring had made a 'last minute' appeal to the Government not to go on with the Appellate Division Bill but to introduce to a Joint Sitting at the beginning of the following session the Separate Representation of Voters Bill as originally passed, and submit it to a Select Committee before the second reading, in effect Mr. Eaton's suggestion. The appeal was addressed specially to the Prime Minister and Mr. Havenga, and Mr. Havenga had let it be known that if there was any substantial part of the Opposition who were prepared to consider the separation of the Coloured voters, he felt they should be given their chance to be heard, and to take their stand.

When the Prime Minister took the unusual course of speaking to the motion to introduce his Bill to the Joint Sitting, it became clear that the case had been pretty thoroughly canvassed and a behind-the-stage agreement had been reached between the two major parties that this proposition should be accepted. The Leader of the United Party proposed a lengthy face-saving amendment in which he asked for assurances that the Coloured people should be adequately consulted and their substantial co-operation obtained for any measure the Select Committee might recommend; that this exploration of the Coloured position should merely be a prelude to a comprehensive reconsideration of the whole non-European question and that the Government should give guarantees not to violate the entrenched clauses.

After a skirmish on these fronts, the whole discussion was brought to an early conclusion and the pre-arranged personnel of the proposed Select Committee duly brought out of the bag.

While it could not be said that the atmosphere in which this bargain was struck had any warmth to it, the only really dissentient notes were struck by the Labour Party and myself. Speaking for his Party, Mr. Hepple declared again that in no circumstances could it —or any part of it—be induced to vote for the principle enshrined in the Separate Representation of Voters Bill, and that he had no confidence in the ability of the two major Parties to find any solution to the problem which the Government had created in this regard.

My own case was in essence similar. My experience of communal representation as enshrined in our legislation gave me no grounds on which to support the extension of this system, while my experience of select committees under Nationalist government, by now quite extensive, gave me no desire to embark again on so frustrating and well-nigh useless an endeavour. One of my two new colleagues, the member for Transkei, Mr. Will Stuart, while agreeing with the general case I sought to make against this new move and in favour of a complete rejection of the proposition, felt impelled in the last resort to see the workings of the Select Committee for himself and was therefore appointed as one of the seven Opposition members of the eighteen-member Committee. With the Select Committee accepted, the Labour Party also felt impelled to watch its course, and accordingly appointed one of its members to the Committee.

The one condition which Dr. Malan demanded for the concession of the Select Committee was that it should not be a delaying tactic but must report in time for legislation in the following session. As the 1953 session was then drawing to its close, the Committee was promptly turned into a Commission with power to act in the recess, on the understanding that it might be reconstituted as a Select Committee when Parliament reopened if it had not completed its work by that time, its specific job being to consult the Coloured community in regard to the Government's proposals.

8

Manufactured Majority: The Enlarged Senate

The later stages in the history of Coloured political apartheid, which became law in 1955 on terms that differed only in incidental detail from those laid down in the original Separate Representation of Voters Bill, justified our prognostications in regard to the Select Committee, although not necessarily our tactics except for ourselves. At the beginning of the 1954 session of Parliament, the Commission reverted to the status of a Select Committee; in April its report was presented to Parliament by Dr. Dönges who had been its chairman throughout its various phases, and on May 17th Parliament launched into its third Joint Sitting with another Bill[1] to validate and amend the fateful 1951 Act, with the omens as unpropitious as before.

The Select Committee-Commission had been as unsuccessful in closing the gap as we had anticipated, and, far from the tensions between the two major parties having been relaxed, in fact they showed all the signs of having been heightened considerably with increasing bitterness. Why then had the Government decided to go ahead with this further attempt to carry its proposition of the political segregation of the Coloured people by this procedure?

The answer to this question was to be found in the effective break which had taken place in the official Opposition. The dissidents were now formally out of the Party and functioning under the leadership of Mr. Bailey Bekker as the Independent United Party, with an accentuation of the bitterness which seems inseparable from family division, aggravated in this case by the refusal of the United Party to surrender one of their seats on the Select Committee to Mr. Bekker. As was soon evident, the group, now five in number,[2] had already accepted the Government's demand for change in the Coloured franchise and implicitly on the segregated basis, this in private conversations between Mr. Bekker and the Prime Minister which were to bear their fruit in an amendment moved by Mr. Bekker in the

---

[1] Now called Separate Representation of Voters Act Validation and Amendment Bill, 1954.
[2] Mr. Arthur Barlow had by now joined their ranks.

second reading of the Bill in the new Joint Session. While the United Party, in a lengthy amendment covering all their old grounds of opposition to the original Bill, took their stand against this Bill, Mr. Bekker's rejection of the Bill was based on the failure of the Government to safeguard the rights of those Coloured voters already on the roll, to take cognisance of those Coloured voters in Natal who would have been eligible for the franchise under existing law, and a demand for higher status and more powers for the partly elected, partly nominated Coloured Advisory Council for which the Bill made provision.[1] With this as a beginning, how much wider could the fissure in the United Party be made? It did not need much experience of politics in South Africa to appreciate the drive behind this new adventure.

This renewed attempt to get his Bill accepted by the requisite majority was to prove the final business of Dr. Malan's last session in Parliament—a session of which I was to write as it closed that to the end it retained its unenviable reputation of being the most unpleasant session in the memory of most of its members.

Cross currents and stresses in regard to the Bill were revealed at the earliest stages of its course. On the motion for leave to introduce the Bill, the Labour Party, the Native Representatives except Senator Cowley,[2] and the two Federal Party Senators, Senator Heaton Nicholls and Senator Browne, voted against the motion on the ground that they were unshakably opposed to the principle of separate representation for the Coloured people. The United Party voted with the Government for the introduction of the Bill, arguing that this joint sitting provided the only means by which the Select Committee might review its proceedings for the benefit of those who had appointed it, and that those who, like the Labour Party, had taken part in those proceedings were illogical in refusing this opportunity. The Independent United Party supported the Government for their own reasons, which they were to make clear later. These were to secure an opportunity to air their grievance that they had not been accorded a seat on the Select Committee and in order to pursue their self-appointed task of trying to find a compromise with the Government which, they argued, was the legitimate and appropriate function of a responsible Opposition.

Mr. Stuart (my colleague), who had served on the Committee,

[1] Joint Sitting 1954, Cols. 72–3.
[2] Successor to Dr. Brookes in the Natal-Zululand Constituency.

agreed with the United Party that it was illogical to vote against the introduction of the Bill and thus deny the Select Committee the chance of reporting its proceedings, but he said he preferred liberty to logic and would vote with the minority against the introduction of the Bill.

From the beginning, there was a tendency to recrimination which became more marked as the debate proceeded. In fact it became the keynote of the whole debate. There was certainly plenty of fuel to stoke it up. Not only were the Independents to accuse the United Party, and particularly its Leader, of keeping them off the Select Committee; the members of the Committee themselves had a lot to say about one another, each side accusing the other of a complete lack of any will to negotiate which alone could have made the appointment of the Committee worth while. Finally, Senator Heaton Nicholls, speaking for the Union Federal Party, denounced the whole idea of the Select Committee, as I had done the previous year when it was originally proposed, on the legitimate ground that the Committee was only Parliament in miniature, and that there was no justifiable hope that it would function other than on party lines, with the Government determinedly against any compromise.

The debate itself was one of the dreariest that Parliament had had to listen to in my time. It consisted for the most part of a series of marathon speeches from the members of the Committee, each and all of the speakers, with the assistance of extensions of the regulation time for speeches (then forty minutes with unlimited extension) striving to put on record for posterity his or his Party's share of the arguments that had gone on in the Committee, and for which the rules governing the reports of Select Committees found no place in the Committee's own report. The Committee itself had produced three volumes of the evidence led before it. These volumes became the source of texts for both sides, by which each sought to confound the other, the Nationalists endeavouring to prove that the common roll was a wicked device of the British in days gone by to foist upon South Africa a pattern which was contrary to its whole tradition and which could only destroy the white race in this country, while the Opposition argued that the system under which the Coloureds held their vote was the free choice of South Africa, had never been abused, and was the only road to co-operation between Coloured and European which was essential if we were to avoid the creation of an anti-White non-European block in this country.

What argument there was was strikingly barren, as being more concerned with the past than with the future. It is true, both sides agreed that the enquiry had revealed the existence of a problem, but what they regarded as the essential features of the problem was not made clear, that is, whether it was the danger to white supremacy of the supposedly phenomenal growth of the Coloured people, or the claim that, whatever scheme Coloured witnesses supported—apartheid or common roll—all had one objective, ultimate equality with the whites.

As the final evening of the debate wore on, nerves became more and more taut and tempers unsettled and uncertain. In the course of the day it had been made known that the Prime Minister would not reply to the debate at once but would postpone his reply until the middle of the following week. There was much speculation as to whether the sitting would be resumed at all since it seemed clear that the Government would not get the two-thirds majority necessary to pass the Bill even with the support of Mr. Bekker's group which now seemed fairly certain. (Senator Ballinger in the course of his speech invoked the shade of that great liberal, Mr. J. H. Hofmeyr, whose old constituency's tragedy was to be represented now by a man whose only contribution to the difficult problem of colour was a proposal designed to facilitate the destruction of the Coloured franchise.)

Whatever the ultimate purpose and intention of the postponement, it was generally viewed as an episode in a war of nerves designed to encourage new cracks in the official Opposition. No doubt it was an accumulation of all these strains that led to a conflict between the Speaker and Mr. Lawrence, which was to lead to the introduction of that motion of censure on the Speaker to which I have already referred. The episode itself, in its beginning at least, appeared harmless. Mr. Lawrence rose to a point of order in defence of one of the United Party's main speakers, Mr. Marais Steyn, whose speech was being continually interrupted by the other side. He hoped the Speaker would not count the time of these interruptions against Mr. Steyn. From that moment, certainly from our end of the Chamber, it was difficult to hear or to know just what transpired, but Mr. Lawrence was named by the Speaker and ordered to withdraw from the House. Mr. Lawrence apparently regarded this as an unjust sentence upon him, and demanded an explanation. This ended in an uproar, in which the Speaker named Mr. Lawrence and declared his suspension from the proceedings of the House. Mr. Havenga, therefore, as Leader of the House, moved for the suspension, which was put to the vote, in which all the Oppositions voted together against the Government. Mr. Lawrence therefore left the Chamber, while Mr. Strauss sought to give notice of a motion of censure on the Speaker for his ruling. Since the rules of the House debarred him from doing so at that stage, the United Party, supported by the Labour Party and my two colleagues, left the Chamber and the Prime Minister moved the adjournment of the debate and of the sitting.

In the days that followed, while the House and the country awaited Dr. Malan's next move, rumours of negotiations between representatives of the Government and some of the leading members of the Coloured people began to circulate. Nothing, however, was known as to their character. When this was disclosed, it came as a complete surprise, certainly to all but the very few in the inner circle of the two major parties. As reported to the reassembled joint sitting by the Prime Minister himself,[1] it was in the nature of an offer from a Coloured source to compromise with the Government on the basis of proposals similar to those put forward by the Independent United Party. The offer, he said, had been made in the name of an organisation calling itself the Coloured People's National Union with Mr. George Golding as President, Mr. D. H. Heuvel, Executive Chairman and Mr. I. J. Stober, General Secretary. Asserting their continuing opposition to any suggestion to interfere with the established franchise rights of the Coloured people, these spokesmen for the Union declared their anxiety as to the future if this matter was to continue to be a source of contention between the two major Parties and fear lest, in refusing what was now offered, they might lose all—a fear aggravated, they said, by the known fact that many of the United Party members really favoured their political segregation. They added, 'In this latter connection, we are alarmed at the fact that certain members of the United Party, headed by one of their leaders who plays a very important part in the Party, has already suggested that the way of meeting this Coloured franchise problem is by raising the qualifications of the Coloured vote.' This was a reference to a suggestion for consideration made by Mr. Harry Lawrence, with which much play had

[1] Report of Joint Sitting 1954, Col. 374.

been made by the Government members as demonstrating what they called the dishonesty of the official Opposition's approach to the whole question of the common franchise.

This new development came as a great shock to all those of us who had determinedly resisted any attempt to apply the principle of legislative segregation to the Coloured people. With our experience of the effects of segregation as applied to the Africans, we could only view with the most profound anxiety any suggestion of a compromise on this issue; and with the gravest fear a proposal of this kind from any important section of the Coloured people themselves. We had no doubt as to what the reaction of the majority of the politically-minded Coloured people would be. It was indeed voiced at once in unequivocal terms by a number of prominent leaders of the Coloured community—an emphatic 'no compromise'. But the mere proposal coming from so prominent a quarter as it had done, could only threaten new divisions in the Coloured community which could not fail to reduce their capacity to offer effective resistance to any further invasion of their rights.

Armed with this new weapon, Dr. Malan, in a speech again full of references to the need to establish peace and friendship and the happy effects in that regard of the 1936 settlement in respect of the Native population, announced his intention to postpone the later stages of the Bill in order to explore the possibilities of getting acceptance of a compromise on the lines suggested, in which particular emphasis was being laid on the protection of the existing rights of registered Coloured voters. In itself, the speech was mainly interesting as reflecting some of Dr. Malan's more curious attitudes to the course of history. A speech by the Leader of the Labour Party offered him particular scope in this regard. Moving a motion that the Bill be read this day six months, Mr. Hepple had said what we as representatives of Africans had often said, that instead of reducing the political rights of the Coloured people, we should be extending them —that what we should aim at in South Africa was not a series of kraals for our racial groups but the building of a composite society. This, said Dr. Malan, was tantamount to a charge on his part against the Creator who had created the world with different countries and different people. Mr. Hepple's attitude was that the world should have been created as flat as a table, because then there would be no barriers. But instead, the world was created in such a way that it was impossible to have anything but different countries and different languages, and in addition to that, the Creator had proceeded to create different colours. 'No,' he thundered, 'I say that, basically, is really a charge against Creation and against the Creator.'[1] But, he added, Mr. Hepple was not alone in his view. He had a little cousin in Russia who took the same view—the typical broadly implied accusation which he himself knew to be without foundation.

In due course, in spite of rumours to the contrary, the progress of the Bill was renewed. The period between the second reading and the Committee Stage of the Bill had obviously been a period of frenzied activity on the part of the Independent United Party. This group had taken upon itself the self-appointed task of bringing political peace to the country on the basis of a compromise between the Government and the official Opposition. They had already made it clear on the second reading that their idea of a reasonable compromise was acceptance of the principle of the Bill with guarantees for the political rights of the Coloured voters now on the roll. The problem was how to apply a proposition of this kind in practice. Eventually the result of their labours in this regard was embodied in lengthy amendments which provided for the delimitation of the Cape Province progressively into one, two, three and eventually four electoral divisions, not as the numbers of voters on the separate roll to be provided for new voters increased but as the numbers of Coloured voters on the present roll declined, the conclusion of the process being reached when all Coloured voters should have disappeared from the common roll, the same process to be applied later to the provincial field and to the extended Coloured Advisory Council for which the Validation Bill provided.

Significantly, these amendments were put to the Committee not by the Independents who had initiated them, but by the Minister of the Interior, to whom the Prime Minister (who was now showing obvious signs of wear) handed over this whole stage of the Bill. And Dr. Dönges in assuming his duties made it plain to the House that if these 'concessions' did not produce the desired two-thirds votes, they would fall away and the Government would be free to resume its old position.

Not unexpectedly, all the Oppositions other than the Independents found the progressive elimination of the Coloureds from the common roll no more acceptable than their immediate elimination,

[1] Joint Sitting 1954, Cols. 307–48.

and said so, to the indignation of the Independants, who had taken upon themselves to commend the new proposals to the House and the country.

Thus the third reading found Dr. Malan's hopes still unfulfilled. His last bid for the two-thirds he wanted had failed. Even with the now six 'rebels'[1] he was nine short of his required number.

But this was not to be the end. That he had made clear in his final speech on the subject. 'If a two-thirds majority is not obtained here today,' he declared as he began his speech on the third reading, 'then in effect this Joint Sitting would be giving a mandate and the mandate is "This fight will be carried on". I can only say that if that fight has to be carried on, it will start immediately.'[2] Presumably he had already made up his mind to drop the reins of government in the recess. This he did. They fell, however, not where he had hoped and expected, into Mr. Havenga's hands. They fell into the hands of Mr. Strydom and his lieutenant, Dr. Verwoerd. There was no doubt the fight would go on, and that without any waste of time or effort in seeking unwanted compromise.

Thus the announcement in the speech from the throne at the beginning of the following (1955) session of the Government's intention to ask Parliament 'at the appropriate time' to give consideration to the separate representation of voters and to the question of the sovereignty of Parliament scarcely came as a surprise. The question had long ceased to be whether this would happen, but only what plan the Government would now pursue to attain its ends.

The session had actually run nearly half its course when the Government made its first new move. On the eve of the customary Easter recess, it announced the appointment of five additional judges to the Appellate Division of the Supreme Court and its intention to introduce a Bill to provide a special quorum for the consideration of constitutional cases. This was followed promptly by the publication of an Appellate Division Quorum Bill. When in due course this measure came before the House of Assembly, the Minister of Justice, in whose hands it lay, made no attempt to dissociate it from the constitutional crisis. On the contrary, he linked it specifically with that crisis and what he and his Party professed to see as the confusion of the conflicting judgments of 1937 and 1952, and their

---

[1] The Group had now been joined by a Natal member, Dr. V. Shearer.
[2] Joint Sitting 1954, Col. 567.

determination to get a decision, ostensibly to re-establish the sovereignty of Parliament—in fact, to give them the power to do what they were determined to do. To the Oppositions, which on this occasion included the Independents now become the Conservative Party, this was merely another attempt to circumvent the entrenched clauses. It constituted an undeserved reflection on the integrity of the Appellate Division Bench, and tended to bring the unquestioned reputation of the highest Court in the land into disrepute.

In any case, this move could not of itself solve the Government's problem. What indeed could it do, other than suggest the determination of the Government to handpick five newcomers in the hope of cancelling out the 'six old men of Bloemfontein' when the appropriate occasion should present itself? It was a situation that was peculiarly difficult to handle, since the Government had already announced its appointments.

The Minister himself could scarcely have made a worse case for his Bill when he piloted it through its final phase in the Senate. When from all sections of the Opposition repeated references were made to the short-lived High Court of Parliament, by which the Government had sought to get behind the 1952 judgment and the entrenchments in the Constitution, Mr. Swart at last interjected that he was not responsible for that Bill. Faced with the query as to what the Government hoped to gain by enlarging the Appellate Division, and constituting a quorum of eleven in constitutional cases which might be brought before the Courts for their consideration, he replied that in that case the Government 'wanted a strong court to hear the case'. To the further question as to how that would help to restore the 1937 decision put by Senator Rubin (Native Representative), his only reply was 'wait and see'. Pressed still further to say what would happen if the decision of the Courts was still against the Government, the Minister declared that 'if the steps we take are found to be illegal, we will take other steps, but we must have certainty'—certainty being, it seemed, the Nationalist view of the law.

As soon as the Quorum Bill was through, what had come to be referred to as the Government's secret weapon was revealed—Parliament was to be asked to reconstitute the Senate to manufacture the majority which the Government had failed to get from the electorate. When the terms of the Senate Bill[1] were released to

[1] Act 53 of 1955.

Parliament and the country—which was only after the introduction of the Bill in the House of Assembly—it was at once apparent that, with the passage of this Bill, the Senate as constituted by the Act of Union would cease to exist and the function that it had performed would cease with it. The Bill provided for two basic changes in the composition of the upper chamber. Where each of the contracting parties to Union had hitherto been represented by an equal number of members, henceforward the two smaller Provinces would each continue to have eight seats but the Cape Province would now have twenty-two seats and the Transvaal twenty-seven. Further, where in the past, election to the Senate seats had been by the members of the House of Assembly and the Provincial Council for the relevant Province on a basis of proportional representation, a system designed to give minorities in the electorate a measure of representation in the upper House, in terms of the Bill Senators would henceforth be elected by straight majority vote. In effect, this meant on the then composition of the House of Assembly and the Provincial Councils that the United Party would elect all the eight Natal Senators while all the fifty-seven Senators representing the other three Provinces would be elected by the Government Party. Thus the whole character and purpose of the Senate was to be changed. From having a composite character designed to reflect the relative strength of the forces in the country as well as the federal element behind our unitary constitution, it was to become simply a reflection of the lower House, an echo of the majority party.

Even on this basis, however, the change would not give the Government the two-thirds majority it needed for its purpose. To secure this, the Bill went on to provide for an increase in the number of nominated Senators for which the Act of Union provided from eight to sixteen. That four of the eight to be added to the pre-existing number of appointed members were to be appointed for their knowledge of the reasonable wants and wishes of the non-White races—who stood squarely against the purpose for which this Bill was being enacted—only added an additional element of cynicism to the whole proposition. With the Senate thus enlarged from forty-eight to eighty-nine and a guarantee that all but eight members from Natal and the four Native Representatives[1] would support it,

---

[1] Senator Cowley was prepared to support the Government on the subject of the Coloured vote until the passing of the Senate Act. He found he could not accept that move or its purpose.

U

the Government secured its requisite majority with four votes to spare for eventualities. But at what a price! Even the Nationalists themselves seemed to be shaken by this move. The Cape organ of the Party, *Die Burger*, saw in it a fundamental and far-reaching step with fundamental and possibly untoward results, and both it and individual members of the Party were uneasily defensive, arguing that the step was legal and had been forced on them by an uncompromising Opposition.

The attitude of all the Oppositions was immediate and unequivocal. United Party, Labour and Conservatives alike declared their determination to have nothing to do with such a measure. For the newly formed Liberal Party and the Natives' Representatives, I moved refusal for the introduction of the Bill on the grounds that no proposal for a change in the composition or constitution of the Senate had ever been before the electorate, so that the Government could not claim any mandate in that regard; that the Bill was the declared second step to get the Coloured voters off the common roll without the support of the electorate as envisaged in our Constitution, and was thus an attempt to circumvent the decision of the Courts and a defiance of the law.

As the Bill pursued its course, the attitude of solid opposition on the non-Nationalist side of the House was only marred by the failure of the Conservatives to maintain consistency and to resist the temptation, with which they were constantly assailed, to attack their erstwhile friends, the United Party, and to blame them for all the troubles in which we found ourselves. Apparently themselves convinced as to the shameful character and the national dangers of this manipulation of the Constitution on which the Government had embarked, they accused the United Party of precipitating the crisis by its uncompromising opposition to the Government's determination to take the Coloured voters off the common roll—the usual fruitless argument, linked with the customary appeal to compromise so that 'rest and peace' might be restored to the land.

The Bill made its appearance—as a long title—on May 11th. On June 9th it emerged from the House of Assembly with one important amendment. The same Mr. Norman Eaton who had triggered off the Select Committee and Dr. Malan's last effort to get the two-thirds majority for his Bill, discovered what seemed to be an extra-special danger in this measure—that the law being what it was in regard to the dissolution of the Senate, no change of government could operate in the future, since for four years no other government would be able to carry any measure against the weight of the Nationalists established in the upper chamber. Probably this had not been intentional: at any rate, the Minister of the Interior, Dr. Dönges, the architect of this new device for circumventing the law and the principle of the Constitution, offered amendments designed to rescue his Party from this challenge to their intention to establish a one-party state.

With the publication of the Senate Bill, tensions both inside and outside the debating Chamber had risen to higher levels than they had ever reached over these years of constitutional crisis. At last there was a sense of estrangement between the two sides in the political struggle that had an atmosphere of permanence about it that had not hitherto been present even at the height of the earlier crisis. In the past the Oppositions had been deeply shocked by the means by which the Government had sought to achieve its ends. Particularly was this the case in respect of the High Court of Parliament. But there had been a certain relief in the tension on those occasions in the conviction that these moves were illegal and would therefore be scotched. It was felt that they would leave a scar on the body politic, but that they would not leave a permanent disability. The Senate Bill, coming on top of the Quorum Act, gave little hope of that kind. The Quorum Act was unquestionably within the law, and there were strong grounds for believing that the Senate Bill would prove legal also. While the latter measure would twist the Constitution established in 1909 out of recognition in one of its essentials, namely a representative second chamber, both measures reflected a spirit of uncompromising determination on the part of the Government to achieve the requisite support for its purpose laid down by the Constitution at any cost to the Constitution itself. This inevitably inspired all non-Nationalists with deep fears not only for their own future but for the whole principle of Parliamentary government and representative institutions in this country.

Nor did the Government's handling of its proposals do anything to alleviate their anxieties. When the debate on the Bill opened in the House of Assembly on May 23rd, 1955, neither the Prime Minister, Mr. Strydom, nor the Minister of the Interior, Dr. Dönges, made any attempt to evade the fact that the intention of the measure was to create for the Government the voting majority in Parliament that it had not been able to achieve through the ballot box. Dr. Dönges applied himself throughout a typically lengthy speech to the job of trying to prove that his proposals for the new Senate which the Bill was to create, were neither unprecedented nor undemocratic. To this end he ranged far and wide for parallels both to the act of constitutional change and to the patterns which he proposed now to establish. He ended by claiming that important minorities in the National Convention had at some stage argued and voted against aspects of the existing Senate, such as its proportional representation basis or its partially federal character, as proof that these features were not essential conditions of democratic practice.[1]

The Prime Minister, Mr. Strydom, began simply by announcing again his determination to get the Coloured voters off the common roll and to establish what he called the sovereignty of Parliament. Thereafter he went rapidly through all the threadbare arguments in support of the Nationalists' case on both these issues, arguments which had been answered a hundred times in the course of the numerous phases of this constitutional crisis.

Neither Minister attempted to suggest that the measure was in itself a good one. They were content to justify themselves to Parliament (as their press had been justifying them to the public) as having been forced to this method to achieve their ends by the refusal of the United Party to give the Government the support necessary to carry into effect by the established constitutional method what they claimed to be their mandate and 'the will of the people'.

Even as this tragic session ended, the Government's plans for what was to prove the final stage of this long drawn-out struggle were being prepared. The Senate Act provided for the dissolution of the old Senate at the end of December 1955. Even before that date, there were signs that the scrimmage for seats in the Enlarged Senate, as it came to be called, had become the dominant preoccupation in Nationalist circles, the first condition of entry in the race being a contribution of £50 (R100) to the funds of the Party. When the new session opened in January 1956, the speech from the throne included among its legislative measures for the session 'A bill relating to the Separate Representation of Voters and the competence of the law courts to pass judgment on the validity of Acts passed by Parliament'. On February 13th, exactly a month later, while the session was still in its first youth, the two Houses were assembled

[1] Hansard, Vol. 89, Col. 6009 *et seq.*

again—with considerable physical difficulty, in view of the increased numbers of the manufactured majority—to perform the one function for which this extraordinary constitutional manœuvre had been planned; on February 27th, with 174 votes to 68, this new and strange Parliament decided to destroy the franchise which the Coloured people in the Cape had enjoyed ever since there had been a franchise for anybody. In due course, the official Opposition again challenged the validity of this legislation in the Courts—this time without success. The whole Appellate Division now, with one dissentient, held that, in terms of the Constitution which had provided for possible reconstitution of the Senate after ten years, the new Senate, however monstrous both in character and intention, had been legally constituted. Mr. Justice Schreiner, standing alone, contended that the purpose for which the new Senate had been so wildly transformed constituted merely another attempt to circumvent the entrenched clauses and as such could not be regarded as falling within the Constitution. At last the Nationalist leaders had got what they were determined to have. Five years later—in 1960—having achieved their purpose, which included release from the incubus of the entrenchments—they elected to get rid of the monstrosity they had created. Probably they hoped that, with it out of sight, it would be generally forgotten, as they no doubt were anxious themselves to forget it. But with the body politic as with the human body, there are some damages too deep for complete healing, some injuries that leave an indelible scar. In that category falls the Senate Act of 1955.

9

The Changing Pattern of South African Society

Economic Straitjacket

While the battle of the franchise, and the constitutional crisis which it had initiated, were changing the political shape and character of the South African state in the name of apartheid, apartheid was putting its mark on the social and economic organisation of the country with equal determination if with less public appreciation of all the implications of the process. Dr. Malan had responded to General Smuts' challenge to him in 1951 to resign as being unable to fulfil what he claimed was his mandate to establish political apartheid with the statement that political apartheid was only a part of the apartheid plan and, he suggested, not even the most important part. Apartheid, he said, was a policy to be pursued wherever White and non-White came into contact with one another, and his Government, although held for the time being on the political front, was indeed pursuing it at an ever increasing tempo on the economic and social fronts where there were no obstacles to block their path.

As representatives of Africans we could not fail to know that that claim was amply justified, that the policy of segregation with all its discriminatory implications, far from being on the way out as we had hoped, was ramifying all over the body social and economic, and that in a way that had seemed to us quite inconceivable in a modern state. Many of the earlier and more conspicuous developments in the policy, separation on trains, racially defined population registration, the prohibition of mixed marriages and of extra-marital relations between White and non-White, group areas legislation designed to separate the various racial groups in respect of living space, had little immediate effect on the African population; the separations these measures were designed to effect had for the most part long been operative as between White and Black on the basis either of law or of custom. This did not mean that they were

310

not a matter of concern to us. On the contrary, any extension of the
policy of segregation was a matter of grave concern to us as involving new challenges to our conception of the course which public
policy ought to take and as making the road to saner policies longer
and more difficult.

But the will and intention to pursue the policy of separation which
these developments reflected had their own immediate implications
for the emerging African population that put in jeopardy such advance, economic and social, as had been made over the years,
created new obstacles to further advance, and were to show all the
signs in fact of making the African population not an integral part
of a developing democracy but a rootless and rightless proletariat
in the land of their birth, with all the dangers which that implied.

The record began in the first months of the new Government's
office, with a circular taking up the tale of the White labour policy
where the first Nationalist Government had left it. Whites were to
be substituted for non-Whites in all Government departments
wherever possible, even at the messenger level. A year or so later,
there began that attack on the number and the earnings of the
Africans in the railway service to which I have referred earlier.[1] In
response to claims from his own side of the House that the previous
Government had increased the non-European labour force out of all
proportion to the increase in the European force in this national
service, and had granted it both larger pay increases and larger cost
of living allowances than had been conceded to the European employees, Mr. Sauer took his stand on a controlled ratio both in
respect of employment and of remuneration as between White and
non-White employees in the service of his department, adding,
'When it is a question of letting either a European or a Native go,
I let the Native go. I want to make this perfectly clear.'[2] At the same
time, he refused a request from a member of the United Party,
Mr. Allen of Roodepoort, himself an old railway servant, that
Africans should be allowed to serve Africans in railway booking
offices. There would not, he said, be enough work to keep them
employed—a very doubtful argument in respect of a service in which
African third class travel was of major importance in maintaining
the level of revenue in the passenger service. In any case, White
trade unionists would not like it.

[1] See p. 114.
[2] Hansard, Vol. 73, Col. 8224.

A year later, the Minister of Labour put on the statute book a Native Building Workers' Act[1] which, while creating machinery under which Africans might be trained for such building as is customary in Native areas, laid down that no person should in our urban areas, and elsewhere outside Native areas, employ any Native on skilled work. In 1956, a new Minister of Labour, Senator de Klerk, was to round off a spreading system of control of the labour pattern of developing industry with the notorious amendment to the Industrial Conciliation Act giving legislative shape to the principle of job reservation.[2] Designed to prevent changes in the racial composition of the labour market in the interests of White labour, it was argued that this legislation could also protect other groups, for example the Coloureds, against competition from Africans. In effect the position of the African at the bottom of the economic scale was to be frozen with even that level conspicuously insecure, as was manifested in the enforced dismissal of all African lift attendants in Johannesburg in favour of Whites. It was an order which ousted men from jobs that, in some cases, they had held with satisfactory service for many years; and to my query as to where these displaced workers had gone, the Minister had no information to give. He did not know.

In the meantime, the early foreshadowed removal of the bulk of the African workers from the cover of unemployment insurance had taken shape. In 1949, the Minister of Labour had legislated to exclude from the benefits of the Unemployment Insurance Act all Africans earning less than £180 (R360) per year.[3] In reply to our contention that these, as the most lowly paid section of the labour market, were those most in need of some security against the blasts of unemployment, the Minister argued that there was always work to be had on farms, so that any African falling out of employment in an urban area was not technically unemployed. That farming had continuously failed to attract what the farming community regarded as adequate supplies of African labour by the conditions of employment which it offered had as little effect on the Minister's attitude in this matter as the additional and very important consideration that leaving an urban area to take work on a farm could, and indeed would, involve for the African worker the loss of such

[1] Act 41 of 1949.
[2] Act 28 of 1956.
[3] Act 41 of 1949.

domiciliary right as he might have succeeded in establishing in the urban area.

And as if to weaken still further a position that seemed already to deny all security, a Native Settlement of Disputes Act[1] had translated into permanent form the provision of the War Measure under which all strike action by African workers had been made illegal. It was significant that one of the purposes of the Act was, in the words of the Minister who introduced it, to bleed Native trade unions to death.[2] Trade unionism, he argued, was not a weapon that Africans could handle. With them, it merely became an instrument of political agitation.

Incidentally, by this time, the whole pattern of South African trade unionism was passing out of the hands of the trade unionists, to be shaped to the Government's pattern, that is on a racial basis.[3] What Mr. Christie had feared was coming to pass; the organisation of the workers, like the organisation of industry's labour pattern, was passing into the hands of the Government.

But these were only the more direct attacks in terms of the apartheid policy on the economic position of the people whose interests were our special responsibility. Every session saw some addition to the complex of laws which, by curtailing rights of movement, of access to property, and of domicile outside Native reserve, weakened the bargaining power, even within the range of employment open to them, of an African population progressively dependent on wage-earning employment to live.

One of the first of these was an extension of the disability imposed in the latter years of the Smuts regime on Africans from the Ciskei and the Transkei desiring to travel to Cape Town in search of work. An amendment to the Railways and Harbours Act under which this disability existed gave to ticket clerks in railway offices the right and the duty to demand permits to travel from all rural Africans seeking to move townward before issuing tickets entitling them to travel. In due course, this legislation was overrun by extensive amendments to the Urban Areas Act designed to confine the process of urbanisation within such limits as the Government was prepared

[1] Act 48 of 1953.
[2] African trade unions were not illegal but were unrecognised under the industrial laws of the country.
[3] The Amendment to the Industrial Conciliation Act which established job reservation (28 of 1956) imposed upon the trade union movement a strict division on the basis of colour.

to permit. Under these, all work seekers were channelled through labour bureaux which controlled not only the direction of the flow of African labour but also the nature of the work which an African work seeker might take. This control was rapidly extended to limit his right to move from one job to another to an extent which scarcely left room for the application to Africans of the Labour Department's job reservation powers. It was a system of direction of labour effectively supported by the progressive application over the whole country of the system of labour service contracts, duly entered in reference books which any authorised person could demand, failure or inability to produce constituting a criminal offence. It provided a comprehensive extension of the area of those pass laws on the abolition of which the Natives Representative Council had been progressively persistent, with the whole range now organised for more effective administration. This was done significantly in terms of an Abolition of Passes and Co-ordination of Documents Act which was one of Dr. Verwoerd's earliest achievements as Minister of Native Affairs.[1]

Coupled with these controls over the African worker as a worker went the progressive elimination of any rights of domicile of Africans outside Native reserves. In the final stages of the Smuts regime, in an effort to apply to Africans in the process of urbanisation social welfare services organised on a basis designed to take into account the varying costs of living between town and country, it had been decided at the administrative level to regard five years' residence in a town as evidence of permanent urbanisation. With the advent of a government which insisted that in no circumstances should Africans be regarded as part of the permanent population of the urban areas, no more was heard of this proposal. Now, qualifications for some degree of permanence, including the right to have a house which might accommodate wife and family, were laid down as ten years in the service of one employer or fifteen years' residence in the specific area with an unblemished police record—a considerable achievement in view of the mass of statutory offences, ever extending, that beset the African's path. Birth in an urban area had, even in terms of Hertzogite segregation, been accepted as qualification for domicile. This still constituted a claim in the specific area, but it rapidly became birth and continuous residence. By the time we left Parliament in 1960, both these conditions offering a limited

[1] Act 67 of 1952.

measure of security, and of family life, were on the way out. In the meantime, all such rights of private ownership of property in urban areas as had survived from more mellow days had either been abolished or were in process of liquidation. In terms of the apartheid policy, urban areas were to be and were to remain White areas in which no African might own fixed property.

While these developments struck at the roots of recognisable opportunity for Africans within our system as it had developed, only one thing could have offered some consolation and compensation both to them and to us for the threat to past attainment and future hopes alike: that was not merely the promise of a recognisably adequate alternative, but the evidence of intention to make African loss and gain at least approximately equal both in time and in scope. The record here was profoundly discouraging both in theory and in practice. As time went on, there was indeed much talk of fair play and of separate development, but evidence as to where and how this was to happen was conspicuous by its absence. Even while these economic discriminations against Africans were taking shape within the society which in fact we shared, progressively reducing them to the common level of migrant workers, Government spokesmen emphatically repudiated the idea of any partition of the country which might provide an area, with a share of the developed resources they had helped to create, where Africans might enjoy some of the opportunities and rights which were being denied them in what was claimed as White area. Yet without this, what could apartheid be other than naked exploitation, and by what philosophy could it justify itself in the eyes of the world and in its own eyes?

This was to be a continuing subject of argument and contention over the years. It was an argument in which the political and the economic were inextricably linked, as they still are. It began to emerge in specific form in the first months of the new regime, in the third election for Native Representatives in terms of the Representation of Natives Act, held in November 1948. It was an election in which the Government found itself curiously and deeply interested. Having fought the general election on a programme which included the abolition of the Native Representatives in the House of Assembly, it was now to be found not merely countenancing but actively encouraging the candidature of people representing the policy of the Party.

Up to this point, both major Parties had kept officially clear of
these elections—as indeed apart from this occasion they were to do
throughout the history of this experiment.[1] The departure from this
practice, and in the particular circumstances of the occasion,
naturally became a focal point of attack from the Opposition
benches when Parliament reassembled in the beginning of 1949.
In response to these attacks, Government spokesmen claimed then
and consistently claimed later that in fact the Party never at any
time put up candidates in the elections under the Representation
of Natives Act. The Minister of Native Affairs, then Dr. Jansen,
who had to face the main brunt of the Opposition's attacks, admitted that the Party had put up one official candidate, that was
for the Natal Senate seat.[2] As for the other candidates who stood
ostensibly on the Government Party's programme, these were
independents whose candidature he felt free to support as he had
done in the case of my opponent when addressing the Ciskeian
General Council meeting that year; but he accepted no responsibility for all that they had said in the course of the campaign.

It was claimed by the Opposition, however, that the one candidate whom the Minister did acknowledge as a party nominee had
told the Zulus that a Zulu state would be set up by the Nationalist
Government. Dr. Jansen repudiated this idea with all the force he
could command. He knew of no Nationalist candidate who had
promised the Zulus that they would form a Zulu state, and, he said,
he could find no confirmation of the Opposition's contention that
the candidate and an organiser of the Nationalist Party supporting
him had told a meeting that 'a section of Natal and Zululand would
be given back to the natives'.[3]

By the following year, 1950, the argument had derived new force
and new significance from discussions which had taken place at a
meeting of the Synod of the Dutch Reformed Churches at Bloemfontein on the eve of the Parliamentary session, the first long session
of the new regime. One outcome of these discussions, in which the
Sending Kerk—the missionary church—had been well to the fore,
had been an agreement that apartheid, to be morally justified, must

[1] The only parties which directly interested themselves in these elections were the
Communist Party and, after 1953, the Liberal Party. The Nationalist Party, however, took a very active unofficial interest in the Transvaal-Free State Senate seat
in the 1954 election and found a seat on their own benches for the defeated
Nationalist-minded candidate.
[2] The abolition of the Senate seats had not yet been adumbrated.
[3] Hansard, Vol. 66, Col. 1689.

be complete. This was indeed a challenge to the politicians which they were not slow to recognise. Dr. Malan and Dr. Jansen at once made it clear that this was a proposition that they could not accept. Inevitably strongly pressed on the matter by all the Oppositions, Dr. Malan, with appreciative and conciliatory references to the knowledge, experience and good intentions of the Church Conference, declared that if one could attain total territorial apartheid, everyone would admit that it would be the ideal state of affairs; but that was not the policy of his Party, and was nowhere to be found in the official declarations of their policy. Total territorial apartheid, he said, was in fact impracticable in the existing circumstances of South Africa, where the whole economic structure was 'to a large extent based on native labour', and 'it does not pay any party to endeavour to achieve the impossible'.[1] In the future, for all he knew, perhaps progress might be made along the lines of the resolutions taken at the Church Congress. In the meantime, the first and most important problem was that there were many Natives who had never lived in the reserves, but had always lived in European areas, and if one tried to send them back to their tribal homes, the Native reserves would have to be considerably extended, and much more land would have to be given to them, otherwise there would be tremendous congestion and no work for them, and they would starve. In the circumstances he saw the objective of the policy of apartheid as merely checking 'the harmful flow of Natives from the native areas to the European areas as much as possible without doing harm to the demands for labour in the European areas'. For the rest, it was simply to be that reduction of all social contacts within the common community to which his Government was applying itself so assiduously.

Dr. Jansen, as Minister of Native Affairs, elaborating the Prime Minister's case,[2] made it abundantly clear that so far as he and his leader were concerned, apartheid was in fact merely the old policy of segregation more effectively and extensively applied to meet the new circumstances which had grown up with the progress of industrialisation. To both, any idea of a separate political existence for any non-European group was simply a travesty of their policy, hostile propaganda intended to create economic insecurity and instability and to frighten the electorate. White supremacy over the

[1] Hansard, Vol. 71, Col. 4142.
[2] Hansard, Vol. 71, Col. 4697 *et seq.*

whole of the country, dressed up from time to time as trusteeship, put a limit to whatever rights Africans were to have even in their own areas; and Dr. Jansen made it clear that those areas would not be enlarged even to the extent of the 1936 quota except on evidence of improved use of the existing reserves, and even then only with the consent of the farming community who would have to surrender the land necessary for such extension.

For Mr. Strydom, who was destined to succeed Dr. Malan as Prime Minister, there was not even much room for trusteeship. He had made his approach to the position of the African in the country quite clear in the 1948 general election campaign. It should be that of master and servant-baasskap. There was no need to apply apartheid on the platteland, the rural farming areas of the country, he argued; it already existed there since no African could be legally there except as a servant. There were no circumstances applicable there under which an African could acquire domicile. And what applied there should in his opinion apply generally—White supremacy and the superiority of White interests, supported and maintained by dis-criminatory legislation. That was the only way in which it could be maintained, he argued in a debate in which he challenged the official Opposition, increasingly committed to the fact of integra-tion, to say whether it was prepared to abolish the discriminatory provisions of our law as affecting people whom they were prepared to accept as part of their nation—a position which Mr Strydom again repudiated for himself and the Nationalist Party.

Dr. Verwoerd's accession to the office of Minister of Native Affairs added another—and increasingly dominant—voice to the argument. It did not however add any more encouraging element to the practical situation. On the contrary, while his dynamic drive increased the tempo of the process of separation in the 'white' areas, it not only failed to produce alternative sources of opportunity and advance for the people discriminated against; it seemed in fact designed to do so. While the spreading restrictions on African urbanisation and African access to the labour market denied the African people advance in the developed sector of the economy which might produce some of the accumulated savings necessary to finance such development, Dr. Verwoerd's increasingly rigid inter-pretation of the obligations and intentions of apartheid were to cut the African community off from outside sources of capital and experience for the development of the reserves which alone could have helped to fill the gap. Over the years, he was to elaborate at considerable length the arguments by which he sought to support and provide a moral basis for these two aspects of a policy which, in their practical effects on the life of the African people, seemed to the democratic and liberal spirit completely irreconcilable. For the Whites, he argued that apartheid must not produce a competitive economy to endanger their livelihood. Latterly, as the need to justify the policy from the African side became increasingly pressing, Dr. Verwoerd was to lay more and more stress on the unwisdom, and indeed on the injustice, of encouraging the development of an African economy on lines unfamiliar to African experience and foreign to African tradition.

From the beginning, and continuously, for Dr. Verwoerd as for Dr. Malan and Dr. Jansen, the ideal was total separation; but to him, as to them, it was in the prevailing circumstances an impractical ideal. In his earliest speeches in Parliament, he repudiated emphatically the Opposition's contention that his interpretation of apartheid given to the Natives Representative Council meant, if it meant anything, the fragmentation of South Africa both economically and politically. He denied forcefully that it implied the creation of autonomous states with power to enter into hostile alliances against White South Africa if they wished to do so, and with independent economies to support them, which the sincere apostles of apartheid would have to help them to create, involving inevitably an implicit threat to the 'White' community. Neither he nor his Party had ever suggested anything that could justify this contention. He had indeed told the Council that 'in their own areas' the Bantu might develop to the highest degree of self-government, but he went on to explain that this was local self-government. His opponents had read more into his statements than he had said or implied. 'What they did,' he declared, 'was to announce that we were going to create separate states. There is not a word in my speech about separate states.'[1] But they had gone further, he went on indignantly, and had said 'these states (this was supposed to be our policy) would be able to enter into foreign relations on their own account. My view is this: all these areas can become self-governing, and in this sense they can have baasskap (supremacy) over their own fate; but all these areas will be within the geographic and economic unit of the Union of South Africa and dependent on

[1] Hansard, Vol. 76, Cols. 7817, 7818.

it. Also in respect of any international relations concerning the
defence of this country. It speaks for itself that South Africa is the
trustee and the ruler of the whole. We have always said that the
white man must rule in South Africa, but the National Party favours
local self-government for the Native in his own areas.'

On the subject of international relations, the other side had said
something 'he had never said and never would say', and he wound
up this speech to the House of Assembly with a repetition of his
contention that under apartheid, the white man would not only
enjoy supremacy in his own part of the country, but also 'as trustee
in respect of the outside world and of the interests of South Africa
as a whole'.

Elaborating this theme in the Senate in May of that year (1951),
he was at pains particularly to dispose of the Opposition's contention that apartheid must mean two economies involving not only a
competitive industrialisation of the Native areas but a very considerable enlargement of these areas at the expense of 'White' South
Africa. He had never spoken of two quite separate economies developing in this country, he declared, and he repudiated the
contention that, to be just, any policy of apartheid must involve an
increase in the allocation of land made to the Africans in terms of
the current land laws. 'It is often said . . . that the Europeans own
a much greater portion of South Africa than the Natives have in the
reserves, so that the latter are most unfairly treated. . . . Let us
analyse that position and see whether it fairly states the case. You
cannot just look at the map, as everybody should know. There is a
vast difference not only in the value of the land, but also in the possibility of living on that land. Also there is another factor which
must be taken into consideration, and that is that of the 8,000,000
Natives, only 3,000,000 actually are . . . to a certain extent bound
to the reserve areas. The amount of land set aside for the Natives is
therefore not expected to provide for 70 per cent of the population.'[1]
Dr. Verwoerd went on to argue that under the Native land laws,
while 13 per cent of the land area of the country might ultimately
pass into the hands of the Africans, that 13 per cent in fact represented 30 per cent of the productive area of the country. Indeed,
'often the Native area is productive to a greater degree if properly
utilised than much of the productive portion apparently set aside
for the Europeans, but on which the other 5,000,000 Natives also

[1] Senate Hansard, May 1st, 1951, Cols. 2832-3.

mainly lives, plus giving additional income to reserve Natives'.[1] To this he added the highly significant argument in favour of the existing land distribution: 'When one realises the difference in the standard of living of the European family and the Native family, then it is clear that for a family of five Europeans one should have on an average 105 morgen and Natives on an average sixteen morgen. That means that the Natives could actually exist on one sixth of the productive area on which the European could. But in actual fact you find that 29 per cent of the Native population live on 30 per cent of the productive areas.'

Over the years the argument as to the degree of separateness involved in apartheid developed on both the political and the economic fronts. Inevitably the Oppositions pressed Dr. Verwoerd, first as Minister of Native Affairs and later as Prime Minister, on both the logic and the morality of his case. If the policy of integration (to which the United Party was more and more committed as meeting the facts of the case) must lead to black rule in South Africa, the constant repetitive challenge of the Government side, surely an apartheid policy must in the nature of things lead to a demand for, and a determination on the part of the Africans to achieve, full and complete autonomy with all that that implied. But while he was insistent that the Oppositions should face the logic of their position, so far as his own policy was concerned Dr. Verwoerd progressively took refuge in the contention that it is useless to look too far ahead; it was only possible to set a direction. In 1959, after he had become Prime Minister, he did indeed commit himself to the possibility of ultimate African independence—no doubt under the necessity to justify his decision to abolish all African representation in Parliament, and under pressure of events in the world outside.[2] An all-over Bantustan he specifically repudiated even then. The ethnic groups were to be preserved—for themselves. Once only did he suggest that, one day, these groups might consider establishing a central Council for themselves, but he did not think they

[1] At this time, the declared policy of his party was to get as many Africans out of the towns as possible, but the country areas and the mining industry might legitimately, in terms of the policy, claim any labour resources they could command.

[2] After his return from the Prime Ministers' Conference in 1961, he did commit himself explicitly if reluctantly to the possibility of ultimate African independence. 'We again unequivocally state the policy of the development of the different race groups. The Bantu will be able to develop into separate Bantu States. This is not what we would have liked to see. It is a form of fragmentation which we would not have liked if we were able to avoid it.' (Hansard, Vol. 107, Col. 4191.)

X

would be prepared to accept the surrender of a part of their own authority which this would involve; and so long as he was in control, this would clearly not be encouraged or possibly even permitted. He would no doubt argue that such a development would be a betrayal of his trust to preserve the culture of each group for its own posterity.

But even for the separate ethnic groups, even while he began to talk of the Bantu being able to go to any heights of which they were capable, the implications were carefully circumscribed for both the immediate and the distant future. In a speech in the 1959 session of Parliament on the Promotion of Bantu Self Government Bill in which he was elaborating what was being received as his 'new vision', that is, 'this possible ultimate independence for Africans', he defended himself against the accusation of fragmenting South Africa by claiming to be doing what Britain was doing for Basutoland.[1] 'When one says we are no longer going to give the Bantu representation in the white Parliament, because that white Parliament after all is the governing body of the white man in his own areas, but the white man with his Parliament will carry out the duties of guardianship over the Bantu in the Bantu areas and will give them the opportunity to develop fully in those areas, everyone knows what the future possibilities are'[2]—a conclusion not quite so clear to others as to himself. Feeling that he was getting less credit than he deserved for this new vision, he argued, 'That is what the outside world praises when Colonial powers give independence to territories. That in why England has been praised in regard to Basutoland. I therefore do not understand why we should be attacked in this respect. 'Surely,' he demanded, 'the United Party is not going to persist in its accusation that we want to create Bantustans with consequent dangers to South Africa?'

Pressed further on the issue of potential full African independence, he countered with another analogy drawn from British experience. There were many forms of self-government which fell short of independence. Had not the old Cape Colony enjoyed responsible government for many years under the imperial control of Britain, which certainly meant less than full independence?

Dr. Verwoerd had already borrowed from the imperial record of Britain the idea of the Commonwealth, a conception which still had

[1] Now Lesotho.
[2] Hansard, Vol. 101, Col. 6214. *et seq.*

the attraction to one in his position of suggesting a continuing basic unity of politically diverse groups under the privileged guidance and control of the parent body.[1]

All this seemed to take care of the political shape of things to come without challenging too deeply that passionate intention that nationalism had bred in his own Party to possess and to dominate the whole of South Africa. In any case, the possible implications of the programme were all comfortably cushioned for them by continual insistence on the need to accommodate the tempo of change to the pace of the African himself as estimated by the white trustee. It did not, however, of itself dispose of the question of the economic pattern. On the contrary, as things were developing, the answer to this, as affecting the day-to-day life of all the people—but, in particular, of the African population—was becoming increasingly urgent.

Throughout the debates on the practical implications of apartheid which, over these years, seemed interminable, Dr. Verwoerd was at pains, as Dr. Malan had been, to repudiate the idea that apartheid stood for oppression of the non-Whites, and particularly of the Africans. True, discrimination did exist in present-day South Africa. That, he maintained, was inevitable when you had the races mixed up as they had been allowed to become, and as the European became more and more threatened by the tide of African migration flowing into the 'White' areas. But when that tide had been turned, which was an essential objective of the apartheid policy, the Bantu people would be in a position to enjoy in their own areas the opportunities now denied them in European areas.[2] When and how the tide would be turned became a matter of repetitive contention between the two sides in Parliament. For some time, the argument was blunted somewhat by the existence of the Socio-Economic Commission,[3] appointed by Dr. Jansen to explore this and relevant matters and to plot a course for the practical application of the Government's policy. The specific terms of reference of the Commission were 'to conduct an exhaustive enquiry into and to report on a comprehensive scheme for the rehabilitation of the Native areas with a view to developing within them a social structure in keeping with the culture of the Natives and based on effective

[1] Hansard, Vol. 98, Col. 4158.
[2] Presumably they would also be less discriminated against in the latter area since they would no longer be feared to the same extent, although there was little enough in the presentation of the policy to support this contention.
[3] The Tomlinson Commission, U.G. 61, 1955, appointed in 1949.

socio-economic planning'. It was a large assignment which the members of the Commission[1] took very seriously. While the Commission pursued its investigations, however, Dr. Verwoerd as Minister of Native Affairs offered various glimpses of the way in which his own mind was working in the matter. In the reserves themselves, if the flow of population to urban areas was to be stemmed, there must of course be improved use of land. In this the Government would assist, and was assisting through the special section of the Native Affairs Department concerned with agriculture. Here he accepted my contention that this must necessitate consolidation of holdings into economic units. Indeed, he had already appointed committees to survey the various areas to establish what in each case the economic unit should be.[2] He also agreed that no real improvement in the existing situation could be achieved save by reducing very considerably the number of people on the land. This he proposed to do by developing a plan which in fact the United Party had adopted while in office, namely that of gathering into villages as many as possible of those families domiciled in the reserves who were landless and dependent on wage earning to live. To these would be added the additional surplus which the process of consolidation of holdings must produce.

At this point there naturally arose the proposition that had often been canvassed in the past, that is, the possibility of an economic diversification of the reserves themselves. It was a proposition that had been investigated from time to time, particularly after the formal acceptance of the Hertzog segregation policy, but without any practical results. Under the new dispensation it assumed a new importance—and a new urgency. How far and how fast would Dr Verwoerd's dynamism carry us in this regard?

It was early apparent that the new Minister did not visualise a progressive industrialisation of the reserves as likely to contribute much to the solution of his problem of turning back the tide of African migration. In the first review of the needs of the situation, he expressed it as his view that the nature of the industries which probably might be developed within a Native area within a measurable space of time would be small in extent and limited in

---

[1] It included two members of Dr. Verwoerd's departmental staff and the member of Parliament destined to succeed him at Native Affairs, Mr. de Wet Nel.
[2] He came later to the conclusion that he should not interfere with the traditional practice in regard to landholding in the reserves; that was a matter for the Bantu themselves, he decided.

character. He instanced, as having been referred to by earlier committies of enquiry, the broom industry and a ceramics industry. Later he was to add furniture making for their own people. In the circumstances, since the chances of the Native in regard to his own industrial development within his own area seemed to him so limited, he pleaded, he said, for the development of European industries in the vicinity of Native areas 'in view of the possibility that the Native labourer will otherwise be torn from his community and be drawn into our white community to be integrated there'.[1]

Here finally emerged the idea of border industries which was to become the key factor in his plans for turning back the flow of Africans from the reserves and ultimately for holding the numbers in the white areas at a not unhealthy level. In the succeeding years, we were to hear a good deal about this plan. But since the border industries were to be 'white' industries governed and controlled by the complex of labour and other laws which limited the economic field open to Africans, it continued to be difficult to see what contribution these industries could make to the effective development of the African population inside and outside Native areas.

The release of the report of the Socio-Economic Commission to the Government in 1954 and to Parliament in 1956 (in the abbreviated edition prepared by the Commission itself) raised the issue of the economic implications of apartheid in its most specific and direct form. Interpreting their terms of reference in the widest sense, the Commission made extensive recommendations revolving round the conclusion that 'the separate development of the European and Bantu Communities should be striven for as the only direction in which racial conflict may possibly be eliminated and racial harmony possibly be maintained'. The way to this objective it found to be 'in the sustained development of the Bantu areas on a large scale'.[2] It proceeded to elaborate an extensive programme for the aforementioned development and diversification of the Native areas which called for the co-operative effort of private capital as well as extensive public spending which it placed in the region of (£104,000,000) R208,000,000 in the following ten years. It pressed the urgency of this programme if the reserves themselves were to be

---

[1] May 28th, 1951. Hansard, Vol. 76, Col. 7799.
[2] Socio-Economic Commission, abbreviated edition, para. v, p. 194—U.G. 61, 1955.

saved from the corroding effects of past neglect and resources developed which would provide both for their present inhabitants and for future generations the sources of gainful employment necessary if the flow of migration to the 'white' areas was to be checked. On the basis of this programme resolutely pursued it believed the Government could count on holding the African population in the 'white' section of the country at some 6,000,000 at the end of the century.

Its scheme also proposed as an essential condition of the progress under which the Native reserves would begin to be able to contribute to their own advance, not only consolidation of the fragmentary holdings which constituted the general pattern of these areas, but consolidation of many of the lesser areas themselves. In their recommendations in respect of consolidation of holdings, the standard of measurement for economic units which they applied was one which could guarantee to the owner and his family a cash income of £60 (R120) per annum.

To anyone familiar with the conditions of African life in South Africa, the development of the Native reserves must be a claim upon both the public conscience and public resources of high priority all too long neglected. With the advent of a government committed to rigid curtailment of African opportunity in the developed sector of the economy, it had become insistently urgent. The Commission's report had therefore been awaited with considerable interest and some hope. Its recommendations, stressing both the need and the urgency, seemed reasonable in direction, whatever the political philosophy which inspired them. Whatever could raise the standard of the population of these areas, and thus increase their bargaining power, must carry the support of any liberal-minded person. These recommendations, in many respects modest enough, could encourage some hopes in that regard.

Whether these hopes would be realised or not now depended on the extent to which the Government—in effect, the Minister— would find the Commission's recommendations acceptable. We were not long left in doubt that on at least one important point, Dr. Verwoerd had ideas of his own which were not those of the Commission. Soon after the receipt of the report by the Government, the two members of the Commission drawn from the Native Affairs Department had second thoughts about the recommendation that private capital should be encouraged to establish industries in the reserves, and reversed their decision in this regard. Dr. Verwoerd was unshakably opposed to this proposition.[1] He was to demonstrate the truth of his assertion made in the House of Assembly on another occasion, 'My Department advocates what I advocate.'

We were thus prepared for a measure of disagreement between the Minister and the Commission, with the last word lying with the Minister. We were scarcely prepared for the extent of this disagreement which was to carry away most of the hopes which the report had engendered. It was fully reflected in a White Paper[2] released to Parliament on the eve of a debate to be initiated by the Minister on a motion that the House discuss the report of the Commission for the Socio-Economic Development of the Bantu Areas within the Union of South Africa. It seems appropriate to quote the introductory paragraphs of this remarkable document. No paraphrasing could do justice to the attitude and intention which inspired it, and indeed was progressively inspiring the whole conduct of public affairs in this period.

Commencing with the statement that in connection with the Report of the Socio-Economic Commission it was necessary that the Government should make known its attitude in three respects, it proceeded to specify:

(i) The factual material obtained by valuable basic research of a scientific nature and by the compilation of previously established but often inaccessible data (which together constitute the main objective aimed at in appointing such a commission) is accepted—not only as the basis of the findings and views of the Commission itself but also as a basis for the further development of ideas and the determination of policy, by the Government and the departments concerned, in so far as amplification may prove necessary.

(ii) The Government welcomes the unequivocal rejection of the policy of Integration and of any theories on a possible middle course, as well as the justification by the Commission of the policy of Apartheid (Separate Development) of the Government, gradually but purposefully applied. It also welcomes the endorsement of the standpoint of the Government, maintained through the years, that sufficiently rapid progress will have been made, and the further advancement of the process of separation guaranteed—in

---

[1] Later, Mr. de Wet Nel, then a member of the Native Affairs Commission, was also to revise his opinion on this matter.
[2] W.P.F., 1956.

other words that security would be ensured for white civilisation and opportunities created for both racial groups in all spheres, each in its own territory or among its own people—if after a period of fifty years an approximately equal proportion of whites and Bantu has been reached in European territory. The Government furthermore welcomes the support given its existing practice of planning and developing the Bantu Areas and the community life of the Bantu in such a way that they can serve their own people, and agrees that the pace should be steadily accelerated.

(iii) Choice of the methods by which the agreed aims of the Commission and the Government may best be realised is obviously not, like the determination of facts, a matter of scientific proof but of individual judgment. The Government appreciates the views expressed by the members of the Commission in this respect and carefully weighs each theory and recommendation. In addition the Government must take into account other considered views based upon much wider practical experience of administrative affairs, the possible use of existing state machinery, the applicability of methods suggested and the conduct of the country's finances. Such views can by placed at its disposal by the Public Service or gained by consultation with those in authority. The aim will always be to promote the accepted idea of progressive separation at the desired pace in a manner which will take the financial resources into account, will fit into the general administrative set-up, will not undermine the prosperity of the country or upset the way of life of European or Bantu, and will take into consideration adaptability to the changing circumstances that arise.

Having thus prepared the ground, Dr. Verwoerd proceeded to reject practically all the basic recommendations of the Commission for the attainment of the mutually agreed objective. In the debate that followed the introduction of his motion,[1] he explained at great length the grounds of his rejection. Still endorsing the need for improved use of land and the diversification of the economy of the reserves, he repudiated the suggestion of extensive outside assistance from either private or public sources in either regard. The introduction of private 'white' enterprise into the reserves could only lead either to the complete white domination of the reserves, with the consequent loss by the Africans of their whole inheritance, or— worse still—to an idea of economic partnership which must in-

[1] Hansard, Vol. 91, Col. 5295 et seq.

An historic aerial picture of the African multitude surrounding Sharpeville Police Station just before the shooting on March 21st, 1960

Professor Z. K. Mathews with Professor Duminy and Chief Justice Centlivres on the occasion of his delivery of the annual T. B. Davey Memorial Lecture at the University of Cape Town on August 15th, 1961

The Margaret Ballinger Home for convalescent and crippled African children, initiated and conducted by a group of Johannesburg white women. This Home is to be closed in terms of the Nationalist Government's policy of social separation.

(see pages 355–6)

MR. VICTOR POTO

(Paramount Chief of Western Pondo-land. Leader of the Transkei Democratic Party until 1966 when he handed over to his lieutenant, Mr. Knowledge Guzana.)

MR. KAISER MATANZIMA

(Paramount Chief of Emigrant Tembu-land. First Prime Minister of the Transkei.)

Mrs. Ballinger in Sydney on September 29th, 1960 with two Aborigine children, on the occasion of her delivery of the Annual Dyson Memorial Lectures

evitably lead to a demand for political partnership to which the Government was fundamentally opposed. On the other hand, extensive public assistance to Africans to diversify their own economy would destroy that spirit of self-help and enterprise on which alone a healthy development could be built. In this connection he had a good deal to say about the effects of the 'spoon-feeding' policies pursued by the previous Government in such efforts as they had made for rural rehabilitation. Looking at it from the point of view of the Bantu, he said, was he to be deprived of his only opportunity of self-development? This, the Minister implied, must happen if he was not allowed to develop at his own pace and in his own way. 'The Bantu must start on a small scale. Psychologically he is not adapted to industrial life and certainly not to private enterprise, to be able to start on a big scale. Nor'—referring to the suggestion that Whites or the Government might start industries to be taken over by Bantu later—'would he be in a position in ten or twenty years' time to take over big industries which have been developed there if his relationship towards industry has been simply that of the recipient and the outsider. The psychological mistakes which have been made in connection with developmental work in the rural sphere must not be repeated in the industrial sphere.[1] That is why the Governemnt believes in the principle, not only that the Bantu should start on a small scale, that in his own area he should be given the opportunity, but that in the main he must start on the basis of self-help. It is only when he mainly spends his own money . . . it is only if he seeks his progress on that basis that he has an opportunity of adapting himself psychologically to the demands of industrial life. But,' he emphasised again, 'he will not have that opportunity if the spoon-feeding system, which has been so disastrous in the past in the rural sphere is applied in this sphere.'

In the circumstances there was no need for the large financial allocations which the Commission had recommended; nor for the Industrial Development Corporation which was part of its plan. In any case, governments did not normally budget for more than one year at a time; and at that moment his Government was prepared to allocate £3,000,000 (R6,000,000) for such projects as it felt could reasonably be undertaken.[2]

[1] These were not specified.
[2] In 1959, after he had become Prime Minister, Dr. Verwoerd did establish a Bantu Investment Corporation—with a modest capital of R1,000,000 (£500,000). Act 34 of 1959.

For the solution of the problem of turning the tide of migration, he now depended primarily on the development of border industries. It was a development which should serve the Bantu well, he argued. These industries would not only provide employment near their homes for those dependent on wage earning: they would also provide the resources for expanding tertiary enterprise in the reserves themselves. Perhaps the critics of his plans did not know how a community was really constituted. He proceeded to explain: for every one person employed, services have to be provided for, on an average, five members—the average family. On a basis of that kind, he argued, 'the scope of the superstructure, that is the number of people who fulfil all sorts of duties, is so great. . . . In other words, for every 100,000 to whom employment can be given in the course of the next fifty years with the growing industries in the vicinity of Native areas, it will be possible on this broad basis, within Native areas where they perform all their services for themselves, to make provision for 2,500,000 persons.'[1] And that, he was to explain later and indeed to underline, would take place without danger to the position of the white worker.

But even with the most dynamic drive and the greatest degree of success the turning tide would still leave 6,000,000 Africans in the 'white' areas of what was still to be one country. This meant at its best one African for one European. How did that square with the idea of apartheid? Dr. Verwoerd was ready with 'clear' replies to this query also.

As far as the 6,000,000 were concerned who, it was estimated, would still be in the 'White' area in the year 2000, various points had to be taken into account. 'The first is that the assumption is unfounded that the same persons will always be domiciled here permanently. I foresee an interaction between the White area and the Bantu area; that those who obtain knowledge and skill by experience and training within the White area will use it in their own area, where there is further progress and opportunities of using their knowledge and skill. In other words, this interaction between the White area and the Bantu area is of great importance in considering the question as to whether we are dealing here with 6,000,000 permanent inhabitants.' He added significantly, 'Let me remind honourable members that of the 6,500,000 (*sic*) or thereabouts, 4,000,000 will in all likelihood be on the platteland; in other words,

[1] Hansard, Vol. 91, Col. 5308.

in a place where the problem of apartheid presents no difficulty to us and where apartheid is maintained locally.'[1]

While this last proposition was to take us back simply to Mr. Strydom's baasskap, European supremacy based on the master-servant relationship without rights of domicile for the servant, Dr. Verwoerd was to produce two other arguments to meet the Opposition's contention that the Government was practising integration and preaching apartheid as a justification of the denial of rights, particularly political rights, to the Africans in our midst. The first of these was that by using people as workers you do not thereby integrate them into your society, any more than you integrate the ox and the ass and the tractor which are also instruments of your economic activity. The argument would appear to be that if you concede no rights to your workers to progress and to become an accepted and recognised part of your economic system, they are not a part of your society.[2]

His second argument, which was to be much depended upon by his Party to excuse the rightless status which he postulated for the African worker, was that he was like the Italians who go to France to take up employment there. 'They remain Italians and they remain anchored in their homeland; that is where they seek their rights; they do not expect to ask for rights in the other place.'[3]

It must again be stressed that down to this point Dr. Verwoerd, like his predecessors, stood firmly for both one state in South Africa and one economy; and within that one state and that one economy White interests were and were to remain paramount. From the beginning of 1959, while he propounded his new vision of possible ultimate independence for the several ethnic African groups, if they should prove capable of developing themselves and their areas to that point, the argument in regard to the economic relationship of the respective groups and the 'white' state assumed a new relevance. Surely separate independent states must postulate separate economies; and if so, this must inevitably involve that competition with 'White' industries and 'White' employment which Dr. Verwoerd had been repeatedly insistent upon his intention to avoid.

In answer to repeated questions by me in a finance debate in regard to this, Dr. Dönges proffered the parallel of the common

[1] Hansard, Vol. 91, Col. 5311.
[2] More recently (September, 1965) an Under Minister of Labour explained that job reservation is itself a denial of integration. See also pp. 466–7.
[3] Hansard, Vol. 91, Col. 5312.

market in Europe, which was then much in the news. It seemed scarcely an appropriate parallel in the South African context. I had yet to learn that the contracting parties in that adventure were proposing to place all the control of and all the decisions in relation to their common interests in the hands of one of them. Yet Dr. Verwoerd had made it abundantly clear that it was the very essence of apartheid that no Black man should make a decision for a white man. It was indeed this which had led him to propound the possibility of South Africa taking the form ultimately of a Commonwealth on the British model where 'the various constituent members are not represented in the mother Parliament, but within which organisation there are still links—economic and otherwise—by which co-operation is possible without a mixed Parliament or Government, whether of the country itself or of the federation, ever being established'.[1]

Dr. Dönges responded in the customary way on such occasions, by silence; and Dr. Verwoerd himself complacently ignored these implications of the parallel when he produced the same sugggestion in the course of the debate on the Promotion of Bantu Self Government Bill. Again challenged by the Leader of the Opposition, now Sir De Villiers Graaff, as to the effects on the South African economy of a system such as the Bill postulated, which was to cut the Africans off from any share in the governmental machinery of the South African state and to justify it on the ground that they were being set on a course of their own, Dr Verwoerd who had earlier accused Sir De Villiers of being unable to differentiate between one national economy and one state,[2] declared: 'I just want to put this point again, that political independence here as in Europe, where they are striving for a European market, is compatible with economic interdependence, and is the right course to take in the South African situation.'[3]

This was the background against which African representation in Parliament strove to maintain its case, which was also the case of the Tomlinson Commission—that was, the urgent need for a dynamic development of our African population, both for their sakes and for the country's. Dr. Verwoerd had rejected the Commission—almost as completely and emphatically as he had rejected

[1] Hansard, Vol. 98, Cols. 4156–7.
[2] Hansard, Vol. 91, Col. 5515.
[3] Hansard, Vol. 101, Col. 6229.

us; and when our period of office terminated, the Native reserves remained economically undifferentiated areas of low productive level, their growing populations not less but more dependent on the established areas of industrial development, with both worker and employer in the straitjacket which apartheid had forged for them.

10

The Changing Pattern—
Administrative and Legal Apartheid

Afrikaner nationalism has always been loud in its claims to be democratic. Nothing has angered its advocates over the years more than the accusation that they are Nazi in temper and authoritarian in tendency and intention. Experience of Native representation as we knew it gave us particular opportunities to learn something of the interpretation which they put upon the idea and practice of democracy; and the more we learnt of it, the more appropriate did it seem to remember Dr. Verwoerd's injunction to which I have already referred: 'Now when a person uses a word like baasskap (supremacy), or any other word, then you, the opponents, must stick to the connotation of the word as used by that person.'[1] In considering Nationalist claims in this matter of democracy, it is essential to sort out the implications of language as used by them.

In the course of the long constitutional crisis over the Coloured vote, Dr. Malan said his Government had been accused of acting undemocratically. 'What is democracy?' he asked, and answered his own question thus: 'Democracy is nothing else than the implementation of the will of the people. There is only one superior sovereign in an ordered state which is founded on a democratic basis, and that is the people.' But who are the people—*die volk?* A very pertinent question in this context, and indeed in any context in South Africa. From the beginning much argument was to range round this theme. In his book, *Unity of the Afrikaner people and my experience on the way thereto,*[2] written at the end of his political career, the people (*die volk*) to whom he referred were the Afrikaans-speaking section of the South African population. This does not of itself justify the contention that he claimed on behalf of this section an overriding political control in the community. Indeed, at an early stage in the argument, Dr. Verwoerd was quoted as having written

[1] Hansard, Vol. 76, Col. 7817.
[2] *Afrikaner Volkseenheid en my ervaring op die pad daarheen.*

in the early days of the war in the *Transvaler*, the Nationalist Party's organ in the Transvaal of which he was the first editor, that after political victory 'our fight will become easier in every field and Nationalist Afrikanerdom will be able to dictate'.[1] Dr. Malan, to whom this proposition had been put by a United Party front-bencher, Mr. Sidney Waterson, for his endorsement or rejection, replied that Afrikanerdom might include Mr. Waterson himself. It was a suggestion that Mr. Waterson repudiated with: 'Not me, among people who want to dictate to the rest of the country.'

But Dr. Malan himself had early made it plain that there were conditions for belonging to 'the people' for whom he claimed sovereignty. The first of these, and indeed the essential one, was that those who aspired to belong must have accepted 'the traditional way' of South African life. This in effect meant a particular attitude to people of colour. In 1952, in the no-confidence debate of that year, initiated by the then new leader of the official Opposition, Mr. Strauss, he was quite specific in this regard. Accepting Mr. Strauss' contention that there had been a deterioration in race relations in the country, including those of English and Afrikaner to one another, he said, 'May I say that in this aspect national unity between Europeans completely depends on the question whether we as Europeans are in agreement regarding the maintenance of European domination in the Western Christian civilisation.'[2]

He had made on earlier occasions, and was again later to make the case that in his opinion there was sufficient common ground in this regard between the members of the two major parties to justify the Parties getting together to plan the next phase in the country's colour policy. It was on the strength of this that he made his offer of a joint select committee to go into the whole colour question again in the light of the new circumstances that had developed and the new problems that had arisen with the progress of industrialisation, and he was both surprised and indignant at the refusal of his offer on the ground that it was a condition of the offer that the proposed Committee should proceed from the principle of apartheid which the Opposition was not prepared to accept.

But if he felt that there was, or should be, common ground in this regard between the two main European groups in the country in terms of his declared policy, as I have already suggested, he was

[1] Hansard, Vol. 78, Col. 3944.
[2] Hansard, Vol. 78, Col. 224.

very specific about two exclusions. First, there was no place in his political philosophy for liberals. 'The difference between us and the liberals and communists' (whom it is instinctive in Nationalist thinking as to all extreme conservatives, to put together) 'is an inconceivable gulf' which he regarded as unbridgeable. It was a gulf which he traced back, to his own and his Party's satisfaction, to pre-Great Trek days and pernicious outside elements. This also was a theme which he had expounded on earlier occasions, inducing me to say that it was clear to me that in the state which Afrikaner nationalism as we were seeing it, proposed to build, there would be no place for people like me.

While that might still be prognostication, what was immediate and specific was that there was and was to be no place within the South African nation for any coloured person or group. Dr. Malan might not care at that moment to be as explicit and emphatic in regard to this second exclusion as Mr. Strydom ('If that is their nation'—referring to the Opposition—'it is not our nation'), but his letter to a friend in America, written in his last year of office (1954) and issued by the Prime Minister's office for public information, reflects the same attitude in terms of a philosophy now in process of elaboration to justify apartheid. Responding to a request from the Rev. John Piersma, who had written to him, he said, 'asking for a statement on the much disputed and misunderstood Apartheid policy of the South African Government', he wrote: 'The deep-rooted colour consciousness of the white South Africans—a phenomenon quite beyond the comprehension of the uninformed—arises from the fundamental difference between the two groups, White and Black. The difference in colour is merely the physical manifestation of the contrast between two irreconcilable ways of life, between barbarism and civilisation, between heathenism and Christianity, and finally between overwhelming numerical odds on the one hand and insignificant numbers on the other. Such it was in the early beginning, and such it largely remains. The racial differences are as pronounced today as they were 300 years ago.' 'Small wonder,' he added, 'that the instinct of self-preservation is so inherent in the white South African. He has retained his identity all these years. He is not willing to surrender it now.' It was a victory of survival which they had achieved 'by throwing an impenetrable armour around themselves, the armour of racial purity and self-preservation'.

It was an explanation of the course of history in South Africa over the preceding three centuries which tactfully ignored the existence of that large Coloured group in the population which the Government was at that moment so intent upon isolating politically, and the extensive legislative programme designed to isolate all our racial groups socially which it found necessary to maintain and to reinforce that 'impenetrable armour'. Following up his main theme, he went on to meet his correspondent's possible argument that the desire of 'white' South Africa for self-preservation could be fully achieved by dividing the country into two states with all the whites in one and all the blacks in another. Theoretically he agreed with that argument, but for the foreseeable future, that was not practical politics. 'Whether in time, we shall reach a stage where some such division, say on a federal basis, will be possible is a matter we must leave to the future.'

In the meantime his friend must give white South Africa credit for not being a nation of scheming reactionaries imbued with base and inhuman motives, nor a nation of fools blind to the gravity of their vital problem. 'They are normal human beings. They are a small nation, grappling with one of the most difficult problems in the world. To them, millions of semi-barbarous Blacks look for guidance, justice and the Christian way of life.'

Here followed an account of all that had been and was being done to fulfil these obligations, involving an extremely heavy burden upon the white population. It had been computed, he wrote, that every European taxpayer in our country carried more than four non-whites in order to provide the latter with the essential services involving education, hospitalisation, housing, etc. In the industrial field 'our industrial legislation makes no distinction on grounds of colour'. And in the political field Local, District and General Councils are firmly established in the Transkei and the Ciskei. These Councils play a major part in the administration of the Reserves, at the same time offering the Bantu ample opportunity for self-government, self-expression and increasing development. In addition, he added, 'the Bantu are represented in both Houses of Parliament by white representatives elected by themselves and given very specific charges'.[1]

A Native Representative was likely to find this a somewhat

---

[1] By this time the proposal to abolish Native representation in the House of Assembly had been put into cold storage, thanks to Mr. Havenga.

Y

highly coloured picture of the circumstances of African life in South Africa. Dr. Malan's authority for the cost to the European taxpayer of social services for Africans (to which his party had been so resolutely opposed when in Opposition) seemed to have forgotten or overlooked the contribution of the African himself to the standard of European living in South Africa—as Dr. Malan seems to have forgotten or overlooked the operation of the very rigid colour bar in the mining industry in terms of the Mines and Works Act. What, however, is not disguised in his letter is the subordinate position of the African, and indeed of the non-European generally, in the body politic and the absence of any prospect of a change in that regard.

A policy which explicitly, and for all foreseeable time, accepted four-fifths of the population as in the community but not of it could not fail to influence the shape and character of government. As Native Representatives, we were well placed to appreciate the nature and direction of this influence, since our constituents and we who spoke for them were the immediate target of the policy. It was to prove to us what had been the liberal's contention from the earliest days of the segregation policy, that freedom within any community is indivisible. The pursuit of a policy designed to maintain the privileged position of one group in the community was to prove impossible of achievement without a concentration of power in the hands of the executive, with the progressive exclusion of both the legislature and the judiciary, and the subjection of the rights of all to the declared objective of a section of the population.

The process of power concentration was—naturally—spasmodic —a periodic response to particular circumstances, which made it particularly difficult to focus—and to resist. The record of Dr. Malan's own period of office suggests a somewhat complex attitude on his part to the principle of government by consultation and consent, depending on what section of the population was under discussion. Committed at the time of his Party's first return to power to the abolition of Native representation as having only a nuisance value, in favour of something better, vaguely defined as 'self-government in their own areas', as I have noted in another context,[1] he could still commend the proposal to remove the Coloured people from the common roll and give them also something better which he described as the system the African people then enjoyed. On the

[1] See p.235.

mechanics of the system, as I have also noted elsewhere,[1] he found no difficulty in persuading himself—and Mr. Havenga—that the substitution of four representatives of the Coloured group for a voice in all the constituencies of the Cape Province involved no diminution of rights. Challenged as to whether the Coloured people saw the proposed change in the same advantageous light, asked whether they had been consulted and had agreed as to the merits of the change, his answer was one that we were to meet on many occasions and from other speakers on the Nationalist front—what obligation was there to consult the Coloured people? Had they been consulted in 1909 when the Act of Union was drawn up? Had the Natives been consulted in 1936 when the Hertzog Bills were put on the statute book?

There were, of course, historical answers to these questions. At both points the people affected had constituted part of the electorate and had carried what weight they could against the tide flowing strongly against them, in each case saving something from the threatened complete destruction of their rights. His final contention involved the whole question of the accepted conception of the range of democratic obligation. It was that the matter of the political rights of the Coloureds directly affected Whites. Were they then to be allowed to dictate the political shape of South Africa for the White group? To this there could only be one answer—an emphatic No. It reminded me of my first experience of Nationalist interpretation of constitutionalism in a multi-racial society. Many years previously, in December 1930, Dr. Jansen as Minister of Native Affairs in the first Hertzog Government had put before a nominated Conference of leaders of the African community the Hertzog plan of segregation; that is, he had in fact consulted what he regarded as responsible African opinion on General Hertzog's proposed legislative programme in this regard. But in his opening speech to the Conference, his direction to the members in regard to their discussions placed a clear limit upon the range of the consultation. 'It will be of no use to put forward propositions which you yourselves know cannot be accepted. You must bear in mind throughout that it is not only your own people who are concerned in the resolutions you may adopt, but that the Europeans are also interested, and that, this being a constitutional country, after all the final say rests with them.'

[1] See U.G. 26 of 1932.

When he again became Minister of Native Affairs, in Dr. Malan's
first Cabinet, being pressed on this matter of consultation, Dr.
Jansen took refuge in the trusteeship argument. According to this,
the African population were the wards of the Whites and, as noted
before,[1] he asked those of us who claimed their progressive right to
participate in the making of the laws by which they were governed,
since when had the trustee been called upon to give the ward a
voice in his, the trustee's affairs?

This attitude to Parliament as the White man's preserve was
reflected in angry references by Mr. Serfontein to a speech made
by Selope Thema in one of the last sessions of the Natives Representative Council: 'If the white man wants to make laws, then we must
be in the Parliament where the laws are made,' Thema had said.
An absolute demand for equality, declared Mr. Serfontein. 'The
Native wants to come and sit with me and with those members
(the Opposition) to make laws for the country,'[2] he ex-
claimed indignantly, and proceeded to accuse the ex-Secretary
for Native Affairs, Dr. Douglas Smit, then United Party member
for East London, of having encouraged him to make those
demands.

Mr. Serfontein went on to repeat Thema's demand, to which had
been added this very pertinent proposition: 'If you do not want
that' (that Africans should sit in Parliament to help make the laws
by which they were to be governed), 'then divide the country and
do not make laws for our side.' My interjection that that was surely
a logical proposition only served to stoke up Mr. Serfontein's wrath
and to draw me, no new experience, into the line of fire. 'Exactly,'
said Mr. Serfontein, 'there we have the hon. member for Cape
Eastern (Mrs. Ballinger) who was present at that Council meeting.
She agreed with Selope Thema. She shook hands with him and
congratulated him on his speech.' (I have no recollection of this, but
it was likely to be true in spirit if not in fact.) 'I ask her whether she
said a single word against that speech'—which is highly improbable,
since it so fully represented my own view of the logic of the situation, as I was to do my best to make clear on many subsequent
occasions. Indeed in 1956, when the report of the Tomlinson
Commission had given new point to specific planning for the future,
by which time it had been made clear that in no circumstances

[1] See p. 239.
[2] Hansard, Vol. 76, Cols. 7778-9.

would non-Whites be acceptable where decisions were to be made for Whites so long as Nationalism remained in control, I proposed a line of demarcation that would give the African people some of the developed resources of the country in which to build that separate development we had already heard so much about. My suggestion, which would have put the ports of East London and Durban on the black side of the line, was so fantastic in the eyes of the disciples of apartheid that it drew no more response than an idle interjection from Mr. Hans Abraham, now Commissioner-General to the Transkei—'Since when have they been a sea-faring people?' To which it was easy enough to reply, in the context of South African society, and particularly to a Party which conspicuously draws its support from a predominantly farming community, 'What has that to do with it? Since when have you been a sea-faring people?' It is not without interest that more recently the first Prime Minister of the incipient Bantustan of the Transkei has adumbrated a claim for an extension of his own frontiers even further west than the line I proposed. What the Zulus may claim in due course remains to be seen.

By the time this argument arose, the shaping of the machinery of government, like the moulding of the social and industrial organisation of the country in terms of the apartheid policy, had in effect passed into the hands of Dr. Verwoerd. Indeed, even as Dr. Malan was fumbling with the position, finding political answers to awkward questions, Dr. Verwoerd was adjusting both theory and practice of government to meet his own conception of the appropriate political framework of apartheid, drawing a clear dividing line between White and non-White. The significant feature of the emerging system was that progressively, all non-white groups were to become the preserve of the Government, insulated from the white electorate and even from Parliament itself. It was a process in which Parliament was to become its own executioner through the uncompromising application of majority rule which conveniently preserved the appearance of white democracy and disguised the essentially revolutionary character of the changes in progress. When his appointment as Minister of Native Affairs in 1951 provided Dr. Verwoerd with an entry into the House of Assembly, he had already held his curious, interesting and revealing meeting with the Natives Representative Council which had ended in the Councillors' challenge to his interpretation of politics, and their decision to put that interpretation to the Courts in terms of the Act under which the Council had been constituted. With that dynamic energy and relentless determination which marked all his political course, he set immediately about the business of re-shaping the whole political structure as it affected the African population, to set the pattern of political apartheid into which all non-white groups should be fitted in due course with appropriate adaptations.

The first and basic instalment of the process was the Bantu Authorities Act introduced in 1951, his first year as Minister. This Act not only fulfilled the declared intention of his Party of abolishing the Natives Representative Council; it planned an entirely new system of local government machinery in Native areas to replace the system of local Councils,[1] which had been developing for over half a century.

Introducing his Bill[2] as 'a constructive Bill' in which there was nothing that should be contentious, he acknowledged that there was some feeling over his proposed abolition of the Natives Representative Council. After our experience of that body, however, he felt that this proposal should not cause any trouble. He then proceeded to elaborate his new scheme of local government. This was to be built on the tribe and the tribal authority—the Chief and his Councillors. Out of two or more tribal authorities so constituted would develop a regional authority, and out of two or more regional authorities a territorial authority for the whole ethnic group would be constituted. This system, according to the Minister, would restore 'the natural Native democracy'. In each and all of the authorities, the constituent elements would be traditional and not elected, the Government—that is the Minister or his deputed officials—deciding who were genuinely and acceptably traditional in each case.

This system, the Minister claimed, was essentially the Africans' own, out of which something truly African might develop. It would not automatically replace the largely elective Councils that had developed to the level of General Councils in the Transkei and the Ciskei, but if the people of these and other areas where the old system was less advanced came to feel that the new system held more promise for them than a system derived from foreign sources

---

[1] The system to which Dr. Malan had made appreciative reference in his letter to Mr. Piersma.
[2] Hansard, Vol. 74, Col. 9807 et seq.

and based on foreign ideas, the changeover would take place.[1] It was a system significantly commended to the African people in an explanatory pamphlet drawn up in the Minister's department, on the ground among others that 'the Territorial Authority's word will be law and the people will more readily respect and obey it. The Councillors will perform their tasks without fear or prejudice, because they were not elected by the majority of votes.'[2]

The Bantu Authorities Bill, the Minister noted, made no provision for 'a general Union-wide authority, a kind of umbrella authority'. The reason for this, he explained, was that the Government proposed to build from the bottom up and not from the top down, as he claimed previous governments had done.

In any case, as his proposed system would take a very considerable time to develop, anything further could be left to the future when 'he himself (the Bantu) would have to decide whether he wanted any further forms of authority'—the ever-present hope that the logic of apartheid would never have to be faced.

It was clear that the Natives Representative Council, with its largely elective composition and its national range, could have no place in Dr. Verwoerd's scheme. His own explanation of its irrelevance was that it presented the classic example of the attempt to develop 'a sort of authority' from the top downwards. 'That is to say,' he declared, 'only a limited number of people were selected as members of a body by a method of election which was not in fact based on the principle of self-government. That small group assembled on behalf of the Natives without having been elected by existing self-governing bodies and without any own experience of self-government on a lower level.'[3]

In so far as I understood what all this meant, it seemed to me then, and still seems to me, a travesty of the history of this institution, as did Dr. Verwoerd's analysis of the reasons for the course which the Council had taken in its later years and the crisis point which its affairs had ultimately reached. General Smuts had seen the new Council as the apex of a system of local government which had been developing since 1894 and which Dr. Verwoerd himself

[1] We may appropriately note here that in due course the Transkeian and Ciskeian Councils did find themselves committed to the new system, in which the Minister's feelings and emotions were deeply involved, and the old Councils, with their half century of growth behind them, accordingly disappeared.
[2] Quoted by Dr. Eiselen, as Secretary for Native Affairs, in *Optima*, March 1959, under the title 'Harmonious multi-community'.
[3] Hansard, Vol. 76, Col. 9811.

at that moment was prepared to say had an important record of growth behind it. With that machinery, all the rural members, elected and nominated alike, were closely familiar, while the urban members had both knowledge and experience of urban Advisory Boards, the annual Conference of which had been assuming increasing importance over the years. It was in any case a course of argument which, applied to Parliament itself in a country in which one Province only had evolved a system of local government, might bring him to the conclusion that this too had been a mistaken development, an attempt to develop 'a sort of authority from the top down'.

Incidentally it may be noted here that the Advisory Boards Conference for which General Smuts had foreshadowed a place in his plans for a Natives Representative Council enlarged in numbers and powers was soon to follow the Council into oblivion. With the new policy of ethnic grouping in African urban townships which flowed from the proposed tribal authority organisation and the contention that urban Africans should seek their political rights and their social and economic opportunity in their own tribal areas and among their own tribal group, there was no more place for such an institution than for the Natives Representative Council itself.

The next move in the re-moulding process, with its emphasis on the tribal pattern of African life, was the application to the whole African population of a uniform system of administrative control symbolised in and crowned by the office of Supreme Chief. By implication African in inspiration and character, this office was to be held nominally by the Governor-General, in effect by the Minister of Native Affairs.

The requisite legislative framework for the system was supplied by an amendment in 1956 to that Native Administration Act of 1927 which had more and more come under criticism in the latter days of the Natives Representative Council and had from the beginning been the subject of periodic attack by us as Native Representatives, as embodying a system of arbitrary government that had no continuing place in a developing society committed to Western standards and principles.[1] Ironically enough, this amendment was framed to extend the range of those powers of the Supreme

<hr/>

[1] Dr. Verwoerd attacking the official Opposition for its refusal to support this Bill, said he gave the Native Representatives credit for having been consistent in this regard. Hansard, Vol. 91, Col. 4898.

Chief which the Councillors had endeavoured to have at least modified if not removed as being foreign to their tradition and completely inappropriate to their changing character and needs. Originally embodied in what purported to be a code of Native customary law drawn up in 1871 for the management and control of the Zulu people in the then new colony of Natal, they had given to the Governor of the Colony complete political power over the Native people, in terms largely influenced, as Selope Thema had argued in the Council, by the dictatorship which Chaka had succeeded in establishing for himself.[1] With him lay the appointment and removal of chiefs; he decided questions of heirship to deceased chiefs; he could divide and amalgamate tribes; he might remove tribes or portions of tribes or individual Natives; he might call out armed men or levies and had power to call upon Natives to supply labour for public works; he was the upper guardian of Native orphans and minors; he could punish political offenders and impose penalties for disobedience to his orders; he might impose a fine upon a Native community as a whole for suppressing evidence of crime; and finally, his actions as Supreme Chief were not cognisable in the Courts.[2]

These were very wide powers indeed, clearly designed to meet the special circumstances of the time. In 1927, when the segregation policy was in the making, and General Hertzog's drive towards a uniform Native policy was getting under way, this code had been extended to the Transvaal and the Orange Free State, where something similar had been in operation since the first days of white settlement but in less formal shape. However the proposal at that time to include the Cape in its range had been withdrawn by General Hertzog himself on the strength of representations made in the Senate by two of that Province's leading liberals, Sir Walter Stanford, at one time Chief Native Commissioner of the Transkei, and Mr. F. S. Malan, one of the Cape members of the National Convention out of which Union grew and destined to become President of the Senate. The grounds of their objection to the proposed inclusion of the Cape in this system was that nothing comparable to it had ever applied in the Cape Colony, and that the Cape, with its record both in politics and education, had long out-

[1] See p. 183.
[2] In terms of the Code as set out by Howard Rogers for the Department of Native Affairs. See *Native Administration in the Union of South Africa* by Howard Rogers of the Department of Native Affairs; 2nd edition revised on behalf of the Department by P. A. Linington, Ex-Native Commissioner. G.P.-S4438, 1948–9, p. 2.

grown conditions in which such a system could have any justification. The Province was indeed well launched on the road of western
civilisation and the standards that inspired it, and now to apply
this Code, enshrining the practice of administrative law enforced
by sanctions outside the control of the judiciary, would be a tragic
and disastrous step backwards, and one certain to be deeply
resented.

Now, some thirty years later, Dr. Verwoerd decided to reverse
General Hertzog's decision. His reason for so doing, as presented to
Parliament, was 'to make the position uniform throughout the
country and secondly to stress the basic principles of Native law and
the fact that the principle of having Bantu Authorities had been
accepted by the Bantu throughout the country'.[1] In reply to an
Opposition which had largely come to support our view of the
system and, like us, refused to have anything to do with the proposal to extend it, the Minister argued that a similar system con-
ferring even wider powers on the administrative authorities already
existed in the Transkei in terms of the Annexation Acts and that, in
fact, many of the powers which the Code introduced could be
applied to the Cape by proclamation if the Government so desired.
He acknowledged that these powers extended to Whites as well as
to Africans,[2] that is, they had been drawn without colour bar, and
he argued that they were thus unlikely to be applied. The powers
which he now proposed to take would apply to Africans only. These
included two significant new powers over the Africans in the Cape
Province. The first of these was the power to imprison without trial
for three months persons considered a threat to law and order and
administrative peace. It was a power of which we had had no
experience, and of the existence of which few people were even
aware until Dr. Verwoerd himself found it necessary to use it soon
after his accession to office. He now assured the House[3] that it was
a power which he had used reluctantly and had no intention of
using again. That would seem, he said, an argument for removing
rather than extending it, but he made no move in this direction.

The second power he now proposed to assume over the Africans
in the Cape was embodied in that clause of the Code which specifically excluded the Supreme Court from questioning or pronouncing

[1] Hansard, Vol. 91, Col. 4410.
[2] A signicant illustration of the non-Colour Bar tradition of the Cape Colony.
[3] Hansard, Vol. 91, Cols. 9204–5.

upon the validity of any act done or order given by the Supreme Chief in the exercise of his powers or from granting any interdict against the actions of any officer acting as representative of the Supreme Chief.

For the rest, the Bill was designed to clarify the extent of those powers of banishment which the law already conferred on his administration. These had recently been brought into doubt at one important point on an appeal to the Courts by an African who had been ordered to remove from his home in the Transkei to a distant part of the Transvaal. The ground of the appeal, which the Appellate Division upheld, was that the complainant had not been given notice of the removal order and was thus deprived of an opportunity to be heard in his own defence. Dr. Verwoerd's argument in this regard was that the decision of the Court in the complainant's favour could negate the whole purpose of the power of banishment which was at issue, by giving the person regarded as a troublemaker the opportunity either to abscond or to use the interval which recourse to the Courts could provide to create a great deal more trouble. The exclusion of the Courts was therefore now made explicit and final.

With the Bill duly put on the Statute Book, in administration and law the African population was set on a course—not necessarily of their own, since it was not of their own choosing, but different from the rest of South Africa. In its legal aspects, the difference was in fact to be considerably narrowed in the next few years by the extensive use of the anti-communist legislation and by progressive amendments to the general criminal law of the country, drawn without colour bar and including conspicuously such provisions as the ninety-day detention clause. South African experience would seem to suggest that laws and currency are subject to the same law—the bad drives out the good.

II

Cultural Apartheid: Educational Insulation

While the foundations of that separate development on which the exponents of the apartheid doctrine were more and more seeking to justify their policy were being laid in tribal organisations and the system of law which, it was claimed, had sustained them, what guarantee was there that something truly African would rise on them, with the complex contacts which the developing South African society was producing even where it did not set out to do so?

Dr. Verwoerd had already shown that he had plans to meet that situation also. The first and basic one was 'Bantu education', the reorganisation of both the content and the control of the education of the African population to make these conform to the pattern and intention of apartheid. This involved that assumption of control of a centralised service by the Department of Native Affairs to which the Natives Representative Council had been so consistently opposed. It was a change which Dr. Verwoerd justified on the very grounds on which the Council had repudiated it, that the education given to the African people 'must not clash with Government policy' and that it should not 'create wrong expectations on the part of the Native himself'—which was bound to happen if it was given under the control of people who 'believe in a policy of equality'—clearly his idea of what was happening within a system mainly founded by and still at that time (1953) largely in the hands of English-speaking missions. Such people would, he contended, by the very nature of the education they would give 'both as regards the content of that education and as regards its spirit, create expectations in the mind of the Bantu which clash with the possibilities in this country'.[1] Elaborating his standpoint in the Senate later,[2] he contended that there was no place for the Bantu in the European community above the level of certain forms of labour. In the past, however, he had been subjected to a school system which drew him away from his own community and practically misled him by showing him the green pastures of the European but still

[1] Hansard, Vol. 83, Col. 3585 et seq.
[2] Senate Hansard 1954, Vol. 2, Col. 2619.

did not allow him to graze there. The essential function of his education must be to encourage him to find his satisfactions in serving his own people and in helping them to produce something that would be essentially theirs.

It was a process that was more likely to develop, and to develop to the satisfaction of the people themselves, if they were financially responsible for it, Dr. Verwoerd considered. People did not appreciate what was given to them, but only what they paid for themselves—a long familiar theme wherever and whenever the matter of services for Africans or the subject of African development came under discussion. Dr. Verwoerd did accept, however, that at that moment (1953) it was not possible for the Africans to finance even the then existing level of their educational services themselves. The Government had therefore agreed to assist by continuing to provide annually the amount of money then being spent on this service, an amount of £6,500,000. (R13,000,000) Further development would however have to depend on the return of direct taxation from African sources—from which part of the allocation already derived. This decision foreshadowed an increase in the incidence of the personal tax on Africans. It was in fact sharply increased in 1956.

The first legislative instalment of this plan was the Bantu Education Act passed through Parliament in 1953. In terms of this Act the Department of Native Affairs took over the control of all teaching agencies in the field of Native education, involving the almost complete exclusion of that wide range of missionary effort on which Native education had been founded and had grown, and which the Minister viewed with such disfavour. Four years later, the second instalment appeared on the stocks. This was the proposal to stamp on the field of higher education the pattern of apartheid which the Bantu Education Act had applied in the fields of primary and secondary education. Here the situation to be met was somewhat different in character from that in the lower field. While racially separate schools were the established practice on the lower educational levels, on the upper levels there had been in recent years a marked trend towards a measure of multi-racialism. While the University College of Fort Hare, established in 1916 specially for non-European students, had come to provide higher education for increasing numbers of students representative of all the country's non-European groups, increasing numbers of non-Europeans had sought entry into the so-called white universities many of whom

350 FROM UNION TO APARTHEID

had been accepted in the English-medium universities of Cape Town, the Witwatersrand and Natal.

Such a development could not but be a major challenge to the arch-apostle of apartheid. Here surely was the forcing ground of Western ideas and, as such, the greatest encouragement to Africans to abandon their people and their culture in favour of the green pastures of white society. By 1957 Dr. Verwoerd was ready to grasp this nettle. The Minister of Education, Arts and Science, with whom the responsibility for higher education lay, was induced to introduce a Separate University Education Bill which set out to do three things. The first of these was to close to non-Europeans what had come appropriately to be known as the open universities; the second was to provide separate university colleges for Coloured, Indian and each of the African ethnic groups; and the third was to pass over the control of the colleges for Africans to the Minister of Bantu Administration and Development, the new title of the Minister's Department.[1] Since the principle of racial exclusion was to apply to these institutions as rigidly as to 'the white' universities, the proposition contingently implied the disintegration of Fort Hare as it had developed over the years, and the substitution for it of a college for the Xhosa people.[2]

The whole proposal involved a wide invasion of that autonomy of the universities which had characterised the growth of higher education in this country. As set out in the Bill, it also involved the creation for the non-White groups of a type of state-controlled institution foreign to South African tradition. As such it evoked a wide and determined opposition from the side of all those immediately affected. This may or may not have had something to do with the Minister's decision to allow the Bill to go to a Select Committee. At any rate he did so, but only after the passing of the second reading, establishing the principle of separate institutions. Since the session was nearing its conclusion, in due course the Committee was reconstituted as a Commission to enable it to carry on with what was to prove a quite extensive programme of evidence-taking in the recess.[3]

[1] It may be noted here in passing that, in due course, the control of the Coloured College passed to a new Department of Coloured Affairs and the Indian College to an also new Department of Indian Affairs.
[2] Fort Hare is situated within the 'White' area of the Ciskei; hence the Transkei Government exercises no control over it.
[3] Another 'Parliamentary' Commission.

Whether the gesture of a Select Committee was worth contending for or accepting was doubtful even at the time, but since it had been conceded, it had to be explored, and the Leader of the Labour Party, Mr. Alex Hepple, and I took our places on the Committee with three members of the official Opposition and seven members of the Government. From the beginning the Committee divided rigidly along the main political dividing line, the Government majority on one side, the Opposition parties on the other. No sooner was the taking of evidence completed than the obviously departmentally prepared report began to emerge, not from the Department of Education but from the Department of Bantu Administration and Development. It significantly contained Dr. Verwoerd's ideas logically developed to include the amazing proposition that each new institution should be governed not by a Senate composed of the senior teaching staff and a Council representing all the parties interested in promoting the institution according to the familiar and established pattern of our university institutions, but by a Senate and an advisory Senate and a Council and an Advisory Council. The line of differentiation, needless to say, was one of colour. The actual membership of each body was to be in the control of the Minister himself, as indeed was to be the case in respect of all the organisation and activities of the proposed new institutions.

The destructive effect of the pursuit of apartheid on long-established and respected institutions founded on Western principles obviously held many desolating experiences for a liberal, but surely none more desolating than this one to one like myself, whose professional training and experience had been gained in these institutions, and had evoked a deep loyalty to the university tradition of this country. I had seen the system blossom from the examining university of the Cape of Good Hope, serving the first university institutions of the old Cape colony to a progressively diversified university system for the whole country, freely adjusting itself to the needs and demands of a developing community. Now it too was to be put into a straitjacket fashioned in terms of an ideology that was already proving incapable of establishing itself in a free society. Here most clearly the rights of all were to be curtailed in the pursuit of the privilege of some. There was to be no more free association for White students than for non-White students, or for 'White' universities than for 'non-White' universities.

For a time, while the taking of evidence was in progress, there seemed a hope that this would not happen, that better judgment might still prevail. It was inspired by the approach of the spokesmen of the Afrikaans universities, known generally to be supporters of the Government. Each and all, while endorsing the proposition of separate university colleges for the various racial groups in the country, were as definite as were the representatives of the 'open' universities that there should be no legislative interference with the right of universities generally to decide whom they would admit, and that whatever institutions the Government should decide to establish should be moulded on the tried and proved pattern upon which our university system had grown up, attracting their students by what they had to offer. When it became clear that, despite the weight of this evidence, the majority report was to maintain and in fact, as I have said, to extend the pattern of the original Bill, at least one minority report was inevitable. Even before the majority report began to emerge, I had made it clear that the Government side's case was unlikely to be mine.

With the back history of the legislation from which the Commission derived, I had hopes that all the non-Government members might be able to agree on a common case. In the issue, the conditions under which any minority report had to be produced were so exceptionally difficult as to make an agreement in this regard particularly valuable as avoiding a dispersal of our limited and much strained resources. The proceedings of the Commission had been interrupted by a general election in which one of our most important members, Mr. Hepple, had lost his seat and had felt impelled to resign from the Commission. He was replaced by an additional United Party member, Dr. Jan Steytler.[1] This happened just as the taking of evidence was nearing its conclusion. Since the prospective post-election short session was unlikely to provide time for more than the most urgent legislation, there seemed reason to expect that the time necessary to make adjustments to this position, as well as to study the evidence, would be available to the Commission. The Minister, however, already clear as to what he proposed to do, as he had been in regard to the findings of the Socio-Economic Commission, was pressing for the conclusion of our work. Indeed, so urgent was he in this regard that the majority report was rushed out from his Department in sections, in one language only, without the delay necessary for a comprehensive release or for that customary

[1] The Labour Party having now disappeared from the Parliamentary scene.

translation into the other language which our constitutional bilingualism calls for in the field of public service. To the indignant remonstrances of one of the United Party members, Mr. P. A. Moore, to the whole of this procedure, the chairman, Mr. de Wet Nel, the Minister's faithful follower destined soon to inherit his office as Dr. Verwoerd moved up into the premiership, angrily retorted with an ultimatum that any minority report should be ready in twenty-four hours.

All the circumstances were imposing a considerable strain on Mr. Nel. We had seen little of him for days, the chair being occupied in his absence by another of Dr. Verwoerd's devoted followers, Mr. Maree, then also on his way up towards important office.[1] A seat in the Cabinet had fallen vacant through the death of the Minister of Education, Mr. Havenga's old lieutenant, Mr. Viljoen, and with Dr. Verwoerd's powerful support, the way was being prepared for Mr. Nel's entry into the Cabinet ranks by this door. The emotional stress of this prospective elevation and, no doubt, the manœuvres associated with it, combined with the demands of his patron that he get the Commission out of the way as soon as possible, would appear to have operated to throw him somewhat off balance and induce him to make this extravagant challenge. A break for tea afforded a breathing space for some reconsideration and counsel the result of which was a decision on his part to extend to three weeks the period allowed to the minority to get their case together.

With this extremely limited time at our disposal it was clear that any effort to make our case must be a concentrated one, concerned to highlight whatever seemed to us the most significant points of difference between us and the majority. Even this presented difficulties with members of Parliament anxious to return to their homes in various parts of the country after a particularly tense and exacting general election, to which all the work of the Commission had been added, again under Dr. Verwoerd's relentless pressure. In the issue, the United Party members asked Mr. Moore to prepare their statement, and if possible by agreement with me, as now the only non-United Party member of the minority group. After considering the line which Mr. Moore proposed to follow, as endorsed by his colleagues, I was glad indeed to co-operate in the production of one report which should set out our common case.

---

[1] As already noted, he was to become in due course Minister of Bantu Education and later also Minister of Indian Affairs. See p. 114.

z

Since that was essentially an academic case, it was agreed between us that the best use we could make of the brief time at our command would be to quote the evidence of the representatives of the Afrikaans universities, the views of the English-medium universities having been widely publicised even before the Commission was appointed, and being therefore well known. This seemed to me an appropriate and valuable exercise as designed to concentrate attention on the academic implications of a move on the part of the Government that was primarily political in inspiration. Where the Minister really responsible had turned a deaf ear to all representations from non-Nationalist quarters, the underlining of the attitude of the witnesses from universities which generally supported the Government's policy might induce him to have second thoughts about the advisability of his proposed departure from the country's established academic tradition in the cause of apartheid.

There were evidences in the months that followed that the Commission itself, and particularly the publicising of the Afrikaans witnesses' views on the Minister's proposals, had stirred a considerable degree of anxiety in Afrikaans academic circles as to the responsibility of the academic profession in this matter. This found its expression in the meeting of SABRA in Durban in December of that year, 1958. Here the whole question of universities and their appropriate line of development was the major subject of discussion. In the meantime, however, two significant developments had taken place. The first of these was the return to the stocks at the very beginning of the short post-election session of Dr. Verwoerd's plan under the grand new title of a Bill to provide for the Extension of University Education, with the contingent liquidation of Fort Hare provided for in a Bill 'to transfer the maintenance and control of the University College of Fort Hare to the Government'. The second was the elevation of Dr. Verwoerd to the premiership on the death of Mr. Strydom in September of that year.

Faced with these two events, involving the clear determination of the Minister become Prime Minister to pursue his own appointed course, the academic voice of SABRA decided that, whatever the academic spokesmen might think and feel about their own profession, it was for the Government to decide what should be done; and the Afrikaner front which Dr. Verwoerd was busy consolidating for Afrikanerdom remained intact.

In the meantime, evidence had been accumulating to show that the assumption of control of the education of the African people at all levels was for Dr. Verwoerd only the formal aspect of a process of cultural insulation which the objective of apartheid and separate development demanded. Social contacts between private persons and groups across the colour line could be as dangerous in stimulating false hopes on the part of Africans and encouraging mistaken ambitions and misdirected effort as any wrongly guided system of education. Africans must learn to do things for themselves, and that those things should be done in an African way, they must be done by themselves. What assistance they might require in the process of learning could adequately—and appropriately—be supplied by what was first his Department and later his Government, by officials who knew and understood both the Government's policy and the people for whom it was designed, as private persons could not do; by people who could be trusted to exercise their influence in the right direction.

Over the years, with this objective in view, there had taken place a strengthening of the controls over non-African entry into any African area, urban or rural, intended to reduce the possible points of social and cultural contact to the minimum, if not to wipe them out altogether. This process was new in range rather than in kind. Since the earliest days of the segregation policy, urban authorities had been empowered to regulate any and all entry into their Native townships by permit. It was a control which operated in respect of all racial groups, including Africans themselves visiting from one area to another. In practice, the extent of the control varied considerably from place to place, and had in fact become progressively less restrictive, leaving ample space for a widening range of those charitable exercises on the part of Whites with which an awakening public conscience sought to alleviate the stresses of modern life for our emerging African population. Its effect in the rural areas had been more discouraging, progressively making less simply a matter of personal choice, and more and more the subject of administrative attention, visits of the kind which I had enjoyed on more than one occasion in the home of a Zulu woman friend, and with her for a few days in the home of Chief Luthuli shortly after his elevation to the chieftainship. It was a development which I had deprecated strongly in the days of the Smuts Government as threatening a cultural isolation of our African population which it was still the objective of public policy to lead along the path of Western civilisation.

The assumption of apartheid as public policy was to give a new impetus to, as it was to provide a new philosophy for such isolation, and new barriers began to arise to block the road to any co-operative effort or social contact between Black and White in town and country alike. On the urban side, over the years, new legislative and administrative controls were brought into operation to reverse the trend which had expressed itself not only in social services for Africans but in cultural activities of various kinds on the part of Europeans with Africans and members of other non-White groups. Philanthropic effort on the part of Europeans for or in association with Africans was progressively curtailed by administrative checks upon non-African services with or for Africans. The sinews of such service might be provided—money might be raised for services for Africans, but over a widening field, it could no longer be administered by non-Africans on their behalf, or by combined bodies of Africans and non-Africans. The exercise of the virtue of Christian charity by one race towards another seemed less important in Dr. Verwoerd's scheme of things than the maintenance and survival of a pure African culture which, it appeared, would be unaffected by day-to-day dependence within a common economy but could not survive contact in civilised social activities.

Where cultural or purely personal contacts were involved, Dr. Verwoerd found it necessary to provide more stringent safeguards against the undermining of the South African way of life as defined by Afrikaner Nationalism. In 1957 he introduced a Native Laws Amendment Act which became notorious for what came to be known as the church clause. This sought to prohibit attendances of Africans at churches in so-called white areas where their presence created a nuisance for the white inhabitants of the area. It was a power which, after considerable public clamour, he agreed to use in consultation and agreement with the local authority concerned. At the same time he took power to prohibit on his own authority the establishment of any inter-racial organisation such as international clubs of which two were then functioning in Natal, at Durban and Maritzburg, or any social contact between Black and White which he considered a challenge to accepted social practice. This latter he explained[1] might amount to a ban on a particular flat or house where people made a point of holding mixed parties which might be an annoyance to their neighbours or cause the concentration

[1] Hansard, Vol. 94, Col. 3238.

in a White area of numbers of Africans. Indeed, he felt that the Government should have power to act even where no nuisance or even any great congregation of Africans was involved but where it seemed that the intention was to defy the policy of apartheid by purposely bringing Whites and non-Whites together—as the activities of the recently formed Liberal Party he felt were designed to do. As he said, 'In view of the Liberal Party's attitude of coming with threats about causing mixed conditions in various spheres of social life, it is not at all unnecessary for Parliament to take steps timeously to curb these activities of theirs.'[1]

In the rural areas, entry of non-Africans into Native reserve became a matter of strict administrative control, the only exception to the general rule of exclusion save by special permission being that of the elected Parliamentary representatives of the African people. In 1960, when that representation ceased to exist, this last remnant of the right of entry went with it.[2] This was one of the less obvious but none the less important and significant effects of that Act for the Promotion of Bantu Self Government which provided for the abolition, not only of the remnants of the Cape Native franchise as represented by our three seats in the House of Assembly, but of all representation of Africans in Parliament.

[1] Hansard, Vol. 94, Col. 3239.
[2] The activities of the White representatives of the Coloured voters in the Cape have been made subject to a rigid administrative control which has operated to prevent these representatives from entering rural Coloured areas—mission stations —for report-back meetings.

12

Political Insulation

Dr. Verwoerd celebrated his elevation to the office of Minister of Native Affairs by abolishing the Natives Representative Council. Among the first fruits of his elevation to the office of Prime Minister was the Promotion of Banti Self Government Act which wiped out the rest of General Hertzog's political settlement of 1936.

His succession to the premiership was achieved through the votes of Nationalist members of both Houses of Parliament, the rival aspirants being the Free State leader of the Nationalist Party, Mr. C. R. Swart, destined to become the first President of the Republic, and Dr. Dönges, the representative of the Cape Province. His success in what was a closely fought and tense contest which took place in the middle of the short post-election session in 1958, just after Mr. Strydom's death, was generally attributed in non-Nationalist circles to the loyalty of the serried ranks of the enlarged Senate to its erstwhile colleague and leader. The accident of the continued existence after it had served its purpose of this institution which even the Nationalist Party could not contemplate without a sense of shame, was probably indeed mainly responsible for this decision. At the same time the decision itself undoubtedly reflected two all-important facts in the development of Afrikaner nationalism and of South African politics: the progressively dominating position of the Transvaal within the Nationalist Party itself, and the dominating influence that Dr. Verwoerd had increasingly clearly exercised within the Party, in the shaping of its policy in what was rapidly becoming recognised as the most important issue in public life, that of race relations.

The first speech from the throne of his premiership, that with which the 1959 session opened, was highly significant as an indication of the confidence with which the Minister of Native Affairs had merged into the Prime Minister. It declared: 'The recent division of the Department of Native Affairs into two separate state departments, namely of Bantu Administration and Development and of Bantu Education, clearly testifies to the value attached, in the interests of Europeans as well as non-Europeans, to promoting the positive elements of the policy of separate development. Measures towards this end will be laid before you, including a Bill to provide university facilities for the various groups of non-Europeans; a Bill to establish a Bantu Investment Corporation, legislation which will link up the Bantu employed in the European areas with the Bantu Authorities in the Bantu areas, and legislation which will give the Bantu Territorial Authorities direct access to the Union Government for the promotion of Bantu interests which will replace the present system of representation by Europeans.'[1]

Most of this programme was already familiar ground of discussion. The final statement, particularly as part of a programme of immediate action, startled even the new Prime Minister's own press. The Leader of the Opposition, Sir De Villiers Graaff, could argue, as he did in the no-confidence motion with which he opened the session's business, that in proposing the complete abolition of the representation of Africans in Parliament, Dr. Verwoerd had no mandate from either the electorate or his own Party.[2] It was a proposition that would change the whole relationship between Parliament and the African people. Where, Sir De Villiers asked, had this extension of the familiar plan of his Party, to abolish the lower House representation but to maintain the Senate representation, come from? Nothing had been heard of such a plan even as late as the election of the previous year. There had apparently been some reference to such a plan in the Party congress which had followed the election, but obviously without any clear decision, or even intention, in the matter. Now there were convincing evidences that the declaration of the new Prime Minister's proposal to put the idea into operation at once had thrown his own Party into some confusion. Had not the *Transvaler*, Dr. Verwoerd's own political organ, reacted by stating that the Prime Minister, Dr. Verwoerd, had quite recently made it abundantly clear that the Government did not intend to create a vacuum, that the existing Native representation would only disappear when the Bantu authorities system had made adequate progress to provide for Natives in the reserves and in the white areas an approach to the Government. What, Sir De Villiers asked, was the Government really offering the African people in lieu of their existing representation, 'this small voice in

[1] Hansard, Vol. 99, Cols. 4–5.
[2] Hansard, Vol. 99, Col. 28. *et seq.*

the central Government of the country'? It was a question to which he gave his own reply—access through Bantu authorities whose members could at any time be dismissed by the Minister if, in his opinion, their continuance in office was not in the general interest of the Native, and whose powers were entirely subject to a Governor-General who could amend, or entirely alter, any by-law made by them and promulgate it in their name.

In my turn I could add the obvious alarm with which the *Burger*, the Cape Nationalist organ, had received the announcement of the Prime Minister's intention. Expressing his anxiety about the proposed removal of the whole African representation and the opinion that there was going to be 'a devil of a row' about it, the columnist Dawie had written:

'In any case, here is again an important policy matter about which we as usual have heard the negative side first, while the positive side is apparently still unrevealed. I hope and trust that the positive side will be very, very strong to help to remove the impression that South Africa is moving backwards in connection with its Native population while the rest of Africa is moving forward. It must be strong not so much to convince the Opposition or world opinion, because these will refuse to be convinced anyway' (which I noted was probably right), 'but to convince many Nationalists.'[1]

Unmoved by any and all of the anxious reactions to his plans, and confident of his ability to hold and to use the power which had fallen into his hands, Dr. Verwoerd determinedly pursued the logic of a course upon which in fact he had been set for a long time. With the bold assurance that, within another year, the Bantu authorities system would have developed to the territorial level in all the reserves,[2] he notified his intention to terminate all immediate contact between Parliament and the African population at June 30th, 1960, when the current period of office of the representatives of Africans should expire.

His plan was a comprehensive one which among the more sycophantic of his followers was hailed as another new vision, but, among the more thoughtful, was the source of considerable perturbation and anxiety, not untinged by alarm, and indignation at the fact that no one had been consulted about it—it was, indeed, Dr.

[1] Hansard, Vol. 99, Col. 87.
[2] An optimistic prognostication, still (1968) far from fulfilment.

Verwoerd's vision. According to the preamble to the Bill,[1] it was proposed to 'provide for the gradual development of self-governing Bantu national units' (of which eight were specified) 'and for direct consultation between the Government of the Union and the said national units in regard to matters affecting the interests of such national units', which, Dr. Verwoerd was to argue, not only made the representation in Parliament unnecessary but made it in fact illogical and misleading. In elaboration, the preamble declared that the Bantu people of the Union of South Africa do not constitute a homogeneous people, but form separate national units on the basis of language and culture, for whom it was expedient to develop and extend the Bantu system of government for which provision had been made in the Bantu Authorities Act in 1951 'with due regard to prevailing requirements, and to assign further powers, functions and duties to regional and territorial authorities'.

The eight cultural units were to be reduced to six for political and administrative purposes. For each of the six, a commissioner-general was to be appointed to act as guide, philosopher and friend, to provide a link between the units and the Minister and 'to advise the Minister (of Bantu Administration and Development) in regard to the needs and wishes of the population'. Provision was also made for the linking up of each national unit with its members in the urban areas by means of 'a Bantu person to represent the Territorial authority (or Board) in the areas of one or more local authorities with that portion of the Bantu community in the said areas which belongs to the national unit concerned'.

Characteristically, the White commissioners-general were to furnish guidance and advice to the African authorities to whom they were accredited in respect of all matters affecting administrative development, and the social and educational, economic and general progress of the population, and to promote the development of the administration of justice and of courts of law.

Introducing the scheme, Dr. Verwoerd[2] said the country was at the crossroads. It must now definitely choose which path it would follow. The United Party stood for a policy of a multi-racial South Africa governed in partnership. That could only lead, not to equality for the blacks, but to black domination. The National Party on the other hand supported a policy that aimed at retaining

[1] Act 46 of 1959.
[2] Hansard, Vol. 99, Col. 6214 et seq.

domination for the white man over his part of the country, for which the white man was prepared to pay a certain price, namely, giving the Bantu full rights to develop in their own areas. 'The Bantu,' he said, 'will now be placed on a new rung of the ladder of a development which can continue as far as he is able to take it. . . . It is within the power of the Bantu and if the territories in which he lives can develop to full independence, it will develop that way.'

According to the white paper[1] accompanying the release of the Bill and setting out the main points of the Prime Minister's case for it, the realisation of the political autonomy envisaged for the Bantu national units demanded that all factors which retarded this development should be removed. Of these, the greatest impediment was the representation of the Bantu in the highest institutions of European government. It was an impediment of a two-fold nature. On the one hand it was a source of European fears of being swamped by the Bantu in the political sphere and on the other, it failed to stimulate the development by the Bantu of Bantu institutions because it fostered expectations of greater participation in European political institutions and promoted the desertion of trained human material from service within its own community.

In any case, representation in the guardian's Parliament was 'not a factor which plays a role in the attainment of self-government by the dependent territory' as appeared clearly from the history of the British Commonwealth. As it existed here in South Africa, such representation was in effect a signpost in the alternative direction which had 'been rejected as utterly impracticable'. It would therefore be abolished.

Here the white paper summarised Dr. Verwoerd's plan for the future in highly significant terms. 'The Minister and his representatives, including the Commissioners-General will be in direct contact with the Bantu by means of conferences with competent bodies and persons better informed than the present elected representatives regarding the legitimate needs and desires of the different Bantu national units, and because of their close contact with the Government, the Bantu leaders will be able to pay positive attention to such real needs. Consequently Bantu interests in Parliament will whenever necessary be effectively attended to by the Minister, and in this task he will be assisted by the Deputy Minister, the

[1] Memorandum explaining the Background and Objects of the Promotion of Bantu Self Government Bill 1959. W.P. 3–59.

Minister of Bantu Education and those members of the Native Affairs Commission who are also members of the House of Assembly as well as the Senators who have been nominated on account of their special knowledge of the non-European population.'

As to the shape of South Africa which might ultimately emerge, the white paper noted that the Prime Minister had already given a definite lead in that regard. He had stated[1] that if the various Bantu national units showed the ability to attain the required stage of self-sufficiency, they would eventually form a South African Commonwealth together with white South Africa 'which will serve as its core and as guardian of the emerging Bantu States'.

To many who heard or read the Prime Minister's statements, it seemed that Dr. Verwoerd had travelled a long way along the logical road of apartheid to the point of accepting the principle of partition which it must imply. Among those who interpreted his 'new vision' in this way was the Leader of the Opposition, who moved to reject the second reading of the Bill on the ground that it

1. aimed at the division of South Africa into black states and a multi-racial state (in effect, the so-called white state, in which more than half of the Africans were employed, and would continue to be employed for as long as anyone could see), and, if implemented, would involve grave dangers for all South Africans;

2. was repugnant to principles of natural justice in that it removed longstanding rights without giving anything of substance in return, and left the Native population without any voice in the Parliament which governed them; and

3. sought to establish in the black areas a system of government in conflict with Western democratic ideas, and would leave the millions of Natives permanently settled outside the reserves without any means of political expression whatsoever.[2]

Sir De Villiers supported his case with the argument that although little or nothing of substance was being given to the African people by this Bill and the system it sought to establish, the very act of establishing the national units as entities was setting them on a road the end of which could not be in doubt. If and when the Black states which the Minister foreshadowed came into existence, what was to prevent them competing against us in the economic field and entering into foreign alliances against us?

[1] Hansard, Vol. 98, Col. 4156, quoted p. 332.
[2] Hansard, Vol. 101, Col. 6024.

Imagine the vulnerability of a country whose working population were not its own subjects, but those of a potentially hostile state. The whole plan, he argued, was a policy of desperation begotten of lack of faith in the capacity of the white man to maintain his position in a multi-racial state.

To us, as representatives of the African population, it seemed that the terms in which the Prime Minister expounded his new vision had so many qualifications and conditional clauses that in fact it offered no practical prospect of political advance for the African population outside the range of white South Africa, while depriving it of the meagre platform it had retained against the corroding influence of Afrikaner nationalism and the trekker spirit. Consequently, seconded by Mr. Stanford, I moved[1] to reject the second reading of the Bill because

1. it sought to lay the foundation of a political separation of white and black which would deprive the African population of all say in the government of the country to which it belonged and of which it formed an essential part;

2. in return it conceded to the African population a system of local government controlled by a Minister and subject to a Parliament in which it would have no representation;

3. it was being introduced without consultation with and against the wish of the African population whose future it sought to shape;

4. it would reduce the African population to the position of a completely subject race;

5. it was a deviation from the established practice in South Africa (which had not been to separate but to draw the African people more and more into the general life of the community), and it repudiated the conditions and foundation of Union [a reference to the determination of the Cape Colony at the time of Union to maintain at least its own political tradition];

6. it was based on a false premiss and supported by fallacious analogies (a reference to the Prime Minister's claim that what he was doing for our African population was what Britain was doing for Basutoland);

7. it was a denial of the trust of the European, brought South Africa into contempt both at home and abroad, and endangered the peace and security of the country.

Throughout the progress of the Bill through Parliament, argu-

[1] Hansard, Vol. 101, Col. 6125.

ment was to range back and forth over all these points. Dominated mainly by the efforts of the Opposition to get clarification as to the practical implications of the Prime Minister's scheme, it returned naturally and insistently to the subject of consultation and consent as the basic principles of democratic government and the only sure foundation of a peaceful and stable solution of our complex problems. As the record shows, the topic was not a new one. Ever since Union, with its insistence on a 'white' Parliament, and the exclusion of large sections of the population from any representation in Parliament, it had been raised recurrently. But it sprang into new and continuing significance with the advent of a Nationalist government committed to a policy of apartheid, particularly in the political sphere. It was of immediate concern to Africans and their representatives with the threat to House of Assembly representation and more particularly to the Natives Representative Council. It was to prove one of the main points of discussion on every measure designed to establish the apartheid pattern. In the process, it came to present two facets—not merely the question of who should be consulted but latterly and of almost greater political significance, who should consult. As the argument developed, there was to emerge a divergence of opinion between the two sides of the political field on both these aspects of the case that involved their whole approach to the operation of the party system and to the position and function of Parliament itself.

The difference began to take shape as early as 1951 in the first debates on the Bantu Authorities Bill which was to abolish the Natives Representative Council and to set the predominantly elective local councils on their way out. Putting up his case against the Natives Representative Council as having failed to serve the real interests of the African people, Dr. Verwoerd declared himself in favour of a return to the practice of the hand-picked Conference of the type which Dr. Jansen had summoned in 1930 in terms of the Native Affairs Act of 1920 to discuss the Hertzog Bills, although neither then nor later did he show any inclination or will to summon such a Conference as the 1920 legislation envisaged—that is, a national conference openly constituted and conducted. In any case, I felt that his reply to the Opposition's case for consultation with the African population on a measure so much affecting them as did this Bantu Authorities Bill more than justified my contention that that system was outmoded and highly unacceptable as denying to the people the right to choose who should speak for them. Challenged as to the attitude of the African people to his plans for their future, he asked,[1] 'Where was I to have that consultation? With the Natives Representative Council, which also shares the opinion of members on the other side, namely that the Bantu should be Europeanised? Must I go and consult them about a system that links up with the traditional system of the Natives themselves? Of course not. It stands to reason they will disapprove of it. And besides, they have forfeited their opportunity of discussing it properly. That body wants other rights, absolute equality of rights for the Natives, and they are not satisfied with a Natives Representative Council. So I was not going to consult them on this matter. Or was I expected, as has been suggested here, to go and consult the advisory councils in the various cities? They have nothing to do with this. Naturally I did not go to them. Was I expected to consult the bungas (the familiar name of the General Councils in the Transkei and Ciskei)? That is an institution based on the other method, and that body has already tried to get rid of the Native chiefs which they have there. That body has already been drawn away from the old traditional system of administration in the past fifty years. Naturally I could not go there either.' He went on to offer what was to become a familiar and significant ground of action by Nationalist ministers; he had had talks with and letters from unnamed individuals strongly supporting his ideas and encouraging his plans.[2]

In the following year, 1952, the question of consultation again arose over the introduction of a comprehensive programme of legislation designed to increase the controls over the entry of Africans into the towns, empowering the Minister to prescribe other areas to which the restrictive provisions of the Urban Areas Act might apply, and in the rural areas to remove limitations on the power of the Minister to remove squatters and to extend his arbitrary powers of removal from their homes of persons who showed what the administration itself regarded as critical or unco-operative

[1] Hansard, Vol. 76, Col. 9814.
[2] Hansard, Vol. 76, Cols. 9901–2. My first experience of this type of approach occurred soon after the Nationalist Party's accession to office, when the new Minister of Health, Dr. Stals, announced his intention to amend the Nursing Act to deprive all non-European nurses of the right to be elected to the Nursing Council or the Board of the Nursing Association on the strength of a letter he had received from a nurse with a strong colour bar instinct. The Nursing Act, introduced by me in 1943 at the request of the Nursing profession and taken over by the then Minister of Health in the Smuts Government, Mr. Harry Lawrence, had been drawn by the profession itself, and passed by Parliament, without colour bar.

attitudes. The Minister's reply on this occasion to Opposition arguments in favour of consultation with the people affected was that
his best advisers on all these matters were not groups of people like
the Natives Representative Council, but the officials of his Department and, for the rural situation, the agricultural societies and other
people 'who are familiar with the position'.[1]

I was, naturally, highly critical of this approach to consultation.
My feelings in this regard had been growing over the years in which
the Native Affairs Department had, under the pressures of the
segregation policy, increasingly tended to become an *imperium in
imperio*, regulating all the activities and the lives of the African
population. It was a development to which I and my colleagues in
both Houses of Parliament had been consistently opposed as unsound in principle and contrary to democratic practice. Now the
whole apartheid approach was inevitably strengthening the bureau-
cratic trend, and with the disappearance of the freely elected
African representation of the African people, and in the circumstances of South African life which reduced the contacts between
Black and White to the minimum at so many levels, it was easy for
a Minister of Dr. Verwoerd's temperament and outlook to argue
that his officials always knew best—except of course for the Minister
himself.

My inevitable objection to this attitude was to annoy Dr. Verwoerd considerably, and to induce a response from him that was
highly revealing in a number of directions. He professed to see in
my objection to his insistence on the authority of the civil service in
what I regarded as matters of policy a personal attack on the
members of his staff. It was 'an attack which was apparently useful
and necessary in her opinion', he said. This led him to expound to
the House what he regarded as the implications of my insistence on
consultation. His exposition began with a somewhat typical statement of his attitude to me personally which was to suffer no modification as time went on; indeed, all the evidences are that the trend
was in the opposite direction. 'I maintain that the officials have
much more experience than the honourable member who exercises
this criticism,' he declared. 'She wants to claim that she knows more
about everything than everyone else. Then I may as well tell her
that I have a completely different impression both of her experience
and of her judgment. My impression is that she is so strongly under

[1] Hansard, Vol. 77, Col. 442.

the influence of a small group of Natives who are not even representative of the true feelings of the great mass of the non-Europeans in
South Africa that she is useless as an interpreter of their views when
I deal with Bantu affairs.' He went on, 'She talks about consultation
but she does not really want it. In other words, she is not advocating
consultation for the sake of consultation: she is doing so in an effort
to get her way by other means'—presumably by getting expressions
of African opinion that would not square with the Minister's intention. 'I may as well tell her now once and for all that as long as this
Government is in power, it will carry out its own policy and not her
policy, and if she thinks she will manage to have her plan executed
by means of consultation, she is making a very big mistake.'[1]

At the end of that year, 1952, the country was shaken by the
development of a defiance campaign 'against unjust laws' of which
I shall have something to say later. As a result of this unhappy
episode, in the short session preceding the election which gave it
its second victory (January–February 1953) the Government put on
the statute book the first series of its special laws designed to deal
with any recurrence of such demonstrations of feeling against its
policies—the Public Safety Act and the Criminal Law Amendment
Act. Both before the introduction of these measures and in the
course of the debates on the Bills themselves, a good deal was heard
and said about the failure of the Government to establish any
co-operative relationship with the African population. Having
already abolished the one freely elected African voice, the Natives
Representative Council, Dr. Verwoerd as Minister of Native
Affairs, to whom the challenge was more specifically made, had
again many questions to ask as to whom the Opposition wished him
to consult, and something against every name he himself mentioned,
from Chief Luthuli to Professor Matthews, Paul Mosaka and Selope
Thema. And of course he would not have consultations with law-
breakers like the leaders of the Resistance Movement and the
African National Congress. What did consultation mean? he asked,
and answered his own question in characteristic fashion. 'Does it
mean that one has to have consultation in regard to political
questions only with a body such as the Natives Representative
Council, or does it mean something more? According to my view,

[1] Hansard, Vol. 77, Col. 772 *et seq.* All report-back meetings were open to all
sections of the African population and were widely attended by the enfranchised
and the unenfranchised alike. And in a non-official atmosphere, those who
attended expressed their views and feelings freely.

real consultation means that you must keep in touch with the Native from the lowest ranks upwards, right through all the various forms of authority: the Department of Native Affairs is the machinery placed in my hands by which the Government maintains that contact throughout the country by means of a multitude of officials who are in direct contact with the Natives.' He added, 'A second form of contact one can have is by going round personally as I am doing, and visiting the places where the people live. In other words, consultation should not be there to give the agitators a good time and give a few educated men the chance to get on to the back of the masses and make them feel that they are now half white.'

He concluded significantly that there was one form of consultation which one could undertake, and that was to have discussions with 'the Native leaders who hold the same views as we do and who are prepared to co-operate with the Government for the benefit of their own people'. That, he said, they were doing. Asked who these leaders were, he said he was not going to say, as he was not going to expose them 'to the propaganda of hostile people and agitators, and to the abuse by the latter of their knowledge of persons among the Natives who are well disposed towards us'. He had set up a new department of information which was to be 'a source of continuing contact' between himself as Minister 'and the real leaders of the Native people'.[1]

This question of consultation is of course closely linked with the function of Parliament and of members of Parliament. If only those are to be consulted who agree with government policy, what is the position, and the purpose, of an Opposition in Parliament? We were to have two revealing sidelights on this subject from Dr. Verwoerd, one at this time and one in the debate on the Promotion of Bantu Self Government Bill in 1959.

In the year following the Nationalists' second electoral victory, that is 1954, Dr. Verwoerd brought to the House a Bill to amend the Native Trust and Land Act. It was designed to remove the check upon the Government's power to move African squatters from land outside scheduled or released areas, and thus to enable the Minister to move these people without the obligation to provide alternative domicile for them. For us, it immediately raised again the question of homes and opportunities for the people who would be affected. Consequently I spent some time in the course of the

[1] Hansard, Vol. 81, Cols. 301–303.

2A

second reading debate on the Bill pressing the Minister about the progress of his plans for the development of the reserves. It was a case which was strongly supported by Mrs. Helen Suzman, then United Party member for Houghton.

To elucidate the Minister's reply on a point of fact, the Liberal Party, of which I shall have something to say later, had come into existence in May 1953, on the back of the Nationalist victory in the general election of that year, and I was at that time its National Chairman. Here let me quote the Minister's own words:

'The hon. member asks that question every year (about the development of the reserves), and I reply to her every year, but she does not understand it. Now I just want to say this to the hon. member. As Leader of the Liberal Party, that hon. member has not the slightest right to ask anything that concerns the principle of the apartheid policy. She now no longer objectively represents the interests of the Natives so that she can ask this Government questions in the interests of the Natives.' He went on: 'She is the Leader of the Liberal Party; she advocates the opposite of apartheid and as an advocate of the opposite of apartheid, she has no right to ask me or this side of the House or that side of the House to do anything based on the principle of separation.' Here a member of the United Party interrupted with 'She is a member of this House'. The Minister, paying no apparent regard to the interruption, proceeded, 'May I now tell that hon. member what she ought to ask to be consistent in terms of her policy? She ought to ask that the Natives in the whole of South Africa—for this is their principle—should have equal opportunities and equal rights. That must imply that the reserves should be abolished. To be consistent, it must mean that if we want to give the Natives equal rights in European South Africa we have no right to protect them against the Europeans in a certain area. Then everyone will have to fend for himself and as an advocate of the liberalistic policy, she only has the right to make one request to me, and that is to abolish the Native reserves and to introduce equality for European and non-European throughout the country. That is all she has the right to ask for. But those who believe in apartheid believe in developing these territories for the Natives to the maximum extent and such people have the right to ask me to introduce improvements there, but she no longer has that right. Also the Native Representative who does not take sides with the Liberal Party but who says "I stand apart. I try to get what I can for the Natives from every Government" can ask me such things, but not the hon. member for Houghton and not the hon. member for Cape Eastern.'[1]

At this point an automatic adjournment of the House provided a breathing space in which members might endeavour to digest a proposition which had startled others besides myself. Resuming the discussion after the dinner interval, the Minister, who had obviously had time to consider the implications at least of the inclusion of a member of the official Opposition in his lecture to me, proceeded to explain that he had been clarifying a point which in his opinion was of the utmost importance not only in respect of the Native Representatives but in regard to all 'liberalists' in all parties in the House. He proceeded again to argue that 'when the Liberalists come along and ask us to do something to create a better population capacity in the reserves, they are asking something which, in terms of their policy, they no longer have the slightest right to ask'—a proposition which he proceeded to extend to the United Party as a whole, which seemed definitely now, he considered, to have chosen the road to integration against that of separation.

The Minister's doctrine as thus set out caused a considerable amount of Press comment, none of it favourable to the Minister's theory of the rights of Oppositions, and both he and his Party were clearly uneasy about the position into which his statement had betrayed him. Naturally, I myself challenged the Minister's attitude to me and his interpretation of the implications of my policy. He was consequently at great pains to tell the House in the third reading debate on the Bill that my interpretation of what he had said could not be right—and since I had quoted the English version of his speech, he must, he said, have been mistranslated.[2] For twenty minutes then he argued and 'explained' that anyone who stood for the opposite of apartheid, as I did, might ask him questions about his policy but had no right to ask from him, from the Government, or from the Opposition, anything which depended upon the principle of the maintenance of separation. Liberals, he repeated, had the right to ask only one thing—the abolition of the Native reserves and the equality of European and non-European in the whole of South Africa. Only Native Representatives who stood outside party had the right to make demands on the Government. To my inter-

---

[1] Hansard, Vol. 84, Cols. 1127–8.
[2] Hansard, Vol. 84, Col. 1833 *et seq.*

jected question as to why, in that case, his Party had contested the
elections under the Representation of Natives Act in 1949, the
Minister made the, to me, somewhat inconsequential reply, 'on the
basis of the apartheid policy. What is the difficulty in that?'

This exposition of the Minister's approach to the spokesmen of
parties whose policy differed from that of the party in office was
naturally of great interest to all sections of the Opposition. It stimulated various attempts at elucidation. Mr. Harry Lawrence wanted
to know whether in accordance with the policy which the Minister
had adumbrated, a socialist member of the House who advocated
the nationalisation of industries was not entitled to ask the Minister
of Labour for wage increases in a capitalist industry, and another
front-bencher asked whether, in terms of Dr. Verwoerd's approach,
a party in the House which opposed the war had the right to put
questions in connection with the Defence Force. By the time
Dr. Verwoerd had finished explaining in relation to these questions
and my position, the difference between asking and asking for,
which appeared to be the central theme of his discourse, it seemed
to me that the only adequate comment was that of the *Cape Times*
leader the following morning which read, 'In general terms, the
Minister seems to be trying to establish that members shall not
demand anything theoretically in conflict with the *reductio ad
absurdum* of their stated policy. According to this view, a pacifist
would be out of order in demanding that soldiers be properly fed
and entertained. This is as absurd as anything else that the Minister
has said. . . . We incline to the view that he continuously mis-
understands himself.'[1]

[1] *Cape Times*, March 11th, 1954.

13

Political Apartheid and Parliament

We had now reached the point where Dr. Verwoerd as Minister of Native Affairs had in effect challenged the right of any political party other than that of the Government in office to speak for the major part of the population for which Parliament was still legislatively responsible. The monopoly of the right of the Government to speak to as well as for the African population to which the Promotion of Bantu Self Government Act was to give shape,[1] was already being organised behind the scenes. The steps in the process were to offer illuminating examples of Dr. Verwoerd's conception of consultation in operation. A powerful instrument ready made for the purpose was in existence through the increasing practice in legislation of leaving with the Minister concerned wide powers to define details by regulation. It is a system fraught with great dangers where the spreading disease of voluminous and hasty legislation tends to leave a wide margin for subjective determination of the dividing line between principle and detail. In this regard, the Bantu Authorities Act was to offer particular—and revealing— scope to a Minister of Dr. Verwoerd's ambition, purpose and temperament. Drawing the outline of an unfamiliar system, it left to his discretion the filling in of the design. It left him scope to define not merely the composition, the powers and the procedures of the Authorities at every level for which the Act provided, but the contact of the Authorities with the outside world as well. In due course, having framed his regulations to leave complete control of every aspect of the Authorities in his hands, he closed the door to influence—interference, he would have called it—from without by laying down that no one other than the specifically designated officers might attend any meeting of tribal or regional Authorities. Full reports of all meetings were to be transmitted to him, and he and he alone could determine how much of this information at his disposal should be made available beyond his official circle.[2]

The implications of these developments were largely hidden even

[1] It was to set the pattern to be applied later to other non-White groups.
[2] See Government Notice 939 of 1953 and Government Notice 1178 of 1957.

from the most immediately interested parties by the method of their implementation, reinforced by the widening gap between Black and White which was inherent in the Government's policy and essential to it as conceived by Dr. Verwoerd. In any case, the whole apartheid plan continued to appear so unrelated to the facts of South African life that it was difficult for the ordinary citizen to comprehend in practical terms the nature of the process upon which the Minister was engaged. An outburst in the Senate on the last day of the pre-election session of 1958 which foreshadowed the way his mind was working passed practically unnoticed except by those immediately concerned, and even they had no reason to regard it as more than a reflection of desire rather than of practical intention. The occasion was the motion to adjourn the House on the eve of the general election. While the other Opposition groups agreed to accept the motion, Senator Rubin speaking on behalf of the Native Representatives opposed it on the specific ground that it deprived him of the right to reply to a motion he had moved earlier, on which several Ministers had expressed their views at some length. With a degree of anger which the occasion seemed scarcely to warrant, Dr. Verwoerd who as leader of the Senate had moved the motion retorted that this opposition from the benches of the Native Representatives was just what might have been expected. It was easy to have a big mouth and puff yourself up but it was usually a frog which puffs itself up to look like a cow, he declared. There was good reason why Senator Rubin should not have an opportunity to reply to the debate on his motion. To tell the truth, he declared, he should actually not have had an opportunity at all to have his motion considered and he had so abused the occasion that there was every reason not to permit him to take up the time of the House again. If there had ever been persons who had abused the time of the House it was those Senators representing the Natives and what they said was of no value. 'They usually give vent to the type of thoughts which go round in the brain of small people,' he declared. He added significantly, 'The more I am placed in the opportunity of preventing them speaking, the more will I prefer to do this in the general interest. . . .' Here he added, 'I must, however, honestly admit that the conduct, particularly of the Native Representatives in this House, is useful because they make it clearer and clearer to South Africa that the time must come when the Government of the country should rather have consultation directly with the Bantu, namely through the medium of their territorial authority leaders and that the apparent channel which they now have will have to disappear because these members are indeed of no value in the fulfilling of their normal interests and requirements.'[1]

In the course of the election campaign, as Sir De Villiers Graaff, Leader of the Opposition, noted later, nothing was heard of this new proposition; but in the months that followed the election, there was accumulating evidence that this had not just been a passing speculation on the part of the Minister, that in fact the next moves designed to smooth the course of this revolutionary proposition were being prepared with the minimum of publicity. In this regard, special interest attached to the speech of my colleague, Mr. Stanford, in the opening debate of the post-election short session.[2] From an intimate knowledge of the Transkei which he represented, Mr. Stanford gave the House a glimpse of both the nature and the extent of these moves. Stating it as his opinion, on information at his disposal, that the Government had secured the acceptance of the system of Bantu authorities by the old Transkeian General Council by a combination of promises—of extended powers for the chiefs and assistance to make these powers effective in the public interest— and threats as to what they stood to lose if they did not adopt the Government's plan, he said an endeavour was now being made 'to create a façade of consent' for the plan which the Minister had adumbrated in the Senate of the substitution of a direct approach to the Government for the existing—or any—Parliamentary representation. While both the chiefs and the people had not yet recovered from the shock of the discovery of the extent to which the Authorities were to be subject to Ministerial control, the Territorial Authority had assembled for a meeting in Umtata, in April of that year—1958. The under-secretary for Native Affairs, who attended the meeting, delivered a number of addresess to the assembled members. One of these dealt with the question of the Territorial Authority in the Transkei having direct access to and consultation with the Minister so that they could put the views of the people of the Transkei before him. He (the official concerned) said he had gathered the impression in casual consultation with councillors that the Territorial Authority wanted contact with the Minister, that they were now a properly constituted body of chiefs

[1] Senate Hansard, February 12th, 1958, Cols. 1125–6.
[2] Hansard, Vol. 97, Col. 74 et seq.

and leading men, and that therefore they fully represented the
Transkei and were the proper body to contact the Government
direct through the Minister of Native Affairs. As against this he
placed representation by 'certain people or classes of people with
personal interests or with other motives' who 'tend to cloud the
issues or to misinterpret or misrepresent views or directly oppose
measures intended for the benefit of the Bantu or in the national
interest'. If all the members of the Authority felt this way, 'they
might consider it advisable to pass a resolution agreeing in principle
to this manner of contact', he concluded.

According to Mr. Stanford, shortly after this speech, an official of
the Native Affairs Department handed to one of the councillors a
typewritten resolution which Mr. Stanford claimed to have in his
hand at that moment. It read: 'As the Transkei Territorial Authority is so constituted as to be fully representative of the people of
the Transkeian Territories (through the Paramount Chiefs, chiefs
and leaders of the tribes residing therein), this Territorial Authority
approves in principle that it is the proper medium, without the
intervention of intermediaries, for direct contact with the Government as represented by the Minister of Native Affairs in all matters
affecting the political, material, social and economic life of the
Natives in these Territories and requests the Government to
devise ways and means in which such direct contact can best be
effected.'

Mr. Stanford's story continued: 'The matter thus raised, without
previous consideration by the Council, was referred to the Caucus
of the Authority, where the significance of the words "without the
intervention of intermediaries" immediately became a matter of
primary consideration and rejection. It was felt, however, that in
the circumstances some resolution must be moved. In the issue, the
draft as submitted to the Territorial Authority was accepted with
the omission of these words and the insertion of the words "in
addition to the present system of political representation". After
further discussion, the mover wished to withdraw the whole resolution, but (according to the minutes of the meeting) the Chairman—
the Chief Native Commissioner—would not permit him to do so.
In the course of further discussion, however, another Councillor,
Moshesh of Matatiele, moved an amendment to make the attitude
of the Councillors quite explicit. This was to add after the words
"political representation" the words "in the Union Parliament, in

the Senate and in the Cape Provincial Council". This was accepted by the mover, but before any agreement was reached on the whole proposition, another Councillor proposed that the whole matter should be deferred and referred back to the people of the Transkei, and should come up again in the following year; the ground of the proposal being that the motion had not come from the Territorial Authority itself, but had been planted on them from outside.'

If the matter had been left there, Mr. Stanford argued, it would have been bad enough—this attempt to get a façade of consent for the Minister's proposition; but on May 9th an article appeared in what purports to be the medium of reliable information in Native Affairs, the journal *Bantu*. Referring to this meeting of the Authority, it was stated in this article that 'another recent milestone in the development of Bantu administration was recently reached when many tribal chiefs accepted the Government's invitation to appoint special representatives in urban areas to act as direct intermediaries between the Government and the members of the respective tribes working in the cities.' The article had gone on to quote the Prime Minister as saying that the system of Bantu representation in Parliament would be reviewed when the Government was satisfied that there were sufficient avenues of approach to the Government through the representative institutions in the Bantu areas themselves.

Dr. Verwoerd's reply[1] to Mr. Stanford's case clearly foreshadowed the extension of the threat to Native representation from the House of Assembly to Parliament as a whole. Denying that pressure had been brought to bear on the Africans to accept the Bantu Authorities system, he came to the question of a direct approach to Government. 'That is said to have been the great sin,' he declared. It seemed to him that the member for Transkei was beginning to be afraid for his own skin and the skins of his co-representatives. What, however, was the logical consequence of consulting the Natives—'the thing they are always pleading for'? he asked. 'Is it not that as the Native increasingly learns to manage his own affairs (particularly in his own areas) he should then have direct access to the Government of the country, rather than have to speak at second hand, mainly through these persons who in fact allow themselves to be made the spokesmen of those who are dissatisfied and not the interpreters of Bantu needs? Therefore it is certainly

[1] Hansard, July 11th, 1958, Vol. 97, Col. 196 *et seq.*

true that the logical consequence of the Bantu development is that the Bantu should increasingly be given the opportunity to put his case to the Government direct.' To Mr. Stanford's interjected question, 'Here in Parliament?', 'No,' came the immediate and emphatic reply. 'No, not here in Parliament. It is not his task to consult with the white man on matters which also affect the white man. He must put his case to the Government of the country as the Basutos of Basutoland put their case to England, and not in the British Parliament.'

Two days after he became Prime Minister, Dr. Verwoerd was asked by Mr. Harry Lawrence whether it was his intention to introduce legislation in that session to abolish Native Representation in the Senate and the House of Assembly. The reply was that the matter had not yet been considered. That was on September 5th, 1958. By the time the 1959 session opened, some three and a half months later, he had persuaded himself that the Bantu Authorities system had indeed developed far enough to justify the disappearance of Parliamentary representation. The Leader of the Opposition might follow his announcement of his intentions in this regard with the pertinent questions I have already noted as to his mandate for this legislation.[1] Mr. Stanford was to use the occasion to give the House a further instalment of the record he had put before it in the previous session.[2] This related the continuing efforts that had been made to get at least a façade of consent from the one Territorial Authority so far constituted—to lend that semblance of mandate for a move the new Prime Minister was determined to make. The highlight of these efforts was an invitation to the leading Chiefs of the Transkei to meet the Prime Minister in Pretoria in the recess. This they had done, accompanied by the Chief Magistrate and the Chief Secretary of the Territorial Authority. At that meeting the advantages of accepting the Prime Minister's plan were pressed upon the Councillors, reinforced by the argument that the money spent on the existing Representatives really belonged to the African people and, in the event of the abolition of this representation, would come to them. The newspaper *Imvo Zabantsundu* (the paper originally established by Tengo Jabavu, but now a government-controlled newspaper), had recorded the sense of the Prime Minister's words as reported by those present at the meeting as follows:

[1] See p. 359.
[2] Hansard, Vol. 99, Col. 98 *et seq.*

'I have called you here so that I can tell you that I am ending the white representation in Parliament because these people I find have big claws. They are eating the fat (or the fattest portion of the joint) from your table which should have been eaten by you. The money that is paid out to these whites who represent you in Parliament will be given back to you.'

The Prime Minister had repudiated this version of what he had said to the deputation. He had, however, failed to tell the public what he really had said. Mr. Stanford's own information was that the Prime Minister had told the Councillors that the present Native Representatives were acting in their own interest, and that we were really professional politicians. (It was the type of argument that we had heard so often that it would not have surprised us if it had been used on this occasion.) That the reports in *Imvo* carried at least the impression made on the minds of the members of the deputation Mr. Stanford maintained was corroborated by the record of the report-back meetings of the members of the deputation. And with a hand-picked deputation drawn from a Bantu Authority all of whose members had to be acceptable to the Government, and with the support of Chief Kaizer Matanzima (now, 1968, first Prime Minister of the Transkei) the occasion was sufficiently successful to encourage the Prime Minister to go ahead with his plan.

When, in due course, the Promotion of Bantu Self Government Bill reached the stocks a few weeks later, the debate on the clause repealing the 1936 Act and thus abolishing all representation of Africans in Parliament was to make practically explicit the exclusion of all Opposition groups from any interest in or rights in respect of the African population. In support of his decision to abolish the representation, the Prime Minister[1] produced two arguments of the greatest political significance. The first related specifically to the question of consultation. Asked why this representation should go when African independence was obviously still far off—why not wait until the Bantu states which the Prime Minister's new vision seemed to envisage should have developed further and have become truly independent, his answer was, in the first place, that this step was necesssary now for the sake of clarity as to the direction in which the country was going. 'For the sake of clarity of the mind of the Bantu and of the world, in Africa and amongst our own popula-

[1] Hansard, Vol. 101, Col. 6237 *et seq.*

tion, a definite choice should be made, and one of the greatest symbols of this choice is the removal of the Native Representatives from this White Parliament.' In the transition period leading to the developing self-dependence of the Bantu areas, he added, 'the White Parliament, as the guardian, has a duty to perform, but whilst the task of emancipation is being performed by the guardian, it is not necessary at the same time to shelter the ward in Parliament, just as little as Britain finds it necessary to do so in regard to Basutoland'.

His other argument in favour of taking this step now was that if the Native Representatives remained, the emancipation of the Bantu areas would be delayed because 'there would still be arguments about the principle and continual demands from the liberals in the United Party and from the Native Representatives still here, and from the Bantu in the cities who refuse to join their own people and their own communities, for an increase in this representation, notwithstanding the fact that independent Bantu states are envisaged'.

But a third, and obviously determining factor in his decision to remove the Native Representatives now was that 'they are the declared enemies of the policy of emancipation'. What they said in Parliament, he said, was not so important, 'but it is because of the access they have to the Natives and the status they have acquired to create the wrong impressions in the mind of the Bantu masses, to try to dissuade them from this process of growing independence, that they should be deprived of the opportunity to abuse their position. For that reason they should not be in Parliament.'

But in a matter so closely affecting the African people, surely they should have been consulted as to whether this change should be made. 'A further argument was that there should have been consultation with the Natives,' the Prime Minister said. His significant reply to this was, 'We know what type of Native is in favour and what Natives are against the measure and we also know why some of them are in favour and some against it. But we also know that the great mass of the Bantu are not able to decide on a matter of this nature.'[1]

He added, again with obvious political significance beyond the immediate occasion, 'Apart from this, however, this is not only a matter where the guardian has to decide for the great mass who are

[1] Hansard, Vol. 101, Col. 6239.

unable to judge, but in the first place it concerns something which primarily affects the survival of the whites. The Bill does give rights and privileges to the Bantu. It is, however, white policy coupled with fairness and justice because basically this point of view is essential for the survival of the whites, as was proved by my whole argument here today. For that reason we are not called upon to ask the Bantu to be the arbitrator in this case.'

So far as we ourselves were concerned, the argument had been advanced that as Native Representatives we constituted no danger. That he agreed was true. But 'It is a question of giving status amongst the Bantu to people who do not deserve any status there. Although they are no danger in Parliament, they have proved by their actions over the years that they were no asset and could be no asset to the Bantu, particularly as far as his future development on these lines is concerned.'

So far as I personally was concerned, I had been made a particular issue in this regard by the member for Namib, who was to leave the Nationalist Party over this Bill. Mr. Japie Basson had found he could not support the abolition of the Native Representatives, certainly not at this stage. In the course of his statement he made appreciative references to us all and in particular to myself as Parliamentarians, quoting in his own support a paragraph from the Nationalist organ in the Cape Province, *Die Burger. Die Burger*, while stating that I had defended a bad case in the Assembly for more than twenty years, graciously said I had done so in an excellent manner, earning a reputation as a first-class Parliamentarian. It was a case, this Nationalist organ felt, that should be stated, but which would in future not be stated so clearly.[1]

Dr. Verwoerd obviously did not agree with his Party press in this latter regard with its obvious political significance. But he also did not agree with it on its personal side either. He was content 'to leave the hon. member for Namib to his admiration for the hon. member for Cape Eastern. I am also able to admire her debating skill but debating skill has nothing to do with the matter of principle which is now relevant here. Apart from this, I can only add: Their actions as far as the real Native interests are concerned, as long as I have had to deal with it, was nothing more than pitiful [sic].'[2]

Dr. Verwoerd did not like opposition. I have no doubt his one

[1] Hansard, Vol. 101, Col. 6173.
[2] Hansard, Vol. 101, Col. 6239. Official translation from Afrikaans.

regret at that moment was that he had not seen his way to abolish us forthwith, but had felt impelled to let our term of office run to the point of its automatic expiry a year ahead.

In the opening debate of the session the Leader of the Opposition, Sir De Villiers Graaff, had reviewed the progress of what he called the erosion of the foundations of democracy and liberty which had taken place over the twelve years of Nationalist rule. Summing up the record, he noted that more and more Parliament and the Supreme Court had been excluded not only from the administration of the Native reserves but also from increasing fields of Native life outside the reserves. In this almost the last debate of the session, Mr. Marais Steyn, the Opposition front-bencher to follow the Prime Minister, was not slow to point the extended threat to Parliament as we had known it, implicit in the Prime Minister's approach to Native representation. What the Prime Minister had said in essence was that where there are differences in principle in this Parliament, and members exercise their right and use their status as Members of Parliament to differ from him in principle, he is justified in removing them from Parliament. . . . 'If it is a true principle in the case of these three hon. members, the two hon. gentlemen and the lady who leads them, it should be equally true of the total Opposition,' he declared. 'I want to express my gratitude to the hon. members opposite for making it possible once more for the Prime Minister to reveal his attitude towards democracy and towards the Parliamentary institution.'[1]

<hr />

[1] Hansard, Vol. 101, Col. 6242.

14

Nationalism and Native Representation

Against the background of the progress of apartheid as recorded in the preceding chapters, it will be readily appreciated that the task of representing Africans in Parliament during the last years of our office was a peculiarly difficult and discouraging experience, with the exploitive character of the policy in operation narrowing opportunity and increasing the instability of the whole African population, while promises of new rights and opportunities remained unfulfilled. But the burden of continuous rearguard action, which was in effect our lot over these years, was itself aggravated by special circumstances affecting us as a group.

I have recorded earlier that the third election in terms of the Representation of Natives Act was due to take place at the end of 1948, the year of the General Election which brought Dr. Malan and his party into office; and I have told of the decision of Nationalist-minded candidates to contest these seats, with one straight Nationalist Party candidate in the Natal Senate seat where Dr. Edgar Brookes was the sitting member. These candidates had in effect only a nuisance value, but my opponent certainly had that for me. My constituency had recently been enormously enlarged by delimitation, not on the basis of the number of potential voters or of population, but of actual qualified and registered voters. I therefore found myself having to travel an area which extended from the outskirts of East London in the South-East to Kimberley and Mafeking in the North-West.

There was no doubt how the constituency would vote. What Dr. Malan freely admitted in regard to the Coloured vote we were to demonstrate again in respect of the African vote, that, left to themselves, the voters, and the people behind them, would not have Afrikaner nationalism. The result was a sweeping victory in the Assembly election for non-Nationalist candidates, and in the Senate elections, where there was any change, the same success attended those candidates who most nearly reflected the opinions of the original team. With this result certain, I used the occasion of the election campaign principally to discuss with my electorate what I thought the Africans should do in the new circumstances that faced us with the change of government. I emphasised that Native affairs had been the dominant issue in the general election, and that now, all parties were talking and thinking Native policy. In the circumstances I thought the Africans should themselves be heard in this regard, and advised them to draw up an African policy for South Africa which would set out their view of the steps by which our common society could progressively be transformed into a truly democratic society based on the old liberal principle of equal rights for all civilised men. Asked at one of the larger educational institutions in the constituency what organisation I thought should be used as the vehicle for such a move, I said it was not my business to decide that question, but that it seemed to me that the African National Congress, which had survived many vicissitudes, could be built up again for the purpose. This would surely be the most economical procedure. At any rate, it would avoid the possibility of a clash and a dispersal of forces which the creation of a new organisation would almost certainly engender.

I may say here that, at that time, it seemed that the African National Congress had suffered from the improvement that had taken place in the economic status of the African population in the war years, and the feeling of impending change in Native policy engendered by General Smuts' move to negotiate with the Natives Representative Council and his declarations in favour of meeting the problems of our new society in more modern terms. When I say 'suffered', I mean it had lost most of such dynamic as it had built up in the campaign against the Hertzog bills and the segregation policy, and showed no conspicuously positive spirit to meet the new challenge which apartheid was to offer. True, the action of the Natives Representative Council in practically going on strike had found a widespread response among the rank and file of the African population, giving rise to a cry for boycott of all segregationist machinery from urban Advisory Boards, through the Natives Representative Council, to Provincial and Parliamentary representation. But the members of the Natives Representative Council, to whom those who raised the cry looked for a lead, and who were themselves among the leading members of the African National Congress, refused to lead in this direction, as I witnessed at first hand at report-back meetings of members of the Council in my own constituency. I myself have always been against political boycotts, particularly in the circumstances of South Africa, where it has always seemed to me that any political representation is better than none. Hence, where my opinion was sought, my advice always took this direction. It seems to me worth while to record these facts in view of the accusations which Dr. Verwoerd so freely made against both the members of the Natives Representative Council and myself. After ten years of experience of the business of making propaganda for an unpopular cause in a highly conservative country, I was fairly accustomed to accusations from the less responsible and less prominent members of both the major Parties. What interested without disturbing me were the addenda of seemingly carried tales with which Dr. Verwoerd garnished his attacks on what I had said or done in the company of Africans, and the degree of antagonism which I, my policy and my manner seemed to induce in him. Although the freely elected representative of a very politically conscious community where members of all classes and both sexes came to report-back meetings all of which were public, I was to Dr. Verwoerd from the beginning of his period of office simply the tool—or the inspirer (the accusation varied with the occasion)—of a handful of agitators who, like myself, were simply out for themselves.

This experience, however, was still to come, with a number of others that we could scarcely have foreseen at that moment, including the revival of the African National Congress, not for the purpose which I had had in mind, but in increasingly aggressive reaction to the denial of African hopes which apartheid was to engender with such tragic results.

Here a certain interest would seem to attach to the history of my efforts to get my African friends to produce a programme of their own that would establish their claim to a progressive emancipation —an evolutionary approach to the making of a democratic multi-racial society which was essentially their objective, as it was ours. I had put this proposition to Dr. Xuma, then the president of the African National Congress, as, I believed, the most constructive job for the Congress to tackle at that moment. I discussed with him what lines such a programme might follow, whereupon he asked me if I could put my ideas on paper and let him have them before the meeting of the Executive of the Congress, due to take place before the end of that election year (1948). In response to this request, I drew up a document which followed the lines of that which I had earlier submitted to General Smuts as Prime Minister. The essential feature as I remember it was the conversion of the pass system, with its negative approach to the process of African urbanisation and the needs of African workers, and its destructive, costly and generally indefensible penal sanctions, into a constructive system of registration for employment that would aim at bringing the worker and the job together, with contingent public responsibility for relieving the burdens of unemployment where it occurred, of accidents, of old age and disability and such other distresses as our industrial society might throw up—in brief, a charter for emerging African labour in a modern society, based on Western ideas and standards. I sent the document to Dr. Xuma on the eve of the meeting. I also, however, sent copies of it confidentially to two or three other prominent members of the Congress belonging to my own constituency who, I knew, would be at the meeting. I expressed the hope that Dr. Xuma might indeed introduce the topic of an African policy for South Africa, when they might then be more prepared for the discussion than was otherwise likely to be the case.

As it happened, this important topic never did come up for discussion at the meeting; the African National Congress was, I gathered, at that moment much more preoccupied with more personal matters. But my efforts in this regard did not suffer complete eclipse. In fact, they achieved a quite unexpected if very transitory success in a most unexpected quarter, as I was to discover by accident. Soon after this date, 1948, one of the friends to whom I had sent a copy of my draft programme, Mr. S. P. Sesedi, a successful business man in Kimberley, became chairman of the Advisory Boards Conference which was still an effectively functioning part of our administrative machinery. A year later I received a letter from him asking me to produce another presidential address for him to present to the forthcoming meeting of the Conference. He had used my document on the previous occasion with marked success, he said. Dr. Eiselen, who had then recently been brought from the academic world into the Civil Service in the important office of Secretary for Native Affairs as being sympathetic towards the Government's policy, had declared that it was the most constructive address he had heard on the subject of a programme for progress for the African people.

The results of the elections faced me with immediate problems which left me little time to meet more than the day-to-day demands of my office. The most immediately threatening of these derived from the return of my husband for the Transvaal-Orange Free State seat in the Senate. The filling of this seat was to face the Government with the problem to which I have already referred,[1] of carrying any proposition in that Chamber. What steps the Government would have taken against any other successful non-Nationalist candidate to get the seat again open, and thus to give them a few more months to manœuvre, I do not know. But when my husband's return was announced in the Chamber, and before his colleagues could introduce him, Dr. Verwoerd, whose Party had brought him into the political arena via the Senate when he failed to win the seat he had contested in the general election, challenged his right to be a member of Parliament at all on the ground that he was not a South African citizen.

In fact my husband, a British subject by birth, at the time of his coming to South Africa was still a member of the Parish and Town Councils of Motherwell in Scotland and an official of the Motherwell (Scotland) Trades and Labour Council. He had been invited to come to South Africa as adviser to the first large African Trade Union, the Industrial and Commercial Workers' Union, an invitation which he had agreed to accept. But in political circles in South Africa, where the first Nationalist Government under General Hertzog was newly in office with the support of Colonel Creswell's white Labour Party, there was considerable anxiety about this new development among the African population, mingled with a good deal of fear. The result was extensive—and intensive—diplomatic activity behind the scenes, ending, after numerous delays, in the granting of a temporary permit only for his entry into the country.

That was in 1928, when under the then existing law governing South African citizenship, British subjects by birth automatically acquired South African citizenship after two years' residence, and from the time of his arrival until his successful Parliamentary contest in 1948, the question of my husband's permit had never been raised again. On the contrary, in due course, when he applied for a renewal of his passport, in 1934, his British passport was taken in and a South African passport automatically issued to him; and from that date onwards he had carried all the responsibilities and performed all the duties of a South African citizen, as indeed he had done ever since his arrival in the country. Now Dr. Verwoerd

[1] See pp. 223-4.

claimed that in fact he had no such responsibilities and no South African rights.

This issue had been raised by a member of the Nationalist Party as soon as the election result was known. It was thus already a public challenge for which the President of the Senate was duly prepared. He ruled that until the courts had declared this claim valid, my husband must be allowed to take his seat.

While this was happening in the Upper Chamber, a similar challenge from the Government benches was being made to my return to the House of Assembly, since under South African law a woman takes the nationality of her husband. At the same time, attention was drawn to the penalty which attaches to wrongful occupation of a seat in Parliament under our law, that of a fine of £100 (R200) per day for the period during which such wrongful membership lasts.

The Speaker of the House of Assembly, also prepared for the occasion, took up the same attitude as the President of the Senate. So far as the fine was concerned, that was a matter for the member herself, he held.

It may be appropriate to record here that the case against my husband's citizenship hung over our heads for some twenty months. In the end, when it came up in the Supreme Court in Pretoria before a bench of three judges, my husband's Counsel decided to subpoena the Prime Minister, Dr. Malan, as Minister of the Interior on whose authority the original permit was granted. While I believe the judgment in the case was never in doubt, I appreciatively record the spirit in which Dr. Malan met the questions put to him on the implications in his mind of the limits of the permit granted. Without hesitation he admitted that from the time the permit was granted, neither he nor the Government to which he belonged had made any effort to apply the limitations it seemed to imply, or had ever taken any action that could suggest that my husband's right to acquire citizenship and to exercise South African citizenship was in doubt.

In the meantime, with the Speaker's decision in my favour—at least temporarily—I was led into the House by the Whip of the Labour Party and one of the Whips of the United Party. Thereby also hangs a tale of some political interest and importance. It is the custom of Parliament that a member coming into the House other than with the duly elected body after a general election, should be introduced by two sitting members. These would normally be two members of his own party. But since we as Native Representatives had no party, but were in effect independents, we had, initially at least, to seek sponsorship outside our own ranks. In the past this had presented little or no difficulty since the United Party Government had accepted the basis of our presence in Parliament and had always been willing to co-operate in this friendly service. Indeed, on the occasion of our second entry into Parliament, the Minister of Native Affairs had sought the co-operation of the official Opposition, a gesture designed to mark the 'national' character of our representation. Dr. Malan and his team, however, would have nothing to do with such a proposition. This was no doubt a logical stand on their part in view of their contention that General Hertzog had departed under pressure from what they claimed was the general agreement in 1936 that Native representation should be confined to the Senate. It is true that they were then not yet committed to a policy of abolition of our seats, but after our vote on the war issue, they had decided upon reduction in our powers, and were moving steadily towards the more extreme position in our regard. So on that occasion the Minister himself, Major Piet van der Byl, and the front bench member then representing the Transkei, Mr. A. O. B. Payn, declared the United Party position by sponsoring us as the group that we had in effect become.

Now, however, a new factor had arisen to complicate the situation. My two earlier colleagues had departed from the Parliamentary scene, one, Mr. Hemming, by death, the other, Mr. Molteno, to return to his earlier profession of law. In their places the Transkei returned Mr. W. Stuart, who had been the runner-up for my seat in my first election, while from the Western Cape constituency came Mr. Sam Kahn, a prominent member, indeed the most prominent member of the Communist Party in South Africa.

With this diverse character of the representation, the problem of our introduction in the first long session of the new dispensation opening on January 21st, 1949, was again a personal one. To Mr. Stuart, with a background of Cape liberalism, this presented no serious difficulty and, as I have noted, Whips of the United and Labour parties performed this friendly service for me. The question was what was to happen to Mr. Kahn. The new Government Party, already loudly committed to fight what it professed to see as the major danger of communism in South Africa, would of course have nothing to do with Mr. Kahn's entry into Parliament. As in my case, the Labour Party was willing to share the responsibility of the introduction with the United Party. The United Party, however, would also have nothing to do with a professed communist, and in the circumstances the Labour Party's offer fell away. Since I was the only established member of our group, and obviously placed to become the liaison not only between my colleagues but between them and the other parties, I felt that the problem of Mr. Kahn's introduction became my responsibility.

In the circumstances I had to inform the Speaker of the House before the opening session that I could not find two sponsors for Mr. Kahn. As I explained to my constituents later, I was not prepared to accept the implication of this situation, namely that Parliament itself should do whatever lay in its power, however little that might yet be, to prevent a duly elected representative of the people from expressing views it did not like. I would therefore, I said, introduce Mr. Kahn alone. But if two sponsors could not be found, the rule requiring them had to be abrogated before Mr. Kahn's introduction could be effected. This Mr. Speaker had to arrange with the Prime Minister.

In due course, having been introduced myself, I rose to announce that Mr. Kahn was waiting to take the oath which rules of the House demand of new members. Mr. Speaker then asked me, in the established form, to bring him to the table in the company of another member. I had thereupon to say that there was no other member available for this service. Dr. Malan as Prime Minister was just getting to his feet to move that the rule be suspended when, to the surprise of all and the admiration of many, Mr. Morris Kentridge, a front-bencher of the United Party, moved out of his bench stating that he would accompany me.

Against this background it is perhaps not surprising that the speech from the throne, which we were to listen to immediately afterwards, sounded particularly ominous in my ears. It announced[1] that after investigation, the Government was gravely concerned at the considerable dimensions already assumed by communistic activities amongst certain classes of the population and was considering the necessary steps to combat them effectively. In my own experience there was singularly little communism among the African community, a thesis which I was to elaborate in Par-

[1] Hansard, Vol. 66, Col. 8.

liament on more than one distressing occasion. What there was, however, was a strong and rapidly growing national consciousness among large sections of the people which was making them less willing to accept without protest policies which threatened such rights as they still possessed. But there was little evidence to suggest that Dr. Malan and his colleagues could differentiate between these two things and apply themselves with vision and generosity to the real sources of potential trouble.

The history of the steps which the Government did take in this regard speak for themselves. In the following year, 1950, the Minister of Justice introduced an Unlawful Organisations Bill which was at once referred to Select Committee. From Select Committee it emerged as a Suppression of Communism Bill with a definition of communism of such wide range that it could cover all political opinions, objectives and activities which the Government did not like. It gave to the executive authority to ban not only the Communist Party of South Africa but any other organisation which, and any person whom the Minister of Justice chose to put in the same category. The penalties for individuals whom the Minister might choose to bring within the scope of this legislation included exclusion from any office and all political activity, with the proviso that in the case of a member of Parliament or of a Provincial Council, this penalty could only be applied after enquiry and report, by the Senate in the case of a Senator and by the House of Assembly in the case of a member of that House, or of a Provincial Council. The relevance of this latter provision lay in the election to the Cape Provincial Council of Mr. Fred Carneson, who, like Mr. Kahn, was a declared communist.

This legislation was carried in the face of the determined opposition of all the Opposition groups with the exception of my colleague from the Transkei, Mr. Will Stuart, who felt that the Government had a case to make against communism. (He was to change his attitude to this particular method of making its case the following year.) The focal point of attack was the indeterminate nature of the offences that were being created by the Bill and the extensive and arbitrary power which it put in the hands of the Government to the exclusion of the Courts. For me, both as a representative of Africans and as a liberal, it seemed fraught with special menace which the progress of events has more than justified. I was convinced then, as I stated in the debate on the second

reading of the Bill, that the intention was to muzzle the propagandists for a multi-racial society in which all groups might share
political power and responsibility. The Minister himself, in introducing the Bill, read out from the programme of the Communist
Party that it was among the principles of the Party to encourage
the African people to fight for their liberties, to fight for the abolition of colour bars and for the extension of political rights. As I
referred to this in my speech on the Bill, one Nationalist member
interrupted with 'That is what you are advocating', to which my
obvious reply was, 'That is exactly the point', which brought me
and everyone like me within the ambit of this legislation.

But what was of even more immediate concern, I felt that the
new powers of the Bill were designed to deprive the growing
African nationalism of all its leaders. That, I was sure, was what
they were intended to do, leaving the African national movement
without leadership in the hope that it would thus disintegrate and
disappear.

So far as the Bill's immediate purpose was concerned, that was
to put Mr. Kahn out of Parliament, this was to take a little longer
than its sponsors had anticipated. The first moves to apply the law
revealed a number of technical weaknesses which induced the
Minister to come back to Parliament in 1951 with amendments to
stop the gaps. The chief of these was doubt as to the retrospective
character of the Act. In the specific case of Mr. Kahn, could he be
subjected to the penalties of the Act as a member of a party which
had been legal when he belonged to it, and which had gone out of
existence before the gazetting of the law under which it would have
been declared an unlawful organisation? The amended law established the continuing culpability of any person who had ever been
a member of the Communist Party. It also, however, made provision for at least the appearance of the right of a member of
Parliament accused of communism to be heard in his own defence,
a semblance of a trial by his peers, and of the maintenance of the
privileges of Parliament. The machinery provided for the purpose
was that of a select committee before which both the accuser, in
this case the Government, and the accused might be legally represented. From this committee, constituted in the customary manner
with a majority of Government members, a report should be submitted to the Minister as to whether the accusation was well
founded. If this should, in the opinion of the majority of the com-

mittee, be established, the decision as to whether action should be taken against the accused or not was to lie with Parliament, which should recommend to the Minister accordingly.

Armed with this revised legislation, on the opening day of the 1952 session the Minister of Justice, Mr. C. R. Swart, announced the terms of a select committee of enquiry into the cases of Mr. Kahn and Mr. Carneson. The United Party accepted the proposition as falling within the law, even while deprecating the retrospective clause in the indictment. The Labour Party sought by amendment to get this retrospective aspect removed, an effort that was as unsuccessful as was my own appeal to the Minister to withdraw the whole proposition (which was in his discretion) as not in the interests of the country.

In due course, the Leader of the Labour Party and I took our places on the Select Committee and endured with what fortitude we could, as did the other members of the Opposition side of the Committee, the travesty of a trial in which the accused conducted their own defence with a skill that few could have equalled, and with the result a foregone conclusion, as indeed have been the results in all committees and commissions which it has been my lot to serve on under the Nationalist Government. According to the majority, the accused were guilty on all counts.

It has to be recorded to their credit that the official Opposition put up a strong stand against the verdict on the ground that, whatever communism the two accused had professed—and they had professed their allegiance openly at all times—it bore no resemblance to the definition in the Act. In addition, from the moment the Act was applied to make the Communist Party illegal, they had scrupulously observed the law both in fact and in spirit. This was their case, and ours when the matter was brought to Parliament itself, with the same result—a majority vote for the expulsion of these two gentlemen from their office and a continuing ban on any political activity on their part.

On May 26th, 1952, Mr. Kahn ceased to be a member of Parliament, having delivered a final speech that stirred a faint presentiment of coming troubles in all but the most insensitive or ignorant. From that moment, to the best of my knowledge, he obeyed the terms of the ban upon him. Certainly he was never accused of having contravened the provisions of the law. Yet in the emergency of 1960 which followed Sharpeville, he barely escaped the arresting party which arrived at his home to pull him in with all the others who were to prove only the latest victims of this type of legislation. He has been in exile since that time.

From the date of Mr. Kahn's expulsion from Parliament until our own political demise in 1960, the Assembly representation was only briefly at its full strength of three members. While the law as it then stood made it possible for the Government to put a member out of Parliament, it proved for a time unequal to the task of controlling the entry of those whom it did not approve. At the by-election to fill the Cape Western seat, an electorate whose spokesmen had made it abundantly clear that they had elected Mr. Kahn not as a communist but as the best candidate offering, that they knew little about communism and did not care much for what they did know, indignant at the interference with their rights as voters which this treatment of their duly elected member involved, determinedly voted for another candidate who had been a lifelong member of the Communist Party. This was Mr. Brian Bunting, son of one of the earliest and best known members of the Communist Party of South Africa. Mr. Bunting, whose nomination was unsuccessfully challenged in the Courts by the Government, was duly elected on November 5th, 1952, and, sponsored by Mr. Lovell of the Labour Party and myself, he took his seat in the final brief session of the Nationalist Party's first Parliament in January 1953.

The session itself lasted barely a month and, with a general election pending, the Government had no time to spare for anything but essentials. With its return to power, however, and that with an encouragingly increased majority, it lost no time in setting the now familiar machinery in operation. The first session of the new Parliament met on July 3rd, 1953. On its first full working day, July 6th, the Minister of Justice announced the Select Committee on Mr. Bunting's case, and on September 29th his period of office was terminated. This occasion found only the Labour Party, myself and my other colleague, Mr. Stuart, in continuing opposition. The official Opposition had been shaken both by the challenge of Mr. Bunting's candidature and some of his campaign propaganda, particularly a sympathetic reference to the passive resistance campaign against unjust laws into which African dissatisfaction had erupted in 1952 with tragic results. Additional factors in the situation were that this was a new member, and a new Parliament, in which the United Party's own ranks had thinned considerably with an obvious swing to the right in the country. My colleague and I naturally felt the need to defend the right of an African electorate to the exercise of a free choice of representation, and I therefore moved with his support that the Minister, accepting the report of the Select Committee as he was sure to do, would take no action but would leave Mr. Bunting in his office. I strove to make my case on the general principle of Parliamentary government, to underline the fact that what was at stake in this case, as in Mr. Kahn's case, was not the right of Africans to be represented by members of their own choice, but the right of all voters to have a free choice of representatives, limited only by the accepted exclusions of the proven criminal or the insane.

With the unfortunate link between these cases and Native representation the whole situation, which any liberal and democrat must have found deeply disturbing, imposed an exceptional tax upon us. And it looked as if the strain might be unending when another named communist, Miss Ray Alexander, accepted nomination in succession to Mr. Bunting, and the Courts, having been called upon to adjudicate in the matter, found that she had no power to withdraw when called upon to do so by the Minister of Justice. The machinery ground on to her election on April 27th, 1954, when Parliament had been again in session for over three months. In the meantime a further amendment to the Suppression of Communism Act, introduced in the early days of this 1954 session, had made it illegal for any named communist, that is, anybody who had ever been a member of the Communist Party or of any other organisation declared by the Minister to be illegal in terms of this law, or any person whom the Minister deemed to be a communist, to enter Parliament, as a member. Thus when Miss Alexander headed the poll in this second by-election, her return was immediately declared invalid and the seat was thus again vacant.

It was to remain vacant until the latter part of that year, when what was to prove the final election of Native Representatives took place. This election was again to bring me two new colleagues in the House of Assembly, Mr. Walter Stanford from the Transkei which he won as a member of the young Liberal Party from Mr. Stuart, and Mr. Lee Warden who, although a political friend of his two predecessors, had never been a member of the Communist Party and who therefore did not, at least at that time, fall under the ban which curbed the political activities of listed communists.

That, however, was not to prove the end of our difficulties in maintaining the meagre strength of our representation. In the early hours of the morning of December 5th, 1956, and the immediately succeeding days, the police rounded up some 156 persons on a charge of high treason, and among the number was Mr. Lee Warden. The treason trial which followed, becoming a matter of world-wide interest, kept our colleague away from Parliament for all but a few days of the long 1957 session, and the whole of the pre-election short session of 1958. Being one of the first to be discharged at the end of the fourteen months' preparatory examination, he joined our ranks again after the general election, and, until our joint removal from the Parliamentary scene in 1960, he gave brave support to the cause which Mr. Stanford and I had sought to maintain between us in his absence. In these closing years of my Parliamentary experience, I saw nothing to suggest that Mr. Lee Warden's political views differed in any essential way from those of the liberals I had known over the years, but since we all disappeared from Parliament, the Government has found some grounds, unspecified, to justify banning him in terms of the Suppression of Communism Act and confining his movement to an area just wide enough to take in his home and the premises on which he conducts his printing business on which his livelihood depends.

In the meantime his predecessor, Mr. Bunting, after periods of house arrest and actual detention affecting both himself and his wife, applied for and was granted an exit permit and has joined the mounting ranks of South African exiles overseas.

15

Reactions to Apartheid

The course of events had already drawn South Africa into the limelight of international disapproval even before the accession of Afrikaner nationalism to the position of power in the country, as Dr. Verwoerd and his predecessors in office were often to remind their critics of the official Opposition over the years. The achievement of the Nationalist Party in office in this regard was progressively to promote her to the position of central figure on the world stage, a position she was more and more coming to occupy in unenviable isolation as time went on. That stemmed naturally and automatically from the nature and course of the apartheid policy with which South Africa as a whole was equated. The inevitable anxiety of anyone professing liberalism in the South African context was whether the political forces in the country could be induced to see the essential cause of this unhappy situation before it was too late, a danger to ourselves and a threat to all we enjoyed in life.

When we went to Parliament as Native Representation, as I have shown, we were politically alone in our approach to Black-White relationships. Our hope was that the country would move in our direction, a hope encouraged by the conviction that that was the natural course of development of that Western Christian civilisation from which we claimed to derive. I have also recorded the signs which lent some support to those hopes in and immediately after the war years. They were all, alas, indeterminate, with those on whom they depended drifting in an atmosphere of complacency, as if all time was at their disposal to make the necessary accommodations between white privilege and prejudice on the one hand and rising African needs and demands on the other that a modern society and the modern world were rendering appropriate. These accommodations called for both intellectual effort and emotional adjustment on the part of the white electorate, and both were lagging conspicuously. Even before the change of government in 1948, it was becoming clear that a good deal of new political thinking would have to be done to

produce a pattern to suit South African needs, that the old Cape
liberal slogan of equal rights for all civilised men, inherited from
Rhodes and conceived in the spirit of nineteenth century optimism,
although still a good answer, was not going to be the whole answer
to the problems of our multi-racial society in the twentieth century.
And much propaganda would be needed to make any truly liberal
conclusions a working force. In 1948, the question still remained—
when and how would this thinking be effectively stimulated, and
how far would it carry us in the time at our disposal in a world that
was moving fast.

The very first steps in the application of the apartheid policy
were to create a new awareness of things political among sections
of the electorate which had not hitherto been conspicuously concerned with the responsibilities of political enfranchisement; and
they were to set in motion a process of differentiation between
Nationalism and all non-Nationalist elements that was to emanci-
pate us as Native Representatives from the position of isolation in
which, as a political minority, we had continued to function during
our first two terms of office. From the early days of Nationalist
government, we were never to be without some element of support
on the Parliamentary front, however variable and uncertain it
might be.

The process began to take shape with the new Government's
challenge to the Coloured vote, and particularly their challenge to
the Constitution. The official Opposition, still essentially conservative in a conservative country, indeed took its stand on the *status quo*
as established by the 1936 settlement, but at least it would not
retire beyond that in the matter of political rights. What was to
become more immediately important, it would not tolerate the
challenge to the Constitution inherent in the Government's plan to
override the entrenchments. In this regard, it was to lead and to
conduct that major legal battle which I have already recorded,
involving both financial and emotional strains of a very considerable
order for which it has had le.s credit than was its due.

This particular struggle was to evoke two significant political
developments on the non-Nationalist side which have become part
of the history of this momentous and troubled period. The first of
these I have already noted. This was the emergence of the War
Veterans' Torch Commando, that spontaneous organisation of ex-
service men and women roused to action by the threat, as they saw

it, to the principles of democratic government for which they had fought. The movement swept into life on the back of the Government's first defeat in the Courts, and what seemed Dr. Malan's threat to proceed to his objective regardless of the legal decision against him. As growing tension in the country only seemed to strengthen the Government's intention in this regard, the leading spirits of the new movement proposed a converging march on the legislative capital recruiting, it hoped, kindred spirits on the way. The intention was to try to persuade the Prime Minister and his colleagues of the strength of the opposition to, and the dangers inherent in, the course which they were pursuing.

The march was spectacularly successful. It reached Cape Town on May 21st, 1951, and after parading the streets with the lighted torches which were its emblem and its symbol, it gathered 10,000 strong at the mother city's traditional centre of public demonstration, the Grand Parade, to endorse the resolution setting out its case against the course which the Government seemed set to pursue. In the light of all that was to follow, the terms of the resolution seem singularly moderate. They read:

'We, ex-service men and women, believe that the recent happenings indicate that our Constitution is being tampered with to the detriment of South Africa's name and honour and the disgrace of her people.

'The War Veterans contend

(a) that pledges honestly given and honestly accepted as between man and man that the franchise and language safe-guarding clauses of the South Africa Act would remain inviolate and sacrosanct must be honoured.

(b) That whatever the law may be, there is a moral obligation not to alter the entrenched clauses otherwise than in accordance with the intention of the founders of the Constitution, and only as a result of a clear expression of opinion by the overwhelming majority of the electorate.

(c) That a failure of the white man to keep his word to a non-European will undermine race relations in South Africa and destroy the very foundations of our economic and political way of life.'

The objective of the Commando, it declared, was to win sufficient support to convince the Government of the error of its ways. It concluded: 'We call upon the Government to withdraw this shameful legislation, and to acknowledge the sanctity of the Constitution.'

Failing this, 'we pledge ourselves to work to ensure its defeat at the next election'.

The decision of the gathering was that the resolution should be carried to Parliament by the leaders of the Commando and there presented to the leaders of the Government and of the Opposition groups. In the issue, it was in fact presented, quietly and without ostentation, by the leaders of the Commando to Mr. Strauss, representing the United Party, Mr. Christie for the Labour Party and to myself for the Native Representatives—my inclusion in the ceremony being, as I remember, at the invitation of Mr. Strauss and Mr. Christie themselves. Government representatives were conspicuous by their absence. Mr. Swart, as Minister of Justice, was to tell the House of Assembly the following day that the leaders of the Commando had said they would reach Parliament at 10.15, and that he had given the police instructions to permit the passage of twelve people for the purpose, but that they had not arrived until after the House had adjourned.

Unfortunately, while the final act in this part of the drama was taking place quietly on the steps of the House of Assembly, trouble had broken out lower down in the city on the fringes of the crowds which the demonstration had attracted. This had led to baton charges by the police, whose forces had been conspicuously augmented in the preceding weeks as if the Government feared for its safety or wished to suggest that it had reason to do so. In the course of the trouble a number of people, including fifteen members of the police force, suffered injuries of varying degrees of seriousness, and when Parliament assembled on the following day, acrimonious exchanges on the subject of these happenings tended to deflect attention away from the Commando's resolution, with its carefully and emphatically underlined constitutional character. The Opposition at once demanded an enquiry into the facts of the disturbances which had taken place. The Government, refusing the demand, countered with an accusation that the demand in itself was an attack on the police which it would not countenance or consider. At the same time it made it plain that it would not be deflected from its appointed course by any demonstrations of opposition strength.

The leaders of the Commando, having failed in their first objective, now applied themselves to their second line of attack, organisation to defeat the Government in its first appeal to the electorate on its record as a government. As the election approached, fortified by the decision of the Courts as to the continuing validity of the entrenchments in the Constitution, the Commando, the Labour Party, and the United Party lined up together in a United Front. The objective was specific and limited—to get what all these groups regarded as a dangerously sectional government out of office. It was an objective which Dr. Malan stigmatised as 'ridiculous and dishonourable', while the very terms in which he elaborated his accusation could only serve to heighten the anxieties which had inspired it: 'They want to force the Government to resign,' he thundered. 'They want to get rid of this Government which, as everyone knows, represents by far the greater part of one of the biggest language groups in the country and receives its support from it.' To Dr. Malan, clearly the 'racial' issue as between English and Afrikaner was very much alive.

When, in due course, the election decision of 1953 brought the Malanites back to office with an increased majority reflecting the beginning of that process of Afrikaner integration which has coloured the operation of the party system in the country ever since, the Commando, without a policy to make it a positive political force, began to disintegrate. Its members had gone to war in defence of democratic principles and practice. The Government's acceptance of the fact, if not of the spirit, of the court decision, and its claim to act completely legally in all circumstances, seemed to cut the ground from under their feet. They were constitutionalists, not revolutionaries. And as their preoccupation with practical politics more and more brought the matter of black-white relationships into the forefront of political discussion, the difficulty of finding a positive and common foundation for so diverse a membership became too distracting and inhibiting a handicap to be overcome.

But as the Torch Commando faded out, almost as rapidly and imperceptibly as it had emerged, heightening tensions in the political field were to produce another, less spectacular but more enduring response to the challenge of the situation. This was the Women's Defence of the Constitution League, to become widely and familiarly known as the Black Sash. It followed on the rejection by the Appellate Division of the farce of the High Court of Parliament and the decision of the Government now, by the reconstitution of the Senate, to manufacture the majority their objective demanded and the electorate had failed to provide. Deeply shocked

2C

by the cynicism of this plan to circumvent the Constitution, a group of women decided to focus attention on the character of a Government that could adopt such tactics and pursue such a course by a new and special type of demonstration. This was to search out the movements of Ministers and to stage a silent protest along their route, pointed by the symbol of a black sash denoting mourning for the rape of the Constitution and the destruction of the principles upon which it had been founded which the Senate Act denoted.

This organisation, like the Torch Commando, came to impressively vital life on a specific constitutional issue. It was, however, in the very nature of South African society that it too should begin to find itself faced with the essential problem from which all others in this country derive—that of colour and the question of a policy in that regard. But as its initial momentum began to pass with its failure to make any effective impression on the Government, and its original numbers fell away before the apparently insurmountable difficulty of finding a generally acceptable platform on which to function, the nucleus of a continuing organisation survived, dedicated to a struggle against apartheid, particularly where its most discriminatory manifestations and its most depressive effects on human life and dignity exposed themselves.

In pursuing this course, the Black Sash was in fact reflecting the course of political development in the country generally. Here the dividing line between Afrikaner nationalism and all other sections of the community was progressively being drawn as that between apartheid, separation, on a colour line and the conception of a single society within which some way must be found to satisfy the needs and the legitimate aspirations of all while maintaining the values and standards of the Western world. Indeed, colour policies were becoming the almost obsessive preoccupation of the country, destined to produce new political groupings and to reshape old ones.

Even as the first Nationalist Government's attack on the Constitution was bringing the Torch Commando into existence, liberal discussion groups and associations were meeting at various points throughout the country, concerned to concentrate attention on the need for a clear challenge to apartheid. When the 1953 election resulted in renewed strength for the Malanites, the Liberal Party emerged, committed not only to the general principle of a common society, but specifically to the abolition of all colour bars and to a citizenship open to all races.

It was an infant endeavour, without adequate preparation and with no financial resources and, as such, it drew to its banner only the most committed of the old liberals of Cape tradition. But it also provided a political home for younger and more radical elements. This in itself was to form an inhibiting factor for many professing liberals, particularly in view of the banning of the Communist Party, although the new Party's constitution provided for a careful scrutiny of the political affiliations of applicants for membership, with the object of curbing the danger of its becoming a home for the politically exiled whose doctrines it did not endorse. Indeed, its first political adventure was to fight the communist condidates in the following two by-elections occasioned in the Cape Western seat under the Representation of Natives Act by the expulsion from the House of Assembly first of Mr. Kahn and then of Mr. Bunting.

A pioneering adventure in party politics, it had plenty of vicissitudes to face. Nowhere does the party system offer a welcome to new parties, while the very forces that were building up increasing majorities for Afrikaner Nationalism predetermined a particularly difficult future for a party dedicated to the liberalising of black-white relationships. Indeed, early in the history of the Party, the passion for justice which inspired it carried it a good deal farther than even many of its first members were prepared to go. Soon the slogan of 'one man, one vote', which owed little or nothing to the old Cape liberal tradition built on the history of the Mother of Parliaments, began to complicate its internal politics as well as the public response to its existence, and many of the more conservative liberals came to feel that there was still more to be done for their cause by working outside the Party, and even inside the official Opposition.

The mere emergence of the Liberal Party, however, did make of the liberal case a positive thing in the South African political scene, and its racially comprehensive character[1] was to be a valuable, if now costly, contribution to the political life of South Africa. While it never won a 'white' seat in Parliament, during our last term of office as Native Representatives it could point to four members of the Party in Parliamentary office. These were my colleague, Mr. Stanford, still officially a member of the Party, and myself in the lower House, and in the Senate, Mr. Leslie Rubin, also an official Liberal Party candidate, and my husband who, like myself,

[1] Membership of the Party was open to all races without qualification.

although a member of the Party, appealed to his electorate on his personal record as a Native Representative.

In the same month in which the Liberal Party was formed, that is, May 1953, what was in effect a hiving off from the United Party took place in Natal in the emergence of the Union Federal Party (I noted earlier in another connection the formation of the short-lived Conservative Party as a dissident splinter from the United Party). Inspired by fear for the future of the English language in the country begotten of the Government's attitude to the entrenchments in the Constitution, and the contingent prospect of the establishment of a unilingual Afrikaner republic, it was mainly concerned to propagate the idea of constitutional change towards greater decentralisation of authority and the right of any Province to secede from the Union in circumstances which, in its opinion, violated the principles upon which that Union had been founded. The Party had a very brief history. Senator Heaton Nicholls resigned the office of leader of the Opposition in the Senate which the United Party had bestowed upon him after its defeat at the polls in 1948, in order to lead this new Natal venture. The Party put up seventeen candidates in the Provincial elections in 1954, but in spite of what seemed a highly emotional reaction on the part of the electorate in Natal to what was called the Natal Stand against the Government, in which the Federalists were particularly active, it failed to carry any of its nominees to victory. This was a blow which destroyed its chances of survival. The significance of its brief existence for us, however, lay in the extent to which its programme departed from the strict segregationist principles to which Mr. Heaton Nicholls had been so deeply committed in the early days of the United Party. Accepting economic integration as a fact of South African life, it declared the right of non-Europeans to enter all fields of employment for which they could prove themselves fit, and propounded the claim of fully urbanised Africans to freehold title in the urban areas. On the political front, it proposed limited direct representation of non-Europeans other than Africans in the Senate and the Provincial Councils, with the retention of the Cape Coloured franchise on the common roll. For Africans, Senator Nicholls, now speaking as a Federalist, moved in the Senate to amend the 1936 Act to allow Africans to be represented in the Senate by Africans. This latter was perhaps less revolutionary than it might appear at the time, since in the early days of the making of General Hertzog's policy, both Mr. Nicholls and Advocate Strydom had found common ground in the proposal to limit African representation to the Senate but to allow Africans to represent their own people. But the emotional content of the proposition had changed considerably in the intervening years, while the proposed retention of representation in the lower House now put the proposal in a new and different context.

While these developments were taking place, the small Labour Party, which occupied the benches next to ours in the House of Assembly, had been undergoing a quite remarkable change in character and direction that was to end by giving its Parliamentary team something of the appearance of an advance guard for liberalism.

The process had in fact begun with the passing of the old leadership before the end of the Smuts regime. It had indeed largely occasioned that passing, when the main though attenuated body of the Parliamentary representation refused to follow Mr. Madeley in his support of Dr. Malan's attitude to the Asiatic Land Tenure Bill of 1946 and, later, to the proposal to abolish Native Representation in the House of Assembly. On the eve of the 1953 election, the extent of the break with the Party's past was revealed in the adoption by the Party's Conference of the fact and the process of African integration into the economic life of the country, and the substitution of the principle of the rate for the job for legislative and other protection of the position of the white worker which had for so long been its basis.

A year later, in 1954, the Party released to the public a revised political programme. Its foundation was the acceptance of the principle of universal franchise for all adult literate persons. As an immediate step towards this objective, it proposed the retention of the then still existing common roll franchise of the Cape Coloured people, with its extension to Coloured women, and to Asian men and women in the Cape and the Transvaal with the requisite qualifications; for the Asians of Natal, on the basis of the same franchise, it proposed a group representation of men and women by three members of the House of Assembly, three in the Provincial Council and two Senators.

For the African population, it proposed to maintain the existing representation of the Cape in the House of Assembly, but to extend the franchise to women possessing the qualifications for male voters laid down in the Representation of Natives Act. On the basis of a Stanbard V qualification it proposed, further, to extend the franchise to African men and women of the other Provinces and to enable the Transvaal Africans to send three members to the House of Assembly and Natal and the Orange Free State two each, with similar representation in the Provincial Councils. For the Senate it proposed an increase in the number of elected representatives to two for each Province, to be elected not on the electoral college system but by the same voters as the representatives in the House of Assembly.

The final provision of this (for Labour) revolutionary programme was that there should be no discrimination in the matter of nomination for Parliamentary or Provincial office on grounds of colour in respect of any racial group.

In the following year, 1955, the new Leader of the Labour Party, Mr. Alex Hepple, put this programme, so far as it related to Africans, to the House of Assembly in a private member's motion which read:

'That this House is of opinion that, in addition to the present right of Natives in the Cape Province, the Native people of the other Provinces should be entitled to elect members to this House, and therefore requests the Government to consider the advisability of taking the necessary steps to extend Native representation to include the whole Union and South West Africa.'[1]

Two years previously the two members who then represented Labour in the Senate had voted with the official Opposition against practically the proposals which this motion was to cover, when moved by my husband as a first step towards an ultimate common franchise.

It may be pertinent to note here that in the debate on Mr. Hepple's motion I moved as an amendment, again supported by Mr. Stanford, 'that, recognising the interdependence of all racial groups in our population and the rights of all to aspire to full citizenship based on a common franchise, this House urges the Government as a first step in this direction (a) to abolish the separate roll now existing for Africans in the Cape Province and to transfer the Africans registered on that roll to the common roll, and (b) to place on the common roll all Africans of twenty-one years and over whose educational attainments equal those acquired by Europeans under the terms of existing Provincial ordinances (which

[1] Hansard, Vol. 87, Col. 702.

provide for compulsory education for European children), and to embark upon a policy of expanding educational opportunities for Africans which will aim at providing them with this qualification.'[1] My argument in support of this proposition was that South Africa had got, not universal suffrage for Europeans, but universal suffrage based on compulsory education for Europeans, which it was our objective to establish for all our populations.

The difference between us and the spokesmen of the Labour Party on the whole subject of political rights had now become one of time and not of principle. Indeed, for the last five years of the Parliamentary life of the Party, there was rarely an occasion when their case and ours did not coincide. It was a case which had always had strong support from an English language press consistently more liberal than the electorate. Indeed, the conversion of the Labour Party to this case, coupled with the ability and determination with which the small Parliamentary Labour team propounded it, made so strong an appeal to that press that when, in the 1958 election, the United Party decided against renewing the arrangement by which Labour had held its seats in Parliament ever since 1943, there was considerable press agitation against the decision. But if elections are designed to reflect the electorate, the end result of the 1948 election more than justified the United Party's decision, regrettable though that might be and was to people of our liberal persuasion. The crushing defeat of the Labour candidates with their fine debating record and with the very considerable support which the press continued to give them throughout the election campaign was to confirm our own experience of the tardy pace of change among the electorate as a whole.

But apart altogether from this matter of the pace of change in political thinking, for the tardiness of which the official Opposition might be—and often was—blamed as giving too little or too indeterminate a lead—the decision of the United Party not to renew the electoral pact with Labour was understandable on other grounds. The Labour Party had not only moved conspicuously away from its war-time ally; in the process it had done little to maintain friendly relations on the Parliamentary front. Indeed, it made no secret of its distaste for the pace which the leaders of the official Opposition felt called upon to maintain. On the contrary, over their latter years, they were continuously insistent on points

[1] Hansard, Vol. 87, Col. 1538.

of difference, often seeming to manœuvre to force the Opposition to vote with the Government on important issues involving a liberal versus reactionary approach. It was a tactic which, as an independent hoping one day to find the major non-Nationalist Party clearly on our side of the line, I had always opposed and had sought to avoid, arguing that every decision registered by vote against what I regarded as the liberal principle in any case was going to make the road back so much longer. No doubt this was essentially the attitude of an independent, and unlikely to appeal to a party politician.

In fact, over the years of opposition, first over the constitutional issue and then generally over apartheid, the United Party had been moving nearer to our point of view, although sometimes almost imperceptibly. It is of course important to remember both the history and the consequent composition of the official Opposition. A combination of the parties of Smuts and Hertzog, of English and Afrikaner, of town and country, it inevitably felt the need to appeal to both language sections of the electorate and to all economic interests in it. As such, its leaders had to face recurrent accusations of trying to be all things to all men. Indeed, its own experience as a party provided some solid ground for the endeavour. In the course of the constitutional struggle, as I have shown, it lost seven of its members on the conservative side, two of whom now sit on the Government's benches, while one reached Cabinet rank without previous service to the governing party, thanks to his English extraction and name. And in our last year, filling, indeed in numbers more than filling, the places hitherto occupied by our Labour Party friends, and fulfilling towards us something of the role which they had played, sat ten liberal dissidents from the United Party under the name of the Progressive Party.[1] Progressive was a less challenging name than liberal and reflected a less radical outlook than that which the Liberal Party had assumed. Unable to tolerate the pace of change in the party with which they had entered Parliament, these ten decided to separate, taking their stand as the Liberals had done on a common roll, but on the basis of a qualified franchise for all races with guarantees for racial minorities.

The period of political thinking had begun in South Africa. The United Party itself, while continuing to support the principle of

[1] Joined later by my colleague, Mr. Stanford, who was to find the Progressive Party's franchise policy more acceptable than that of the Liberal Party.

social and residential separation, had come to take its stand firmly on the basis of one state with a Parliament in which all groups should have representation. The nature of the representation proposed at and accepted by its earlier Conferences in this period of our history did not break much new ground. Its main point of emphasis was that a United Party government would put the Coloured voters back on the common roll, that is, they would restore the Coloured franchise as it had been. So far as the Africans were concerned, it was content to promise the two more elected Senators for which the Representation of Natives Act had permissively provided. As the argument between apartheid and non-apartheid developed, however, it proposed to enlarge the African representation by extending it to the other Provinces, to provide a possible eight members in the House of Assembly, giving a guarantee to its own supporters not to go beyond this without a clear mandate from the electorate. For the Asians it also postulated Parliamentary representation but left the form to be decided by consultation when the prospective occasion for implementation should make it a matter of immediate concern.

Each and all of these representations, however, were to be subject to one condition—that the candidates for office should all be white. Just as the Native Representatives left Parliament, however, the Leader of the Opposition, Sir De Villiers Graaff, announced a major development in his Party's policy in this regard. This was the intention, when the Party was in a position to do so, not only to bring the Coloured population back into political partnership with the Whites on the old basis, but to take the colour bar out of the law governing nomination for election to Parliament. Legally this meant, as the Government benches were keen to establish, that a Coloured man might be nominated for and elected to Parliament even to represent White voters, involving the ultimate challenge to Afrikaner Nationalism and apartheid.

The proposal to crown the edifice of the United Party's political plan with a possible race federation undoubtedly owes most of what it has to offer to the pressures of its opponents for a clear picture of the future as the United Party sees it. Presumably contemplating the extent to which the present Government will impose its own pattern of political separation on Black and White alike, and the degree of territorial separation which the existence of the Native reserves provides, the plan would seem to represent an attempt to weave into the framework of a common multi-racial society to which the United Party is pledged, whatever African political entities may be brought into existence by the apostles of apartheid before a change of government takes place. It is thus the counter, and the challenge to Dr. Verwoerd's commonwealth idea in that it postulates a multi-racial Parliament, at least at the upper, federal level. The proposal in regard to the Coloured people similarly postulates the rejection of an all-white Parliament at the level at which Parliament normally functions.

All these developments have to be seen against the background of movements and events in the non-European sector of South African life, and particularly among the African population.

As I have endeavoured to show, African tempers were considerably strained before the advent of the Nationalist Government. While African social and economic standards had been rising under the stimulus of war-time labour demands, resentment had been steadily increasing against the legislative and administrative limitations to the process of advance, particularly the pass laws and the Urban Areas Acts, the restrictive effects of which had spread both geographically and socially under the official policy of segregation. And with all the advance, there remained a great area of African poverty, aggravated in its social effects by the serious backlog in housing and the extensive slum conditions that prevailed. These provided a dangerous breeding ground of unrest which had already more than once erupted into conflict between the people and the police whose unrewarding duty it was to invade such privacy as slum and near-slum living conditions permitted in the application of pass and liquor laws which by their very nature could not otherwise be made effective.

As it had developed, it was a situation which, while presenting peculiar problems in the maintenance of law and order, in its root causes also presented a challenge to statesmanship to whosoever should have control of government in this rapidly changing period. Faced with it in something in the nature of crisis form in the last years of his period of office, General Smuts had adumbrated at least a measure of change both in policy and in practice to meet the new circumstances and the new demands to which they had given rise. What approach to the situation the policy of apartheid would dictate was soon to be revealed, with effects on the African's mood and the course of African action that was to become an immediately dominant factor in the political life of the country as a whole in the years that followed.

The first eruption of violence the new Government had to meet was in itself a curious and unusual one. This was the outbreak of serious riots between Africans and Indians in Durban and its environs. The trouble began on January 29th, 1949, at the terminus of the Indian-owned buses which mainly serve the African workers in the Durban area. It rapidly spread outwards to the adjoining business areas, and further afield into the neighbouring suburbs and bordering townships. Over the several days during which the police sought to get the situation under control, some fifty-three Indians and eighty-three Africans lost their lives.[1]

The outward circumstances, in which the Africans were the attackers and the Indians the victims, suggested a deep-seated animosity between the two groups, engendered by the superior economic position of the Indians vis-à-vis the Africans, which eventually erupted in this violent form. One curious feature of the event, however, was a wide-spread claim by the Africans in justification of their attacks on Indians, that when they had dealt with the Indians they would inherit the Indians' possessions. Where and how had this claim arisen? This was a question which kept on recurring in letters from my friends in Natal, who had heard the story from their own African servants. Did I think the Government could have had anything to do with it?—a reflection of the impression which past Nationalist propaganda had made on the mind of the English-speaking electorate. My view was that such a thing, with all its implications, was unthinkable in our society whatever its prejudices might be. Later, information given to me by Dr. A. B. Xuma, at that time President of the African National Congress and an old friend, offered a suggestion as to how this idea had arisen and spread among the Africans in this Province. He himself considered that the claim had stemmed from propaganda that had been widespread in the previous months in the course of that election for Native Representatives in which the Government Party had officially contested the Natal Senate seat. This propaganda, as Dr Xuma subsequently informed a public meeting in Cape Town, and as I recorded it in Parliament on May 18th, 1949, was to the effect that it was the policy of the Government to repatriate the Indian population, which would be to the advantage of the Native population

[1] Hansard, Vol. 66, Col. 58.

who would inherit their property and their rights. This had been put to Dr. Xuma himself, in his own house, he informed me, by an organiser of the Nationalist Party in an effort to persuade him to put his weight as leader of the African National Congress behind the Nationalist candidate. His reply to this was, 'What have the Indians got in the Free State?' It was a pertinent question, since the Free State admits no Indians to domicile. Once in 1946, when, in the course of the debates on the ill-fated and highly controversial Asiatic Land Tenure and Indian Representation Bill, I suggested that we could solve Natal's problem, which had inspired this measure, by opening the Provincial barriers to Indian immigration so as to allow the Indian community to spread more evenly over the whole country, the response from the Nationalist benches had come violently from the speaker who followed me with 'The first Indian that comes into the Free State, I shoot'.[1]

Conforming to a more familiar pattern were the riots that broke out on the Witwatersrand in the closing months of 1949, and re-curred spasmodically there and elsewhere throughout a good part of the following year. These were, as the Minister of Justice declared, attacks on the police in the course of their ordinary duty— in effect, on raids to check passes and permits and the possession of illicit liquor. These raids were carried out in the late hours of the night and the early hours of the morning, when the police might expect to find the people at home.

Woven in with these was an unsuccessful attempt of more politically minded groups to organise a May Day stay-at-home demonstration in support of demands for better wages, which was also to end in conflict with the police in the Witwatersrand area, and a considerable addition to the already over-large prison population.

The following years were to see numerous variations of these unhappy events, but the basic pattern, with a quite considerable history behind it, encouraged Government spokesmen to argue, as Dr. Malan, and more particularly Dr. Verwoerd, were to do, that these eruptions into violence were but a reflection of a world-wide disease begotten of the war, which had afflicted the former Govern-ment to a greater degree and at greater cost in life than it had the present Government. And where the situation suggested new economic and political demands, they contended that the respon-sibility for these should be placed fairly and squarely on the

[1] Hansard, Vol. 68, Col. 6019.

shoulders of the previous Government for its folly in dragging the non-European population into a conflict which had nothing to do with them or us.

These arguments, in the mouth of a Government determined to make no concession to changes which it disliked and to which it was vocally deeply opposed, led simply and directly to the conclusion that what the situation demanded was a firm hand to restore a healthy respect for law and order badly eroded by the weakness and sentimentality of its predecessors. Our counter-argument as Native Representatives, strongly supported by the Labour Party and increasingly also by the official Opposition as the days of its opposition lengthened, that these disturbances were not episodic, but were the symptom of deep-seated social ill-health begotten of segregation policies, were either ignored or were repudiated as the irresponsible propaganda of hostile and irresponsible people.

But if in fact these earlier manifestations of a spirit of unrest, and indeed of tension, which were to achieve an increasing intensity in the following years, seemed to fit into a familiar pattern, the developing situation was soon to throw up something that could not be so simply catalogued, and was to prove politically highly significant. It began with the decision, at the end of 1951, of the leaders of the African National Congress, in association with the Indian National Congress, to organise a nationwide campaign against what they regarded as unjust and racially discriminatory laws. The timing of this move is significant. The Parliamentary session of that year had seen the abolition of the Natives Representative Council. In place of freely elected spokesmen had come the framework of Bantu Authorities, traditional tribal heads maintained by and answerable to the Government. This had been followed by the passing of the Suppression of Communism Act to add a new threat to Parliamentary representation which had so far survived the declared intention of the Government to extrude it from the lower House.

A year earlier, Group Areas legislation designed to kraal each race in separate areas, where its members should live and carry on all their economic activities among their own people, had put the whole position of a totally unenfranchised Indian community in jeopardy, aiming a deadly blow at all those enterprises, particularly in Natal, by which a highly commercial people maintained themselves.

The situation constituted an immediate challenge to the leaders of the various groups. The answer which the Africans gave to it was this proposal of a campaign designed to focus the attention of the Government, and the electorate which had put it in office, on the attitude of the unenfranchised mass to the laws to which they were being subjected.

The details of the plan were elaborated at the annual Conference of the African National Congress in December 1951. Here it was agreed that the first move should be an approach to the Prime Minister setting out the specific laws which, it was considered, should be repealed forthwith, and asking for direct representation of the African population in the Councils of the nation. If these representations should fail, a nationwide call should be put out to the people to defy discriminatory regulations such as the limiting of the use of seats in public places, waiting rooms on stations and other public amenities to Europeans only, and to court imprisonment for such contraventions of the law.

The particular Acts specified in the list to be sent to the Prime Minister were the Pass Laws, the Group Areas Act, the Bantu Authorities Act, the Suppression of Communism Act and, presumably in recognition of the readiness of a Coloured people's organisation to stand in on the campaign, the Separate Representation of Voters Act. Less defensible within the terms of the Land Acts, which were not included in the list, were 'the so-called rehabilitation scheme and the cattle-culling policy'. These were additions to the list obviously designed to enlist the support of the people in the reserves.

It was agreed that the Prime Minister should be approached forthwith, with a request for urgent and favourable consideration of these claims; failing this, he should be informed that in the absence of constitutional avenues through which the case might be pressed, there would be no alternative to an endeavour to focus attention on the grievances and demands of the people by extra-legal action. In the likely event of an unfavourable response, it was proposed to plan the opening of a campaign of defiance to coincide with the celebration of the tercentenary of the first permanent white settlement in South Africa, of which the Nationalist Government proposed to make a great occasion organised to the slogan 'We build a nation'.

The Prime Minister's response was both prompt and unfavour-

able, concluding with a warning against any contravention of the
law of the land. The Government would deal firmly with both those
who defied the law and those who encouraged them to do so.

Despite this warning, mass meetings were in fact held at various
centres on April 16th, 1952, the date of the final tercentenary
celebration, and volunteers for the campaign of defiance were called
for. The campaign itself was formally launched on June 26th in the
names of the two Congresses and a Franchise Action Council, later
to become the Coloured People's Association.

The hopes of a nation-wide response to the call were not realised.
Only in the Cape Province did the campaign reach any considerable
proportions. This was itself significant in that, over the years after
the adoption of the segregation policy, it was in the Cape Province
that Africans had conspicuously lost long-established civil rights,
and where the sense of freedom was possibly greater than in other
parts of the country where habit had accustomed the people to
discriminatory practices. All over, however, between June 26th and
the end of the year, over 8000 men and women made the challenge,
and most of them served from thirty days to three months imprisonment as the price of their demonstration.

Unfortunately, but not without precedent, the campaign afforded
a cloak to rabble elements of which the conditions of urban African
life produced all too many. This resulted in mob riots at Port
Elizabeth and East London, with loss of life on both sides of the
colour line, and inspiring very considerable fear among the white
population not only in these centres but throughout the country.[1]
To a Government which in any case was not prepared to make any
concession to any opposition, these disastrous and lamentable events
offered ample justification for the contention that the campaign and
all that went with it was the work of dangerous extremists, anti-
white elements communistically inspired that must be suppressed
if white civilisation was to survive in South Africa. The Government's whole response, then, to the demands of the situation in the
following session of Parliament, the curtain-raiser short pre-
election session of 1953, was the passage of two drastic measures

---

[1] In Port Elizabeth, a large cinema for Africans was burned down and the proprietor murdered by the mob; in East London, a nun who was a regular social
worker in the African township was burned to death in her car. Rumour had it
that the body was subsequently mutilated and parts of it consumed by rioters.

Only a judicial Commission could have established the facts and this the
Government consistently refused.

designed to strengthen the hand of the Minister of Justice. These were a Public Safety Act, empowering the Governor-General, or if the occasion seemed to him particularly urgent, the Minister himself to declare a state of emergency where the ordinary law of the land might be superseded forthwith by powers of summary arrest and detention, and a Criminal Law Amendment Act creating two new offences, carrying heavy penalties, that of advocating resistance to any law and that of collecting money to assist the families of resisters.

Already the powers of banning taken by the Government in its anti-communist legislation had been quite extensively used to undermine the leadership of any organisation that tended to show an active political anti-apartheid spirit. Numbers of leading figures in the trade union field had been ordered to give up their jobs, a process of what the Government regarded as cleaning up which was considerably extended after another abortive call to strike action on May 1st, 1953, which had ended in conflict between those who were prepared to answer the call and those who were not. Now it was to be extended to the political front, with Mr. Albert Luthuli's case only the most conspicuous and characteristic.

Chief Albert Luthuli, having become president of the Natal Branch of the African National Congress in 1952, was summoned to Pretoria in September of that year and told that he must either give up his chieftainship or his activities with the A.N.C. He chose the former. In December, with this independent stand to recommend him, he became national president of the A.N.C. Early in the new year, 1953, he was banned in terms of the Suppression of Communism Act, which meant that he was confined to his home in Groutville and prohibited from attending meetings for five years.

By this time the Defiance Campaign had largely spent its force, itself compromised by gangster (skolly) elements that it had nothing to do with and shattered on the rocks of an uncompromising Government. Its ambitions had far outrun its organisational ability; but to anyone with any past knowledge of the African political field in South Africa, it marked a landmark not only in African but in South African political history. Some ten years previously, my husband and I had listened to demands at an annual conference of the African National Congress in Bloemfontein that Africans should now be ready to suffer and even to die in the cause of African freedom. The words were passionate—and evaporated into thin air, an academic gesture in a cause that nobody yet believed was sufficiently desperate to call for such sacrifices. Now some Africans were prepared to make sacrifices, if not to die, in that cause, with the odds against them much greater than they or we could have foreseen at that time. And those odds were to lengthen as the Government became more deeply committed to the course it had chosen and more determined to pursue it.

Undiscouraged, the Congress and its co-operating bodies,[1] which now included a European group calling itself the Congress of Democrats, a strongly left-wing organisation, proceeded to plan a new attack on the situation. The ultimate objective now was a new National Convention[2] which should frame a new constitution for South Africa under which the rights of all sections of the population should be guaranteed. An elaborate plan of action designed to lead up to the calling of such a Convention was drawn up and endorsed by a meeting of representatives of the Congresses in Durban in March 1954. The meeting took place under the chairmanship of ex-chief Luthuli who, with other leaders previously banned, was temporarily in circulation again thanks to a court decision declaring banning without warning invalid.

The first step in the programme was to be a Congress of the People to take place at a prearranged centre in July 1955, this Congress to be constituted of delegates from local cells and committees all over the country. The delegates would arrive at the chosen venue by special trains or on foot in 'freedom marches' bringing statements of grievances collected by the way, which were to form the basis of a Freedom Charter, to be drawn up at the Congress as a guide to the hoped-for National Convention.

In due course when the Congress met in one of Johannesburg's great African townships, Luthuli and many of the other moderate leaders in the field of African politics were again under ban in terms of amended legislation, and the Freedom Charter was drawn up without their presence. It set out all the familiar grievances of the non-European groups in the population and called upon the Government to abandon its discriminatory policies and to extend the rights of citizenship to all.

While the Government made no attempt to interfere with the

[1] The Indian National Congress, the Congress of Democrats and the Coloured People's Organisation.
[2] The idea of a new Convention was very much the subject of political propaganda at this time on the more liberal side of the political field.

2D

organisation of the Congress and gave no sign of concern about this new demonstration of the rising tide of non-white feeling, it was in fact watching the situation with a concentrated attention which was to culminate in the mass arrests of December 1956 on charges of treason to which reference has already been made.[1] It was a sweep which again struck at many of the earlier leaders of the African National Congress, in spite of accumulated and accumulating evidence of both their moderation and their stand against violence.

But, as yet, neither banning orders nor prosecutions for treason involved the silencing of those thus subject to the rapidly growing powers of the Minister of Justice. The Minister had not yet armed himself with the powers which were subsequently to accrue to his office to make it a criminal offence to publish the words of a banned person. So with Luthuli still discharging his function as President General of the A.N.C. from his home in Groutville, Natal, as another general election approached, the African National Congress now planned a new course of demonstrations aimed at inducing the white electorate to abandon the policies of the Nationalist Party and the Government that inspired and directed them. These included a stay-at-home demonstration by workers on the eve of the election which was fixed for April 16th, 1958. It was designed to focus attention on both the absence of political rights and the inadequacy of prevailing wage rates among a population to whom the right of collective bargaining was denied.

The Government's answer to these manifestations of the African attitude to its policies was to ban all meetings of more than ten Africans in any of the larger urban areas without the permission of the Native Commissioner or the Magistrate except church services, funerals, sporting events and meetings of the representatives of Africans in Parliament. These were evidences that it was now taking the situation seriously indeed. As the election day approached, all police leave was cancelled and the Union Defence Force was ordered to stand by. Arrangements were made to maintain essential services in the event of a widespread response to the stay-at-home call, and employers were urged to discourage their employees from participating in the demonstration.

The demonstration in itself was a complete failure. For one reason or another, it evoked signally little response from the main body of workers. Possibly an incipient economic contraction which was

[1] See p. 396.

producing a widening area of African unemployment made those in work less willing to jeopardise their own position. But the attempt in itself was not without significant effects. By the threats implicit in it, at so critical a moment as a general election always is, it had raised the level of the Government's reaction to these repeated challenges to its policy and authority; and that on the eve of the transfer of ultimate authority to the most uncompromising member in the Nationalist ranks.[1]

At the same time, it struck a blow at the prestige of the African National Congress from which it was not to recover completely before it was banned; and this it did at a critical moment in the history of the Congress, when its leadership was being challenged from within as unequal by age and temperament to the demands upon it created by progressively strengthening Afrikaner National-ism.

To appreciate the importance of both these effects, it is important to remember what had been happening to the African National Congress in the preceding years. I have already recorded the position when the Nationalist victory of 1948 startled everybody, including the Africans, into a new awareness of the importance of public policies in regard to colour, and my advice to those who consulted me in the course of my Parliamentary duties. At that time, as I noted, the African National Congress, although still the only African political organisation of any importance, could not be regarded as a great political force. The progress of events in the first years of Nationalist rule, and particularly the threat to the existence of the Natives Representative Council and Parliamentary repre-sentation of Africans, gave it a new appeal to the African com-munity, as it gave a new purpose to African leadership. The result was the Defiance Campaign. This in turn, though a failure in itself, drew the people to the Congress ranks in ever-increasing numbers. It roused them to a new level of political consciousness and an appreciation of the nature of the struggle they would have to face to achieve any measure of political freedom. The result was a rapid and impressive rise in the membership of the organisation, which not only encouraged but demanded renewed effort to counter the spreading daily pressures of apartheid.

The declared objective of the Congress was what it had always been—a share in a multi-racial society that would accord oppor-

[1] Dr. Verwoerd became Prime Minister on September 3rd, 1958.

tunity to all groups. Its method was to pursue this objective in co-operation with whatever representatives of the other racial groups in the population would be prepared to co-operate. The franchise being what it was, with its contingent effect on the character of Parliament itself, the course to be pursued would per-force be largely extra-Parliamentary. Insistence, however, was re-peatedly laid by the leaders on the obligation to avoid violence. In all the circumstances, this might be difficult to achieve, but, it was stressed, where the intention failed, the blame must lie on other shoulders.

As its efforts to make the desired impact upon the Government suffered one defeat after another, as, in fact, the pressures of apart-heid multiplied and spread, a new generation of young men in more of a hurry and with less respect for power began to make itself heard in criticism of both the objective and the method to which the older leaders were deeply and conscientiously committed. Against a background of emerging Africa and apparently intran-sigeant South Africa, this new element began to call in question the policy of associating with other groups which, since the Defiance Campaign, had acquired an almost formal character. Particularly were they opposed to collaboration with the left-wing white group. They also began to repudiate the idea of a multi-racial society. Where earlier leaders had approached the problem of political adjustments in our complex society with a singular appreciation of white fears of swamping by non-white numbers, there began now to be talk of Africa for the Africans. In this, the only concession to the fact of racial difference was to admit the right of anyone pre-pared to accept the rule of the majority to be accorded citizen status as an African, the emphasis being on persons and not on groups.

In this developing situation, the older leaders now sought to recover for the Congress the ground lost in the failure of their pre-election plans with new plans to exploit the next emotional occasion in the Nationalist calendar, the jubilee of Union due in 1960. Immediately the differences within the organisation began to assume definite and explicit shape. By the end of another year, with the new Prime Minister's decision to break the last political link between the African and the European communities legislatively formulated in the so-called Promotion of Bantu Self Government Act, the rift became open and final. While the African National Congress in its December 1959 Conference elaborated plans to mark the jubilee year with a major campaign against the pass laws and the intensification of a boycott of Nationalist firms and products which had been initiated some time before, the dissidents, under the name of the Pan-African Congress, met in a conference of their own to plan what they had determined would be a more dynamic challenge than they believed the A.N.C. could or would mount. The focal point of this was also to be the pass laws, but the tone of attack which they planned was to be 'decisive and final'. The instruction to all members was that on a given date they should leave their passes at home and offer themselves at the nearest police station for arrest. Like their parent body, they took their stand against violence —but they added the injunction 'no compromise'. Their slogan was to be 'no bail, no defence, no fine'.

Thus were competitive forces lining up to give the African version of half a century of Union, with both sides underlining the theme of non-violence. However good the intention, the issue is now world history in the tragic episodes of Sharpeville and Langa. What is less well known, although highly significant, is that the state of emergency which followed them was to gather behind bars, in addition to the Pan-African leaders, not only Albert Luthuli, Z. K. Matthews and others of the old guard of moderate men already exonerated by the Courts in the Treason Trial, but the first fringe of a Liberal Party pledged to the constitutional pursuit of a multi-racial democratic society. In this jubilee year, 1960, South Africa's major problem was coming home to roost, and in doing so was giving convincing proof that freedom is indeed indivisible.

16

Jubilee Year: Year of Crisis

The final disappearance of African representation from Parliament in the jubilee year of Union was no doubt fortuitous. Dr. Verwoerd, under whose direction and indeed on whose sole authority, it seemed, the abolition of all African representation had been substituted for the earlier policy of limitation to the Senate (itself put in cold storage by Dr. Malan), had chosen to allow the sitting representatives to complete their term of office. This was due to expire on June 30th, 1960, in terms of an early amendment to the original Representation of Natives Act designed to guarantee as far as possible that no session of Parliament should be without African representation. But no doubt if his attention had been called to the circumstance that Africans would cease to have a voice in Parliament in this jubilee year, he would have regarded it as an appropriate coincidence. Did it not stand for the fulfilment of Nationalist Afrikaner hopes in one all-important regard, the triumph at last over liberalism of the Trekker spirit partially defeated at Union by the Cape's determination to maintain its own tradition? The North was at last to enter into its heritage. True, by this time, four representatives of the Cape Coloured people had taken their seats in Parliament; but the pattern of White–non-White relationship had been set, making this an obviously temporary anomaly. Time would take care of that situation.[1]

The abolition of African representation, carrying with it all the hopes with which we, who had decided to try to use it, had set the 1936 settlement on its course, must in any case have made this year for us a singularly depressing and discouraging one. Before it came to an end, it was to prove a year of tragedy for many others and of crisis for the whole community.

The record began, not inappropriately, with the Prime Minister himself. It took the form of an announcement by him on the second working day of the Parliamentary session[2] of his intention to hold a

[1] As already noted, the Coloured representatives are to disappear at the end of the present Parliament, due in 1971, this in terms of the Separate Representation of Voters Amendment Act 56 of 1968.
[2] January 20th, 1960, Hansard, Vol. 103, Col. 98.

referendum on the conversion of the Union into a republic. The method and the timing of the announcement were alike typical. With the speech from the throne silent on a matter of such importance, Dr. Verwoerd chose the first major debate of the session, the no-confidence debate initiated by the Leader of the Opposition, to make his declaration. The issue would be put to the white electorate, whose majority decision the Government would accept, whatever it was, and whatever the size of the majority vote. No more was heard of that substantial majority which Dr. Malan had spoken of as the condition for him of a mandate in this important political issue. The necessary legislation to provide the requisite machinery for the referendum would be presented to Parliament in the near future.

While the shock of this move was still being absorbed, the visit of the British Prime Minister, Mr. Macmillan, culminating in his 'winds of change' speech, raised the political temperature on more fronts than the immediately obvious one, that of the differences of approach between the British and the South African Governments to the subject of colour and race. Inevitably it gave new content to the discussion as to the nature of the republic aimed at by the Government, and how this was to affect not only the domestic situation but South Africa's membership of the Commonwealth and her relationship with her neighbours in Africa.

Even as the argument in this regard developed, events in various parts of the country were both reflecting and creating new tensions among both Black and White. The Government's urgency to extend the Bantu Authorities system in an endeavour to lend colour to the claim that this new system had been accepted and had progressed to the point where Parliamentary representation was both unnecessary and out of place, had already led to serious disturbances in a number of rural areas, notably Sekukuniland in the north and Zeerust in the west. The end of 1959 saw a wide extension of the field of disturbance in which considerable areas of the Transkei were deeply affected. On the urban side, the session had scarcely got into its stride when there occurred at Cato Manor, a large slum area on the outskirts of Durban, one of the worst and most costly riots of the more familiar kind, resulting in the murder of four white and five African policemen. The occasion was a police raid on a Sunday afternoon for illicit liquor.

It was into this highly charged atmosphere that the Pan-African

Congress launched its campaign against the pass laws. From that moment it seemed as if nothing could halt the flowing tide of crisis.

The starting point was a press conference held by the president of the P.A.C., Mr. Robert Sobukwe, on March 1st, in which he announced his organisation's plans for a campaign designed to achieve 'freedom and independence' for the African population of South Africa by 1963. The campaign would start on Monday, March 21st. Its immediate target as originally planned was the abolition of the pass laws. In pursuit of this objective, members of the organisation were instructed to leave their reference books at home on that day and to present themselves at the nearest police station for arrest. If the police refused to arrest them and ordered them to depart, they should go home quietly and return later in the day again inviting the police to apprehend them. The Commissioner of Police had been informed of the plan by Mr. Sobukwe himself who had stressed the intention—and instruction—of the Congress that the campaign should be conducted in a peaceful and orderly manner. He had asked that the police should aid in this regard by not making impossible demands upon the Africans.[1]

Whether the leaders of the P.A.C. really believed that a programme such as they envisaged could be carried out without conflict between the demonstrators and the authorities, even as Parliament met on the afternoon of Monday, the 21st, to discuss the vote for the Prime Minister's department under which the now pending referendum and republic were sufficient source of strain and contention, rumours of more immediate trouble were seeping through from the north. Rising to open the debate, in an already tense atmosphere, the Leader of the Opposition, Sir De Villiers Graaff, expressed the hope that the Prime Minister would be able to give the House full information in regard to reports that there had been serious rioting at Vanderbyl Park 'with wounding if not loss of life', and that Saracens (armoured cars) had been ordered out.[2] When he had concluded his speech on his main topic, that was the Prime Minister's plans for the referendum and the nature of the republic he proposed to establish, he was immediately followed by the member for Vanderbyl Park, Dr. Carel de Wet. Dr. de Wet proceeded to give the House his information about the morning's

[1] For a valuable summary of the events of the following days, see S.A. Institute of Race Relations, Fact Paper No. 5, 1960, *Days of Crisis in South Africa*.
[2] Hansard, Vol. 104, Col. 3721.

events in his constituency. This was that there had been serious rioting and that one black man had been shot.[1] He went on to add that what he was concerned about was that where there were riots whether on the part of whites or on the part of blacks, if it was necessary to shoot, only one person was shot dead. It was a remark which was to echo not only round the House and the country but round the world in the days that followed, in spite of the efforts of his colleagues and of the Prime Minister himself to modify the effects of his words by arguing that what he intended to convey was his belief that enough force—but only enough force—should be used on such occasions as was necessary to restore law and order. It was a gloss on his words which Dr. de Wet was happy to accept.

When the Prime Minister himself entered the debate later in the afternoon, he had to inform the House that in addition to the events in Vanderbyl Park, about which rumour seemed substantially correct, more serious trouble had occurred at Sharpeville location near Vereeniging. There a crowd estimated originally at 2000 but subsequently swelling to 20,000, had concentrated around the police station and in circumstances in which there was as yet no clarity, shots had been fired, killing twenty-five Africans and wounding fifty more. There had in addition been demonstrations at points in the Cape Town area. More than 1000 arrests had been made at Wynberg, a suburb of Cape Town. Outside these areas it seemed that the demonstrations, if any had taken place, had been quite peaceful or had failed.

Taking the initiative in typical fashion, Dr. Verwoerd concluded his statement by deploring the fact that the effect of the propaganda made to throw doubt on the Government's handling of the Natives 'which necessarily had an inciting effect on the Bantu', had encouraged a certain organisation to attempt the impossible, namely, to defy the state and the good order for which the state was responsible'.[2]

In an atmosphere of increasing tension and anxiety as to the range and character of the day's happenings, the House continued for the rest of the afternoon to conduct a sometimes heated but more often desultory debate on the referendum and the republic. By the time of the evening session, there were rumours of serious trouble in the Cape Town area involving the use of Sten guns by the police

[1] Hansard, Vol. 104, Col. 3732.
[2] Hansard, Vol. 104, Col. 3759.

and of cars being set on fire. Against that background, Mr. Harry Lawrence, now speaking as a front-bencher of the Progressive Party, felt that the whole discussion as to the future shape of South Africa had an air of unreality.[1] What was needed was to know and to get to grips in some constructive fashion with the existing situation. Before the House rose for the night, the Prime Minister gave his latest report. According to this, the death roll at Sharpeville had risen to fifty-three, and the record of wounded to 156.[2] Information as to the situation at Langa (Cape Town) was obscure, although the trouble there was serious too. His information was that the police had been fired on from a flat and that they had returned the fire.[3] He had no details to report.

When the House reassembled on the following day there was little thought for anything but the record and the course of events in the troubled areas. The Prime Minister's latest report, given at the opening of the afternoon session, was that on the whole, things were quiet, although the situation remained tense in the Cape Town area. In Johannesburg, 132 Bantu had been detained for being without identify books, among them R. W. Sobukwe, leader of the P.A.C. and Kitchener Leballo, secretary of the organisation, against whom charges of sedition were being considered. In other areas in which signs of trouble had developed, quietness seemed now to reign if perhaps insecurely, under the shadow of police patrols.

The record so far as it went—and much of it was still very general—was sufficient to induce the Leader of the Opposition to describe the occasion as one that both sides of the House would recognise as something in the nature of a national calamity. While supporting the Government in its responsibility to restore and maintain law and order, he urged the Prime Minister forthwith to appoint a commission of enquiry to explore the deeper causes of the recurrent trouble which was afflicting the country in ever more dangerous proportions, the commission to be a national one in the sense of representing both sides of the political field under an agreed chairman and with agreed terms of reference.

It was a proposition that all sections of the Opposition could and did support, although I had little conviction as to the need for such a commission in the light of all our accumulated and accumulating

[1] Hansard, Vol. 104, Col. 3790.
[2] The final record for Sharpeville and Langa was 71 dead and 217 Africans and 17 police injured. Hansard, Vol. 104, Col. 4292.
[3] Hansard, Vol. 104, Col. 3822.

knowledge, and little faith in its results in the light of our past experience. But it was immediately apparent that the Prime Minister had no intention, certainly no immediate intention, of conceding such a commission.[1] He too felt that he knew enough of the causes of the troubles we were experiencing to make such a commission unnecessary. The Oppositions insisted on placing the blame for these disturbances on the Government and its policy of apartheid. He felt that the situation was being viewed from the wrong perspective by the other side of the House. They had in mind only one thought, or point, namely the disturbances which had taken place during the last few days together with those which had taken place in recent weeks or months. That was not enough to give one a proper insight into these incidents. One should look further in order to get a correct perspective. The trouble which we were experiencing should not be regarded as a purely South African phenomenon. One should see whether it was symptomatic of the time and whether it was symptomatic of the continent of Africa 'as a result of all sorts of ideas expressed in the world and inspired in other parts of the world'. In fact it would seem to have afflicted us less than some other countries. So far as we ourselves were concerned, these disturbances were not a new feature of our lives. They were periodic events 'which came in cycles as a result of incitement in regard to some or other matter of law'. The fact was that this simply happened in South Africa. True, it might be said that on this occasion a fairly large number had been killed on a single occasion. He granted that. The explanation was to be found in the fact 'that they are now more bold than they were'.[2]

As for a commission such as the Leader of the Opposition asked for, he wished to issue a warning that instead of being a means of solving a problem, that might just become a platform for agitation which could give rise to greater trouble. He would not lightly give an answer to that proposition today. He would consider it carefully but he felt it was fraught with great dangers.

On the following day, March 23rd, Dr. Verwoerd announced his decision to appoint two one-man commissions to establish the facts of the riots and the shootings at Sharpeville and Langa, the com-

---

[1] Hansard, Vol. 104, Col. 3875 *et seq.*
[2] The words 'more bold' would seem to reflect Dr. Verwoerd's meaning better than the official translation which reads 'more courageous'. He said: 'Die posisie het nou so ontwikkel dat hulle nou meer manhaftig is as toe.' Hansard, Vol. 104, Col. 3878 *et seq.*

missioner in each case to be a judge. The Government, he said, was also giving serious consideration to the appointment of a commission with a judge as chairman to enquire into the whole position and to see how these dangers could be avoided in future.[1] In the circumstances, he appealed to the House to discuss this matter no further.

In spite of this appeal, the situation continued to be the subject of increasingly bitter debate between the two sides of the House, the temperature no doubt considerably raised by the accumulating evidence of the reactions overseas to the events of the preceding two days. Of these, the most conspicuous and startling was a prepared statement read at a press conference in Washington by the press representative of the United States State Department. It read: The United States deplores violence in all its forms and hopes that the African people of South Africa will be able to obtain redress for legitimate grievances by peaceful means. While the United States as a matter of practice does not ordinarily comment on the internal affairs of governments with whom it enjoys normal relations, it cannot help but regret the tragic loss of life resulting from the measures taken against the demonstrators in South Africa.[2]

Particular significance attached to this unusual action on the part of the United States in that South Africa was already facing a concerted attack from the Afro-Asian countries at U.N.O. on the policy of apartheid generally. It was to be followed by a request to the Security Council to take action in regard to these recent riots—as Dr. Verwoerd declared, reporting to the House a few days later, 'where a small detachment of police was for the maintenance of law and order, obliged to fire upon thousands of rioters, causing the death of some seventy-one persons'.[3]

By the following morning, Thursday, March 24th, there were mounting evidences that the storm which had shaken us earlier in the week had by no means spent its force. The A.N.C. had originally refused to stand in with the P.A.C. in its campaign. It had argued that the ground had been inadequately prepared for such a campaign as the P.A.C. proposed and that more harm than good could flow from a tactic that had no reasonable prospect of success. Now, influenced possibly by the response which the call had evoked

---

[1] Hansard, Vol. 104, Col. 3915. This commission was never appointed.
[2] Hansard, Vol. 104, Col. 4004.
[3] Hansard, Vol. 104, Col. 4362.

from the African population, and no doubt genuinely concerned for the victims of the disturbances that had taken place, it called for a day of mourning for the tragic events of March 21st. It asked the people to stay away from work on Monday, March 28th and to mourn quietly in their homes. The P.A.C. decided to stand in on this and called upon their members to observe the day in the way proposed.

In the meantime the situation in Langa and the neighbouring township of Nyanga continued to be tense. Since the events of March 21st, increasing numbers of people had stayed away from work, no doubt in response to a message from Robert Sobukwe to continue the anti-pass campaign until victory should be won; and on the morning of Thursday, March 25th, some 2000 Africans under the leadership of a young student, Philip Kgosana, congregated at the gates of the Caledon Square gaol, in proximity to the Houses of Parliament, offering themselves for arrest as being without reference books.[1] Kgosana and another of the demonstrators were arrested and put into the cells but the police officer in charge, after some talk with them, asked them to disperse the crowd on the understanding that reference books would not be demanded until conditions became more normal. The crowd agreed to disperse if Kgosana and his companion were released, which was allowed on their own recognisances.

On the following morning, March 26th, the Commissioner of Police gave notice through the press that reference books would not be demanded until further notice. Reporting the suspension to the House of Assembly the Minister of Justice explained that this had been done as a temporary measure 'to avoid a congregation of people at police stations and possible bloodshed, and so as not to tie the hands of the police in combating riots, as well as giving protection to the public at those places where it is most essential'.[2] While the Progressive Party and the Native Representatives welcomed this move as an encouraging augury for the future, the United Party Natal Provincial leader, Mr. Douglas Mitchell, stigmatised it as 'a shocking exhibition of complete weakness'.[3]

[1] Among the onlookers at this demonstration was my husband who found it at least an interesting addition to his many experiences in South Africa to see police with Sten guns posted to prevent Africans from going into gaol.
[2] Hansard, Vol. 104, Col. 4301. The suspension was withdrawn on April 10th. See Fact Paper No. 5, 1960, South African Institute of Race Relations, pp. 28–9.
[3] Hansard, Vol. 104, Col. 4202.

While this situation was developing, the Government was preparing its own response to the challenge implicit in the combined mourning-day call of the two Congresses. On the evening of March 24th, a proclamation was signed by the Governor-General banning all meetings without distinction of race, in a number of magisterial districts, the ban to operate until June 30th; and on March 28th, the day of mourning, the Minister of Justice introduced an Unlawful Organisations Bill designed to give him the power to ban both the A.N.C. and the P.A.C. and any other organisation he put in the same category. The Bill also contained provision stepping up tenfold the penalties for intimidation provided in the Riotous Assemblies Act of 1956.[1] The Minister justified this latter provision on the ground that much of the trouble which had eventuated over the past few days was due to 'the cruel and barbaric intimidation and victimisation' which he declared had been taking place among the African population on a large scale.[2]

While the House anxiously awaited news of the response to the day-of-mourning call (which had been addressed not merely to Africans but to all South Africans), all the Opposition groups put up what resistance they could to the introduction of the Bill. The grounds of their objections to it did not always coincide. The Progressive Party and the Native Representatives were entirely opposed to the measure on the wide general ground that, in the political circumstances of South Africa, to ban these mouthpieces of African views and feelings was simply to drive agitation underground and to play into the hands of more and more extreme elements. While the United Party were also critical of the proposal designed to destroy channels of African political expression, they based their decision to oppose the introduction of the Bill mainly on the absence of any time limitation in the use of the powers which the Government sought to take under it, involving a new wide area of administrative action out of the control of Parliament. When, on the second reading of the Bill, the Minister agreed to limit the duration of any ban to twelve months, they found it possible if not palatable to accept the Bill. According to the Leader of the Opposition, they had been much influenced in this direction also by the Minister's case in regard to the degree of intimidation to which the

[1] In respect of a fine, from £50 to £500 and in respect of imprisonment from six months to five years. Act 17 of 1956.
[2] Hansard, Vol. 104, Col. 4305.

law-abiding mass had been subjected, although in 'the shocking picture of a reign of terror carried on in certain townships, which the Minister had painted', he, the Minister, had in fact painted a shocking picture of the breakdown of the administration of the Government and of its complete failure to protect the law-abiding people who wanted only to go about their lawful occasions and to keep out of political troubles.

By the morning of March 29th, the record of the day of mourning was fairly clear. In Cape Town the response had been almost complete, between 90 per cent and 95 per cent of the workers having stayed at home on the previous day. In Johannesburg, the response was estimated at 85 per cent to 90 per cent and in Port Elizabeth at something between 85 per cent and 95 per cent. In Durban, some 20 per cent to 25 per cent of the workers stayed at home. In the smaller areas there had been a varying response, on the whole on the low side.

With this evidence of the support which the Congresses could still command, the question now was, what would follow. The A.N.C. had called for one day of mourning, to end at midnight on March 28th. The P.A.C. however, had initially planned a continuing campaign and there had been no move to rescind the instructions in that regard. On March 29th there were still large numbers of workers at home in the townships in the Cape Town area; and on the morning of March 30th there occurred what was probably the most spectacular episode of this momentous period. This was the march of a column of Africans estimated at 30,000, again under the leadership of Philip Kgosana, along the main highway from Cape Town's southern suburbs to the Caledon Square gaol to repeat again, in proximity to Parliament, the tactic with which the campaign had begun, that was to offer themselves for arrest as being without reference books.

The news of the march was received both within the precincts of Parliament and in the city with mounting anxiety. The probable price of any untoward incident in circumstances such as these was too great to be contemplated without anxiety. With signal discipline and self-control on all sides, the column reached its destination without misadventure. The leader was received by the Deputy Commissioner of Police. The news as it filtered through was that he had asked for an interview with the Minister of Justice and, under the impression that the officer had agreed to arrange this, he had advised the demonstrators to depart quietly to their homes.[1] In the belief that at last their leaders were to reach the ear of authority, the crowd had dispersed as requested.

That afternoon in Parliament the Prime Minister made a statement on the situation in the country generally in which he referred to 'the influx of a large number of Natives who are mainly congregated at Caledon Square', and added, 'but these Natives are busy moving back to Langa and Nyanga in two columns'.[2] He could give the House and the country the assurance that the Government would not have the least hesitation in using enough force to ensure that peace and good order were maintained. Consequently in so far as it was necessary to employ defence force units that was being done. He added a warning—those who abused any influence they might have amongst the Bantu in order to incite them would also receive the full attention of the Government.

Immediately thereafter the Minister of Justice announced to the House that the Governor-General had issued a proclamation declaring a state of emergency in terms of the Public Safety Act of 1953 in some eighty districts of the country; and in the early hours of that morning, even before the public were aware of this development, there had taken place the first sweep of those arrests under the powers given to the police by the proclamation, to which reference has already been made.[3]

Among the first to be arrested was Philip Kgosana. The effect of this and of the arrest of other prominent African leaders was to rouse the people to further demonstrations to which the Government's reply was to throw a tight cordon of heavily armed police, troops and sailors round the three Cape townships of Langa, Nyanga East and Nyanga West with instructions to let no one enter or leave the township after 7.30 a.m., extended on the following day to 8 a.m. For a week thereafter the bulk of the African people of these areas remained practically sealed off from the life of the city and the country, dependent, as their immediate resources were

---

[1] When the events of these days were under investigation later, Kgosana said he had understood the Deputy Commissioner to say that the interview would be arranged. The officer said he had merely undertaken to convey the request to the appropriate quarter.
[2] Hansard, Vol. 104, Col. 4361. At this time Parliament was under heavy guard by police with Sten guns and Saracens manned by soldiers.
[3] See p. 421. On April 22nd the Minister of Justice told the House of Assembly that 1569 persons had been detained under the emergency powers, of whom 94 were whites, 24 Coloured and 1451 Africans (Hansard, Vol. 105, Col. 5803).

consumed, on the philanthropic services of the Red Cross and groups of private people who set themselves to collect and distribute food where the need was greatest. At the end of the week, their resources exhausted, they began to drift back to work in increasing numbers. The cordon round Langa was raised on April 7th and at Nyanga on the 8th. In the weeks that followed, the police were exceptionally active, rounding up thousands of Africans in town-ships throughout the country for offences of diverse kinds ranging from incitement and intimidation to statutory offences such as illegal entry into the urban areas.[1] All this kept alive the atmosphere of tension and anxiety among all sections of the population.

As if to crown the record of disaster came the staggering news on April 9th of an attack on the life of the Prime Minister at the opening of the Rand Agricultural Show in Johannesburg. It was an episode that, otherwise unrelated to the political scene, inevitably imported into it an emotional factor of the first order. While the country as a whole expressed its relief that our history had not been stained with a senseless assassination, Dr. Verwoerd and his fol-lowers were to see in his escape from death new and most significant evidence of his great destiny and the will of Providence for its fulfilment.

In the weeks that followed, for a considerable part of which Dr. Verwoerd was immobilised and inaccessible, recovering from the wound he had sustained, a widespread stocktaking was taking place, with some remarkable results. The succession of shocks which all these events had involved could not fail to affect the whole community. The economic effects were grave indeed. They in-cluded an early plunge on the stock exchange which deepened significantly with the news of Sharpeville and Langa and the world's reactions thereto. In the days following the riots, the industrial and commercial sectors of the economy ground almost to a standstill in the larger urban centres, where, as I have shown, the stay-at-home call, reinforced by intimidation, made the im-mobilisation of the labour force almost complete. It was a situation which, having arisen, called for firm action, and the drastic action which in fact was the Government's immediate and almost auto-

---

[1] On May 6th, the Minister of Justice said 18,011 Africans had been arrested since the declaration of the state of emergency (Hansard, Vol. 105, Col. 6818), of whom 5294 had no permit to be in urban areas, 569 were told to leave and go to the reserves. Of these, 5 had no home in the reserves and were therefore allowed to stay in the urban area.

matic response, the declaration of the state of emergency and the banning of the two African political organisations, undoubtedly had a large part of the electorate behind them.

However, as the position was brought under control what was more important and significant was the wide preoccupation with what was to follow. As I wrote at the time,[1] with the state of emergency still in operation, 'There is general agreement that it cannot go on without disaster. In the sense of insecurity that it creates at home, with civil liberties for all sections of the population closely circumscribed, and the feeling of hostility that it and all its attendant circumstances have engendered abroad, the whole of our economic and political life is creaking dangerously.'

The significant element in the discussions which took place up and down the country was the need to restore confidence abroad in the stability of the country and the conviction that this could only be done by restoring some degree of confidence between White and Black within the country. The basis of the case that we had been making for so long was at last being accepted, and indeed quite widely canvassed, that Africans had legitimate grievances and progressively fewer channels for their expression, that whatever future was postulated for them must be one the potential benefits of which were apparent and acceptable to them, which itself postulated consultation with representative African opinion. Nor was this thesis confined to anti-Government circles. Even among the Government's own supporters, where the first concern had been and still was to keep control of the political machine, and where criticism had therefore been frowned upon, this case was to be heard with varying degrees of emphasis. Generally, care was taken to endorse the basic principles of Government policy—apartheid was still the essential condition of happy race relations—although the loyalty of the Coloured people in the time of crisis, gratefully acknowledged by the Minister of Finance, Dr. Dönges, as spokesman for the Government in the Prime Minister's absence,[2] suggested that it might not be of such general application after all. But it was suggested that in its application to the Africans, who were the immediate concern, there had been faults in administration. There began to be talk of the need for a modification of the pass

---

[1] *The Times*, London, September 13th, 1960.
[2] Hansard, Vol. 104, Col. 5511. 'I want to assure them that they will not find us unappreciative of their courageous and loyal attitude.'

laws and the liquor laws to reduce the points of friction between the people and the police. SABRA indeed called for a comprehensive enquiry into all aspects of administration and policy which caused unnecessary friction and discontent, and specified four features of the prevailing position which it considered demanded immediate attention. These were the control of movement of Africans which involved the pass laws, the right of Africans to a share in the management of their residential areas, the need to step up wages and to increase productivity to meet the increased cost of life in a modern society and under modern conditions, and finally the control of the supply of liquor and all it involved. In addition they forthrightly urged the most rapid development of the reserves with the assistance of white capital, initiative and skill, the whole pro-gramme to be pursued in consultation with responsible African opinion.[1]

While this might be regarded as the approach of the intellectuals and possibly discounted as such, it was noteworthy that representa-tions in similar vein were being made to the Government by the Afrikaanse Handelsinstituut, the Afrikaner organisation represent-ing commerce and industry. Indeed, the Executive of the Handel-sinstituut associated their organisation with the Association of Chambers of Commerce, the South African Federated Chambers of Industries, the Steel and Engineering Industries Federation of South Africa and the Transvaal and Orange Free State Chambers of Mines in representations to the Prime Minister himself covering much the same ground. These combined organisations, representing employers of some one and a half million African workers, approxi-mately two-thirds of the whole African labour force, in a memor-andum setting out their case, underlined their conviction that Africans had genuine grievances that must be removed if the country was to avoid disastrous repetitions of the state of tension and emergency it was then enduring.[2] While some control of the movement of a population in process of urbanisation was no doubt necessary, the existing system of controls and the pass system which supported it must be modified to remove their penal aspects. The liquor laws must be changed to do away with the harassing and oppressive practice of police raiding; wages must be raised either by government action or by private initiative, or best of all by collec-

---

[1] S.A. Institute of Race Relations, Fact Paper No. 5, 1960.
[2] Quoted by Sir De Villiers Graaff, Hansard, Vol. 105, Col. 8110.

tive bargaining, envisaging rights of trade union organisation. (This latter proposition was in fact one which the Federated Chambers of Industries and Commerce had been pressing upon the Minister of Labour even before the crisis.) Above all, they urged that the urban African must no longer be treated as a migrant worker but must be recognised as a permanent town dweller and as such given property rights and a share in local government at least in his own townships. Finally they too pressed the need for the rapid development of the reserves, if necessary with the assistance of European capital and initiative.

Indeed, as the Leader of the Opposition was to note in his last major speech of the session, the most significant factor in the political scene at that moment was that for the first time in our history, representations had been made to the Government by virtually every big organisation representing the employers of Native labour calling upon it to alter or modify its policies in respect of the non-Whites in South Africa. The uniformity of the proposals coming from such diverse quarters had all the appearance of a latent but deep desire for change, for something more constructive than the endless record of ideological legislation which had kept the country in a state of tension over the years. Its release at that moment was no doubt encouraged and stimulated from two important political quarters. The first of these was the Government's own press. Throughout the course of the argument over integration versus apartheid, *Die Burger*, the organ of Cape nationalism, had been guardedly critical of the time factor in the application of the Government's policy and in particular of the application of the positive side of the programme. It had also been clearly uneasy about the extension of the policy to the Coloured people. It now came out with an emphatic demand for a speeding up of the constructive aspects of the Government's programme if South Africa was to be saved from the fate of being regarded as the polecat among the nations of the world.[1] *Die Transvaler*, Dr. Verwoerd's own paper, while adhering strongly to the Party line on general policy, also expressed anxiety about international reactions to its effects as it had been pursued so far.

But undoubtedly the greatest encouragement to the idea of the need for some more humane accommodation with the emergent African population derived from a speech by Mr. Paul Sauer, Leader

[1] *Die Burger*, April 7th, 1960.

of the House of Assembly to his constituents at Humansdorp on April 19th, ten days after the attack on the life of the Prime Minister.[1] Reviewing for his audience the events of the immediate past, he said the old book of South African history had been closed at Sharpeville. South Africa was now faced with the need to reconsider 'in earnest and honesty' her whole approach to the Native question. A new spirit must be created, to restore faith in South Africa overseas in both white and non-white countries. There would have to be an important change in the practical application of Government policy, although it would not mean a deviation from the set policy, he added circumspectly. The 'pinpricks' which had laid the people open to the propaganda of the African National Congress and the Pan-African Congress must be removed.

From there he tentatively adumbrated the programme which SABRA, whose Conference was opening on that day, was to underline in its concluding resolutions, revised administration of the reference book system to make the African feel it was a benefit and not an oppression, amendment of the liquor law to get rid of the raids which made the African 'feel inferior'; the creation of representative bodies of Africans in the urban townships through which 'that healthy contact between people and authority' which he claimed existed in the rural areas might be achieved in the towns; higher wages and encouragement to increased productivity—a recurrent theme over all this period due to an increasing awareness of the range of African poverty stepped up by an incipient trade recession; and finally 'Giant development schemes in the reserves'. All this would mean immense sacrifices both financially and physically but critical overseas countries could offer practical help by supplying technicians and qualified personnel. This suggested opening the doors to immigration. True, Afrikaner nationalism had tended to discourage immigration (this had indeed been a major point of difference between Dr. Malan and General Smuts). That was a reflection of the fear of the Afrikaner of being swamped. But with the republic now practically an accomplished fact, he implied that that attitude would change.

With this extensive area of common ground to encourage them, all shades of opposition in Parliament pressed the same case from their varying standpoints. And surely it offered hope and scope for change. The programme proposed was modest enough but it could

[1] *Cape Times*, April 20th, 1960.

be the beginnings of a saner and more humane adjustment to the needs and demands of our multi-racial society. It did not challenge the ultimate objectives of government policy but it did endeavour to meet the immediate and pressing stresses of African life, particularly in the towns. What, I asked at the time, were the chances of its being sympathetically received and how far would it carry us along the road to internal peace? The answer to the first question lay with one person, the Prime Minister; the answer to the second lay contingently with the African population.

There was much speculation, and that not only in political circles, as to what the Prime Minister's reactions to the situation were to be. Would he emerge from his enforced isolation with new thoughts, another new vision; and if so what would be their nature, what direction would they take? We were not long left in doubt as to the answer, which was conveyed to us in circumstances and by a method which themselves confirmed the nature of the trends which the pursuit of apartheid had imported into our political life.

The extensive celebrations planned for the Jubilee were to culminate at Bloemfontein at the end of May. The Government had early let it be known that it would organise its business for a brief session to enable members of Parliament to join in the final festivities. It had, however, not foreseen the course of events which, as the foreshadowed date of adjournment approached, was to find the country in the grip of a state of emergency with all its attendant circumstances. It seemed unthinkable that any Government should propose that Parliament should go into recess for months in circumstances such as these. Yet it was soon apparent that that was exactly what the Government did propose. On May 17th, with the closing date generally rumoured as three days ahead, May 20th, the Minister of the Interior, Mr. Tom Naudé, rose to move an omnibus guillotine designed to give the Government power to put through any measure it wished to deal with within that period. Suspending the standing orders governing the duration of the daily sessions of Parliament, his proposals gave to a Minister or a Deputy Minister the right to declare any measure—Bill or motion—as of an urgent nature, whereafter the Government might allot the time for all the later stages at his discretion. It was a proposition which, to all intents and purposes, wiped out the rights of Opposition which the accepted rules of Parliamentary procedure were designed to protect. As the Minister noted, however, it was not entirely new in

South African experience. It had significantly found its way into our history soon after the beginning of the Nationalist regime. It had in fact been introduced in the upper chamber by Dr. Verwoerd himself as leader of the Senate in 1952, at a time when the Government was still experiencing considerable difficulty in carrying its legislation in that Chamber. It was now achieving a new notoriety which, the Minister implied, might be considerably extended by its inclusion as a permanent part of our Parliamentary code. Was it not part of the ordinary Parliamentary procedure in Australia? Not that Mr. Naudé was enamoured of it, he declared; but it had always been understood that Parliament would adjourn for the final phase of the Union festival and now, he claimed, the Opposition were endeavouring to block that intention by spreading themselves on unimportant business. There was, he argued, nothing really important remaining on the order paper; and with the motion passed against the votes of the combined Oppositions, with whom the Government had failed to get any agreement on the adjournment, the Minister of Justice rose to move one of those pieces of business which apparently fell within Mr. Naudé's category of unimportance. This was nothing less than the request to the House for its endorsement of the regulations which the Minister of Justice had issued in terms of the declared state of emergency which, unless so endorsed, would lapse with the prorogation of Parliament. Under these regulations, hundreds of persons drawn from all groups in the population were making us familiar with the anxieties and insecurities inseparable from the right of the police to arrest and detain without trial anyone they chose to treat in this fashion; and with a ban on meetings over wide areas of the country, the political life of the country outside Parliament was in something closely resembling a straitjacket.

This proposal, like the guillotine motion, not unexpectedly found all the Opposition groups as determinedly opposed to the concession of such uncontrolled power as they were to a prorogation of Parliament that would silence the one still free voice of political criticism. As the representative speaker of each group—which was all the operation of the guillotine allowed—made this case in the name of his Party, the occasion had for me a very special significance. It was my last speech in Parliament—the culminating point of twenty-three years of effort to induce those with whom power lay to avoid the disaster which had overtaken us. It was made to the terms of the final amendment moved in the name of African voters which read:

'This House declines to approve the emergency regulations and amendments thereto because

1. The Government has failed to justify (a) its declaration of a state of emergency and (b) its intention to continue that state;
2. large numbers of persons are being held in custody and can be so held indefinitely without any charges being preferred against them or proof given of their danger to the State; and
3. by its intention to govern by means of these emergency regulations, the Government not only denies the rule of law but deprives South Africa of its rightful place among civilised nations and leaves us friendless in a dangerous world.'

The Minister in introducing his motion had said that he was quite persuaded that the troubles we had just experienced were not simply the result of objections to the reference books and the demand for better wages. It was the only point in the Minister's case with which I could agree. The reference books and the prevailing poverty of the African people, which had focussed special attention on the question of wages, were only part of the whole complex of laws and restrictions and controls and limitations of freedom of the African population that had been steadily developing over all these years, creating a state of tension among the African population which was the gravest danger to South Africa as a whole.

As I have noted, we were particularly qualified to speak of its dangers, since the tentacles of arbitrary power had reached out to the Liberal Party itself, pulling within prison walls a number of the local leaders of the Party—a warning, I felt, to any and all political parties who differed from the Government about the future shape of South Africa.

Nor was this the only new category that had been added to our gaol population by the state of emergency. For the first time in our troubled history a number of women had been arrested and put behind bars for political offences and languished there without trial, their personal and their domestic cares the concern of whatever charitable assistance might offer. Who could contemplate the closing down of Parliament with anything but the gravest anxiety while these conditions continued to prevail?

On the following day, May 19th, the Minister of Finance, introducing his Appropriation Bill, made it clear that the Government machine was set to complete the course that had been plotted for it. He was prepared to admit that the situation in the country was not quite so good as when he had introduced his budget on March 2nd. The actual costs of the events of the previous weeks had still to be evaluated. The immediate task was 'to restore the confidence in the stability of our economy which to a certain extent had been shocked'.[1] This was a task for the Government, but it was also the duty of every South African, and he called upon 'everybody who loves South Africa to place South Africa first in this instance and to contribute towards this important object which is in the interest of all of us'.

It was an appeal which the Leader of the Opposition met with a comprehensive analysis of the inner causes of the crisis in which we had landed and from which there still seemed no prospect of deliverance. Calling upon the Government to abandon its policies on racial affairs which had failed to bring racial peace to South Africa, had endangered our economic and industrial development and had increasingly isolated us from our natural friends in the Western world, he drew attention to the manifestations of a wide-spread desire for release from the tensions which had marked our political life for so long. Reviewing the representations that had been made to the Government from so many and such diverse quarters, one got the impression, he said, that there was general agreement that what we wanted in South Africa was more government by discussion and less government by decree and dictation.[2]

The debate which followed, rigidly limited as it was under the Government's schedule, held at least this consolation that so much of what was said from all the Opposition benches was to so large an extent the case which we had to make at that moment. Our disappearance from Parliament would therefore not be the end of it. Our responsibility had passed to others and in some measure it was being accepted by them. I began this record with the story of our discovery of what we were going to have to contend with to establish our case. Those whom we might now legitimately regard as our successors in what was in effect the struggle for a single society in South Africa committed to the democratic principle had already had some experience of the forces arrayed against them. They were

[1] Hansard, Vol. 105, Col. 8099 et seq.
[2] Hansard, Vol. 105, Col. 8107 et seq.

now to have startling evidence of the strength and determination of the major force that confronted them. With the time factor in this debate, as in the duration of the session, in the discretion of the Government, the Minister began his reply to the second reading of his Bill within a couple of hours of his known intention to move the adjournment of the House. This in itself was no occasion for surprise. The adjournment was itself a foregone conclusion, and the Minister's own reply to the debate was unlikely to hold any surprises. Yet the occasion was to prove a momentous one, deciding the fate of the country for as far as one could see.

Having dealt at some considerable length with the debate as and where it related to finance and the country's economic stability, Dr. Dönges announced that he had been authorised to read to the House a statement prepared by the Prime Minister himself on behalf of the Government on the questions raised by the recent events and the approaches which had been made to the Government in that regard. In what followed, it was abundantly clear that the Prime Minister had emerged from his isolation more convinced than ever that, both in objective and in method, his was the essential wisdom. The recent disturbances which the country had experienced had given rise to general reflection, his statement began. Various bodies had submitted ideas and proposals to the Government. He warned, however, that the people who made these proposals often were inadequately informed to be able to test the effects of their proposals. It therefore remained the task of the Government, with all the facts at its disposal and after consultation with its experts, to make the necessary decisions. 'In addition we must guard against the tendency which has arisen in certain quarters as a result of internal and external propaganda to see the disturbances in the wrong perspective; and in the second place against the attempts of opponents to try to encourage a change to a supposedly altogether new policy or a revision of policy. This in the end appeared to be nothing but an attempt to revitalise the policy of integration which has already failed here and elsewhere in Africa.'[1]

With that preface, Dr. Verwoerd proceeded to reaffirm his faith in his own policy of separate development as the only road to peace and good order. The unfortunate circumstance, he said, was that the Government was so seriously hindered in its efforts to promote

[1] Hansard, Vol. 105, Col. 8337 *et seq.*

this development as rapidly as possible by the unfavourable atmosphere created by hostile organisations and persons 'some of them
white and imbued with communistic aims sowing suspicion and
inciting the non-whites'. It was also significant, he considered, that
the disturbances had taken place especially in areas where the local
authorities were controlled by opponents of the Government's
policy, 'and it is well known that the principles of separate development have not always been applied in the same good spirit as
underlies the aims of the Government'.

In the light of all this, the Government would have to take steps
to prevent incitement and agitation whether direct or indirect from
continuing as in the past. It would also see that in every city with
a large Bantu population, the Department of Bantu Administration
was equipped to exercise on behalf of the Government proper
supervision over the administration 'to ensure that the Bantu are
properly informed on the aims of government policy', and to expand
the already existing opportunities available to the urban Bantu for
establishing direct contact with the Government or its representatives on matters of policy—an extension to the field of urban local
government of the principle which the Prime Minister had enunciated as his justification for the removal of African representation
from Parliament. The proposal was not new, he reminded the
House. Five years earlier he had prepared a Bill to provide for the
substitution of representatives of the Bantu themselves in the urban
areas for the 'practically useless' partially elective Advisory Boards.
That plan had been hampered by the opposition of white city
Councils and their organisations, by urban Bantu individuals and
organisations who had been made suspicious of the objects of the
plan in advance, as well as by political organisations. The atmosphere, he believed, had now changed in the light of experience
and it was now the Government's intention, 'in accordance with
its policy of separate development', to go ahead with it. It would
give the Bantu in the Bantu residential areas an increased measure
of authority over their own people in those areas.

Having thus disposed of the question of principle, and issued his
warning to any and all those who did not agree with him in that
regard, he proceeded to consider the specific representations that
had been made to him. Much had been made of the Africans' resentment of the reference books. That also was essentially the work
of inciters. Reference books, like influx control, were really a pro-

tection for the law-abiding worker. The format of the books had not
been entirely satisfactory. That was under reconsideration, and the
Department was also applying itself to the devising of means whereby
the benefits of the system would become more apparent to the
people themselves.

On the subject of wage rates and the pressure on the African
worker of the rising cost of living, the Prime Minister considered
that this was a matter which should not wait upon Government
action. Employers were free to meet the demands of this situation
themselves, nor did they need trade union pressure to drive them
to it. The liquor laws he was prepared to admit had been a source
of conflict between the people and the police. As they stood they
could not be administered except by a system of police raiding
which the police themselves had found most unsatisfactory. This
was a matter which had long been under consideration. Now it
seemed public opinion was ready here for a change. The Government was investigating the experience of other countries in Africa
where the laws in regard to the sale and consumption of liquor had
been relaxed and, 'in spite of certain doubts which are still felt and
certain difficulties which are expected', it intended with the necessary degree of caution to effect certain changes in this regard 'so
that the necessity for the system of raids might fall away'.

For the rest, the Government recognised that the policy of
separate development made it essential that the Bantu homelands
should be enabled properly to provide both for the future increase
of the African population and for the return flow which his policy
envisaged. It was with this in mind that it was pushing on with the
encouragement of border industries which gave private enterprise
the opportunity to assist in this matter by providing work and the
wages which the people might spend in their own areas to stimulate
their own economic life, 'and will thus form the basis of large-scale
developments in those areas'. Towns would be established 'and the
Bantu will practise all the tertiary occupations which will follow, in
which the Bantu Development Corporation[1] recently established
would be there to assist with advice and financial aid'.

In order to accelerate the development of the Bantu areas, the
Government had therefore decided 'to concentrate immediately,
after consulting the newly established Advisory Economic Council,
on the development of the border industrial areas'.

[1] See pp. 329n., 359.

Hoping that all these well-meant steps would be given the best chance of success 'unlike in the past', he concluded 'I have nothing to add.'

Before this debate began, which was to conclude with this highly important communication from the Prime Minister, Dr. Dönges had informed the House that it must end at 6 p.m. on that day, the purpose being to enable the Senate to put its stamp on the final business of the session that evening. When he reached the end of the statement, less than forty minutes of the allotted time remained for the representatives of the electorate to consider the Prime Minister's response to the greatest internal crisis the fifty-years-old Union of South Africa had so far sustained. It might prove to be true, as the only Opposition speaker on the third reading of the Bill, Mr. Marais Steyn, said, that the contents of the statement added up to the mixture as before with an infusion of alcohol. The occasion and the circumstances alike called for the closest scrutiny of all its implications and the fullest discussion in the highest political forum of the wisdom and soundness of the Prime Minister's decisions. In fact, the business of the House was suspended at 6.8 p.m. It was resumed at 10.55 to hear the Minister of Finance move the adjournment of Parliament to January 20th, 1961.

Could the Government, and its controlling source of authority, have shown its contempt for Parliament and Parliamentary government more explicitly and more convincingly? The outward trappings of the system indeed remained; the spirit that had inspired it and had given us a place among the civilised nations of the world had, like African representation, been turned out. When, if ever, would it return?

Epilogue

17

The Coming of the Republic

This is 1968. What have the intervening years contributed to the South African political scene? And with what effect on the shape and character of South African society?

The first and most immediately important contribution was surely the coming of the Republic with its contingent termination of South Africa's membership of the Commonwealth. The setting up of the Transkei Legislature in 1963 may be regarded as the second significant contribution to the country's political shape; and undoubtedly the legislative decision taken this year to wipe out the Coloured franchise at the end of the present Parliament, taken with the far-reaching implications of a Prohibition of Political Interference Act, designed to prevent concerted political action between different racial groups, has imported another radical change into our constitutional set-up and our political life.

On October 5th, 1960, the white electorate by a slender majority —850,458 votes for, 775,875 against—voted in favour of the conversion of the Union of South Africa into a republic. Armed with this mandate, Dr. Verwoerd, now fully in harness again, proceeded to make his plans for the launching of the new phase in our history on May 31st, 1961, Union Day, now to become Republic Day. On that day, the Republic of South Africa would be set on its way with the induction of its first President, Mr. C. R. Swart, in the capital of the old Transvaal Republic, Pretoria.

For years Afrikaner nationalism had argued that the establishment of a republic alone could, and would, create that so far elusive thing, white national unity in South Africa, a unity urgently necessary to enable us to tackle our great problems of white–non-white relationships, and to set the country firmly on the path of peaceful and stable progress. This much desired end, seemingly, it would achieve by simply substituting a South African President for the Queen, thus releasing the English-speaking section of the population from the bondage of a divided loyalty.

In announcing his intention to implement his mandate, Dr. Verwoerd had sought to encourage the doubters who had voted

against him in the referendum by assuring them that the republic he
planned to establish would be a democratic one, that there would
be no radical change in the country's Parliamentary institutions or
constitutional practices. Further, in deference to the feelings of
the English-speaking section of the population, who mainly although
not entirely made up his opposition, he would do his best to keep
the new republic within the Commonwealth. In the course of the
referendum compaign he had addressed a letter in this strain to all
the voters.

However, with their experience of some twelve years of Nationalist government in which they had seen so many changes within the
framework of an apparently familiar Parliamentary system, culminating in the radical change involved in the removal of all
African representation from Parliament and the political isolation
of Africans from the main stream of South African life, all opposition
groups both in Parliament and outside continued to be doubtful
of the value of these assurances.

The nature of their doubts and the anxieties which prompted
them were revealed at the beginning of the new (1961) session of
Parliament on the occasion of the request by the Prime Minister for
leave to introduce his Republic of South Africa Constitution Bill.
Adopting the tactic reserved for a special degree of opposition, that
of opposing the proposed legislation at this early stage, Sir De
Villiers Graaff for the official Opposition made his Party's assent to
the proposition conditional upon an assurance that the prospective
republic would in fact remain in the Commonwealth, and that provision was or would be made on a legislative basis for 'guaranteeing
such basic rights as would advance national unity in South Africa'.[1]
In his turn, Dr. Steytler, Leader of the Progressive Party which
still held eleven seats in the House of Assembly, asked specifically
for a rigid constitution and the protection of minority rights, for
adequate decentralisation of powers to the Provinces and for the
participation of all responsible citizens in the government of the
country, irrespective of race or colour.[2] While Sir De Villiers Graaff
stressed the hope that South Africa would retain what connections
it still had with a world that was moving in a direction diametrically
opposed to the one being pursued by the South African Government, the speakers for both parties placed a significant emphasis

[1] Hansard, Vol. 106, Col. 12.
[2] Hansard, Vol. 106, Col. 24.

on the need for us to carry with us in any policy the support of the whole population of the country.

Indeed as the debate went on, both opposition groups expressed their deep concern at the complete exclusion of all the non-white groups in the population from any say in the vital issue of the nature of the state to which they belonged, and expressed their anxiety about the effect of this exclusion on the temper of these groups.

Nor, even as the Prime Minister himself was assuring Parliament and through Parliament the country that 'South Africa is enjoying a wonderful peace',[1] were their anxieties without foundation, as Government spokesmen were themselves soon to confirm. Already there were signs that, despite the drastic action taken by the Government against their organisations and their leaders on the back of Sharpeville, the Africans were again on the move with plans to focus attention on their views and their wants. In December 1960, some forty leading personalities among them, mainly professional and commercial men and Ministers of religion, had come together in the African township of Orlando, Johannesburg, to consider ways and means of uniting the African people against a republic about which they had not been consulted, and of exercising pressure on the Government to call a national convention entrusted with the task of drawing up a new constitution for South Africa which should recognise and make provision for the rights of all sections of the population.

Their deliberations blossomed early in 1961 in a call to Africans of all shades of opinion and from all walks of life, to attend an 'all-in' Conference to be held in Pietermaritzburg on March 25th and 26th. The terms of the call were set out in pamphlets which were distributed widely throughout Johannesburg and the Witwatersrand over the weekend of the 14th–15th February. As recorded by *Die Burger*, they were in themselves highly significant. They read:[2]

'The 3,000,000 white voters have chosen to declare a republic with complete disregard for the standpoint of our 12,000,000 people.

'By this action, they have endorsed and justified the oppression of our people under the pass laws and the other discriminatory laws of this Nationalist Government. A new democratic constitution must be drawn up on the principle of a vote for each person.'

In the days that followed, the initiating body failed to keep

[1] Hansard, Vol. 106, Col. 85.
[2] *Die Burger*, February 16th, 1961.

together. The old line of cleavage between those like the A.N.C. who wished to co-operate with other racial groups, and those who, like the P.A.C., wished to stand alone, early resulted in a number of resignations from the organising committee. Plans for the Conference went ahead however, and, in spite of the arrest of a number of the leaders four days before the dates fixed for the Conference (including several of those who had already resigned from the organising committee), the Conference did in fact take place. The resolutions of its more than 1,000 delegates were put on record in full in the House of Assembly by the Minister of Justice, Mr. F. C. Erasmus, on May 8th.[1] They read:

'A grave situation confronts the people of South Africa. The Nationalist Government, after holding a fraudulent referendum among only one-fifth of the population, has decided to proclaim a White Republic on 31st May and the all White Parliament is presently discussing a constitution for it. It is clear that to the great disadvantage of our people, such a republic will continue even more intensively the policies of racial repression, political persecution and exploitation and the terrorisation of the non-white people which has already earned for South Africa the righteous condemnation of the entire world.

'In this situation, it is imperative that all the African people of this country, irrespective of their political, religious and other affiliations, should unite to speak and act with one single voice.

'For this purpose, we have gathered here at this solemn All-in African Conference and on behalf of the entire African nation and with a due sense of the historic responsibility which rests on us, we declare:

'That no constitution or form of government decided without the participation of the African people who form an absolute majority of the population, can enjoy moral validity or merit support either within South Africa or beyond its borders.'

'We demand that a National Convention of elected representatives of all adult men and women on an equal basis, irrespective of race, colour, creed or other limitation, be called by the Union Government not later than May 31st, 1961. That the Convention shall have sovereign powers to determine in any way the majority of the representatives decide, a new non-racial democratic constitution for South Africa.

Hansard, Vol. 108, Cols. 6064–5.

'We resolve that if the minority Government ignore this demand of the representatives of the united will of the African people

(a) we undertake to stage country-wide demonstrations on the eve of the proclamation of the republic in protest against this undemocratic act;

(b) we call on all Africans not to co-operate or collaborate in any way with the proposed South African Republic or any other form of government which rests on force to perpetuate the tyranny of a minority, and to organise and to unite in town and country to carry out consistent actions to oppose oppression and win freedom;

(c) we call on the Indian and Coloured communities and on all democratic Europeans to join forces with us in opposition to a regime which is bringing disaster to South Africa and for a society in which all can enjoy freedom and security;

(d) we call on democratic people the world over to refrain from any co-operation or dealing with the South African Government, to impose economic sanctions and other sanctions against this Government whose continued disregard of all human rights and freedoms constitutes a threat to world peace.'

To implement these resolutions the Conference elected a National Action Council which should decide upon and organise whatever action the people should be called upon to take should the Government turn a deaf ear to its representations.

These resolutions, the Minister informed Parliament, had been distributed widely over the country under the heading 'Reject Verwoerd Republic. Prepare for Action at the end of May.'

In due course, with no sign of yielding on the part of the Government, the National Action Council decided that the African population should be called upon to stage a three-day stay-at-home demonstration at the end of May, culminating on the Republican celebration day, May 31st.

In the meantime, significant developments had been taking place among the Coloured community. Here too, among a population traditionally deeply divided, there was a new movement towards unity, a unity also designed to challenge and repudiate the emerging Republic and its architects.

Even before the opening of the 1961 Parliamentary session which was to see the formulation of the new Republican constitution, there had been spreading rumours that the leading personalities among the Coloured people were drawing together to establish a united Coloured front in opposition to apartheid. There was talk also of a new and highly significant movement on their part to consult with the Africans. On February 23rd,[1] the pattern of events began to emerge. The daily press reported that on the previous evening, a meeting had been held in Cape Town where plans had been laid for the calling of a 'National Convention of the Coloured people of the Union which should work for the abolition of the Colour bar and full citizenship for all South Africans'. The list of the persons present was impressive, including as it did well known, educated and highly respected persons generally accepted by Government supporters and Opposition alike as men of moderate views.

In the publicity which surrounded the meeting, the rapprochement between the Coloureds and the Africans was considerably high-lighted in both Government and Opposition press. On the eve of the meeting *Die Burger* columnist, Aat Kaptein, under the heading 'This new political development must not be underestimated', wrote:[2] 'What must be regarded as important is the fact that the Coloureds have had consultations over the plans for the Convention' (which they hoped to hold in the middle of the year) 'and undoubtedly will still have with well-known Bantu and that the form and the content of the Convention even now, four months before its opening, have been tested by the opinions of the Bantu. There is no doubt that a considerable measure of agreement has been reached and that out of that, a great measure of co-operation can develop.

'This is a new political development of the first order and whoever underestimates its significance makes a great mistake.'

This drawing together of Coloured and African leaders was a matter of uneasy concern in political circles.[3] In the past, the Coloured community had on the whole tended to stand aloof from African movements,[4] partly in response to appeals and implied promises made by successive governments, and partly in the conviction

---

[1] *Cape Times*, February 23rd, 1961.
[2] *Die Burger*, February 22nd, 1961. 'Hierdie Politieke Novum kan nie onderskat word nie.'
[3] Mr. Abe Bloomberg, Coloured representative in Parliament, urged the Coloured leaders not to act hastily in forming a liaison with the Africans. *Cape Times*, February 24th, 1961.
[4] The Coloured People's Organisation which co-operated with the Congresses in the fifties represented a small left section of the Coloured community.

that in fact they must be accepted as part of that 'Western' type of state that even Afrikaner Nationalism professed to be building. And in the very recent past, their hopes in this regard had received special encouragement in the appreciative speeches of Dr. Dönges and Mr. Tom Naudé on the steadfastness and the loyalty of the Coloured people in the days of crisis.[1]

What was the key to this change in attitude? It was given by the Coloured leaders themselves in interviews which followed the launching of their campaign. In the days that followed the riots, as has already been noted, in the heart searchings as to the root causes of the troubles that had so seriously and calamitously erupted in March 1960, there was a new concern among the White electorate about the rights and claims of the Coloured people. This was particularly evident among the Government's own supporters, especially in the Cape Province which had always been uneasy about the place assigned to the Coloured people within the framework of the apartheid policy. While the general proposition that the Coloured community should be aligned with the Whites was widely canvassed, considerable support seemed to be forthcoming for the recognition of the claim of the Coloured people to be represented in Parliament by their own people. So far had this gone in the months succeeding Sharpeville that on July 23rd, 1960, Dawie of *Die Burger* referred to this suggestion as 'the most dramatic idea' in this field of discussion and gave it as his impression that 'the Nationalist Party is already more than halfway in agreement with this principle and can be completely won for it by strong leadership'.

All this naturally engendered an atmosphere of optimism and hope among the Coloured people. So much greater then was the reaction when Dr. Verwoerd decided that the time had come to deal firmly with this situation, to make it clear that he would have no more invasions of the apartheid policy in respect of Coloureds than in respect of Africans. So long as he was in control, there would be no opening of the doors of Parliament to Coloured members. Such a development could only be a springboard for further demands that would destroy the whole policy of separation.

He set out his attitude in two lengthy statements released to the press on November 24th and December 8th, 1960. In the first he argued that the greatest need of the Coloured people was economic and educational development and experience in the field of local

[1] See p. 434.

government in the service of their own people. In the second, he elaborated at considerable length a 'new deal' for the Coloured people along those lines. It had a singularly familiar ring about it for those who had followed the course of the Government's African policy, more and better housing, more jobs, more educational facilities and new powers in the field of local government for a Coloured Council which had come into existence against the will of the Coloured people and without their support after their removal from the common roll. There was promise also of a Minister of Coloured Affairs who would be given responsibility for Coloured education, and a Coloured Development Corporation to encourage and assist Coloured economic activities, all with the same flavour of apartheid about it.

In the meantime, he had made what came to be known as his granite wall speech to a conference of the Nationalist Party on the Witwatersrand. Expressing himself forcibly on the dangers implicit in all the discussions that were going on about a possible new approach to the Coloured people, he urged the leaders of the Party to realise that they must stand like walls of granite on their colour policy since the existence of 'the nation'[1] was at stake. He followed this up by calling a meeting of the Federal Council of the Nationalist Party at which he stressed his now insistent theme that principle could not be sacrificed to unity.

This drew from the Council a comprehensive statement[2] designed 'to counteract confusion about official Nationalist Party policy towards the Coloured community arising from vigorous discussions recently in the Press and among Nationalist supporters'. This statement welcomed and endorsed fully the Prime Minister's two statements and with him repudiated as a matter of principle any idea of Coloured representation in Parliament by Coloured persons. Like the Prime Minister, the Council expressed its belief in 'a policy of parallel streams which cannot flow into each other' as the only basis on which good friendship can be permanently acquired through good neighbourliness. 'In the interests of Coloured people as well as Whites points of friction may not be re-created through partnership or mixing in any form.'

Thus was the door to citizenship slammed decisively, even

---

[1] 'Die nasie'—clearly the Afrikaner nation.
[2] *Cape Argus*, January 23rd, 1961. 'Nat Party kills all doubt about policy on Coloured people.'

forcefully, in the face of the Coloured community. From the statements of their leaders, it would appear that the granite wall speech came to them as a particular shock, inducing them to close their own ranks and drawing them to the other victims of the Government's exclusive policies. In a mood of deep disappointment and frustration, they followed the progress of the African movement and promised their support for the demonstrations planned for the end of May while continuing to plan to hold their own supporting Conference later in the year.

The Government's reactions to all these signs of unrest among the non-White population were sharply characteristic. The arrest of leaders of the All-in Conference in an attempt to prevent the meeting of the Conference has been noted.[1] On the back of the Conference, on April 5th, the Minister of Justice renewed the ban on the A.N.C. and the P.A.C. On May 3rd, he introduced a General Laws Amendment Bill,[2] the first of a new series of enactments which was greatly to increase the power of the executive and to make new inroads on the liberties of all sections of the population on the grounds of threats to law and order and the security of the state.

The most significant feature of this Bill was an amendment to the Criminal Procedure Act empowering the Attorney-General, where he considered it in the interest of the state or the maintenance of public order, to issue an order that a person arrested on suspicion that he had committed a crime should not be released on bail or otherwise within twelve days of his arrest. It also extended the wide range of cases in which the Minister of Justice might order trial without jury. It further amended the Riotous Assemblies Act to extend the Minister's power of banning meetings and widened greatly the definition of intimidation.

Armed with these new powers and resources, the Minister proceeded to ban all meetings, with some specified exceptions, from May 19th to June 26th. In the meantime, the police had been heavily engaged in massive raids throughout the country rounding up Africans suspected of having committed any of the diverse statutory offences with which their path was and is beset. And to round off the drive to see that the great day was not marred by serious trouble, during the last ten days of May, all police leave was cancelled, as was the leave of certain Citizen Force units, and the

[1] See p. 452.
[2] Hansard, Vol. 108, Col. 5784.

Citizen Force generally and Commando units of the Defence Force were brought to a state of preparedness for service.

On May 23rd the Leader of the Opposition, Sir De Villiers Graaff, asked the Prime Minister whether he would give an undertaking that the House, before it rose on May 26th (for the recess to cover the launching of the Republic), would be given an opportunity of debating the Government's action in (a) banning gatherings and meetings, (b) having large numbers of persons arrested and (c) partially utilising the Citizen Force, with particular reference to (i) the evidence which had led the Government to believe that violence or unrest might arise between then and June 26th, (ii) the need to prolong the banning proclamation until June 26th, (iii) the state of the nation as revealed by these actions on the part of the Government.[1]

The Prime Minister refused the debate and deprecated the questions put as implicitly encouraging the prospective trouble makers. The intentions of these trouble makers had been widely publicised by the press, he said, and thus were well known but the Government, as was its duty, would be prepared to meet the situation. He considered that there were members of the public who were playing with fire. He referred specifically 'to the very recent agitation for a multi-racial National Convention'. This was an effort to bring down the Nationalist Government and/or to attempt to join the English-speaking South Africans with the non-Whites against the Afrikaners. In this he saw the hand of the communists, and everyone who lent support to the proposition, whatever his personal aims, became jointly responsible for what their aims were—a clear warning which experience of the range of our anti-communist legislation already on the statute book could point effectively.

In the event, the planned three days' demonstrations designed to focus attention on the exclusion of the majority of the population from the political processes involved in the transformation of Union into Republic were only limitedly supported, and by the third— and vital—day, had practically faded out altogether. But the nature and the extent of the preparations which the Government had found it necessary to mount to meet the threat scarcely gave to the great occasion of the launching of the Republic the appearance and atmosphere of the harmonious, united, happy adventure that its supporters were anxious to claim for it.

[1] Hansard, Vol. 108, Col. 6943 *et seq.*

18

The Republic in Operation

As has been noted, the Leader of the Opposition had been much concerned to get guarantees from the Government that the Republic would remain within the Commonwealth. It was a demand which had been consistently made by the official Opposition from the moment the Prime Minister's determination to establish the Republic became clear and certain. While Dr. Verwoerd's response to this demand was that he saw no reason to accept the principle that the assurance of continued membership should precede the establishment of the Republic, he said again that he would do his best to remain within the Commonwealth. It was not what Nationalists would have wished but they were prepared to make this sacrifice out of respect for the feelings of the English-speaking section of the population and in the cause of that national unity at which the Republicans aimed.

There is reason to believe that Dr. Verwoerd did what he could at the Prime Ministers' Conference where the decision lay to keep South Africa within the family of nations which it had helped to create but, as we know, the pressures against apartheid were more than he could resist and he had perforce to accept the fact that South Africa was not an acceptable member of the family so long as that policy prevailed. And the surrender of his policy was a sacrifice he was not prepared to make.

But his experiences at the Conference were not without their effect upon his thinking on apartheid. They had called for a facing of the ultimate implications of his policy if it was to establish any claim to a moral basis. As already noted[1] this was reflected in his first major speech to Parliament on his return from the Conference. Where before there had been varying emphasis from time to time on the process and extent of separation, it was now unequivocally stated that the Bantu would be able to develop into separate Bantu states. 'It is a form of fragmentation which we would not have liked if we were able to avoid it,' he said. 'In the light of the pressure being exerted on South Africa, there is however no doubt that eventually this will have to be done, thereby buying for the White man his

[1] See p. 321 n., also p. 331.

459

freedom and the right to retain domination in what is his country settled for him by his forefathers.'[1]

The problem of political rights for the Indians and the Coloured would then still exist. Here he reluctantly accepted 'the rejection of the old proposition that one cannot have a state within a state'. He went on to elaborate: we would have to give the Coloureds opportunities for development firstly by means of their own local governments, secondly by way of managing the sort of thing now falling under the control of the Provincial Councils, viz. their own municipal affairs, the education of their own children and similar matters. Thirdly he accepted that, 'within the White state and therefore within the same borders, an institution should be established or a method should be evolved to give the Coloureds further rights of self-government over their national interests. However, the time to decide precisely how and in regard to what this must be done could wait until the development had progressed to the second stage.'

Asked by Mr. Gray Hughes,[2] United Party member for the Transkei, whether the Coloureds would eventually lose their Parliamentary representation, Dr. Verwoerd said that until we had reached the stage where the Coloured Council was fully performing its functions, no decision would be taken in that regard. Coloured representation would remain as it was then.

So far as the Indians were concerned, the same sort of provision would be made for them as for the Coloured population except that in no circumstances would there be representation for them in Parliament.

He then added in respect of both groups 'we limit their development to that of a Council which will exercise authority over their own affairs similar to the powers now enjoyed by the provincial authorities. If it is necessary to have further development on those same parallel lines then we shall have to do so.' But he did not visualise that there would be any necessity for representation in a common Parliament. He foresaw that 'some other machinery might be evolved by which each of these groups could be given full authority and a full life, separate from each other in the political sphere'.

With the irresistible dynamic which characterised all his political life, Dr. Verwoerd was ready with the main lines of his first Bantu

[1] Hansard, Vol. 107, Col. 4191.
[2] Hansard, Vol. 107, Col. 4193.

state within a year of this declaration of policy. In the first big debate of the 1962 session of Parliament he announced his hope that a Bill to convert the Transkeian Territorial Authority into a self-governing territory might be laid before Parliament before the end of that session—the first full Republican session. It might however be impossible to get it there before 1963 since so much of its pattern had still to be decided by the members of the Territorial Authority to which its final form must be officially submitted. He could, however, give the House and the country some idea of what the change would involve. He did not claim that the Government was prepared 'to permit a drastic development'. He did claim, however, that it was an important development of which everybody in the country and the outside world should take due note.[1] He added:

'Inasmuch as people did not believe that we were in earnest, and that we were prepared to implement it, the development which we are arranging here is in fact a democratic one.'

He then proceeded to foreshadow the shape of the new constitution. There would be a Parliament which, so far as the Government was concerned, would have to have an element of representation in it. There would no doubt also be a place for the chiefs but that was a matter on which the Bantu themselves would have to express their views.

The elected members would be returned by voters living in the Transkei and outside it on a franchise still to be determined. It was not necessary, he felt, to underline the fact that the Transkei Parliament would consist of Bantu members only, elected by Bantu persons only, in effect that White and Coloured people living in the Transkei would not fall under its jurisdiction.

The Parliament would have to have an executive body. The Government was proposing a cabinet at the head of which should be a Prime Minister who would choose his own Ministers. To this Transkeian Government would be committed initially responsibility for a number of matters that would seem to be within their competence such as agriculture, education, health and welfare, which would be added to as the people concerned gained experience. In the meantime, the South African Government would continue to carry the rest of the responsibility for the Transkei as far as the rest of the country was concerned. At the same time, it would supply administrative officers to guide the Bantu administration which the

[1] Hansard, Vol. 2, Republic of South Africa, Col. 74 *et seq.*

new state would have to have and to train it 'in the process of democratic government'.

These developments would result in Transkeian citizenship for the Transkeian Bantu. The implications of this in the transition period would have to be worked out by constitutional lawyers, but 'the principle of a distinctive national identity must', he declared, 'be coupled to the principle of a distinctive citizenship'.[1]

All these developments would cost a lot of money but Dr. Verwoerd felt that it was worth it all since in their doing this 'the international struggle against South Africa would be deprived of whatever background there was for it', and, he added, 'If there is any justice in the world, this should strongly counteract the international animosity and suspicion which have such a detrimental effect on our country.'

In the event, the Transkei Constitution Act reached the statute book in 1963. Its terms provided for a Legislative Assembly to consist of all the chiefs at the head of tribal units, sixty-four in number,[2] and forty-five elected members. The enfranchised electorate was to be all Xhosa persons of twenty-one years and over, and taxpayers of the age of eighteen years, that is, all males of that age. Provision was also made for a Cabinet of six members. Of these, the Chief Minister, who should also be the Minister of Finance, would be elected by the members of the Assembly; the other five were to be selected by him from the members of the Assembly. To these should be entrusted the portfolios of Agriculture and Forestry, Education, Justice, Interior and Roads and Works.

The status of the new state was to be symbolised in a national flag which should be flown alongside the Republican flag and a National Anthem which should be sung with the South African national anthem. The Act further created a Transkeian citizenship which was to cover all the Xhosa people both inside and outside the Transkei. The Xhosa people wherever they might be were to be one nation.

But not as yet an independent nation. As Mr. de Wet Nel, Minister of Bantu Administration and Development, was at pains to underline in the course of the debates on the Transkei Constitution Bill—as Dr. Verwoerd himself had done in his speeches in the previous year—the Transkei remained part of South Africa. In

[1] Hansard, Vol. 2, Col. 77.
[2] All paid officers of the Government and removable by it.

the circumstances, its citizens would not be treated as foreigners in the Republic. And since its citizenship would not be recognised internationally, all its external relationships would be regulated by the South African Government—an answer, at least for the time being, to the repeated challenge from Opposition benches as to the danger of creating independent states on our borders which might form hostile alliances against the Republic.

The question was, what was all this to mean in the life of the ordinary Xhosa. A citizenship, a flag and an anthem could not be without some significance.

These five years since the Legislative Assembly of the Transkei came into existence[1] have seen very significant changes in the status and position not only of the Xhosa people but of all the African people in South Africa. As if the establishment of a modified system of local government in the Transkei had established a separate African citizenship throughout South Africa, the Nationalist Government has progressively treated all Africans in South Africa, that is all South African Africans, as if they were in fact citizens of a foreign country. Where the majority of them, some two-thirds, still live in what the Government calls the White area, many of them born there, by a series of Bantu Laws Amendment Acts, it has sought to loosen all foundations of permanence which might suggest claims to residential and political rights in that area.

Its primary concern in this regard has been in respect of the urban population. As we have seen over the years, even under Nationalist rule, some accommodations had been made to the facts of urbanisation. These had included the recognition of the right to be in a particular urban area of persons born and continuously living there, or persons with ten years' continuous employment with one employer or fifteen years' residence without any conflict with the law.[2] The assumption by the Department of Bantu Administration and Development of ever-widening control over the distribution and use of African labour has now put these rights in jeopardy. The present Minister of Bantu Administration and Development, Mr. M. C. Botha, has now expressly stated that these provisions can 'by no means be construed as citizen rights acquired in the homelands of the Whites by the Bantu'; they are merely categories of influx control exemptions. And he has warned that any continuing

---

[1] The first elections were in 1963.
[2] See p. 314.

propaganda to the contrary might necessitate measures to clarify the legal position beyond doubt.[1]

And it is reported that in the spirit of this approach, draft regulations have already been circulated to public authorities proposing that Africans falling into these categories, in certain circumstances including being out of employment for more than a month without proof of illness, should be evicted from their homes, and contingently endorsed out of the area.[2]

Against this background, the existence of an established middle class has posed a special challenge to the protagonists of apartheid, that is the African business men, industrialists, doctors, lawyers and other professional men whom Mr. Blaar Coetzee as Deputy Minister of Bantu Administration and Development lists as 'unproductive' in terms of South Africa's labour needs. These are the people who, according to an ex-Secretary of Bantu Affairs and one of the architects of the apartheid policy, Dr. Eiselen, are really putting the position in the urban areas as the Government seeks to plan it 'out of balance' in that they are not in the service of the European people but form a Bantu middle class which hopes to stay in the urban areas permanently.[3] Steps, Dr. Eiselen said, were being taken to reverse that situation and to encourage this class to go to the homelands to carry on their activities there.

No doubt Dr. Eiselen had in mind, among other pressures, the directive given in 1963 to local authorities in regard to the granting of trading licences even in the African townships—which included a complete embargo on the establishment of new businesses which do not confine themselves to the provision of daily essential domestic necessities, and the rigid control of existing business against expansion or acquisition of property rights in respect of premises.[4]

In line with all this is the recent directive from the Department in respect of home ownership in the urban African townships. This relates to a system of 30-year leasehold of land on which Africans might build their own houses. It was a system conceded by Dr. Verwoerd himself to the emerging middle class before the policy of separate development achieved its present level of rigidity. Local authorities have now been informed that it is to come

---

[1] Senate, May 15th, 1967.
[2] S.A. Institute of Race Relations Summary, 1967, p. 168.
[3] *Cape Argus*, December 6th, 1967. Report of an interview by touring party of sixty South African town councillors, municipal officials and business men.
[4] Circular Minute No. A12/1–A8/1 quoted S.A.I.R.R. Survey 1963, pp. 145–9.

to an end and while the present owners and occupiers will not
be disturbed 'until further notice', in the meantime the houses
built under the scheme, including some 8000 in the Soweto complex of Johannesburg that would do credit to any good middle-
class suburb in the 'white area', may not be sold to anyone other
than the local authority nor can the owners bequeath them to
their heirs.

Accompanying all these efforts to establish the claim of the im-
permanence of the already urbanised African population has gone
a strenuous tightening up of influx control limiting both the number
of workers entering the urban labour market and the duration of
contracts of service. At the same time, there has been a progressive
extension of the areas to which all the restrictive conditions of the
Urban Areas Act may be applied to cover not only developing
industrial areas but in fact any area to which the Minister wishes
to apply them.

Thus today, with the African population still in process of shifting
from country to town under the pressure of economic need and
following the recognised course of socio-economic development in
modern societies, it is to all intents and purposes impossible for an
African to establish domicile in an urban area.

In the rural areas, where approximately one-third of the African
population, together with a considerable body of immigrants from
neighbouring territories, provide the labour force for an agricultural
industry which is always crying out for more labour, Nationalist
spokesmen in the past have contended that there was no apartheid
problem since Africans could only live there as servants on white
men's land. Now, however, it would appear that there is an urgent
need in government circles to establish a uniform pattern for separate development throughout the country. An effort is therefore
being made to whittle away the labour tenancy system in favour
of individual as against family contracts. This is no doubt to bring
about a reduction in the number of women and children now in
these areas. These will now presumably have to go to the homelands
of their ethnic groups.

At the same time, machinery is being forged to establish a link
between individual and tribe on which can be built a uniform
migrant labour system for country and towns. In 1967, the Deputy
Minister of Bantu Development announced that it had been decided
that all Bantu labour should be mobilised through the active

2G

agency of the Bantu authorities. A scheme, he said, was being worked out for the decentralisation of labour bureaux to the tribal and regional authorities and for the compulsory registration of every Bantu [sic] in the homelands as a work-seeker. These Bantu would then be allotted to specific labour categories according to prescribed norms so that all sectors would receive their rightful share of the available labour.[1]

On April 1st, 1968, a proclamation was issued under which this system has been established. According to one of the Government's front bench speakers on these matters, Mr. G. F. van L. Froneman,[2] a tribal labour bureau has been established at each Tribal Authority. These bureaux, he explained, receive requisitions from the White homeland for the recruitment of labour. The Authority now recruits labour in its own area amongst the members of its tribe. Under that requisition, the Bantu (sic) then comes to work for a year. This, he added, is virtually the same pattern as the one now operating in the case of workers from Malawi according to which the Bantu leave their area to come to work for a certain period, which in the case of Malawi is a maximum of two years or eighteen months. For the South African African, the period of contract is for one year only, at the end of which time the worker must return to his tribal unit before a new contract can be entered into.

This purposeful extension of a social instability which a healthy economy would normally choose to do all in its power to avoid or to counteract, is the price that the community is called upon to pay for that separation which is designed to give the White man security in his part of South Africa, and justified on the ground of giving the several African groups rights of self-development in their areas. While even the most ardent supporters of apartheid are coming to acknowledge that Africans will always be in our midst and that in fact they are indispensable to our economy, it is ever important to them to underline that they do not belong here. The argument with which this contention is supported owes much to Dr. Verwoerd's claim,[3] noted earlier, that labour is no more integrated into a society by being employed in it than is the ox or the ass or the tractor. A new Minister of Bantu Administration and Development, Mr. M. C. Botha, argues from the premiss that in terms of the

[1] Vide *Cape Argus*, April 27th, 1967.
Hansard, Vol. (1968), Col. 6601.
See p. 331.

Government's general policy the Bantu, although in the 'white' area for labour, do not enjoy the same labour opportunities as the whites; they have access only to certain traditional and demarcated categories of work. It is absolutely wrong, therefore, to call their mere presence on such an unequal basis integration.[1]

Mr. Botha, in the course of a comprehensive policy statement in the Senate on May 15th, 1967, foreshadowed a new proposition to meet the otherwise intractable facts of the situation. This is in fact to equate the position of South African Africans with that of the foreign Africans. The latter now have to carry passports and to have a permit from the South African administration to take work in a particular area. In a major announcement on the next phase in the implementation of the Party's policy, the Minister adumbrated the extension of a similar system to the 'Bantu nations' of South Africa. Postulating the identification of every African with his ethnic group and its tribal authority he suggested that 'As the nations develop and become more attached to their own national authorities and exercise greater powers, White-Bantu administration can be based increasingly on international agreements'. This could mean that 'many matters which are now arranged by such laws as the Urban Areas Act, the Reference Book Act, the Labour Act and so on can then operate under agreements between the Bantu nation and the White nation'.

He went on to explain that this could lead to a revision of the whole system of documentation now in operation. 'Each Bantu person in a White area can then carry a document of identity from his own national authority and a document from our Government showing where the Bantu person works and lives.' This, he argued, would make it clear that the limitations on Bantu in the White areas would not be discrimination between people in a mixed context but differentiation of the local White people on the one side and members of the remote Bantu nation on the other.

In the meantime, while separate states and the separate opportunities which they are to provide continue to present a mirage-like quality, separation in both rights and opportunities becomes ever more insistently the reality of African existence in the Republic of South Africa.

---

[1] Senate Hansard, May 15th, 1967, Col. 2827 *et seq.*
2G*

19

Coloured Separate Freedoms: and Inferiority

This year, 1968, the Nationalist Party celebrated twenty years of Nationalist rule. In an article[1] written for the occasion, the Prime Minister, Mr. B. J. Vorster, claimed that the hardest nut the Party as a Government had had to crack was that of the relationships between the diverse groups in the population, particularly between the Whites and the non-Whites. This, he considered, the Party had done most successfully through its policy of recognising the identity and the right of existence of each different nation, language and colour group, by eliminating points of friction between groups and by providing for each group, as well as for their members, opportunities to develop according to their own character and ability, and with the maintenance of their own identity which had brought peace and quiet to the land.

In the light of these claims, a special interest attaches to the trilogy of Acts which were put on the statute book in that year, setting the position of the Coloured—and Indian—population within the framework of the apartheid policy. These are the Separate Representation of Voters Amendment Act, the Coloured Persons Representative Council Amendment Act, and the Prohibition of Political Interference Act.[2]

The first of these Acts completes the process of the disfranchisement of the Coloured population of the Cape Province on which the Nationalist Party embarked as soon as they got into office. As already noted, all representation of this group will disappear from the Parliamentary scene at the end of the life of the present Parliament due to take place in 1971.

The second amends a Coloured Persons Representative Council Act passed in 1964 during Dr. Verwoerd's period of office, but never so far implemented. Where the previous Act provided for a Council with an appointed majority and closed sessions, this provides for a Council of sixty members, forty of whom are to be elected and twenty

---

[1] Article 1948–1968 entitled . . . en nou die Toekoms (. . . and now the future), quoted *Die Burger*, May 18th, 1968.
[2] Introduced as the Prohibition of Improper Interference Bill in 1966.

appointed by the Government. It also makes provision for an Executive of five members of whom one shall be designated by the State President as chairman and four will be elected by the members of the Council from their own number. Its sessions will be open. A building is being provided for it in which there will be accommodation for members of Parliament and other interested parties, including the press.

To this Council will be committed responsibility for finance, local government, education, community welfare and pensions, rural areas and settlements and such other matters as the State President may from time to time determine by proclamation. The Chairman of the Executive will, like the Prime Minister of the Transkei, be responsible for finance. The electorate for the Council will be all adult Coloured persons throughout the Republic. The Act provides for compulsory registration of voters. The Minister responsible for the Bill hoped that it might be possible to get the Council into existence by the second half of 1969, commending it warmly 'as making an important contribution towards establishing the Coloured population as a nation and towards their happiness'.[1] He himself and others of his political persuasion were to argue that now the Coloured population were being given political rights for the first time in their history.

The Act provides no specific channel of communication between Parliament and the Council or the Coloured community for which supposedly the Council will speak. This the Minister said would be the subject of consultation with the Council when it was effectively constituted. On the results of such consultation the Government would decide whether the liaison to be established would be with Parliament or with the Government—a decision of deep constitutional importance which the Minister seemed scarcely to appreciate.

The third Act of the trilogy, the Prohibition of Political Interference Act, is designed to establish complete political apartheid by laying down that no person of one population group may be a member of any political party of which any person who belongs to any other population group is a member or render assistance in any way across the colour line in an election for Parliament, the Transkei Legislature or the Coloured Persons Representative Council or any other body to which the State President by proclamation in the Gazette applies this provision. As simply stated in the preamble

[1] Hansard, 1968, Col. 2927.

to the Act, it is an Act 'To prohibit interference by one population group in the politics of any other population group'. The Act also makes illegal the receipt by political parties of financial assistance from abroad.

While this Act clearly applies to all Parties and all population groups as defined under our laws, its history associates it particularly with the Coloured population group and their position in terms of government policy. In the years which followed the constitutional battles of the fifties and the removal of the Coloureds from the common voters' roll, except for the reaction against their exclusion from the referendum and the making of the constitution of the Republic, the Coloured people had taken little interest in the political scene and the *quid pro quo* machinery which had been conceded them in return for the rights they had lost in 1955. In 1964, however, a new interest in politics began to manifest itself among the community. This was undoubtedly related to the decision of the Progressive Party to contest the two Coloured seats in the Provincial Council in the elections due in 1965, and their plans to put up candidates for the four Parliamentary seats in the general election due in 1966. The Party's very active pursuit of their objectives resulted in their winning the two Provincial Council seats against United Party competitors and an unofficial Nationalist candidate and that with majorities that amply justified their hopes for the Parliamentary election.

The effect of the Party's success in government circles was what might be called electric. It was generally known that Dr. Verwoerd had hoped to wipe out the Progressive Party in the election which he had held unexpectedly in 1961 on the back of the establishment of the Republic. These hopes had suffered a set-back in the return of one Progressive Party member, Mrs. Helen Suzman, in her Johannesburg seat of Houghton. A set-back but not the abandonment of his hope that this objective would yet be achieved and proof given to the world that South Africa was convincedly rejecting the liberal line. Now the prospect of a strengthening of the Party's numbers in Parliament, and that on the votes of Coloureds whose acceptance of his policies he insistently proclaimed, was something that must be avoided.

He began to talk of the duty of the Government to ensure that the Coloureds 'of their own volition' should send to Parliament 'those Whites who they believe will best represent their true and real interests'. There was much speculation as to the course he would pursue to achieve this. As has been noted, his Government had legislated in 1964 to provide what promised to be a modestly improved Coloured Council which had not so far been brought into existence. Rumour had it that he would change the basis of choice of the Parliamentary representatives by placing it in the hands of this body which with its nominated majority and its closed session might be guaranteed to return members acceptable to the Government. While the debate was going on the Minister of the Interior introduced an amendment to the Separate Representation of Voters Act to make the term of office of the Coloured representatives a fixed five years—as the Native Representatives had had—in place of the provision that placed their election not less than eight days before the polling day for white voters. This would mean that while the 'White' election was due in May 1966, the Coloured election would not take place until late in that year. This had the merit of giving the Government more time to work out its plans. In the meantime, the Progressive Party continued its activities.

In May, the general election duly returned the Nationalist Party with an increased majority inflated by the creation of ten new constituencies.[1] And in August, when the new Parliament assembled, the Prime Minister was no doubt ready with the Prohibition of Improper Interference Bill when he fell victim to the assassin's knife. That the Bill eventually saw the light under his successor, Mr. Vorster, does nothing to put its paternity in doubt. Mr. Vorster, however, may have been more accommodating in agreeing to send the Bill to a Select Committee destined to become yet another Parliamentary Commission in which the scope of the enquiry was widened to include not only the terms of the Bill (A.B. 81–66) but also 'any matters concerning the political representation of the various population groups'.

This put the matter in cold storage for some two years while the Commission travelled the country and took evidence from all and sundry. In the meantime, the elections for the Coloured seats were again postponed pending the Commission's recommendations on the future of Parliamentary representation.

In due course, the Commission's report appeared, in the now familiar form of such Commissions, with a brief statement of findings by the Government majority setting out what nobody doubted was already settled Government policy. This was to take legislative

[1] It also returned Mrs. Suzman.

shape with minor modifications in these three measures, with the Opposition side of the Commission contending that the proposal to abolish the Coloured Parliamentary franchise and to interfere with the rights of parties to propagate their policies across the colour line was not only against the weight of the evidence submitted to the Commission but was a further dangerous retreat from democratic practice which had suffered so much erosion under Nationalist rule.

Thus the Coloured people have been given their place within the framework of apartheid, a place which is to be duplicated for the Indians. And the whiteness of the white Parliament has been established. But it is a solution of the Nationalist problem of making and keeping Parliament white which has its awkward features. Without separate national homes, the Coloured and Indian groups must always remain subject to the South African Parliament and the moral justification for separate development which Dr. Verwoerd had been forced to accept, at least in theory, in the case of the African population: that is potential separate states and separate sovereignty, must for them be continuously lacking.

But Dr. Verwoerd had already faced that difficulty in 1965 when the question of Coloured representation became an immediate issue for him, and had marked out the line of argument for his Party.[1] Given the vote, he said, a minority party had little chance of getting into power but it might hold the balance between two equally strong parties which was a highly undesirable eventuality which would certainly lead to trouble. In the circumstances was it not much better to give such a minority group limited powers and opportunities? It was true that, under his plan for the development of the Coloured Council as the field of political activity for the Coloured people, they would continue to be subject to the authority of the entire State as controlled by the majority group but 'we must ask ourselves . . . in what way we can best serve the interests of everybody even if it means that the one gets slightly less than the other'.

That the pattern which he then proposed for the Coloureds—and the Indians—meant perpetual exclusion from a share in government has been accepted by his successor and his Party. This was frankly stated by the Minister of the Interior in the Senate in the final phase of the disestablishing measure. So far as he and the

[1] Hansard, Vol. 14, Col. 4245 *et seq.*

Nationalist Party could foresee, he explained simply, the Coloured people would never have exactly the same say as the White man in the country which was governed by the White man . . . but there was no reason to give the same political rights to the Coloured people as those enjoyed by the Whites if this were impossible from a practicalpoint of view.[1]

[1] Senate Hansard, May 20th, 1968, Col. 3169 *et seq.*

20

Further Reactions to Nationalist Pattern

The Nationalist Party has consistently claimed that its policy and the pattern which this has progressively imposed upon South African society has more and more been accepted by White and non-White alike. In support of its contention so far as Whites are concerned, it points to its increasing majority in Parliament over the years,[1] and so far as all sections of the population are concerned, to the peace and quiet that prevails, the absence of those troubles which so many other countries are experiencing and to which, according to Mr. Vorster,[2] the presence of people of different colours, races, languages, beliefs or political conceptions makes us prone. How well do these claims stand up to the facts of the case?

So far as the white population is concerned, there is no doubt that in addition to its massive consolidation of the Afrikaner volk which has been its great achievement, the governing Party has gathered in the votes of a section of the English-speaking group which, frightened by what has happened in the rest of Africa, has come to believe that this Party offers the best guarantee of the survival of the White man in South Africa. But the Parliamentary Oppositions, the United Party and the now sole representative of the Progressive Party, still speak for 40 per cent of the electorate and they have consistently opposed the course which the Government has pursued and continues to pursue. They have stood four-square against the Bantustan policy with its implicit—and eventually explicit—fragmentation of the country. They have underlined repeatedly the danger of making a rootless, rightless proletariat of the African population upon whom the economic structure of South Africa as a whole depends. They have exposed relentlessly the unreality and the injustice of treating Africans *now* as members of Bantu states which in fact do not exist, and may never exist; and they have warned persistently of the dangers that lie in creating independent states on our borders, particularly in a world which,

[1] It now holds 126 seats to the Opposition's 39+1—with 4 Coloured seats.
[2] *op cit.* See p. 468.

474

if it is deeply divided on many things, is significantly united in its abhorrence of both the theory and the practice of apartheid.

They have continued to take their stand on the unity of the South African state with one Parliament in which all groups in the population must be represented.

This does not preclude the provision of differential local government machinery designed to meet the needs of varying localities— a policy which in fact has a considerable history behind it in respect of African areas. But they repudiate the suggestion that local councils can take the place of full citizenship rights. That is, they repudiate the idea that such groups as the Coloureds and Indians shall be forever without a share in the making of the laws by which they are governed at the level at which those laws are made.

Both parties go further and postulate the right of at least the Coloured people to enter Parliament, while the Progressive Party continues to stand for a common franchise for all groups with the right of all voters to nominate whom they choose as candidates for Parliament.

All of which means that there has emerged clearly and unequivocally an apparently unbridgeable gap between the two sides of the political field. It was sufficiently deep as early as 1961 for Dr. Verwoerd to warn that if the Opposition should get into office and seek to re-establish the pre-Nationalist political pattern with the Coloureds again enfranchised on the common roll, there would again 'be hatred and opposition not only against the United Party but against Britain' because it would be considered that Britain was 'sitting behind this move'—which he stigmatised as using the non-White vote to thwart the will of the White community.[1]

By 1965, he could declare that he was prepared to defend the system of which he was indeed the architect, by force.[2]

All of which creates a position that surely calls for a serious re-appraisal of the whole political situation and of the whole concept of the party system by which it ostensibly works.

So far as the minority groups in the country are concerned, the Coloured community will no doubt accept the new Council and

[1] Hansard, Vol. 106, Col. 81.
[2] Hansard, Vol. 13, Col. 632. 'I believe in the supremacy of the white man over his people in his own territory and I am prepared to maintain it by force.'

use what it has to offer.[1] Apart from the abortive efforts of 1961 to induce the Government to reconsider the course which it has chosen and to strive by consultative means to find an accommodation that would be acceptable to all groups in the country, as has been noted the Coloured community has over the years given little evidence of political interest, except for their part in the 1964 Provincial election which sparked off the movement for the complete elimination of the Coloured franchise. But whether this is a reflection of acquiescence in a policy which puts a very low ceiling on the political advance to which they can aspire or to discouragement at the prospect, only time can show.

In the meantime, it is interesting to see again signs of uncertainty and some anxiety among members of the ruling group as to the wisdom of the course which the politicians have chosen. Among these is the announced decision of SABRA to conduct a full-scale enquiry into the future development of the Coloured people.[2] Notable also is an article by Professor N. J. Rhoodie[3] of the University of Pretoria under the heading 'Coloured Homelands' in which he asks some very pertinent questions which no doubt the Coloured leaders will also ask if and when the Coloured Council becomes a real debating chamber. Once the Government has finally decided to treat the Coloureds as a nation-to-be to what extent, he asks, will it be morally permissible and justifiable to prescribe the lines along which the nascent nation must evolve? (a question that might be asked in respect of all the non-white groups), 'that is to decide the conditions for national growth and the type of nationhood that must eventually crystallise? Do we have the right to offer these people a form of nationhood which will, at the stage of political adolescence, be inferior to that which is foreshadowed for the Xhosa in the Transkei?'

And surely the political emancipation of the Coloured people 'cannot be timed for a date later than that earmarked for the Transkei, especially in view of the indisputable fact that the Coloureds are in all respects a more sophisticated and developed group than the Xhosas. . . . Neither will it be equitable to prescribe to them how

[1] The Indians also would seem to have no alternative. But leaders of the Transvaal Indian Community have rejected the recently appointed South African Indian Council until it becomes elective and said they would never give up their claim to be represented in Parliament. Vide *Sunday Times*, Johannesburg, August 4th, 1968.
[2] *Star*, Johannesburg, April 11th, 1968.
[3] *New Nation*, June 1968.

they will shape and exercise their future nationhood.' Finally he asks a question that should give serious food for thought to those who apparently lightly assume, as the Minister sponsoring the disfranchising Bill did, that the Coloured people will never have the same say as the Whites—would the Afrikaner have bowed to similar conditions imposed by the British after the Boer War?

In the establishment and the functioning of the Transkei Legislative Assembly, the Government would appear to have more solid ground for its contention that its policy of separate development is being accepted, particularly by those most immediately affected by it and whose existence and position initially inspired it. Before the end of this year, (1968) the Assembly will have completed its first five years of existence and will go to its second election with all the appearance and trappings of an established Parliamentary system.

There are however certain factors in this situation which have still to be evaluated. The first of these lies in the composition of the Legislative Assembly as constituted by the elections of 1963; the second lies in the circumstances in which that election took place, and in which the new Assembly has functioned in the intervening years.

While there were no clearly defined party lines between the candidates who offered themselves for the forty-five elective seats in the Assembly in 1963, the candidates tended to range themselves behind two leading personalities representing two widely divergent points of view. These were Chief Kaizer Matanzima, a qualified attorney and a graduate of the old University College of Fort Hare who had long been the chief supporter of the Government's policy of separate development and had been chairman of the Transkeian Territorial Authority, and the Paramount Chief of the Pondos, Chief Victor Poto, who had been a member of the Natives Representative Council and a consistent opponent of the Nationalist policy of apartheid.

In the absence of party labels, and party organisation, the actual balance of power could not be effectively revealed in the election itself. That depended upon the voting for the office of Prime Minister. In this Chief Matanzima won the day by fifty-four votes to forty-nine. In the count, Chief Victor Poto claimed the votes of thirty-eight of the forty-five elected members[1] with the

[1] See S.A. Institute of Race Relations Survey 1963, p. 98, for analysis of voting.

appointed members voting mainly for Chief Matanzima. In the circumstances, it would appear that many of the chiefs voted against the weight of opinion of their tribesmen which by tradition they are supposed to voice and to represent.

In the very first session of the new Assembly, the situation crystallised out into a party system with Chief Matanzima leading a Transkei National Independence Party committed to the objective of an independent Transkeian state and a Democratic Party operating under the chairmanship of another lawyer, Mr. Knowledge Guzana, representing Chief Poto's stand in favour of a common multi-racial South African society.

While the line of division is sharp and clear cut, it has been contained within the party framework with the two sides finding considerable common ground on economic issues of which the most pressing is the need for more land to meet the demands of a rapidly growing population already too great for its resources. However, the decision by a considerable majority of the Assembly this year, 1968, to press the Republican Government to do everything in its power to prepare the Transkei for full independence in the shortest possible time found the Democratic Party still urging that the Transkei should be permanently retained as an integral part of the Republic of South Africa.

But while the Transkeian Territorial Authority would thus seem to have effected a smooth constitutional transition into an incipient sovereign legislature, there had in fact been widespread disturbances particularly over the eastern areas of the Territory since the latter part of 1959 which had caused the Government to establish what was to all intents and purposes a state of emergency throughout the territory.

These disturbances, which took the form of violent clashes between tribesmen and chiefs and headmen, were confusedly related to the establishment of tribal authorities and the powers which the chiefs were to acquire under the Bantu Authorities system. The Government's reponse to this situation was to proclaim special regulations for the administration of the Transkei.[1] Under these regulations the Minister of Bantu Administration and Development acquired the power to prohibit any person from entering, being in or leaving the Transkei. Provision was also made for the prohibition

[1] Proclamations R400 of November 30th, 1960, R413 of December 4th, 1960. See S.A. Institute of Race Relations Survey 1961, p. 43 et seq.

of meetings of more than ten Africans with certain exceptions, save on the authority of the Native Commissioner who might impose conditions as to who might be present or address any meeting for which permission might be given. Chiefs were given wide powers of arrest of White 'agitators' operating in the Territory who were to be handed over to the police. They were also empowered to order the removal of their own tribesmen and their families within their jurisdiction, while they were protected by provisions that made it an offence to do or say anything that was intended or was likely to have the effect of interfering with the authority of the state or any of its officials, to organise or take part in a boycott of a meeting convened by any state official or a chief or headman, or to refuse to obey a lawful order of a chief or his headman or to treat either with disrespect.

Of particular importance were the wide powers given to the Native Commissioner, a police officer or an N.C.O. to arrest without warrant any person who, the particular officer was satisfied, had committed an offence under the regulations or any law or intended to do so, or any person suspected of having information relating to such an offence. Persons arrested in terms of this provision might be held in custody until the Native Commissioner or police officer was satisfied that they had fully and truthfully answered all relevant questions put to them or until the Minister ordered their release. Persons arrested under these provisions would not be allowed to consult a legal adviser save with the Minister's consent.

It was against the background of these drastic regulations that the opponents of the Bantustan policy had to conduct their propaganda. It was against this background that the 1963 elections were fought and all the business of the first Transkeian Legislative Assembly has been conducted over the five years of its existence. It would seem that the second general election would be held under similar circumstances.[1]

Year after year, the Democratic Party has called for the repeal of the proclamations under which these conditions are established as involving a denial of the people's rights of freedom of speech and assembly; and year after year, the ruling party with its main support still among the chiefs, has insisted that they are still necessary to safeguard internal security and peaceful administration.

[1] This was in fact the case.

In the light of this situation, it would seem that even the Transkei provides less solid ground for the Government's claim that its policy is being generally accepted than the Government itself would like us, and the world outside, to believe.[1] Events in the rest of the country over these years hold all too many evidences of the extent to which the policy has in fact been rejected and the price which its determined pursuit has exacted from its opponents and from the country as a whole in personal freedom and in national security.

The failure of the demonstrations planned by the All-in Conference's continuing committee for the end of May 1961, and the absence of any untoward incident on the occasion of the inauguration of the Republic, coupled with the disappearance of most of the leaders of the movement, some by arrest, others by flight, no doubt encouraged the Government to feel that its handling of the situation had been effective in spite of the criticisms and forebodings of the Oppositions. And the sweeping support which it got from the electorate in the election which Dr. Verwoerd had decided to hold in October of that year (1961), two years earlier than he need have gone to the country, seemed to suggest that many others who had not voted for his Party before, had come to feel the same. Thus it came to the first full Parliament of the Republic in a mood of triumphant self-assurance.

Yet before the session was completed, indeed early in May 1962, the Minister of Justice, now Mr. B. J. Vorster, was piloting a General Law Amendment Bill through Parliament which, designed to establish the new offence of Sabotage, also provided new and frightening extensions of ministerial powers and new areas of exclusion of the Courts.

Introducing the second reading of the Bill,[2] the Minister was repetitive in his assurances that the country was quiet, calm and peaceful 'in spite of the artificial agitation' made outside—a reference to the reception which the publication of the Bill had met from the non-Nationalist press and public. Because the country was peaceful, and because he wanted to keep it that way, he was introducing this measure timeously. One of the reasons for this

[1] In the second Transkei election held on 23rd October, 1968, Chief Matanzima's Transkei National Independence Party scored a considerable victory, winning twenty eight of the forty-five elective seats against the Democratic Party's fourteen, a circumstance which the Government is not slow to claim as practical evidence that its policy of separate development is being more and more accepted by the African population.
[2] Hansard, Vol. 4, Col. 6058 et seq.

quietness and peace, he was convinced, was that in the purely political sphere, the advantages inherent in the Government's policy of separate development of all population groups in the country were being realised.

In this atmosphere of quiet and calm why was he taking these powers? His justification was that the cold war throughout the world was being stepped up and that the Communist Party in South Africa was getting its second wind. It had come to the conclusion that force was now necessary to achieve its objective which was the bringing down of the Government and the taking over of the country. It had in fact already used force, he said. There had been cases of sabotage in seven to eight places at a time—obviously well organised by people in close touch with one another. It was 'accurately calculated sabotage'. He felt the time had come to devote more attention particularly to the White agitators in South Africa—most of the non-White communists had fled but the majority of the White members of the organisation had remained. By implication, these people provided the plans and the organisation behind these acts of sabotage, which were part of a programme to liberate all Africa by December 1963. As yet the plan was non-violent where people were concerned but sabotage against specific parcels of property was the No. 1 goal.[1] Declaring emphatically that it was not his intention or that of his Government to restrict freedom of speech in any way, he proceeded to set out his plans, 'with the aid of the existing legislation and this amendment', to make communists harmless in South Africa.

In future, in addition to prohibition of attendance at gatherings —now so widely defined as to seem to include all social as well as political occasions—and to restriction to particular areas, provision was made for house arrest with the obligation to report at regular intervals to the police, reports which would include any change of address or occupation. But it was not enough to impose a ban on attendance at meetings; the written word must also be controlled. Hence provision was made whereby no statement might be made to the press by banned persons nor might such persons be quoted by other people.

Further the press which might carry communist propaganda must be more closely controlled. While powers already existed to ban already registered newspapers, the sponsors of any new regis-

[1] Quoted by the Minister from an article in the *New York Post*.

tration might be called upon to deposit R20,000 which could be confiscated in the event of their publication proving a medium of communist propaganda.

In addition to these attempts to stop what the Minister regarded as loopholes in the existing legislative machinery for the restraint of communists, where the State President already had power to ban organisations which he, that is in effect the Minister, regarded as pursuing and furthering the aims of the banned Communist Party, the process of enquiry and report which the provisions of the existing law required were now removed and the banning could now be applied without these delaying procedures.

Embarked on this course of removing restraints on executive powers, the Minister took the occasion to remove the condition in the Unlawful Organisations Act of 1960 under which the State President could ban organisations for twelve months only. In future the State President might ban organisations declared unlawful under that legislation without any limitation of time or reference to Parliament. Thus was set on its course the process of making permanent the temporary[1] which has come to be a feature of legislation of this kind over recent years.

The Bill also extended for another year the twelve-day delaying provision in regard to bail initiated in 1961. And finally, it established the substantive offence of sabotage hitherto unknown to South African law, placed the onus of proof on the accused to establish his innocence and provided for the offence the penalties laid down for treason.

While the Minister insisted that the Bill aimed solely at curbing communist activities and dealing with sabotage, the Leader of the Opposition, Sir De Villiers Graaff, reflected the general attitude of the non-Nationalist press and public to its provisions when he said that there were provisions in this Bill which involved the civil death of persons whose offence was that they had incurred the displeasure and the suspicion of the Minister which to his mind were more serious than the provisions dealing with the new offences the Bill created 'vicious' as these were.[2]

In the months that followed, the Minister used his powers under this Act extensively. He published a list of 102 persons, including

---

[1] See *The South African Law Journal*, February 1966, 'The Permanence of the Temporary' by A. S. Matthews and R. C. Albino.
[2] Hansard, Vol. 4, Col. 6080.

Government's ex-chief Luthuli, whose speeches and writings might not be published. He closed the Johannesburg City Hall steps and the Grand Parade, Cape Town, by tradition places of public meeting. He banned the Congress of Democrats—the 'white' arm of the Congress movement. He initiated the system of house arrest by serving drastic orders on a Treason Trialist, Mrs. Helen Joseph[1] under which she was to be confined to her home where she lives alone, from 6 p.m. to 6.30 a.m. on weekdays, from 2.30 p.m. on Saturdays till Monday morning and on all public holidays. She was to have no visitors other than her doctor and her lawyer, provided they were not banned persons. She was ordered to report at police headquarters between twelve noon and 2 p.m. every day except Sundays and public holidays. These orders were to run for five years. Mrs. Joseph's name was already on the list of persons whose writings might not be published.[2]

Similar orders were served on some eighteen other persons before the end of the year with even more stringent conditions, in several cases involving twenty-four hours' house arrest.

In the course of the year, one of the already banned leaders of the A.N.C., Mr. Nelson Mandela, for whom a warrant of arrest had been issued, was eventually arrested and brought to trial charged with incitement and leaving the country unlawfully. His trial, at which he chose to conduct his own defence, created considerable reaction among the opponents of the Government's policies as a consequence of which the Minister banned all protest meetings against the arrest, custody, trial or conviction of any person for any offence in South Africa and South West Africa from October 20th, 1962, to April 30th, 1963.

In spite of these evidences of executive powers and the will to use them, sabotage seemed to be on the way to becoming more rather than less frequent in South Africa, with the banned national organisations, the A.N.C. and the P.A.C., attracting attention to themselves under new guises—Poqo succeeding the Pan-African Congress and Umkonto we Sizwe, the Spear of the Nation, succeeding the African National Congress—under new and more extreme leadership, now committed to meeting force with force; and after violent riots in Paarl in November 1962 and the murder

---

[1] Mrs. Joseph was not a listed communist, that is, she had never been a member of the Communist Party.
[2] She had just completed a book called *If This be Treason* on the subject of the Treason trials.

of a White family at the Bashee River in the Transkei, Mr. Vorster was back in Parliament seeking ever more drastic powers to contain what he himself conceded was to a large extent a question of the franchise but he claimed had become a demand for the control of the country.[1] In terms of a further General Law Amendment Act powers were now given to Magistrates to refuse bail at their own discretion and the Minister acquired the power to detain in custody for a period of twelve months a person who had completed a sentence imposed under one of a number of Acts if he considered that the release of such a person was likely to further the achievement of any of the objects of communism as defined in the Suppression of Communism Act. This was to enable him to hold in custody Mr. Robert Sobukwe whose term of imprisonment on the charge of incitement to break the law relating to passes was due to expire on May 3rd of that year, 1963.[2]

The Act further extended the definition of sabotage to cover persons who go abroad to train as saboteurs. It also empowered the State President, that is the Minister, to declare any organisation to be the same as a banned organisation without the lengthy procedure of proving it to be so—this to enable the Minister to equate Poqo with the P.A.C. and The Spear of the Nation with the A.N.C.

But most important, it gave to a police officer of the rank of Lieutenant or higher the right to detain any person whom he might suspect of being connected with crimes affecting the security of the state for a period of ninety days or until the detainee had answered all questions put to him to the satisfaction of the Commissioner of Police. Persons thus detained would be held in solitary confinement and without access to their legal advisers without permission.

Drastic indeed—'the end of another melancholy chapter of the deterioration of the position in respect of race relations in South Africa under this Government', as Sir De Villiers Graaff said in stating his Party's attitude to the measure. And again unequal to the situation. Within another year, Mr. Vorster was back asking for more powers to deal with more sabotage. Speaking in the Senate on March 10th, 1964,[3] he said that from December 1961 when the

---

[1] Hansard, Vol. 6, Col. 4638.
[2] This provision has since been renewed yearly so that Mr. Sobukwe is now (1968) serving his sixth year of administratively extended sentence: now in April, 1969 the Government has announced (Cape Times, April 26th) that he is to be released on conditions not yet disclosed.
[3] Senate Hansard, 1964, Cols. 1980–1.

first large-scale sabotage occurred, to March 10th, 1964 there had been 203 serious cases of sabotage in South Africa. Of these, 182 had occurred before June 30th, 1963, when the ninety day clause came into operation and 21 since. He had reason to believe that the campaign would be stepped up again after certain trials for political offences then pending had been completed, and to meet that situation, he proposed to extend for another year the operation of the ninety day detention clause which in 1963 he had agreed to limit to one year's duration.

In 1965, another year ahead, Mr. Vorster, still waging his war against communists, real or deemed, was to break new grounds of administrative action in several alarming directions little related to communism. A further amendment to the Criminal Procedure Act provided for the arrest and detention of persons likely to give material evidence for the State in any criminal proceedings where there was any danger of tampering with or intimidation of such witnesses, the detention to continue until the conclusion of the particular case or six months, whichever might be the shorter.

The Act also provided for the imprisonment of recalcitrant witnesses for successive periods of twelve months. It repealed the twelve days' delay in the possible application for bail but substituted a provision under which the Attorney General might, if he considered it in the interests of the safety of the public or the maintenance of public order, issue an order that a person arrested on a charge of having committed any of a number of offences, ranging from sedition, treason, murder to housebreaking with aggravating circumstances, should not be released on bail until sentence had been passed or the person had been discharged.

In 1966, two significant developments took place in the field of public law. The first was the extension of the security laws to South West Africa, and the first talk of terrorists, with a provision in the 1966 version of the General Law Amendment Act[1] empowering any commissioned officer of the police of or above the rank of Lt. Colonel to arrest any person without warrant if he has reason to believe that this person is a terrorist or favours terrorist activities or in any other way is connected with terrorists and terrorism or sabotage or has information which could be of use in furthering the objects of communism. Persons so detained might be held for interrogation for fourteen days with the possibility of further periods

[1] Act 62 of 1966.

2H

of fourteen days on the authority of a Judge of the Supreme Court.

It is interesting to note that this was the year in which Mr. Vorster was telling Mr. Allen Drury[1] that he felt we were now in control of the communist situation which was why he was withdrawing—really suspending—the ninety day clause.

In 1967, came the Terrorism Act from a new Minister of Justice, Mr. Pelser— 'a very far reaching measure' for which he was offering not the slightest excuse, he said.[2] The Act created the new offence of participation in terroristic activities very widely defined. It also provided for indefinite detention for interrogation in place of the previous year's fourteen day provision, for summary trial before a judge without a jury and with the onus of proof of innocence on the accused. The Minister said he would not reply to questions in Parliament about persons detained under the Act since any information given would be of value to the terrorist movement.

To bring this record up to date, this year, 1968, has seen no material addition to or retraction from this long tale of legislation of an emergency character. What it has done however, which is not without significance, is to bring Poqo to light again.

[1] See *A Very Strange Society*, p. 415.
[2] Hansard, Vol. 21, Col. 7023.

Conclusion

From a demonstration against the pass laws in 1960, through sabotage to terrorism. And now the news that in the small Cape provincial town of Victoria West, two police sweeps have drawn in some forty to fifty Africans[1]—mainly garage attendants, milk delivery men, shop workers, hospital labourers and messengers—on charges of Poqo activities.

It would seem that all this has little to do with the ordinary law-abiding citizen beyond an obligation to support the Government of his country in its efforts to maintain security against the enemies of the state without and law and order against the machinations of their friends and allies within. This is in fact how the Prime Minister, the Minister of Justice and the members of the governing party can and do represent the situation to themselves and to those to whom they feel impelled to justify their progressive assumption of arbitrary powers to meet the situation with which they find themselves confronted.

But if Mr. Drury's impressions are well-founded, it would seem that even among their own rank and file, there are some doubts and anxieties about the shape which these developments are imposing upon our society. Reporting his interview with Mr. Vorster Mr. Drury records: 'I could not forget, any more than I could during my interview with his legendary predecessor, that this amiable, easy going and charming Afrikaner could, entirely on his own say so—unhampered by legal protections, courts or diplomatic protest, pick up a telephone and have me thrown into jail, there to stay for a day, ninety days, 180 days or whatever it suited him . . . I simply had to acquire a little of that stout protection hugged to themselves so closely by supporters of the Government. *"I haven't done anything wrong, so it won't happen to me."*[2]

'It did not take a great deal of imagination, when in the presence

[1] *Cape Times*, July 12th, 1968. Some 30 were arrested on April 24th and 10 to 20 on July 9th.
[2] Mr. Drury's italics. It is interesting to speculate as to whether the 'protection' to which Mr. Drury refers will seem so adequate since Mr. Vorster's amazing use of the Special Branch of the police to investigate the authorship of a 'smear' letter against him and his policies obviously originating in the ranks of his own Party.

of the two men who actually had the power to do it, to realise how very easily in the Republic of South Africa it can.'

The implications of this situation for those who are not among the supporters of the Government, particularly for people professing liberal sentiments, were pointed—if they needed to be, by the response to Mr. Drury's questions about the position of the Government's critics under the laws which thus armed the executive. 'It is not any question of the political opponents of the Government being banned either,' Mr. Vorster said. 'No action has ever been taken against any politician, or against anyone because he was a member of a particular political party. Action has been taken against him because of his acts as an individual.

'Oh yes, of course, it is true that members of the Liberal Party have been banned but no action has been taken against the Party as such nor is any action contemplated against any party as such.'

Experience has shown that it has scarcely been necessary for the Government to take action against any party of which it disapproves such as is implied in Mr. Vorster's statement. The desired end can be achieved by the simpler process of disrupting or destroying the conditions under which a Party can pursue its objectives even where these are clearly constitutional and legal. This Mr. Vorster's Government has effectively done by its Prohibition of Political Interference Act under which the multi-racial Progressive Party has perforce become an all-white Party to survive, and the Liberal Party, finding it impossible to accept the limitations imposed upon it by this legislation, has terminated its own existence.

And in the days before this attack on the rights of political association of all sections of the population had been thought of as a means of restricting the activities of anti-Nationalist parties, the Liberal Party had already had ample experience of the possibilities and effects in that regard of the indirect attack implicit in Mr. Vorster's practice of action against individuals. From the earliest days of the Republic, the Party found its activities progressively curbed by the immobilisation of its young leaders one after the other by drastic banning orders imposed under the comprehensive terms of the Suppression of Communism Act by a Government and a Minister of Justice who more and more explicitly have claimed that liberalism is simply the forerunner of communism. These attacks on members of the Party have been sufficiently extensive to justify the belief that the Government did in fact hope to destroy the

Party without incurring the particular odium of banning it as a party. And in the absence of disclosed and proved criminal actions on the part of the persons banned, we are entitled also to believe that their sole offence was that their views, legitimately held, and their actions legitimately based on these views, were unacceptable to a Nationalist Government.[1]

Looking back on the record of these first years of the Republic, it is easier to see grounds for anxiety than for complacency. That security of the State which a Nationalist Government has claimed as its first and most immediate objective is curiously elusive, while the high price already paid for it remains a continuing charge on the liberties of all sections of the population.

This alone would seem to call for a sincere and careful reconsideration, if not of the objectives to which we are committed by the majority vote of a privileged electorate, at least of the methods by which and the pace at which we are prepared to pursue them. White South Africa has chosen a self-regarding policy of protection of its own position. Its spokesmen in office have repeatedly said they are prepared to give to the other sections of the population what they seek for themselves. That is demonstrably not true in respect of the minority groups, Coloured and Asian. And it fails signally to take any recognisable shape for the majority group, the Africans.

But the most important aspect of the situation has been consistently sidestepped—Do these groups want what is ostensibly being offered to them? This is a vital question which lies at the root of all our insecurities. It is a question that must be faced sooner or later; and all the evidences are that the sooner the better.

---

[1] A number of people claiming Liberal Party membership were charged with and convicted of sabotage. The Party was deeply shocked at the betrayal of trust by these members of a Party committed to constitutional and non-violent action and demanded the resignation forthwith of those who were in fact members of the Party.

Index

Abraham, Hans, 341
Advisory Economic Council, 444
African/s, 340, 357, 363, 365, 385,
    415 ff., 434, 450, 457, see also
    Bantu, Native
African labour force, 22; middle
    class, 464 ff., nationalism, 392;
    rural population, 22, 465; women,
    51–2; women on farms, 465
African National Congress (A.N.C.),
    47, 123, 368, 384, 385, 386, 412–21,
    428–31, 437, 451, 457, 483
African Unity, Organisation for, 15
Africans, Africa for, 420; and
    Coloured, 454, 457; and com-
    munism, 390–2; consuming capacity
    of, 108; and economic development,
    328 ff., 338; and education, 348;
    ethnic divisions of, 17; Federal
    Party and, 404; and inter-racial
    contact, 355 ff.; and Nationalist
    Government, 384; political advance
    of, 22, 364; and politics, 416 ff.;
    and Poqo, 487; ratio of to other
    groups, 15; and reference books,
    443; and republic, 451–3; and
    separate development, 480 n.;
    social services for, 356; and tribal
    authority system, 342, 346, 359 ff.;
    and trusteeship, 340; and urban
    authorities, 437; urbanisation of,
    20, 436, 438, 464 ff.
Afrikaans, 16
Afrikaanse Handelsinstituut, 435
Afrikander Bond, 38
Afrikaner/s, 16, 272, 401, 458, 477,
    487; Nationalism, 22, 334, 358,
    364, 383, 397, 398, 402, 403, 419,
    437, 449, 454; relationships
    between, 38 ff., 63 ff.
Afrikaner Party, see under Political
    parties
*Afrikaner Volkseenheid en my ervaring op
    die pad daarheen* (by Dr D. F.
    Malan), 272, 334

Afrikanerdom, 16, 354
Albino, R. C., 482 n.
Alexander, Morris, 62
Alexander, Ray, 395
Allen, F. B., 311
All-in African Conference, 451–3,
    457, 480
Anglo-Boer War, 13, 38, 39, 477
anthem, national, 69, 70, see also God
    Save the King, Die Stem van Suid-
    Afrika; for Transkei, 462
apartheid, 14, 19, 20, 151 n., 205 ff.,
    226, 287, 291, 313, 335 ff., 343,
    372, 383, 385, 397, 419, 420;
    administrative and legal, 334 ff.;
    and Africans, 310 ff., 319–20, 420,
    466; and African middle class, 464;
    and bureaucracy, 367; on Cape
    railways—proposed, 132;
    introduced, 230; and churches, 246,
    316–17, 356; and Coloured, 455;
    Coloured opposition to, 453; and
    constitution, 234 ff., 239 ff., 248 ff.,
    296; cultural, 356; in education,
    235–6, 348 ff.; and human dignity,
    402; legislation for, 255–6; and
    Liberals (Verwoerd), 370–1;
    Malan's explanation to Coloured,
    227 ff.; in Parliament, 235 ff.,
    255 ff.; to Piersma, 336 ff.; and
    Natives Representative Council,
    205 ff., 211; pattern of, 248; in
    the Platteland (Strydom and
    Verwoerd), 208, 318, 331, 465;
    political (Malan), 235, 248, 255,
    296; (Verwoerd), 341 ff., 365, 469,
    472; and political consciousness,
    398 ff. (see also Black Sash, Torch
    Commando); positive side of,
    436–8, 455–6; in post offices, 230;
    and race relations, 434; and riots,
    426–7; Smuts on, 232–4; social and
    economic, 310 ff., 319 ff.; in social
    service, 355–6; and Tomlinson
    Commission, 327; and Transkei

490